Revisiting
Professional Learning Communities at Work

New Insights for Improving Schools

Richard DuFour
Rebecca DuFour
Robert Eaker

Solution Tree | Press

a division of
Solution Tree

555 North Morton Street
Bloomington, IN 47404
800.733.6786 (toll free) / 812.336.7700
FAX: 812.336.7790

email: info@solution-tree.com
solution-tree.com

Printed in the United States of America

ISBN: 978-1-934009-32-1 (perfect-bound edition)
        978-1-934009-38-3 (hardback edition)

Dedication

We believe so strongly in the power of educators to impact the lives of others because our own lives have been enriched not only by members of our family, but also by teachers and educational leaders who have served as our mentors and role models. As a teenager, Rick's perception of himself as a student, leader, and person was impacted forever because of the high expectations, encouragement, and support of Father Arthur Lee Trapp. Father Trapp's insistence that we are put on this earth to serve others was a lesson well taught because of the way he modeled it. Dr. Jerry Saimon and Dr. Richard Kamm gave Rick his first position in educational administration and personally guided him through the ups and downs of leading a school. They were the support system he desperately needed as a young administrator. Dr. Jerry Bellon helped him to define his role as a leader rather than manager, a perspective that has had an enormous impact on his work. Finally, living with Becky has had a profound effect on Rick's life personally and professionally. He continues to strive to be more like her each day.

Several exemplary professionals have left significant, positive, and lasting imprints on Becky's life. Ms. Carolyn Bushong, Mr. Bill Skinner, and Mrs. Ann Greene were three exceptional high school teachers who challenged and supported her. Dr. D. L. (Pete) Warren and Dr. Robert Lynn Canady served as caring and skillful advisors, professors, and role models during her undergraduate and graduate studies. Mrs. Estella Ellison, Ms. Barbara Parker, and Mrs. Suzanne Rogers were invaluable colleagues during Becky's teaching career. Principal John Hollandsworth and Superintendent Leonard Gereau provided her with training in the correlates of effective schools and distributed teacher leadership and continued with ongoing support throughout her internship and administrative placements. Becky is especially grateful to Dr. Bob Eaker for welcoming her into the DuFour-Eaker collaborative team; and finally, her deepest gratitude goes to her husband, Rick, for being a constant mentor and loving life partner.

Rick DuFour has been a significant influence on Bob, as a professional colleague, mentor, and most important, as a dear friend. And, like Rick, Bob was fortunate to have Dr. Jerry Bellon as both a friend and mentor. Jerry modeled significant lessons in leadership, but more importantly, about life. Additionally, the late Dr. Richard Marius of Harvard University was a close friend and role model for Bob, along with many others such as Ralph White and Sam Ingram, who mentored Bob in his early days as a university administrator. Bob has been especially blessed in that his most significant mentors have been his family—his wife, Star, and his daughters, Robin and Carrie, and his late parents, Raymond and Jewel Eaker—each of whom has been a constant source of pride, caring, and encouragement.

Rick DuFour

Becky DuFour

Bob Eaker

Acknowledgements

Our work and our thinking have been shaped and influenced by some of the greatest contemporary educational thinkers in North America. We have benefited greatly from the wisdom of Larry Lezotte, Michael Fullan, Doug Reeves, Rick Stiggins, Roland Barth, Mike Schmoker, Jonathon Saphier, Dennis Sparks, Bob Marzano, and Tom Sergiovanni. Like so many educators, we are in their debt, and we acknowledge the enormous contribution each has made to our practice, our ideas, and our writing.

We are also grateful to our colleagues and associates, particularly those who have contributed to this book. Janel Keating, Dick Dewey, Clara Sale-Davis, Lillie Jessie, Bernice Cobbs, Mike Mattos, Chris Weber, Alan Addley, Austin Buffum, Anthony Muhammad, Tom Many, and Cassie Erkens have enriched not only this work but our understanding of effective professional practice.

We also acknowledge the tremendous support we have received for this project from the Solution Tree family. Suzanne Kraszewski is a skillful editor who polished our prose, and Amy Shock designed layouts for the book, both of which greatly enhanced its readability. We are grateful for the enthusiasm and energy they devoted to this endeavor from its inception to its completion.

Finally, we continue to be deeply indebted to Jeff Jones, the president of Solution Tree. We could not ask for a more effective champion of our ideas, a publisher more committed to advancing our work, and, most importantly, a better friend. Our relationship with Jeff is a true blessing.

Rick DuFour

Becky DuFour

Bob Eaker

Table of Contents

About the Authors

The 3Rs of Professional Learning Communities xix

Introduction

Revisiting Professional Learning Communities at Work 1

    A Merger of Research and Practice 2

    Chapter Overviews 4

Chapter 1

New Insights Into Professional Learning Communities
  at Work 13

    What Is a Professional Learning Community? 14

        1. Shared Mission (Purpose), Vision (Clear Direction), Values
           (Collective Commitments), and Goals (Indictors, Timelines,
           and Targets)—All Focused on Student Learning 15

        2. A Collaborative Culture With a Focus on Learning 15

        3. Collective Inquiry Into Best Practice and Current Reality . . . 16

        4. Action Orientation: Learning by Doing. 16

        5. A Commitment to Continuous Improvement 17

        6. Results Orientation 17

    The Big Ideas That Drive Professional Learning Communities 18

    Purposeful Language. 19

    What Has Become More Clear? 20

        1. The Necessity (and Challenge) of Shaping the Culture of
           the School and District. 21

        2. The Tendency for Hard Facts About School Improvement
           to Be Distorted Into Dangerous Half-Truths. 25

        3. The Importance of an Action Orientation, or "Learning by
           Doing" 25

4. The Importance of Frequent, Common Formative
Assessments 26

5. The Importance of Providing Teachers With Relevant
and Timely Information (Not Data) as a Catalyst
for Improving Teaching 26

6. The Importance of a Systematic Response When Students
Don't Learn, and a Process for Enriching and Expanding
Learning When Students Are Already Proficient 27

7. The Importance of Guiding the Work of Collaborative
Teams 27

8. The Importance of Widespread Leadership and the Role of
the Central Office 28

9. The Classroom as a Learning Community 28

10. The Need for a Common Language 28

11. The Benefit of a Contemporary Context 29

12. The Power of Stories 29

Chapter 2
The Rise and Fall of School Reform
The Rise and Fall of School Reform 31

No Child Left Behind: All Students Will Learn, Or Else! 37

The Definition of "Adequate Yearly Progress" 38

The Disparity Among States 39

The Nature of the Assessments 40

Lack of Funding 41

Considering the Impact of Nonstop School Reform 45

The Disappointment of Conservatives 45

The Dilemma of Liberals 47

Finding Common Ground in the Education Wars 51

Another Perspective on Public Education in America 51

National Assessments 51

International Assessments 53

Public Support 54

Education and the Economy 56

Why Educational Reform Has Failed to Deliver 62

Unrealistic Expectations. 62

The Complexity of the Task. 63

Misplaced Focus 64

Lack of Clarity on Intended Results. 65

Lack of Perseverance. 65

A Failure to Appreciate and Attend to the Change Process 66

Can Public Education Be Saved? 66

Chapter 3
Making the Case for Professional Learning Communities. . . . 67

Research Supporting Professional Learning Communities 68

Organizations That Endorse Professional Learning Communities . . . 72

Bridging the Knowing-Doing Gap 79

The Story That Drives a PLC. 82

Changing the Story Can Help Change the System 86

Chapter 4
The Challenge of Cultural Change 89

The Importance of Cultural Change 90

Embracing the Difficulty of the Challenge. 92

Leading the Improvement Process. 97

Common Mistakes in the Change Process 99

Fear as a Catalyst for Change. 102

Leadership Strategies for Changing Culture. 105

First Steps in Reculturing. 107

A Different Metaphor 109

Reason for Hope. 110

Chapter 5
Clear Mission and Shared Vision. 113

A New Mission Requires New Actions 115

The Second Building Block: Shared Vision 119

Creating a Vision of a Professional Learning Community 120

Building Consensus in a Professional Learning Community 122

Mistake #1: Leaders Attempt to "Go It Alone" 122

Mistake #2: Leaders Use a Forum That Is Ill-Suited to the
Dialogue Necessary for Consensus 123

Mistake #3: Leaders Pool Opinions Rather Than Build Shared
Knowledge 124

Mistake #4: Leaders Allow for Ambiguity Regarding the
Standard for Moving Forward 129

Mistake #5: Leaders Set an Unrealistic Standard for Moving
Forward 130

A Story of Shared Vision 130

The Struggle of Consensus 139

A District- or School-Level Vision? 140

Questions to Guide the Process 141

Evaluating the Vision Statement 142

The Benefits of a Clear, Shared Vision 143

Shared Vision Motivates and Energizes People 143

Shared Vision Creates a Proactive Orientation 143

Shared Vision Gives Direction to People Within
the Organization 143

Shared Vision Establishes Specific Standards of Excellence . . . 144

Shared Vision Creates a Clear Agenda for Action 144

A Final Caution 144

Chapter 6
Shared Values (Collective Commitments) and
Common Goals

Common Goals 147

Collective Commitments Contribute to the Action Orientation
of a Professional Learning Community 151

Collective Commitments Clarify How Each Member Can
Contribute to the Common Purpose and Shared Vision
of the School or District 152

Collective Commitments Can Help Create an Internal Focus 152

Collective Commitments Provide a More Effective System of
Accountability 154

Collective Commitments Help to Change the Culture of
   Organizations 156
      Limit the Commitment Statements to a Reasonable Number . . 157
      Be Explicit and Direct Rather Than Vague and Ethereal 157
   Common Goals. 159
   Other Keys to Effective Goals. 161
   The Pursuit of Nonmeasurable Goals 163
   A Solid Foundation Is Just the Start 164

Chapter 7
Teaching in a Professional Learning Community 169

   The Knowing-Doing Gap at Work 171
   A New Image for the Profession. 178
   Time for a New Story 182
   Converting a Hard Fact Into Dangerous Half-Truths. 182
      1. What is it we want our students to learn? What knowledge,
         skills, and dispositions do we expect them to acquire as a
         result of this course, grade level, or unit of instruction? . . . 184
      2. How will we know if each student is learning each of the
         essential skills, concepts, and dispositions we
         have deemed most essential? 186
      3. How will we respond when some of our students do not
         learn? What process will we put in place to ensure students
         receive additional time and support for learning in a timely,
         directive, and systematic way? 187
      4. How will we enrich and extend the learning for students
         who are already proficient?. 187
   PLCs Build Shared Knowledge Rather Than Pool Opinions 187
   A Collaborative Team at Work. 189
      What Did They Do? 191
      What Did They Learn? 193

Chapter 8
Assessment in a Professional Learning Community 199

Summative Versus Formative Assessment 202

Formative Assessment in the Classroom 205

Common Formative Assessments 208

Team-Developed Common Assessments Are More Efficient. . . . 212

Team-Developed Common Assessments Promote Equity 213

Team-Developed Common Formative Assessments Help
Monitor and Improve Student Learning. 213

Team-Developed Common Formative Assessments Can Inform
and Improve the Practice of Both Individual Teachers and
Teams of Teachers 213

Team-Developed Common Formative Assessments Can Build
the Capacity of the Team to Achieve at Higher Levels 215

Team-Developed Common Formative Assessments Are
Essential to Systematic Interventions When Students
Do Not Learn. 216

Creating and Using Common Formative Assessments 216

Building Shared Knowledge of Quality Assessments 220

Chapter 9
A Tale of Excellence in Assessment 227

At Last: The Familiar Territory of the Classroom 231

The First Common Assessment 234

Toto, I Don't Think We Are in Kansas Anymore 237

Unleashing the Potential of Effective Assessment 239

Chapter 10
Intervention and Enrichment in a Professional Learning
Community. 241

Schools That Do Not Leave Learning to Chance 246

Elementary School Examples. 246

Middle School Examples 249

High School Examples 251

A Common Theme in Uncommon Schools 253

Words of Caution About Systematic Interventions. 255

No System of Interventions Will Compensate for Ineffective
Teaching. 255

A System of Interventions Works Most Effectively in Schools Where
Collaborative Teams of Teachers Have Established Essential
Learning, Common Pacing, and Common Assessments. 256

A System of Interventions Should Fit the Context of Your
School 257

Do Not Fall in Love With a Tree—Embrace the Forest 257

Objections to Creating a System of Interventions. 258

Objection 1: Attention Is Given to Students Who Are Not
Learning at the Expense of Average and Gifted Students . . . 258

Objection 2: Systems of Support Put the Burden for Learning on
Educators Rather Than on Students; Interventions Will Only
Enable Students, Encouraging Them to Be Irresponsible . . . 260

Objection 3: The Schedule Won't Allow It 265

Is a System of Interventions the Same as Response to
Intervention? 269

A System of Interventions in Action 271

Planning for and Facilitating Intervention and Enrichment . . . 274

Involving Parents as Partners. 277

Integrating Specials Areas. 278

Using the Child Study Team in a New Way 279

Chapter 11
The Classroom as a Learning Community. 283

Collaboratively Developed Classroom Norms 284

Tips for Effective Classroom Norms 287

Align Classroom Norms With School-Wide Expectations. . . 287

Keep the List of Norms Few in Number 287

Allow Each Classroom to Establish Its Own Norms 287

State Norms as Commitments to Act in Certain Ways
Rather Than as Beliefs 287

Review and Refer to Norms on a Regular Basis 288

Model and Celebrate the Classroom Commitments 288

Strategies for Creating a Learning Community in the Classroom . . 288

Present Clearly Defined Learning Outcomes in Terms Students
Understand. 288

Encourage Student Participation in Assessment of Their
Learning. 289

Use Cooperative Learning. 291

    1. Clearly Perceived Positive Interdependence. 293

    2. Face-to-Face Promotive Interaction 294

    3. Individual Accountability/Personal Responsibility 294

    4. Appropriate Use of Interpersonal and Small-Group
       Skills 294

    5. Group Processing 294

A Word of Caution for Creating Classroom Learning Communities . 296

A Classroom Learning Community in Action 296

Chapter 12
The Role of the Principal in a Professional Learning
Community. 301

The Principal in a Professional Learning Community 308

Principals of PLCs Are Clear About Their Primary
Responsibility 308

Principals of PLCs Disperse Leadership 309

    Reciprocal Accountability 312

Principals of PLCs Bring Coherence to the Complexities of
Schooling by Aligning the Structure and Culture of the
School With Its Core Purpose 317

A New Image of Leadership 324

Mike Mattos, Principal of Pioneer Middle School,
Tustin, California 325

Ken Williams, Principal of E.J. Swint Elementary School—
The Learning Academy, Jonesboro, Georgia. 327

Bernice Cobbs, Former Principal of Snow Creek Elementary
School, Penhook, Virginia; Current Principal of Boones Mill
Elementary School, Boones Mill, Virginia 328

Clara Sale-Davis, Former Principal of Freeport Intermediate
School, Freeport, Texas. 330

Lillie Jessie, Principal of Elizabeth Vaughan Elementary School,
Woodbridge, Virginia 332

Dick Dewey, Former Principal of Eastview High School,
Apple Valley, Minnesota. 333

Clarifying Priorities 334

Chapter 13
The Role of the Central Office in a Professional Learning Community

Community. 337

Is There a Place for Top-Down Leadership? 341

Tight About What? 342

Advice on Being Tight 345

Key 1: District Leaders Must Use Every Aspect of an
Effective Change Process and Present a Compelling
Rationale for Moving Forward 345

Key 2: District Leaders Must Communicate Priorities
Effectively, Consistently, and With One Voice 358

Key 3: District Leaders Must Limit Initiatives to Allow for
the Sustained Focus Essential to a Change Initiative. . . 362

Key 4: District Leaders Must Help Teachers and Principals
Build Their Collective Capacity to Raise Student
Achievement by Embedding Ongoing Professional
Development in the Routine Work of Every Educator . . 364

Positive Top-Down Leadership in Action 371

District A: The Autocratic Approach 371

District B: The Laissez-Faire Approach 372

District C: Loose-Tight Leadership at Work. 372

Pressure and Support 374

Chapter 14
The Role of Parents and the Community in a Professional Learning Community

Learning Community 377

Characteristics of Effective School-Family Partnerships. 380

Implement Regular, Two-Way, and Meaningful Communication
Between Home and School. 380

What Is It We Want Our Students to Learn? 381

How Will We Know If Our Students Are Learning?. 381

Offer Advice and Training Regarding Parenting Skills 382

Make Sure Parents Become Partners in the Education of Their
Children. 385

Provide Multiple Opportunities for Parents to Volunteer in the
School 386

Include Parents in School Governance and Decision-Making. . . 389

Collaborate With the Larger Community and Utilize
Community Resources. 392

Tips for Effective School-Family Partnerships 395

Which Lens Will We Look Through? 396

Mountain Meadow Elementary: A Professional Learning
Community. 398

Janel Keating, Deputy Superintendent of the White River
School District, Buckley, Washington, and Former Principal
of Mountain Meadow Elementary School. 399

Chapter 15
Sustaining the Professional Learning Community Journey. . 411

Dangerous Detour #1: We Need More Training Before We
Can Begin 413

Dangerous Detour #2: Let's Find a Way to Shortcut
Key Processes. 415

Dangerous Detour #3: Someone Else Needs to Do It 416

Dangerous Detour #4: We Pick and Choose Programs Rather Than
Work at Comprehensive Cultural Change 419

Dangerous Detour #5: We Quit When the Going Gets Tough 420

Sustained Effort Requires Creating Short-Term Wins 423

Sustained Effort Requires Celebrating Short-Term Wins 426

Final Thoughts. 427

Appendix. 431

Indicators of Student Achievement: Our Current Reality 432

Synthesis of Research on the Characteristics of Effective Schools . 438

Synthesis of Research on Indicators of a Productive School Culture . 440

Successful School Improvement 441

Professional Learning Communities Required to Improve Schools. . 442

What Works: School Factors That Increase Student Achievement. . 443

Practices of Improving Schools and Districts 445

Six Characteristics of High-Performing Organizations 446

Adlai Stevenson High School Vision Statement 448

Stevenson High School Board/Administrative Leadership Team
    Collective Commitments 453

Stevenson High School Faculty Collective Commitments 455

Stevenson High School Support Staff Collective Commitments . . . 457

Collective Commitments for Stevenson Students 458

Collective Commitments for Stevenson Parents 459

Key Terms and Concepts in a PLC 463

References and Resources 473

Index 509

The 3Rs of Professional Learning Communities

Richard DuFour, Robert Eaker, and Rebecca DuFour—the 3Rs of professional learning communities—are among the nation's foremost authorities on applying PLC principles in the real world of schools. They consult with state departments, professional organizations, and school districts throughout North America on strategies for improving schools.

 **Richard DuFour, Ed.D.,** was a public school educator for 34 years, serving as a teacher, principal, and superintendent. He was principal of Adlai E. Stevenson High School in Lincolnshire, Illinois, from 1983 to 1991 and superintendent of the district from 1991 to 2002. During his tenure, Stevenson became what the United States Department of Education (USDE) has described as one of "the most recognized and celebrated schools in America." Stevenson has been repeatedly cited in the popular press as one of America's best schools and referenced in professional literature as an exemplar of best practices in education.

Rick is the author of 75 professional articles, and he wrote a quarterly column for the *Journal of Staff Development* for almost a decade. He was the lead consultant and author for the Association for Supervision and Curriculum Development's seven-part video series on the principalship.

Rick was presented the Alumni Achievement Award from Illinois State University, the Distinguished Scholar Practitioner Award from the University of Illinois, and the Distinguished Service Award from the National Staff Development Council.

Rebecca DuFour, M.Ed., has served as a teacher, school administrator, and central office coordinator. As a former elementary principal, Becky helped her school earn state and national recognition as a model professional learning community. She was the lead consultant and featured principal in the Video Journal of Education program *Elementary Principals as Leaders of Learning* (2003) and is one of the featured principals in *Leadership in an Age of Standards and High Stakes* (2001).

Becky has written for numerous professional journals, reviewed books for the *Journal of Staff Development,* and authored a quarterly column for *Leadership Compass,* published by the National Association of Elementary School Principals.

Robert Eaker, Ed.D., is a professor in the Department of Educational Leadership at Middle Tennessee State University, where he also served as dean of the College of Education and interim vice president and provost. Bob is a former fellow with the National Center for Effective Schools Research and Development. He has written widely on the issues of effective teaching, effective schools, helping teachers use research findings, and high expectations for student achievement. He was cited by *Phi Delta Kappan* as one of the nation's leaders in helping public school educators translate research into practice. Bob was instrumental in the founding of the Tennessee Teachers Hall of Fame and was a regular contributor to the Effective Schools Research Abstracts series.

Other Resources by One or More of the 3Rs

Books

- *Revisiting Professional Learning Communities at Work™: New Insights for Improving Schools* (DuFour, DuFour, & Eaker, 2008)

- *A Leader's Companion: Inspiration for Professional Learning Communities at Work™* (Eaker, DuFour, & DuFour, 2007)

- *Learning by Doing: A Handbook for Professional Learning Communities at Work™* (DuFour, DuFour, Eaker, & Many, 2006)

- *Professional Learning Communities at Work™ Plan Book* (DuFour, DuFour, & Eaker, 2006)

- *On Common Ground: The Power of Professional Learning Communities* (DuFour, Eaker, & DuFour, Editors, 2005)

- *Whatever It Takes: How Professional Learning Communities Respond When Kids Don't Learn* (DuFour, DuFour, Eaker, & Karhanek, 2004)

- *Getting Started: Reculturing Schools to Become Professional Learning Communities* (Eaker, DuFour, & DuFour, 2002)

- *Professional Learning Communities at Work™: Best Practices for Enhancing Student Achievement* (DuFour & Eaker, 1998)

- *Creating the New American School: A Principal's Guide to School Improvement* (DuFour & Eaker, 1992)

- *The Principal as Staff Developer* (DuFour, 1991)

- *Fulfilling the Promise of Excellence: A Practitioner's Guide to School Improvement* (DuFour & Eaker, 1987)

Videos/DVDs

- *The Power of Professional Learning Communities at Work™: Bringing the Big Ideas to Life* (DuFour, Eaker, & DuFour, 2007)

- *Let's Talk About PLC: Getting Started* (DuFour, Eaker, & DuFour, with Dennis Sparks, 2003)

- *Through New Eyes: Examining the Culture of Your School* (DuFour, 2002)

- *How to Develop a Professional Learning Community: Passion and Persistence* (DuFour, 2001)

Revisiting Professional Learning Communities at Work

In our first book, *Professional Learning Communities at Work: Best Practices for Enhancing Student Achievement* (DuFour & Eaker, 1998), we stated the premise of that book in its opening sentence:

> The most promising strategy for sustained, substantive school improvement is developing the ability of school personnel to function as professional learning communities. (p. xi)

Our conviction in the validity of that statement has not wavered; however, we now have much clearer insights regarding the most effective strategies for helping educators make the transition from traditional schools to professional learning communities (PLCs).

A number of factors have contributed to our new insights. First, we have had the pleasure and privilege of working with and sharing ideas with some of the most influential people in education: Roland Barth, Michael Fullan, Wayne Hulley, Larry Lezotte, Doug Reeves, Jonathon Saphier, Mike Schmoker, Dennis Sparks, Tom Sergiovanni, and Rick Stiggins. These respected colleagues and friends have enriched our lives. They have shared their expertise, responded to our questions, enabled us to understand the complexities of school improvement at a deeper level, and helped clarify our own thinking.

We have also benefited from our association with some of the leading school practitioners in North America, including Tom Many, Barbara Eason-Watkins, Anthony Muhammad, Peter Noonan, Mike Mattos, Matt Miller, Susan Sparks, Austin Buffum, Alan Addley, Tim Kanold, Janet Malone, Clara Sale-Davis, Dick Dewey, Bernice Cobbs, Janel Keating, Tim Brown, Chuck Hinman, Dennis King, Ken Williams, Regina Owens, Lillie Jessie, Charlie Coleman, Susan Huff, Tyrone Olverson, Eric Twadell, Brian Butler, Sam Ritchie, Cheryl O'Leary, Jack Balderman, and Terri Martin. They are what Fullan (2005a) has called "system thinkers in action"—people who have developed deep understanding of what it takes to improve schools by rolling up their sleeves and doing the work. They represent the power of learning by doing, a concept we will return to frequently in this book.

Our great friend and publisher, Jeff Jones, has made an enormous contribution to our work and our lives during the past 10 years. As the president of Solution Tree, he has transformed a once small publishing company into one of the most influential providers of meaningful professional development in North America. He has been tireless in his efforts to promote the PLC concept, and we consider his entry into our lives in 1998 as a key turning point in our work as authors and consultants.

Finally, our personal and professional partnership is entering its fourth decade. Without question, the most important development in our long relationship has been the addition of Becky DuFour to our team. Becky's experience as a successful leader of a PLC, her skill as a presenter, and her empathy for educators have been instrumental both in establishing the credibility of the PLC concept and in extending the concept to others. Many of the new insights we introduce in this revised edition we attribute to her, and we are pleased to have her join us as a coauthor of this work.

A Merger of Research and Practice

The primary objective of this book is to offer educators specific, practical recommendations for transforming their schools into PLCs so that their students may learn at higher levels and their profession becomes more rewarding, satisfying, and fulfilling. We have not, however, limited our study to research, practices, and standards in education. We also examine organizational development, change processes, leadership, and successful practices outside of education. We rely heavily on the work of Robert Marzano, Doug Reeves, Linda Darling-Hammond, Richard Elmore, Charlotte Danielson, Michael Fullan, Andy Hargreaves, Milbrey McLaughlin, Larry Lezotte, Fred Newmann, Roland Barth, Seymour Sarason, Phil Schlechty, Mike Schmoker, Rick Stiggins, Paul Black, Dylan Wiliam, Dennis Sparks, Judith Warren Little, Karen Seashore Louis, and others who have offered powerful insights for improving public schools. But we also have sought out the lessons that can be found for educators in the work of Patrick Lencioni, Burt Nanus, Tom Peters, Barry Posner, Peter Senge, Robert Waterman, Ken Blanchard, Jim Collins, Jerry Porras, Jeffrey Pfeffer, Robert Sutton, Marcus Buckingham, Warren Bennis, James Champy, Stephen Covey, Terry Deal, Peter Drucker, John Gardner, Daniel Goleman, Rosabeth Moss Kanter, John Kotter, James Kouzes, Robert Kegan, Kerry Patterson, Howard Gardner, and others.

A learning organization is willing to learn from its external environment, and the most successful people in any area look outside their narrow field for fresh perspectives and new ideas (Kanter, 1997). We believe that school practitioners can and should learn from organizations outside of education that have struggled with some of the same issues public schools face today. The best of these organizations have struggled to find answers to questions such as these:

- How can we clarify and communicate the purpose, vision, values, and goals of our organization?

- How can we initiate, implement, and sustain a change process?

- How can we provide strong leadership while simultaneously empowering those closest to the action?

- How can we shape organizational culture and provide structures that support the culture we seek?

- How can we create collaborative processes that result in both individual and organizational learning?

- How can we foster an environment that is results-oriented yet encourages experimentation?

- How can we build ongoing learning and continuous improvement into our routine work practices?

In the final analysis, however, while we have become students of research inside and outside of education, our work has been grounded in our experiences in schools and districts throughout North America. We have observed and struggled with the perplexities of school improvement, confronted the obstacles that must be overcome, and gained valuable insights into the practices that enable a school or district to function as a PLC. We have benefited immensely from our association with schools and districts across the continent and our many opportunities to observe educators in a wide variety of settings work their way through the challenges of becoming a PLC. We have tremendous respect and appreciation both for their efforts and for the role they have played in our own learning. We hope this book will provide insights into that learning and encourage educators to undertake the challenging but rewarding process of building their collective capacity to create schools and districts that operate as high-performing PLCs.

Chapter 1: New Insights Into Professional Learning Communities at Work

This book begins with a review of six characteristics of a PLC and three big ideas that drive the PLC concept. It then identifies 12 new learnings that have emerged as a result of our work with schools and districts as they have attempted to bring the PLC concept to life in their organizations.

Chapter 2: The Rise and Fall of School Reform

While this book strives to describe a better future for public schools, this chapter offers a look at the past. Chapter 2 provides a brief overview of the origins of public education in the United States. The chapter then examines the reform efforts of the past quarter century with an extensive discussion of the impact of the most ambitious school reform initiative in American history—the No Child Left Behind Act. It examines some of the reasons past school reform efforts have failed to accomplish their intended objectives. The chapter makes the case that in many ways, public education has been remarkably successful; however, the need to provide the best education possible has never been more imperative than it is today because the consequences of poor schooling have never weighed heavier on the future of our children.

Chapter 3: Making the Case for Professional Learning Communities

This chapter demonstrates the extent to which the PLC concept has been endorsed by educational researchers and professional organizations serving educators. The challenge of improving schools does not depend upon educators discovering new ideas; it depends upon their willingness to implement what is already known regarding best practices for student and adult learning. This chapter begins to examine some of the cultural conditions that interfere with the implementation of PLC practices and offers a story to illustrate the concept at work in a school.

Chapter 4: The Challenge of Cultural Change

This chapter emphatically asserts that creating a PLC requires, and is tantamount to, reshaping the traditional culture of schools and districts. It draws a distinction between structural and cultural change and stresses that changing the structure of any organization is not sufficient to change its culture—the assumptions, behaviors, expectations, and habits that constitute the norm for the organization. Chapter 4 explores the nature of a substantive improvement process, obstacles to be overcome, and whether the best path for results-oriented change comes from the top down, or from the bottom up. It introduces the ideal of a culture that is simultaneously loose and tight, a concept that we will reference often throughout the book. Finally, it makes the case that transforming traditional school cultures to support the PLC concept is indeed difficult, but very doable.

Chapter 5: Clear Mission and Shared Vision

Shared mission, vision, values, and goals are the four building blocks that comprise the foundation of a PLC. Chapter 5 examines the first two blocks: mission and vision. The mission building block answers the question, "What is our purpose?" to which schools often provide a trite and superficial response. This chapter suggests how the issue can be examined in a way that serves as a catalyst for improvement. The vision building block answers the question, "What do we hope to become?" The chapter offers strategies for developing a shared vision, examines common questions related to articulating a vision, provides summaries of research that can be used to inform the process, and suggests criteria for assessing a vision statement. Most importantly, this chapter suggests some of the very specific actions and activities the members of a community would engage in as they move mission and vision from rhetoric to reality.

Chapter 6: Shared Values (Collective Commitments) and Common Goals

Chapter 6 examines the third and fourth building blocks of a PLC: values, or collective commitments, and common goals. The values building block answers the question, "How must we behave, what commitments must we make and honor, in order to make our shared vision a reality?" Value statements articulate the collective commitments members of a PLC agree to put into action to create the school they desire. This chapter offers suggestions for developing such statements.

The remainder of the chapter is devoted to the goals building block, which clarifies the indicators of progress the school will monitor and the timetable of the specific steps that will be taken to move the school toward its vision. The chapter stresses that SMART goals are essential to a results orientation, effective teams, and continuous improvement, and are a key factor in the accumulation of small wins necessary to sustain the improvement initiative. The chapter identifies common mistakes that schools make in developing goals, and it presents criteria for assessing goals.

Chapter 7: Teaching in a Professional Learning Community

This chapter identifies the single biggest barrier educators must overcome if they are to create PLCs in their schools and districts: the long tradition of teachers working in isolation. The chapter asserts that the common practice of teachers continuing to work in isolation today despite all that is known about the benefits of a collaborative school culture is a classic example of the "knowing-doing gap"—not doing what we know we should do. The chapter also challenges educators to avoid the half-truths of pseudo-teams rather than real teams and "coblaboration" rather than collaboration. It suggests the topics teachers would collaborate about if their focus was on student learning and describes the work of a collaborative team in an elementary school to illustrate. The chapter concludes with the story of a team of teachers who worked collaboratively and collectively to raise achievement for their students.

Chapter 8: Assessment in a Professional Learning Community

This chapter points out that historically the goal of assessment in education in the United States was to assist schools in what was universally accepted as their fundamental task: sorting, ranking, and selecting students. It argues that if schools are to fulfill a new purpose—high levels of learning for all students—assessment must take on a different purpose. The chapter draws a distinction between summative and formative assessments and asserts the latter are vital to schools that function as PLCs. While acknowledging that good teachers are constantly assessing student learning through multiple and varied checks for understanding as a part of each day's lesson, the chapter also calls upon collaborative teams of teachers to work together to create a series of common formative assessments as one of the tools they use in their more formal investigations of student understanding. Educators are urged to use assessment not merely to monitor student learning or diagnosis problems in that learning, but also, more importantly, to inform and impact their instruction to improve student learning. The chapter explains the significance and benefits of such assessments and presents a brief overview of some of the principles of good assessments.

Chapter 9: A Tale of Excellence in Assessment

Chapter 8 examines the technical aspects of assessment in a PLC. In chapter 9, we illustrate the potential power of effective assessment practices through the oldest teaching vehicle known to man—a story. Good stories teach us. They convey not only how something should be done, but more importantly, why it should be done. They communicate priorities and clarify what is significant, valued, and appreciated. Chapter 9 tells a story of excellence in assessment in a PLC. The protagonist of the story is a high-school teacher, but the message applies equally and with little revision to middle and elementary schools as well.

Chapter 10: Intervention and Enrichment in a Professional Learning Community

This chapter explores the question, "What happens when a student does not learn despite the best efforts of his or her classroom teacher?" It asserts that the honest answer to that question in most schools is, "It will depend on his or her teacher." The chapter argues that schools committed to high levels of all learning will ensure students who have initial difficulty receive additional time and support for learning in a timely, directive, and systematic way. It highlights nine schools across the United States that have achieved extraordinary results through comprehensive improvement efforts that have included such systems of interventions. The chapter also addresses how schools are using this concept of differentiation of time and support to bring proficient students to higher levels of learning. It asks educators to accept responsibility for creating schedules that allow this differentiation, and concludes with a story of a school that has done so.

Chapter 11: The Classroom as a Learning Community

Although this book is devoted primarily to implementing the PLC concept across schools and districts, this chapter explains how individual teachers can apply the concept to create classrooms that function as learning communities. It explains how teachers are using norms to create collective commitments between students, establishing specific learning targets in kid-friendly language, training students to apply clearly defined criteria for assessing the quality of their work, and using effective cooperative learning strategies to create classrooms of community rather than competition. It argues that since the ability to work cooperatively and collaboratively has been established as an essential workplace skill for the 21st century, teachers should model those skills and create conditions in their classrooms that help students develop the skills. The chapter ends with a story of how a team of high school calculus teachers has used this strategy to create one of the most effective Advanced Placement programs in the United States.

Chapter 12: The Role of the Principal in a Professional Learning Community

This chapter begins with a review of the research on the importance of the principalship and continues with recommendations from researchers and professional organizations in an effort to help those in the position function most effectively. The chapter attempts to simplify the principal's complex role with three specific recommendations:

1. Principals must recognize their primary job is to create the conditions that help the adults in their building continually improve upon their collective capacity to ensure all students acquire the knowledge, skills, and dispositions essential to their success.

2. Principals must disperse leadership throughout the school because their responsibilities are far too extensive for any single person to fulfill.

3. Principals must bring coherence to the complexities of schooling by aligning the structure and culture of the school to its fundamental purpose of high levels of learning for all students.

The chapter offers specific recommendations for each of the three areas and concludes with advice from principals from across the country who have been highly effective in leading PLCs.

Chapter 13: The Role of the Central Office in a Professional Learning Community

This chapter examines the challenge of how the central office can promote the PLC concept districtwide at the same time it provides the autonomy and freedom essential both to organizational flexibility and personal ownership on the part of school professionals. It examines the research on the role of the central office in promoting learning, considers the issue of top-down leadership, and returns to the concept of loose-tight leadership with specific suggestions regarding the practices about which central office leaders should be tight. The chapter examines the research from Howard Gardner, Kerry Patterson, and their colleagues on strategies for influencing the thinking and behavior of others. This section, while included in the central office chapter, is beneficial for every reader. The chapter concludes by examining the research on effective professional development and offering recommendations on how the central office can apply that research to build the capacity of staff to implement the PLC concept successfully.

Chapter 14: The Role of Parents and the Community in a Professional Learning Community

This chapter examines the extensive research on the impact of parent involvement on student achievement and offers strategies for promoting effective parent involvement. It offers specific recommendations in the following key areas identified by the National Parent Teacher Association:

1. Establishing communication between home and school that is regular, two-way, and meaningful

2. Fostering effective parenting skills

3. Making parents partners in the education of their children

4. Providing multiple opportunities for community members to volunteer in schools

5. Including parents and community in school governance and decision-making

6. Collaborating with the larger community and becoming a community resource

The chapter includes real-life stories from a school district that has become the hub of the community it serves and an elementary school that has been described as the "Nordstrom of education" because of its commitment to serving parents.

Chapter 15: Sustaining the Professional Learning Community Journey

The final chapter acknowledges that while it is easy to identify what educators must do to improve schools—build their capacity to function as a PLC—implementing that knowledge is difficult indeed. It stresses that while there is no step-by-step checklist or recipe for becoming a

PLC, there are certain key concepts that must be addressed. The chapter points out five dangerous detours and potholes to avoid on the PLC journey and reminds readers of the imperative of persistence if they are to complete that journey successfully. Finally, it presents consistent advice from the world's leading organizational theorists regarding the very best strategy for fostering persistence while engaged in the challenge of substantive change.

We sincerely hope this book will be used as a tool to stimulate the shared mission, vision, collective commitments, and goals; the collective inquiry; the collaborative teams focused on learning; the action orientation; the commitment to continuous improvement; and the focus on results that we believe are critical to the survival and success of public schools.

Chapter 1

New Insights Into Professional Learning Communities at Work

Strong professional learning communities produce schools that are engines of hope and achievement for students. . . . There is nothing more important for education in the decades ahead than educating and supporting leaders in the commitments, understandings, and skills necessary to grow such schools where a focus on effort-based ability is the norm.

—Jonathon Saphier

New knowledge is the most valuable commodity on earth. The more truth we have to work with, the richer we become.

—Kurt Vonnegut

According to legend, when good friends Ralph Waldo Emerson and Henry David Thoreau reunited after a long separation, each would ask his colleague, "What has become clearer to you since last we met?" It has now been 10 years since we wrote *Professional Learning Communities at Work: Best Practices for Enhancing Student Achievement* (1998). In this volume, *Revisiting Professional Learning Communities at Work*, we answer the question, "What has become more clear to us regarding the promise, potential, problems, and pitfalls surrounding the PLC concept?"

Our conviction regarding the vital role the PLC concept plays in school improvement has only grown over the years. Professional organizations and researchers echo that conviction, and they now routinely call upon educators to organize schools and districts into PLCs to improve both student and adult learning. In fact, the term *professional learning community,* which prior to 1998 was used primarily among educational researchers, has now become part of the routine jargon of educators throughout North America. The term is now used so ubiquitously to describe any loose grouping of educators that it is in danger of losing all meaning.

While the term *professional learning community* has become commonplace, the actual practices of a PLC have yet to become the norm in education. Too many schools, districts, and organizations calling themselves PLCs do virtually none of the things that characterize PLCs. Despite the increasing popularity of the term, actually transforming the culture of a traditional school to reflect the PLC concept remains a complex and challenging task. We are convinced educators would benefit from both greater clarity regarding the PLC concept and specific strategies for implementing the concept. We hope this book will provide both.

What Is a Professional Learning Community?

We define a professional learning community as *educators committed to working collaboratively in ongoing processes of collective inquiry and action research to achieve better results for the students they serve. Professional learning communities operate under the assumption that the key to improved learning for students is continuous, job-embedded learning for educators* (DuFour, DuFour, Eaker, & Many, 2006).

In *Professional Learning Communities at Work* (1998), we identified six characteristics of PLCs, and in *Learning by Doing* (2006), we delved into those characteristics in more detail:

1. Shared Mission (Purpose), Vision (Clear Direction), Values (Collective Commitments), and Goals (Indicators, Timelines, and Targets)— All Focused on Student Learning

The very essence of a *learning* community is a focus on and a commitment to the learning of each student. When a school or district functions as a PLC, educators embrace high levels of learning for all students as both the reason the organization exists and the fundamental responsibility of those who work within it. To achieve this shared purpose, the members of a PLC create and are guided by a clear and compelling vision of what their schools and districts must become to help all students learn. They make collective commitments that clarify what each member will do to contribute to creating such organizations, and they use results-oriented goals to mark their progress. This foundation of shared mission (purpose), vision (clear direction), values (collective commitments), and goals (indicators, timelines, and targets) not only addresses *how* educators will work to improve their schools, but also reinforces the moral purpose and collective responsibility that clarify *why* their day-to-day work is so important.

2. A Collaborative Culture With a Focus on Learning

If shared purpose, vision, collective commitments, and goals constitute the foundation of a PLC, then the collaborative team is the fundamental building block of the organization. A PLC is composed of collaborative teams whose members work *interdependently* to achieve *common goals*—goals linked to the purpose of learning for all—for which members are held *mutually accountable*. It is difficult to overstate the importance of collaborative teams in the PLC process. It is equally important, however, to emphasize that collaboration does not lead to improved results unless people are focused on the right issues.

Collaboration is a means to an end, not the end itself. In many schools, staff members are willing to collaborate on a variety of topics as long as the focus of the conversation stops at their classroom door. In a PLC, *collaboration* is a systematic process in which teachers work together, interdependently, to analyze and *impact* professional practice in order to improve results for their students, their team, and their school.

3. Collective Inquiry Into Best Practice and Current Reality

Educators in a PLC engage in collective inquiry into 1) best practices about teaching and learning, 2) a candid clarification of their current practices, and 3) an honest assessment of their students' current levels of learning. Collective inquiry helps educators build shared knowledge, which, in turn, allows them to make more informed (and therefore better) decisions, and increases the likelihood they will arrive at consensus. Educators in a PLC have an acute sense of curiosity and openness to new possibilities.

4. Action Orientation: Learning by Doing

Members of PLCs are action-oriented: They move quickly to turn aspirations into action and visions into reality. They understand that the most powerful learning always occurs in a context of taking action, and they value engagement and experience as the most effective teachers. In fact, the very reason that teachers work together in teams and engage in collective inquiry is to serve as catalysts for action. Learning by doing develops a deeper and more profound knowledge and greater commitment than learning by reading, listening, planning, or thinking (Pfeffer & Sutton, 2000). Furthermore, educators in PLCs recognize that until members of the organization "do" differently, there is no reason to anticipate different results. They avoid paralysis by analysis and overcome inertia with action.

5. A Commitment to Continuous Improvement

Persistent disquiet with the status quo and a constant search for a better way to achieve goals and accomplish the purpose of the organization are inherent in the PLC culture. Systematic processes engage each member of the organization in an ongoing cycle of:

- Gathering evidence of current levels of student learning

- Developing strategies and ideas to build on strengths and address weaknesses in that learning

- Implementing the strategies and ideas

- Analyzing the impact of the changes to discover what was effective and what was not

- Applying the new knowledge in the next cycle of continuous improvement

The goal is not simply learning a new strategy, but rather creating conditions for perpetual learning. This creates an environment in which innovation and experimentation are viewed not as tasks to be accomplished or projects to be completed, but as ways of conducting day-to-day business—forever. Furthermore, participation in this process is not reserved for those designated as leaders; instead, it is a responsibility of every member of the organization.

6. Results Orientation

Finally, members of a PLC realize that all of their efforts in these areas—a focus on learning, collaborative teams, collective inquiry, action orientation, and continuous improvement—must be assessed on the basis of results rather than intentions. Unless initiatives are subjected to ongoing assessment on the basis of tangible results, they represent random groping in the dark, not purposeful improvement. As Peter Senge and Fred Kofman (1995) have concluded, "The rationale for any strategy for building a learning organization revolves around the premise that such organizations will produce dramatically improved results" (p. 44).

The Big Ideas That Drive Professional Learning Communities

Noel Tichy (1997) contends that great leaders are able to translate the purpose and priorities of their organizations into a few big ideas that unite people and give them a sense of direction in their day-to-day work. We have found it helpful to frame the PLC concept within three big ideas.

First, the fundamental purpose of the school is to ensure all students learn at high levels, and the future success of students will depend on how effective educators are in achieving that fundamental purpose. There must be no ambiguity or hedging regarding this commitment to learning, and schools must align all practices, procedures, and policies in light of that fundamental purpose. Members of a PLC work together to clarify exactly what each student must learn, monitor each student's learning on a timely basis, provide systematic interventions that ensure students receive additional time and support for learning when they struggle, and extend and enrich learning when students have already mastered the intended outcomes. A corollary assumption stipulates that if all students are to learn at high levels, the adults in the organization must also be continually learning. Therefore, structures are created to ensure staff members engage in job-embedded learning as part of their routine work practices.

Second, schools cannot achieve the fundamental purpose of learning for all if educators work in isolation. Therefore, school administrators and teachers must build a collaborative culture in which they work together interdependently and assume collective responsibility for the learning of all students.

Third, schools will not know whether or not all students are learning unless educators are hungry for evidence that students are acquiring the knowledge, skills, and dispositions deemed most essential to their success. Schools must systematically monitor student learning on an ongoing basis and use evidence of results to respond immediately to students who experience difficulty, to inform individual and collective practice, and to fuel continuous improvement.

Purposeful Language

As we were determining the title for *Professional Learning Communities at Work,* we chose each word of that title very purposefully. A *professional* is someone with expertise in a specialized field, an individual who has not only pursued advanced training to enter the field, but who is also expected to remain current in its evolving knowledge base. The knowledge base of education has expanded dramatically in the past 30 years, both in terms of research and in the articulation of recommended standards for the profession. Educators in a *professional* learning community make these findings the basis of their collaborative investigation into how they can better achieve their goals. They *practice* teaching and leading by constantly enhancing their skills and knowledge in the same way a doctor practices medicine or a lawyer practices law.

The term *learning* also carries significant weight in the title. One of the major challenges in the implementation of the PLC concept is convincing educators to shift from a focus on teaching to a focus on learning—to move beyond the question, "Was it taught?" to the far more relevant question, "Was it learned?" We advocate for *learning* communities, not *teaching* communities, and argue that the best way to improve student learning is to invest in the learning of the adults who serve them.

Learning suggests ongoing action and perpetual curiosity. In Chinese, the term *learning* is represented by two characters: The first means "to study," and the second means "to practice constantly." The only hope for creating schools and districts that are continuously improving upon their capacity to raise student achievement is to establish the expectation that educators must engage in the ongoing study and constant practice of their field. If all students are to learn, those who educate them must be lifelong learners.

Much had been written about learning organizations when we wrote our original book, but we have always preferred the term *community*. While the term *organization* evokes images of structure and efficiency, the term *community* suggests a group linked by common interests. As Thomas Sergiovanni (2005) writes, "Communities spring from common understandings that provide members with a sense of identity, belonging, and involvement that results in a web of meaningful relationships with moral overtones" (p. 55). Communities form around common characteristics, experiences, practices, or beliefs that are important enough to bind members to one another in a kind of fellowship (Carey & Frohnen, 1998). Successful communities provide members with broadly shared opportunities to participate, promote collective responsibility, and foster a strong sense of belonging (Clinton, 2007).

In a professional learning *community*, all of these characteristics are evident. Educators create an environment that fosters shared understanding, a sense of identity, high levels of involvement, mutual cooperation, collective responsibility, emotional support, and a strong sense of belonging as they work together to achieve what they cannot accomplish alone.

What Has Become More Clear?

In the time since we wrote *Professional Learning Communities at Work,* we have acquired much knowledge as we have worked with schools and districts to implement the PLC concept. This enables us to offer richer and more helpful ideas to contemporary educators. In short, much has become more clear to us about improving learning both for students and adults. Therefore, this book will not only review the core concepts and practices of a PLC, it will also explore each of the following 12 new and/or deeper learnings in detail:

1. The Necessity (and Challenge) of Shaping the Culture of the School and District

Educators who cultivate PLCs must engage in an intentional process to impact the culture of their schools and districts. When they are successful, their organizations will undergo profound cultural shifts. We certainly stressed the importance of culture—*the assumptions, beliefs, values, expectations, and habits that constitute the norm for an organization*—in *Professional Learning Communities at Work*. What has become more clear to us is that those who hope to reculture a school or district will face two very significant barriers. First, educators have been conditioned to regard school improvement as programs to adopt or practices to implement, rather than as an ongoing process to build their collective capacity to achieve the purpose, priorities, and goals of their organizations. It is not unusual for us to hear a faculty say, "We do PLCs on Thursday mornings"—a telltale sign they have missed the central premise of the PLC concept and have simply added a new practice to their existing school culture. When the culture has truly shifted, a faculty recognizes that they *are* a PLC; they do not *do* PLCs. They subject every practice, program, policy, and procedure to ongoing review and constant evaluation according to very different assumptions than those that guided the school in the past.

The second barrier to reculturing is particularly formidable. Diarist Anaïs Nin observed, "We don't see things as they are, we see things as we are." Every one of us develops patterns of thought or mental models that represent complex webs of our ideas and assumptions about the world in which we live (Senge, 1990). These models filter our observations and experiences and help us make sense of them. New information gets processed to conform to the ongoing stories we tell ourselves. Anything inconsistent with that story or contrary to our mental models is likely to be dismissed or ignored. "People," Emerson wrote, "only see what they are prepared to see."

Organizational theorists advise that a key to improving any organization is honestly assessing the current reality (Collins, 2001) and confronting the hard facts (Pfeffer & Sutton, 2006). Who could oppose such sound advice? We have discovered, however, that the problem in improving schools is not presenting compelling evidence of the need for change, or even demonstrating the most promising strategies for raising student achievement; the problem is that the evidence and strategies often get filtered through the mental models and mythology of the hard-working, well-intentioned educators who are ultimately called upon to do differently.

The case for operating schools and districts as PLCs is compelling; it is supported by research, proven in practice, endorsed by professional organizations, and best of all, grounded in common sense. We cannot recall a single time when we have reviewed the evidence in support of PLCs with a group of educators, and they then opposed the concept. No staff has ever argued schools are more effective when teachers work in isolation, when they focus on what is taught rather than on what is learned, when high-stakes summative assessments are the only tools used to monitor student learning, or when the response to students who are not learning is left to the discretion of each teacher. But later, all too often, the existing mental models and prevailing mythology begin to erode and distort the PLC concept. Examples of the prevailing mythology include the following:

- "Not all kids can be expected to learn at high levels, because learning is a function of ability, and ability is distributed along the bell-shaped curve."

- "It is my job to teach and their job to learn."

- "We won't be able to improve student learning until parents, the administration, the school board, the legislature, and society do a better job of fulfilling their responsibilities."

- "The schedule won't let us."

- "If we give students additional opportunities to learn when they struggle, we teach them to be irresponsible and deprive them of the important lessons to be learned through failure."

- "I am the king of my kingdom, and as a professional, I want the autonomy to make my own decisions unencumbered from the opinions of others in my school."

- "As a teacher, I am only responsible for the students in my classroom, and I do not intend to take on responsibility for other students or have others interfere in my work with my students."

- "As a principal, I am only responsible for what goes on in my own school, and I don't want to take on responsibility for helping to improve other schools."

- "We are working as hard as humanly possible, and everything we are currently doing is vital, so we cannot stop doing anything we are doing or add any more to our already full plates."

- "You can find research to support anything, and researchers do not understand the world of practitioners, so we should not be persuaded by research."

- "People can skew data to say anything they want, so we should not be persuaded by data."

- "I have always done it this way, and I have been successful."

- "It is the administration's job to improve the school, not mine."

- "If we just had more resources, all our problems would be solved."

- "We cannot go forward unless everyone agrees, because you cannot insist that people do something they do not choose to do."

- "I have worked hard to create 'my stuff' for my class, and I do not want to share my materials with others."

- "This is just the latest fad, and it too shall pass."

- "I have too much content to cover to take the time to gather evidence that students are learning."

- "We are doing as well or better than the schools around us, and the parents seem satisfied, so it would be foolish to tinker with success."

- "Teachers do not have the expertise to develop good curriculum, write valid assessments, or analyze data, so this work should be left to the experts."

The words President John F. Kennedy spoke at Yale University in 1962 are uncannily appropriate when applied to the world of public education:

> As every past generation has had to disenthrall itself from an inheritance of truisms and stereotypes, so in our own time we must move on from the reassuring repetition of stale phrases to a new, difficult, but essential confrontation with reality. For the great enemy of truth is very often not the lie—deliberate, contrived and dishonest— but the myth—persistent, persuasive and unrealistic. . . . Mythology distracts us everywhere.

There is no easy way to overcome the obstacle of mythology when engaged in school improvement. It involves making thinking explicit and calling upon people to engage in the difficult task of articulating and examining their assumptions. It calls for building shared knowledge and learning by doing. It requires breaking free of inertia by creating new experiences for people that call upon them to act in new ways. It demands constant and consistent commitment to a sustained direction during an extended period of time. There is no one "A-ha!" moment when the existing culture will give way to new assumptions, beliefs, values, expectations, and habits that constitute the norm for the school or district. The transformation requires fierce resolve, tremendous passion, and relentless persistence. No matter how effectively the case is made for building the capacity of a staff to function as a PLC, much work will remain to be done.

2. The Tendency for Hard Facts About School Improvement to Be Distorted Into Dangerous Half-Truths

Stanford University researchers Jeffrey Pfeffer and Robert Sutton (2006) have concluded organizations often distort clear and compelling evidence of best practice into dangerous half-truths. We have repeatedly seen this phenomenon at work in schools and districts throughout North America. The existing mythology of schooling is so seductive that rather than recognizing the need to create a new culture based on new assumptions, educators are prone to adopt and dilute ideas and concepts to fit their existing culture. They opt for "sorta PLCs," and the concept begins a slow but inevitable death from the constant compromises of its core principles. Throughout this book, we will identify examples of how powerful hard facts are being distorted into dangerous half-truths in education.

3. The Importance of an Action Orientation, or "Learning by Doing"

In *Professional Learning Communities at Work,* we stressed the importance of building the foundation of a PLC through the articulation of shared mission (purpose), vision (clear direction), values (collective commitments), and goals (indicators, timelines, and targets). We offered strategies and templates for leading the dialogue and generating the documents designed to reflect this solid foundation for moving forward. It has become apparent, however, that schools and districts often settle for merely creating documents rather than implementing ideas. In many instances, little is done to align organizational practices or individual actions with the expressed purpose and priorities. We have come to understand that writing a mission statement has often been used as a substitute for living a mission. Dialogue and documents can be used to create the illusion of change and to impede rather than promote meaningful action. Therefore, in this book we repeatedly return to the questions, "What would it look like if we really meant what we said?" and "What specific actions can we expect to see in light of our priorities?"

4. The Importance of Frequent, Common Formative Assessments

In *Professional Learning Communities at Work,* we listed two questions to guide the work of a PLC: "What is it we want our students to learn?" and "How will we respond when they do not learn?" Later in the book, we discussed teachers developing common assessments as part of their collaborative team process. We implied that teachers would work together to answer the question, "How will we know if our students are learning?" But in retrospect, we did not give this issue nearly enough attention. We have come to understand that one of the most powerful strategies available to a school that hopes to become an effective PLC is to engage teachers in the creation of high-quality common assessments. The question, "How do we know if our students are acquiring the intended knowledge, skills, and dispositions of this course, grade level, or unit of instruction?" is the linchpin of the PLC process and a critical component of the work of collaborative teams. Furthermore, the work of Doug Reeves, Dylan Wiliam, Paul Black, Rick Stiggins, and others has helped us come to a much deeper appreciation of the importance and power of *formative* assessments, assessments used as part of the teaching and learning process instead of assessments administered only to provide a grade. We examine common formative assessments in detail in chapter 8.

5. The Importance of Providing Teachers With Relevant and Timely Information (Not Data) as a Catalyst for Improving Teaching

We have concluded schools and teachers suffer from the DRIP syndrome: They are data rich, but information poor. Most teachers are awash in data, but data alone will neither inform nor improve a teacher's practice, and students will not achieve at higher levels unless teachers are becoming more effective in their classrooms. Without relevant information on their respective strengths and weaknesses, teacher conversations regarding the most effective ways to help students learn a concept will deteriorate into sharing of uninformed opinions—"This is how I like to teach it." Improving teacher practice requires informed and precise conversation about effective techniques, and the best way to provide teachers with the tools for that conversation is to ensure each receives frequent and timely information regarding the achievement of his or her students in reaching an agreed-upon standard on a valid assessment in comparison to other similar students attempting to achieve the same standard. We will later review strategies and processes that provide teachers with the ongoing information they need to improve their practice.

6. The Importance of a Systematic Response When Students Don't Learn, and a Process for Enriching and Expanding Learning When Students Are Already Proficient

In *Professional Learning Communities at Work,* we made repeated references to the significance of a collective response when students did not learn. We did not, however, adequately address what such a response would look like in the real world of schools. We attempt to address that here by providing parameters for and examples of systematic interventions that ensure students receive additional time and support for learning when they struggle. We have also asked educators to tackle the issue of how schools can expand and enrich learning for students who are already proficient in the skills being taught.

7. The Importance of Guiding the Work of Collaborative Teams

We have come to a deeper understanding of steps that schools can take to help teachers move from a tradition of isolation to a culture of collaboration; however, it has also become increasingly evident that simply providing educators with time to collaborate will do nothing to improve a school if they spend that time focusing on issues that do not impact student learning. One of the most pressing questions a school must consider as it attempts to build the collaborative culture of a PLC is not, "Do we collaborate?" but rather, "What do we collaborate about?" This book offers more specific and purposeful strategies to help educators engage in collaboration that impacts both student and adult learning.

8. The Importance of Widespread Leadership and the Role of the Central Office

Professional Learning Communities at Work focused on the school as the center of change and devoted little attention to the role of the central office in promoting the PLC concept throughout a district. Furthermore, although it called upon principals to involve faculty in decision-making and to empower teachers and teams, it offered few specific examples regarding widespread distribution of leadership. This book will address both the role of the central office and specific ways to distribute leadership throughout the organization. It will also explore the critical role of leaders in initiating and sustaining a substantive improvement process.

9. The Classroom as a Learning Community

In the past, we focused on restructuring schools to operate as PLCs. We have come to believe, however, that aspects of the concept can also be applied to the classroom. We include a chapter here on how restructuring classrooms to function as learning communities in their own right can provide the structure and climate for enhanced student learning, more effective teaching, and more positive relationships.

10. The Need for a Common Language

Harvard researchers Robert Kegan and Lisa Laskow Lahey (2001) found that changing the conversation in an organization can have a profound impact on its culture and the day-to-day work of the people within it. Changes in conversation, however, require specificity of language.

Many organizations settle for superficiality in language, using terms so ambiguously and loosely that they can mean very different things to different people. We have come to understand that not only a common language, but also precision regarding the meaning of that language, are crucial to the culture of discipline essential to effective schools and districts. This book will attempt to provide clarity and exactness regarding the critical terminology of professional learning communities.

11. The Benefit of a Contemporary Context

Much has changed in public education in the past decade. State standards have attempted to clarify what students must learn, state assessments are being used to monitor schools, and sanctions and penalties are now imposed upon schools and students on the basis of test results. No Child Left Behind legislation has been enacted and continues to be debated. This book addresses the current context of public education.

12. The Power of Stories

Richard Axelrod (2002) once wrote, "Universities come to know about things through studies, organizations come to know about things through reports, and people come to know about things through stories" (p. 112). Kouzes and Posner (1999) describe storytelling as "the most basic form of communication—more prevalent and powerful than facts and figures." They claim, "The strongest structure for any argument is a story" (p. 101). Howard Gardner (1990) argues that the artful creation and articulation of stories constitute a fundamental responsibility of leaders. Noel Tichy (1997) concurs that the ability to create and tell a vibrant story is one of the most powerful teaching tools available to leaders—"an essential prerequisite to becoming a first-class winning leader" (p. 174). In our own work with schools, we have found that stories are what people remember best, because good stories appeal to both reason and emotion—the head and the heart. Good stories teach us. They convey not only how something should be done, but more importantly, why it should be done. They communicate priorities and clarify what is significant, valued, and appreciated. Therefore, we have integrated stories into many of the chapters of this book to help illustrate our points.

Søren Kierkegaard observed that while life must be lived forward, it can only be understood backward. Before moving forward with recommendations for transforming schools, we examine the historical antecedents that have brought contemporary educators to this moment of opportunity. Chapter 2 provides a history of education reform.

Chapter 2

The Rise and Fall of School Reform

Education reform has become the new status quo. Every president aspires to be the education president, every governor the education governor. The reform process has never ended because the reforms have typically led to disappointment—and to constant demands for still more reforms.

—Terry Moe

We cannot solve the problems of today with the same thinking that gave us the problems in the first place.

—Albert Einstein

Although the United States was the first nation to embrace the idea of free universal education for all its children, its schools were specifically designed to sort and select students according to their perceived abilities and likely vocations. Thomas Jefferson asserted that general education was critical to the vitality of the new republic, and he proposed 3 years of public schooling for the children of Virginia. He also, however, designed a system of education that ensured only the 20 boys of "best genius" in the state would be "raked from the rubbish annually" to receive up to 10 years of schooling at the public's expense, and that only half of those would ultimately be admitted to the university each year (Jefferson, 1782). Schools became adept at this process of separating the wheat from the chaff, and for most of the nation's history, there was very little wheat. In 1900, only 10% of high school-aged Americans attended school, and it would be almost 175 years after Jefferson presented his plan for "universal" education before the majority of students who entered public schooling in any given year would complete a high school education.

If sorting and selecting students was the fundamental task of education, the factory model—the prevalent organizational model of the late 19th and early 20th centuries—provided the ideal conceptual framework for completing that task. Frederick Winslow Taylor, the father of "scientific management," argued that "one best system" could be identified to complete any task or solve any organizational problem. According to Taylor, management's job was to identify the one best way, train workers accordingly, and provide the supervision and monitoring needed to ensure that workers would follow the prescribed methods without deviation. Taylor's model demanded centralization, standardization, hierarchical top-down management, a rigid sense of time, and accountability based on adherence to the system. The assembly line embodied Taylor's principles and helped the United States become the world's industrial giant.

Confident they had discovered the one best way to run any organization, business leaders and politicians argued that schools should adopt a similar model to produce the kinds of workers industry required. The uniformity, standardization, and bureaucracy of the factory model soon became predominant characteristics of the school district. The key was to have the *thinkers* of the organization specify exactly what and how to teach at each grade level, and then to provide strict supervision to ensure teachers did as they were told. Decisions flowed down the educational hierarchy to teachers who, like factory workers, were viewed as underlings responsible for carrying out the decisions of their bosses.

The focus was on the process rather than the results. If teachers taught the right curriculum, utilized the correct textbooks, assigned students to the appropriate classes, and adhered to the correct schedule, the results would take care of themselves.

And, just as different assembly lines were designed to produce finished products of differing quality (Cadillacs versus Chevrolets), the educational assembly line was designed to turn out students of various levels. Curriculum and expectations varied significantly to reflect the quality of the raw material (that is, students) to be shaped by the schools. In 1910, the National Education Association (cited in Lazerson & Grubb, 1974) called upon educators to "recognize differences among children as to aptitudes, interests, economic resources, and prospective careers" and to sort and select them accordingly. Students were simply the passive raw material transported along the educational assembly line.

In *Democracy and Education,* published in 1916, John Dewey opposed aspects of the factory model in schooling and offered the conceptual framework for "a new education"—child-centered schools in which the curriculum was determined in large part by the interests of the students, and learning became experiential and social rather than rote. Dewey's ideas, which reflected the reformist era of his times, resonated with many educators, and advocates of "progressive education" proliferated across the country.

By the second half of the 20th century, however, progressive education was under attack from a counterrevolution of traditionalists (Rippa, 1974). Articles entitled "Crisis in Education," "What Went Wrong with U.S. Schools," and "We Are Less Educated than Fifty Years Ago" may have a contemporary ring, but they were published in 1957 and 1958 in *Life* and *U.S. News & World Report.* In that same era, Arthur Bestor (1953) argued in his best seller, *Educational Wastelands,* that citizens should wrest control of the public schools from "educationists" who had "dumbed down" the curriculum. *Why Johnny Can't Read* (1955) by Rudolf Flesch came to a similar conclusion. With the launching of

Sputnik in 1957, many cited the failure of the public schools to provide a rigorous curriculum as the primary reason that the United States had fallen behind Russia in the race to space, and a spate of university-based curriculum reforms, particularly in mathematics and science, emerged as the preferred strategy for resolving the crisis.

A quarter of a century later, the ascendance of Japan as an economic power once again led critics to conclude that the public schools were responsible for an American crisis—this time, the fall from its position of unchallenged economic superiority. In April 1983, the National Commission on Excellence in Education captured headlines with its conclusion: National security was in peril because of substandard education in American public schools. The commission made frequent references to "decline," "deficiencies," "threats," "risks," "afflictions," and "plight." The opening sentences of the report set the tone:

> Our nation is at risk. . . . The educational foundations of our society are presently being eroded by a rising tide of mediocrity that threatens our very future as a nation and as a people. . . . We have, in effect, been committing an act of unthinking, unilateral educational disarmament. (1983, p. 5)

A Nation at Risk served as a catalyst for a flurry of school improvement initiatives throughout the United States that came to be known collectively as the "excellence movement." Within 2 years of the report, more than 300 state and national task forces had investigated the condition of public education in America. But the excellence movement did not offer a new direction; instead, schools simply needed to do *more*! Students needed to earn *more* credits for graduation in courses that were *more* rigorous and required *more* homework. Schools needed to add *more* days to the school year and *more* hours to the school day. Schools needed to test students *more* frequently and expect *more* of teachers, both before offering employment and before extending tenure. The reforms of the excellence movement simply called for an intensification of existing practices. They contained no new ideas. By the end of the decade, the United States Department of Education was forced to report that despite the unprecedented effort to reform American schools, student achievement continued to stagnate at relatively low levels (Alsalam & Ogle, 1990).

The failure of the excellence movement was widely attributed to the fact that it represented a "top-down" attempt to mandate improvement. It had tended toward standardization, increased reliance on rules and regulations, and detailed specifications of school practices at the expense of local autonomy. Impetus for the movement had come from elected officials and business. Control was centered in state legislatures. Practitioners had become mere pawns in the movement, and the vast majority of the reform efforts had simply been imposed on them.

This demise of the top-down excellence movement prompted the "restructuring movement," a new, two-pronged approach to school improvement based on establishing national goals and providing site-based local autonomy to achieve these goals. President George H.W. Bush articulated the strategy when he called for "decentralization of authority and decision-making responsibility to the school site, so that educators are empowered to determine the means for accomplishing the goals and are to be held accountable for accomplishing them" (Bush, 1989). To establish the national goals, Bush convened the nation's governors for an educational summit that, after some tweaking by Congress, led to the creation of Goals 2000, which stated that by the turn of the century:

1. All children in America will start school ready to learn.

2. The high school graduation rate will increase to at least 90%.

3. American students will leave grades 4, 8, and 12 having demonstrated competency in challenging subject matter, including English, mathematics, science, history, and geography, and every school in America will ensure that all students learn to use their

minds well, so they are prepared for responsible citizenship, further learning, and productive employment in our modern economy.

4. U.S. students will rank first in the world in mathematics and science achievement.

5. Every adult American will be literate and possess the knowledge and skills necessary to compete in a global economy and exercise the rights and responsibilities of citizenship.

6. Every school in America will be free of drugs and violence and will offer a disciplined environment conducive to learning.

7. The nation's teaching force will have access to programs for the continued development of their professional skills and the opportunity to acquire the knowledge and skills needed to instruct and prepare all American students for the next century.

8. Every school will promote partnerships that will increase parental involvement and participation in promoting the social, emotional, and academic growth of children.

Two assumptions drove the initiative: First, the ambitious national goals would send a clear message that schools could not conduct business as usual. Schools would need to be completely restructured to meet the monumental challenge confronting them. Second, educators would warm to the challenge because they would be freed from the shackles of bureaucracy and top-down mandates and would have the autonomy to do what was needed to improve their schools. Both assumptions proved to be false.

Studies of the movement's impact consistently found that school practitioners typically elected to focus on marginal changes that did not directly address the quality of student learning (Newmann & Wehlage, 1995). In fact, educators in restructured schools seemed no more inclined to discuss conditions of teaching and learning than their colleagues in schools with traditional structures. Students were left virtually untouched by the reforms that swirled around, but not within, their classrooms. So the restructuring movement, like the excellence movement before it, failed to make a significant difference in the ability of American schools to meet the challenges they face.

No Child Left Behind: All Students Will Learn, Or Else!

With the dawn of a new century, education reform took yet another turn in the United States with the passage of No Child Left Behind (NCLB) legislation in 2002. No Child Left Behind was one of the first items on the domestic agenda of President George W. Bush, and it passed Congress with strong bipartisan support. The law increased testing requirements, mandating annual assessments in reading and mathematics in grades 3 through 8 and once in high school. It called for reporting student test results separately by race, ethnicity, and other key demographic groups, and it required schools to demonstrate "adequate yearly progress" (AYP) on state tests overall and for each group of students. If schools could not demonstrate AYP, they faced interventions followed by increasingly severe sanctions. The law also stipulated that students could transfer to better-performing schools or receive tutoring if their schools did not demonstrate sufficient progress, required states to ensure that every teacher was "highly qualified," and mandated detailed reports to parents on school performance and teacher quality. Finally, the law designated annual increases in the percentage of students achieving proficiency on the state assessment until 2014, when the poor performance of a single student would designate the entire school as "failing."

The law was clearly the most ambitious educational initiative in American history. As one report concluded, "NCLB has affected families, classrooms and school districts throughout the country. Virtually every aspect of schooling—from what is taught in elementary, middle and high school classes, to how teachers are hired, to how money is allocated—has been affected by the statute" (Commission on No Child Left Behind, 2007, p. 14).

Once again, America's very survival was at stake. Advocates of the law contended that the United States faced a stark choice: Would it take bold steps to improve education or "risk jeopardizing the future of our nation's children and our competitiveness in the global economy by maintaining the status quo" (Commission on No Child Left Behind, 2007, p. 11)? We assume the question was rhetorical.

An issue unique (or perhaps, peculiar) to American public education soon emerged. Although it was argued that education was a national priority, the federal role in education had traditionally been quite limited. Less than 7% of the funding for education came from federal dollars, and the responsibility for education had traditionally been left to the states. As NCLB was being crafted, there was great reluctance, particularly among groups that opposed "big government," to either infringe on state's rights or exalt the role of the United States Department of Education. Congress resolved this dilemma by mandating strict sanctions for schools that failed to show they were helping students achieve adequate yearly progress, but allowing each of the 50 states to determine what students should be expected to learn, how they would be assessed, and the rigor of both standards and assessments.

Criticism of NCLB grew as the United States Department of Education implemented the legislation. The following are the most frequently cited concerns.

The Definition of "Adequate Yearly Progress"

Critics of NCLB objected to a system that assessed the quality of a school on the performance of its students on a single test at a single point in time. They also objected to the fact that growth was not a significant factor in determining AYP. A school with a large number of economically disadvantaged students could be deemed failing, even if its students could demonstrate dramatic progress, while a school with a population of students of high socioeconomic status could be deemed successful despite showing no growth or actual decline. For example, in 2004–2005, 62% of Florida's schools did not meet AYP, yet more than a third of those failing schools were graded as either "A" or "B" on the state's 5-scale report card, which awards half of its points on student growth from year to year (West, 2005).

Opponents of the law also criticized its provision that an entire school would be designated as failing because of the disaggregated performance of as few as 30 students in any one of the 37 different subgroups of classification (for example, students with special needs, students with limited English proficiency, and so on). If even one subgroup failed to meet the proficiency standard for 2 consecutive years, all students in the school would be given the opportunity to transfer to a "successful school." As Gerald Bracey (2006) writes, "a school might be doing well by 36 of its 37 subgroups, but in federal eyes it is uniformly failing." In 2003–2004, only one third of the schools that failed to make AYP did so because of the achievement of all students. All others failed because of the performance of subgroups, absenteeism on the day of the test, or other factors identified in the legislation (Stover, 2007).

The Disparity Among States

Because establishing standards, developing assessments, and defining the level of performance necessary for students to achieve proficiency were left to the discretion of each state, states with the highest expectations are most likely to have failing schools under NCLB. In fact, one way for an education governor to show the effectiveness of his or her leadership is to create an assessment system with low enough standards for most students to be deemed proficient.

The state-driven NCLB assessment is not the first attempt to determine the proficiency of American students. Congress established the National Assessment of Educational Progress (NAEP) in 1969 to monitor the academic achievement of elementary and secondary students in the United States and to report findings to Congress and the public. A bipartisan National Assessment Governing Board was created to determine the subject areas to be assessed, establish appropriate student achievement levels, and oversee the creation of the assessments. Results are presented, state-by-state, for students in grades 4, 8, and 12 in what has come to be called "The Nation's Report Card."

There is, however, virtually no correlation between student proficiency on state tests and performance on the NAEP. For example, in 2005 Texas reported that 79% of its fourth-grade students were proficient or better in reading on its state test, but only 29% achieved proficiency or better on the NAEP. Mississippi boasted 89% of its students achieved proficiency on the state test, but only 18% met that standard on NAEP. Missouri, on the other hand, had only 35% of its students meet the state proficiency standard, but 33% were proficient or better on NAEP (Toppo, 2007). Thus, Missouri, whose students scored well above students from Texas, Mississippi, and most other states on a common national assessment, has far more schools in sanctions for not meeting the AYP requirement of NCLB. The data suggest that the single most expeditious strategy for the state of Missouri to increase the percentage of its students achieving proficiency on the state assessment (and thereby reducing the number of schools not meeting AYP) is to administer the Mississippi exam to its students.

As one critic wrote, "The perverse impact of NCLB is to encourage states to lower their expectations for students so fewer schools are identified as failing" (West, 2005, p.1). Another acknowledged, "It was not difficult to determine that asking all states to reach 'universal proficiency' by 2014 but allowing them to define 'proficiency' as they saw fit would create 'a race to the bottom'" (Petrilli, 2007).

The Nature of the Assessments

In 2001, prior to the enactment of NCLB, the Commission on Instructionally Supportive Assessment identified criteria for assessment that supported learning. The criteria included:

- A modest number of curricular aims

- Clear, concise descriptions of each curricular aim

- Instructionally useful reports that help teachers and students alike understand areas of strengths and weaknesses in a student's learning

The Commission recommended that state assessment results be reported standard-by-standard for each student, school, and district.

State assessments typically fail to meet these standards on all counts. W. James Popham, chair of the Commission, contends states have identified far too many curricular aims to teach in the time available and that teachers are unable to learn from NCLB tests because they receive "too general score reports" that fail to provide the specific information teachers need to improve their instruction. As Popham (2004) concludes, "The problem is that most state curricula, against a backdrop of these significant NCLB pressures to improve test scores, are actually lowering the quality of education in a state's schools" (p. 31).

Lack of Funding

Congress authorized more than 91.25 billion dollars over 5 years to help public education finance the new and demanding mandates of NCLB. Only 59.8 billion actually was approved. Critics have charged that one of the problems with the implementation of NCLB is that it was under-funded by over 31 billion dollars.

As this book goes to press, the United States Congress is considering the reauthorization of NCLB. Liberals and conservatives alike are calling for major revisions, although they offer contradictory recommendations. The Forum on Educational Accountability is a consortium of over 100 religious, educational, civil rights, and civic organizations that continue to endorse the NCLB premise of raising student achievement and closing the achievement gap. Nevertheless, this "coalition of the willing" has attacked the implementation of NCLB for its over-emphasis on standardized testing, narrowing of the curriculum and instruction to focus on test preparation, over-identifying schools in need of improvement, using sanctions that do not improve schools, and inadequate funding. The Forum has presented 14 recommendations to Congress for improving NCLB, including considering growth in the assessment of schools, using multiple indicators of student achievement, and reducing the reliance on sanctions.

The 15-member Commission on No Child Left Behind is a bipartisan group established by the Aspen Institute, a nonprofit organization dedicated to fostering enlightened leadership and open-minded dialogue. Although the Commission was decidedly pro-NCLB upon its creation, 5 years later, it too expressed concerns and offered 75 recommendations for improvement. Its proposals, however, call for ratcheting up the pressure on educators and their schools by demanding still greater accountability and even tougher sanctions.

The Commission called for the redefinition of a "highly qualified" teacher to place less emphasis on academic credentials and more emphasis on the teacher's ability to demonstrate growth in student learning by raising test scores for his or her students. Teachers who fell into the bottom quartile of the state would be designated as low performers and would be required to undergo 3 years of professional development. If they still did not meet the standard of an effective teacher, a district could choose to retain them for an additional 2 years, but would be required to advise parents that their students are not being taught by a highly qualified and effective teacher. At the conclusion of the 2 years, the teacher could no longer teach in any school receiving Title I funds. The proposal guaranteed that at least one fourth of the teachers in any state would be deemed deficient.

Principals too would be required to produce improvements in student achievement that were comparable to high-achieving schools with similar student populations. Any individual who could not meet this standard within 3 years could no longer serve as the principal of a Title I school.

The Commission also called for the creation of yet another assessment for all students in grade 12 "to assess content 12th-grade students must master in the 12th grade and that they need to be college and workplace ready" (Commission on No Child Left Behind, 2007, p. 136). The Commission argued the assessment would serve as a measure of a school's effectiveness and, importantly, would hold high schools more accountable.

President Bush himself weighed in for reauthorization of the law and sought to assure the public and the educational community that the law was not intended to punish schools, but rather to help them. The problem, in his view, was not implementation, but perception, and proponents of NCLB simply needed to do a better job of explaining the benevolent intent of holding schools accountable ("Bush," 2007).

Others, however, questioned whether NCLB could ever achieve its lofty purpose of higher student achievement and the elimination of the achievement gap, even if it underwent significant revisions. Diane Ravitch (2007b), the former undersecretary of education in the George H.W. Bush administration, pointed out there was no research-based evidence that the sanctions of NCLB actually improved schools and questioned why federal legislation would be based upon unproven and questionable strategies. Michael Petrilli, a former member of the United States Department of Education in the George W. Bush administration, played a key role in attempting to persuade educators and legislators of the benefits of the law. Petrilli (2007) described himself as a "true believer" and a primary cheerleader for NCLB. By 2007, however, he had lost hope. As he wrote, "Speaking personally, I've gradually and reluctantly come to the conclusion that NCLB as enacted is fundamentally flawed and probably beyond repair. . . . I can't pretend any longer that the law is 'working,' or that a tweak and a tuck would make it work."

Public support for NCLB has waned. By mid-2007, nearly two thirds of American adults prefer the law be rewritten or abolished. The more familiar people were with the law, the more likely they were to oppose it. Even 52 Republican congressmen and 5 Republican senators broke ranks and called for a repeal of the law (Hargrove & Stempel, 2007).

One can argue that NCLB has changed the conversation about education in America. Questions regarding how to assess the quality of a school, what learning is most essential, and how to monitor the proficiency of each student are much more a part of the dialogue both inside and outside of the educational community than they have been in the past. It is likely that far more attention is being paid to the achievement of groups of students who were overlooked prior to NCLB. Throughout most of American history, public education—an enterprise that consumes approximately 400 billion dollars in expenditures each year (National Center for Educational Statistics, 2007)—has been largely unaccountable for demonstrating results. It is self-evident that the practice of assigning teachers with the weakest academic backgrounds and least experience to schools and students with the greatest needs must be addressed. Thus, NCLB has certainly raised issues regarding public schooling in America that needed to be addressed.

Nevertheless, 5 years after the passage of NCLB, even the most benign assessment of the impact of the legislation must acknowledge the U.S. Department of Education was incorrect when it boldly asserted that holding schools accountable for the academic achievement of every student through the application of increasingly severe sanctions would "ensure that no child is left behind." In fact, one comprehensive study of the achievement of fourth graders on the National Assessment of Educational Progress from 1992 to 2006 concluded there were greater gains in student achievement in reading in math in the years prior to the implementation of NCLB than in the years following, and progress that had taken place in narrowing the achievement gap in the 1990s largely disappeared in the post-NCLB era (Fuller, Wright, Gesicki, & Kang, 2007). As one author concluded, "NCLB is to education what Katrina was to New Orleans" (Bracey, 2006). The most ambitious federal program to reform education in the history of the United States has made little, if any, progress toward achieving its goals.

Considering the Impact of Nonstop School Reform

Although we have presented the efforts to reform American education in the past quarter century in three phases—the excellence movement, the restructuring movement, and No Child Left Behind—a case could be made the nation has engaged in a continuous, unabated, even frenzied effort to improve its schools during this time period. What effect has this quarter century of nonstop reform had on public education in America?

The Disappointment of Conservatives

Conservatives staunchly supported NCLB, arguing it had the potential to transform American schools, "to do for the *quality* of America's schools what Brown v. Board of Education did for the *equality* of America's schools" (Chubb, 2005, p. 1). Conservatives were convinced that because public education suffered from the complacency and bloated bureaucracy endemic to monopolies, competition and threats of sanctions were required to shake educators from their lethargy. The application of free-market principles to schools represented the best solution to the problems of education, and conservatives applauded NCLB provisions that allowed parents to send their children to the public school of their choice and gave states the power to take over low-performing schools. As one advocate explained, "When parents are able to vote with their feet, and when they are given alternatives—charter schools or private schools—to the regular public schools, the latter are put on notice that they stand to lose kids and money if they don't perform" (Moe, 2006). Another promised, "If every school in the nation were to face a high level of competition both from other districts and from private schools, the productivity of America's schools, in terms of students' level of learning at a given level of spending, would be 28 percent higher than it is now" (Hoxby, 2001, p. 72).

Alas, the promise of booming student achievement as a result of increased accountability, sanctions, and parental choice has, to date, failed to come to fruition. The NCLB provision that allowed parents to transfer their children out of a "failing" public school had little impact, as only about 1% of eligible students exercised that option (Stover, 2007). States have shown very little interest in taking over failing schools, and their capacity to do so has been called into question (Ratner, 2007). Research regarding the impact of charter schools and vouchers on student achievement has produced mixed results. In 2006, the National Center for Education Statistics (NCES) found that after adjusting for student characteristics, charter schools scored significantly lower than public schools in both reading and mathematics, and charter schools associated with public school districts performed better than those independent of public schools (NCES, 2006). The NCES also attempted to examine differences in achievement between public and private school students in fourth and eighth grade. It concluded that when demographics were factored into the analysis, public school students achieved as well as their private school peers in fourth-grade reading and eighth-grade math, less well in eighth-grade reading, and outperformed private school students in fourth-grade math (NCES, 2006). A 7-year study conducted by the Center for Evaluation and Education Policy (2006) tracked a program in Cleveland, Ohio, that allowed public school students to use vouchers to offset the cost of attending private schools. The Center concluded that roughly two thirds of the students who took advantage of the voucher option had already been attending private schools, and that after controlling for differences in minority status, student mobility, and prior achievement, there were no statistically significant differences in overall achievement scores between students who used a voucher to attend a private school *throughout* their entire elementary school career (kindergarten through sixth grade) and students who attended Cleveland's public schools during those same years.

The failure of NCLB, charter schools, and vouchers to impact student achievement and improve schools led conservatives in search of an explanation as to why their strategies had failed. Some argued that the federal government had simply not been tough enough and made too many compromises that weakened the impact of sanctions (Rudalevige,

2003). Others cited the opposition of teacher unions as the cause of the failure. As Terry Moe (2006), a member of the Hoover Institution, wrote, "The unions could not stop the enactment of No Child Left Behind, the landmark federal accountability law, but they did succeed in weakening some of its key provisions. And since its passage they have done everything possible to impede its implementation, undermine its popularity, and pressure for key changes that would render it impotent." Moe alleged that teacher unions, which he described as "the most powerful force in the politics of education," considered any promising innovation for improving student learning a "mortal threat." Unions opposed school choice "because they don't want one child or one dollar to leave the schools in which their members work." Unions had also undermined attempts to hold schools accountable because "they do not want anyone to lose a job merely because they are no good at teaching."

If, however, state discretion and teacher unions were to blame for NCLB's failure to deliver the promises of its conservative advocates, it follows that states without teacher unions had full discretion to implement the law successfully. There is no evidence that their efforts were any more effective than the states with strong unions.

The Dilemma of Liberals

No Child Left Behind posed a dilemma for liberal politicians as well. On the one hand, they applauded the law's commitment to serving poor and underprivileged students. After all, liberals had long regarded education as a primary weapon of the war on poverty. But legislation does not truly take form until it is administered, and liberals have attacked the implementation of NCLB from the outset.

Richard Rothstein (2004), former education writer of *The New York Times*, presented the liberal perspective when he wrote, "Raising the achievement of lower-class children requires public policy that addresses the social and economic conditions of these children's lives, not just school reform" (back cover). Rothstein cited the litany of problems that, on average, accompanied low socioeconomic status and concluded that the cumulative effect of the "occupational, psychological, personality, and economic traits" impacting lower-class students was so huge that "schools cannot overcome it, no matter how well trained are their teachers and no matter how well designed are their instructional programs and climates" (p. 5).

Proponents of this perspective argued it was the pervasiveness of poverty in America, not substandard schooling practices, that was responsible both for the low performance of American children on international tests and the gap in achievement among students of different races and socioeconomic status. After all, a UNICEF study (2007) of the 21 richest nations in the world found the United States ranked last in almost every indicator of children's well-being. The United States had more children living in poverty (22%), had the worst record in child health and safety services, had the most children living in single-parent families, and had the lowest ranking in the positive health behaviors of its children. Another analysis of poverty in America concluded that "disproportionately large numbers of American children remain poor" with 38% of children under 18 living in low-income families (Education Commission of the States, 2007).

Furthermore, the gap between the rich and the poor in the United States is widening. Between 1979 and 2004, the after-tax income of the top 1% of the population nearly tripled, rising from $314,000 to nearly $868,000, for a total increase of $554,000 or 176% (with figures adjusted for inflation by using 2004 dollars throughout the analysis). During that same timeframe, the average after-tax income of the middle fifth of the population rose a relatively modest 21%, or $8,500, reaching $48,400 in 2004. Meanwhile, the average after-tax income of the poorest fifth of the population rose just 6%, or $800, during the past 25 years, reaching $14,700 in 2004 (Sherman & Aron-Dine, 2007).

Tax cuts enacted by the Bush administration in 2001 made the gap even more pronounced. As a result of that legislation, in 2006, households in the bottom fifth of the income spectrum received tax cuts that averaged $20 and raised their after-tax incomes by an average of 0.3%, while households in the middle fifth of the income spectrum received tax cuts that averaged $740 and raised their after-tax incomes an average of 2.5%. The top 1% of households, however, received tax cuts in 2006 that averaged $44,200 and increased their after-tax income by an average of 5.4% (Leiserson & Rohaly, 2006). As one analysis concluded, "Income is now more concentrated at the top of the income spectrum than in all but two years since the mid-1930s" (Sherman & Aron-Dine, 2007).

From the liberal perspective, closing the student achievement gap required closing this cavernous and still growing gap between the poor and the middle class. The disparity in achievement and academic potential between poor and middle-class students begins prior to children entering school and is only exacerbated during the school years (Lee & Burkham, 2002; Schemo, 2006; Steinberg, 1996; Rothstein, 2004). Children of the poor are far more likely to attend lower-quality schools with substandard facilities, fewer resources, and less qualified teachers than their middle-class peers. They return to homes and neighborhoods that are less likely to support student learning or communicate that learning is important. The problem, liberals argued, did not lie with the schools, but with societal conditions. As one writer argued, "If America's poor children could be provided the same conditions for growing up, including the same quality of schools, as those afforded to middle-class suburban youth, we would have no crisis (in education) at all" (Mehlinger, 1995, p. 27).

So while liberals acknowledged that educators needed to improve school practices, they argued that schools were being made the scapegoat for failed public policy and were being used to divert attention from larger societal issues. As Rothstein (2006) wrote,

> If we truly believe that school improvement alone can close (or even come reasonably close to closing) the achievement gap . . . then we need not worry terribly much about the serious social problems facing American society. All these problems—racial discrimination,

economic inequality, inequitable access to health care, dysfunctional families and neighborhoods—will take care of themselves. But if school improvement alone cannot close (or come close to closing) the achievement gap, then assertions to the contrary have the effect of undermining public and political pressure to take action to reform other social and economic institutions, making a significant narrowing of the achievement gap less likely. In this sense, the rhetoric of school reform is counterproductive and dangerous.

Conservatives attacked liberals for their "soft bigotry of low expectations" (Bush, 2003), their pessimism, and their failure to acknowledge the examples of high-poverty schools that were helping their students to achieve at high levels. As Chester Finn (2006) wrote:

It's also obvious that schools face a huge challenge when they must combat uncooperative forces in other parts of their pupils' lives. What's remarkable, however, . . . is how many terrific schools manage to overcome precisely that challenge. For three decades, there's been a wealth of anecdote, example, and research attesting to the success of individual schools in "beating the odds" and producing well educated youngsters *in spite of* the hostile forces at work in many of those kids' lives.

Rothstein (2006) countered that criticism by dismissing claims that some schools have closed the achievement gap as "unfounded." If test data indicate student success, he questioned whether the make-up of the student body was representative of the general lower-class population, or he argued that the tests only focused on basic, rather than higher-order skills, or he suggested that lower-class students continued to lack noncognitive skills, such as perseverance, self-discipline, and the ability to work with others, which are ultimately more important to an individual's success.

Finding Common Ground in the Education Wars

It seems both sides in the education wars have demonstrated a willingness to dismiss evidence that does not support their respective positions and to cast aspersions on the opposing perspective. If conservatives have tended to oversimplify school improvement—tough accountability measures and parental choice will lead to high levels of learning for all students, regardless of their socioeconomic status— liberals have tended to present significant school improvement as an impossibility and to disregard schools that have been successful in working with children of poverty.

The one area, however, where liberals and conservatives seem to find common ground is that neither NCLB nor any of the nonstop reform efforts of the past quarter century have resulted in the quality schools vital to the future of the nation and its citizens. Conservatives may contend that educators *won't* improve their schools, while liberals may argue that educators *can't* improve their schools; but both groups seem increasingly resigned to the fact that efforts to reform schools are doomed to fail.

Have we reached the point in the history of American education where the performance of public schools is so dismal that there is no longer any hope for widespread school improvement? We are convinced the answer to that question is a resounding "No."

Another Perspective on Public Education in America

It can be argued that the public system of education in the United States has been a remarkable success. Consider the following.

National Assessments

Although it is difficult to analyze national assessment results in one of the few industrialized nations that has no national assessment, there are some trends that can be identified in the limited information that is available.

- In 1960, 41% of Americans 25 years of age or older had earned a high school diploma. By 1980, the percentage had risen to

66%, and by 2000 to 80% (United States Census Bureau, 2006b). Historian Lawrence Cremin (1991) described this explosion as "nothing short of phenomenal" and questioned why this unprecedented expansion of education "brought with it a pervasive sense of failure" (pp. 40–41).

- High school graduates are earning more credits and taking more rigorous courses than ever before (National Assessment of Educational Progress, 2007). Between 2000 and 2006, the number of high school students taking and passing college-level advanced placement exams administered by the College Board increased from 260,658 to 405,999, more than 56%. The College Board (2007) reported, "Across all 50 states and the District of Columbia, educators and policymakers have succeeded in helping a wider segment of the United States student population than ever before successfully complete a college-level AP course before leaving high school" (p. 6).

- Between 1980 and 2005, the average SAT score in reading remained virtually the same, moving from 502 to 503, despite all the efforts to improve American education. But scores for every one of the subgroups identified by the College Board—white, black, Asian, Puerto Rican, Mexican, and American Indian—increased. How could the scores of every group increase and the total remain flat? The answer is found in a statistical phenomenon called Simpson's Paradox—the composition of the students taking the exam has changed dramatically. White students have traditionally scored higher on the test than other groups. In 1980, 85% of the students taking the SAT exam were white. By 2005, that percentage had dropped to 56%. So the headline in 2005 could have been, "SAT Scores Remain Flat Despite School Reform Efforts," or it could also have read, "Educational Opportunities Extend to a Broader Range of Students While SAT Scores Continue to Rise for all Categories of Students."

Each would have been accurate, but the first was far more likely to have been reported.

- As mentioned earlier, when the socioeconomic status of students is controlled, public school students outperform students in private and charter schools in mathematics and fourth grade language arts (Lubienski & Lubienski, 2006; NCES, 2006).

International Assessments

Some argue, however, that student performance on national exams is not relevant since American students are competing with students around the world for a place in the global economy. The United States has not come close to achieving its Goals 2000 target of being first in the world in math and science on international assessments of those skills, and therefore, the public schools are failing. But once again, a different perspective may be offered.

- The Trends in International Mathematics and Science Study (TIMSS) was developed to track student achievement by the International Association for the Evaluation of Educational Achievement (IEA), an international organization of national research institutions and governmental research agencies. The most recent results revealed American eighth graders significantly improved their math and science scores, while the scores of most other countries declined. Furthermore, the study revealed that the "gap in achievement between White and Black eighth-graders narrowed in both mathematics and science over this time period" (Institute of Education Sciences, 2004).

- Of the 35 nations participating in the Progress in International Reading Literacy Study of fourth graders, only 3 nations scored significantly higher than the United States. U.S. schools with low poverty (under 10%) scored significantly higher than the highest-scoring nations in the world. If U.S. schools with poverty rates between 25 and 49% were considered as a nation, they would have scored fourth among the 35 nations. Only schools with poverty rates above 75% scored below the international average (Bracey, 2006).

- Seventeen school districts in suburban Chicago created the "First in the World" (FiW) consortium to assess the achievement of their students on international examinations. The districts were unique because of the relatively high socioeconomic status of the communities they served, with only 7% of their students designated as low income. Students were assessed in math and science in grades 4, 8, and 12. As a study by the United States Department of Education acknowledged, "When benchmarked against an international measure of math and science achievement, FiW students performed exceptionally well in all grades tested. FiW students excelled on the fourth, eighth, and twelfth grade general knowledge tests, and scored among, or just below, the highest performing countries worldwide. . . . The performance of Advanced Placement students was exceedingly high, with their scores placing them in first place internationally" (U.S. Department of Education, 1999). Clearly, reporting of "average" scores on international assessments can be very misleading when a country is as heterogeneous as the United States.

Public Support

Reformers may call for sweeping changes in American education, but public satisfaction with their local schools is at one of the highest points in four decades. Since the publication of *A Nation at Risk*, the percentage of those giving the grade of A or B to their local schools has jumped from 31% to 45%. Parents are even more likely than the general public to assign a grade of A or B to their children's schools, with the percentage increasing from 49% to 67% since the mid-1980s. As the pollsters reported, "the public assigns generally high marks to the local public schools and the level of satisfaction rises the closer the public gets to its schools" (Rose & Gallup, 2007, p. 40).

Although Americans may be fond of their local schools, they have grave concerns about the nation's educational system and the achievement gaps among students. Only 16% of those polled gave the nation's schools the grade of A or B. The public does not, however, believe that schools are the source of the problem. The 2006 Gallup poll reported, "There is near-consensus support for the belief that the problems the public schools face result from societal issues and not from the quality of schooling" (Rose & Gallup, 2006, p. 43). By nearly a three-to-one margin, the public feels the nation should focus on improving existing schools rather than on seeking alternatives to public education. In another poll, 98% of respondents favored the guarantee of a free public education and 96% said it is important that the public schools be strengthened (Teixeira, 2006).

Americans also consistently cite education as the one area in which government spending should be increased. According to the National Opinion Research Center's General Social Survey administered in 2006, 74% of those polled indicated the government was spending too little on education, and only 5% felt it was spending too much. This marked the fifth time in the last six polls that education was the public's top spending priority among 22 options from which participants had to choose. As the director of the survey reported, "In absolute terms, support for educational spending has been very high and has changed little since 1989" (Smith, 2006, p. 2). Results from the 2007 Gallup poll reinforce that conclusion. Whereas the public's greatest concerns regarding education at the time of *A Nation at Risk* were lack of discipline and the pervasiveness of drugs, today the greatest concern is lack of adequate funding, with more than twice as many respondents citing that problem than any other (Rose & Gallup, 2007). The use of the term "our failing public schools" has become almost a cliché among government officials and the media, and yet, there is strong evidence that the very public served by those schools has never been more favorably disposed toward them.

Education and the Economy

One of the most consistent arguments in the calls for overhauling public education is that "our failing schools" put the American economy in peril. The report of the National Commission on Excellence in Education (1983) was particularly emphatic in linking the quality of education to economic survival. The opening salvo of that report proclaimed "the imperative for educational reform" because "our once unchallenged preeminence in commerce, industry, science, and technological innovation is being overtaken by competitors throughout the world" (p. 1). The report warned, "The world is indeed one global village," we are in fierce competition with determined competitors, and schools in America must be reformed "if only to keep and improve on the slim competitive edge we still retain in world markets."

Not everyone found this argument compelling. Historian Lawrence Cremin (1990), for example, dismissed the contention that school reform can solve problems of international competitiveness as "at best foolish and at worst a crass effort to direct attention away from those truly responsible for doing something about competitiveness and to lay the burden instead on the schools" (p. 103). Nevertheless, the practice of blaming schools for the nation's economic woes has continued unabated. Most recently, the National Center on Education and the Economy (2007) warned the nation's standard of living would fall steadily if American schools continued on their current course, because nations around the world would outpace us.

But if the authors of *A Nation at Risk* were correct, if the nation's economic well-being is directly and inextricably linked to the quality of America's public schools, it would seem there is much to celebrate. The 1990s represented the greatest period of sustained economic growth in the nation's history. Between 1987 and 2007, the American economy had grown faster than any other advanced economy in the world. In its 2006 assessment of global competitiveness, the World Economic Forum ranked the United States the most competitive among the 117 nations rated (Bracey, 2006). Certainly, if schools represent the fundamental problem in tough economic times, they should receive accolades when the economy is booming. Instead, they were labeled "failing" and were subjected to the most ambitious and punitive federal intrusion into education in the history of the nation.

We concur with the assessment of educational historians David Tyack and Larry Cuban (1995), who concluded that "the public schools, for all their faults, remain one of our most stable and effective public institutions—indeed, given the increase in social pathologies in the society, educators have done far better in the last generation than might be expected" (p. 38).

And yet, the "failure" of a quarter century of nonstop reform to transform schools has led to unprecedented levels of despair about the possibility of school improvement in the United States. Neither the top-down mandates of the excellence movement and NCLB nor the bottom-up, site-based approach of the restructuring movement accomplished the lofty goals they promised, so reformers inside and outside of education have increasingly argued that American schools are simply incapable of transformation. A nation that has historically placed such high expectations (and demands) upon its public schools seems, for the first time, to be losing confidence in the *possibility* of improving its schools.

The Consortium on Productivity in the Schools (1995) concluded schools resist any meaningful change efforts and are *unable* to learn and improve. The Koret Task Force on K–12 Education (Moe, 2001) charged that schools were incapable of reforming themselves because they were bureaucratic, inefficient, unaccountable, and committed to preserving the status quo. Reforming schools has been likened to untangling the Gordian Knot (Whittle, 2006) and turning around a supertanker, although one critic suggested that analogy is "an insult to the speed and maneuverability of supertankers" (Greene, 2006). Others have declared schools so terrible, so harmful to students, and so incapable of meaningful reform that the only solution for parents is to remove their children from public education and teach them at home (Short, 2004; Turtel, 2005).

Even long-time advocates for public education seem despondent. The American Federation of Teachers (AFT) acknowledged that a "sizable and growing proportion of the American public—especially in urban areas, where many failing schools are located—has lost faith in public schools and in the government bureaucracies that control them" (cited in Fuller & Mitchell, 2006). Seymour Sarason (1996), a longtime observer of America's schools, notes that the single greatest change he has witnessed over a quarter of a century is "the sense of disillusionment with and disappointment in our schools" (p. 345). After 10 years of research on the relationship between the public and its schools, the president of the Kettering Foundation made the following observation: "The research forces me to say something I never thought I would say— or even think. The public school system, as we know it, may not survive into the next century" (Matthews, 1997, p. 741). Richard Elmore (2000) cautioned, "If schools, school systems, and their leaders respond to standards-based reforms the way they have responded to other attempts at broad-scale reform of public education over the past century, they will fail massively and visibly, with an attendant loss of public confidence and serious consequences for public education" (p. 2). Phil Schlechty (1997) warned educators, unless they moved quickly to transform their schools in dramatic ways, "public schools will not be a vital component of America's system of education in the twenty-first century" (p. xi). Michael Fullan (2005a) concluded that educators have been incapable of implementing widespread, sustainable school improvement and that the few apparent success stories are invariably short-lived and a function of "luck."

Educators have become increasingly defensive as they react to this constant criticism. Their defense typically falls into three categories: 1) We are not as bad as everyone says we are, 2) we cannot overcome the poverty and societal problems that impact our students and our schools, and 3) we are victims of a political process led by those with personal agendas. As we have illustrated, one can make a case for these arguments; however, this line of reasoning will do nothing to bring about the improvements that are so desperately required if schools are to meet the needs of the children they serve.

If teachers and principals believe the impetus for student learning remains outside of their influence and there is nothing they can do to overcome these external variables, the idea of school improvement will undoubtedly seem futile, if not downright ridiculous. If educators continue to argue they cannot be responsible for students' learning until all the problems of society are solved, they are essentially saying they will *never* accept responsibility for their students' learning. If they are content with the assertion that "We are not as bad off as everyone says we are," they will not create organizations capable of continuous improvement.

And while educators may rail against the current accountability measures being imposed upon them by governmental fiat, they should also acknowledge that their own failure to address critical issues in the teaching and learning process has contributed to those fiats. If states have become more prescriptive about what students must learn, that prescription is at least in part a reaction to the fact that what students were taught in any given school depended more on the interests and idiosyncrasies of their teacher than on any common agreement about the knowledge, skills, and dispositions considered most essential to student success. If states have imposed annual testing to monitor student learning, one important reason why is that most schools and districts were so inattentive to gathering evidence of that learning. In many districts, the only data on student learning came from grades assigned by individual teachers—with no attempt to establish agreed-upon criteria for assessing the quality of student work or the extent of their learning—and nationally normed tests specifically designed to sort and select students, rather than monitor their achievement of particular standards. Until recently, if formal charges were brought against a school alleging that learning was taking place, most schools in America could be confident the charges would ultimately be dropped for lack of evidence.

If states have demanded scrutiny of the achievement of subgroups of students, it is because for decades educators ignored the achievement gaps of student groups and focused on the comfortable ambiguity of averages. If states have stipulated specific steps that must be taken to address students who had not demonstrated learning, educators must acknowledge that in most schools and districts they have never developed a systematic response to assist students who were not learning, choosing instead to leave the issue to the discretion of individual classroom teachers. If states are reluctant to leave the issue of school improvement to the faculty of each school to address, it is because they have learned that merely giving educators site-based autonomy does not ensure they will use that authority to focus on improving student achievement. *One important step educators can take in the face of pressure for accountability is to stop thinking of themselves as victims and to acknowledge that to a large extent, they are reaping what they have sown.*

We are not prepared to accept the conclusion that it is impossible to improve schools. Nor do we believe that improvement can only occur when parents provide schools with a better class of students, society has solved its problems, and educators are freed of all accountability measures. Although much of the popular criticism of schools has been unfair and unfounded, we contend that educators have both a professional and moral responsibility to constantly seek better ways of meeting the needs of their students. We want to stress that while we are sympathetic to the difficult conditions in which educators find themselves, we are not apologists for the status quo. Educators *must* make substantive changes in the structure and culture of their schools and districts.

Students have never needed effective and committed educators more than now. A chilling editorial in *U.S. News & World Report* (Zuckerman, 2006) warned that education and family background are replacing race and gender as barriers to upward mobility. Throughout most of the 20th century, young boys and girls could choose to drop out of school and would still have access to the middle class. That possibility is increasingly remote in contemporary America. Today a school dropout earns only 65 cents for every dollar earned by the high school graduate and only 33 cents for each dollar earned by those with a bachelor's degree (United States Census Bureau, 2006a). Those with an undergraduate degree are most likely to move up from the income bracket in which they started, but a student from the top income quartile has a 1 in 2 chance of earning a degree, while the chances of a student from the bottom quartile earning a bachelor's degree are less than 1 in 10. A child in a family earning under $35,000 has a 1 in 17 chance (Brooks, 2006). The American dream is receding from reach for many of our children.

Education opens not only economic doors, but other doors as well. Quality of life, health, and even longevity are strongly correlated to education. As *The New York Times* reported, "The one social factor that researchers agree is consistently linked to longer lives in every country where it has been studied is education. It is more important than race; it obliterates any effects of income. . . . A few extra years of school is associated with extra years of life and vastly improved health decades later, in old age" (Kolta, 2007). Creating schools that are more effective in helping students to achieve academic success and to feel more connected to the educators that serve them can literally be a matter of life and death for those students.

The American public is concerned about its schools, and nearly 9 of 10 Americans believe it is important to close the achievement gap that currently exists among students of different races and socioeconomic status. And while few Americans hold schools responsible for *creating* that gap, the majority does assign responsibility for *closing* it to educators (Rose & Gallup, 2006). We believe these findings illustrate the collective intelligence that Surowiecki (2004) refers to as the "wisdom of crowds." Americans, in general, continue to believe in their schools, and they turn to them to help solve the greatest challenges facing their nation.

And despite the history of failed reforms, we continue to believe in both the possibility of improving schools and the collective capacity of educators to play the key role in that improvement. If, however, future efforts to improve schools are to be more productive than their predecessors, educators and policymakers alike should address two questions:

1. Why have past school improvement efforts not achieved the intended results?

2. What course of action offers the best hope for those who seek to make their schools more effective?

Why Educational Reform Has Failed to Deliver

Education reform has failed for a variety of reasons. Before considering a more promising strategy for improving schools, we offer the following observations about the failure of past reforms.

Unrealistic Expectations

A primary cause for the despondency regarding public education's ability to reform itself is the unrealistic expectations foisted upon the schools by policymakers at both ends of the political spectrum. In 1964, President Lyndon B. Johnson, a liberal Democrat, made education a cornerstone of his Great Society initiative arguing, "The answer to all our national problems comes down to a single word: education" (Perkinson, 1979, front piece). Twenty-seven years later, President George H.W. Bush expressed the identical sentiment when he launched the Goals 2000 program by saying, "Think about every problem, every challenge we face. The solution to each starts with education. For the sake of the future—of our children and the nation—we must reform America's schools" (Bush, 1991).

Schools have been called upon to solve every social ill and fulfill every cultural hope. Are teenage pregnancies a problem? Schools need to do a better job of teaching abstinence. Has China gained market share in key industries? Schools need to do a better job of preparing students to compete in the global market place. Is childhood obesity a concern? Schools need to teach nutrition, promote a more active lifestyle, and stop selling soft drinks. Are business executives and members of Congress engaging in unethical activities? Schools need to teach morals. There is no other institution in America that has been called upon to do so much for the nation and for every individual within it.

No Child Left Behind now demands 100% proficiency for every student in the United States by 2014, a goal that no state or nation in the history of the world has ever achieved. Unfortunately, a system has been created to ensure that by definition, every school in America will ultimately be deemed a failure, regardless of how effective it is in helping its students learn. Thus, education reform has been, and will continue to be, labeled a "failure" because the definition of "success" is unattainable for mere mortals. Even Diane Ravitch (2007a), a frequent critic of public education, has concluded the hyperbole about the failure of schools and the creation of a system to ensure every school will ultimately fail are both part of an effort to destroy confidence in public schools and thereby advance the cause of those who favor the privatization of education in America.

The Complexity of the Task

Changing any organization is difficult, but changing something as complex as the American system of education is absolutely daunting—primarily because there really is no American "system" of education. Fifty different very autonomous states are responsible for overseeing more than 14,300 relatively autonomous school districts that operate 95,726 mostly independent schools that employ more than 3.1 million teachers who typically close their doors and work autonomously in the service of more than 48 million students (National Center for Education Statistics, 2005).

But the scope of the effort is not the only obstacle to be overcome. Our educational system is fundamentally conservative, as might be expected given its historical roots in scientific management—the assertion that a successful organization must discover the "one best process" for conducting its work and insist that the process be adhered to without variation. As Fullan (1993) writes, "The way that teachers are trained, the way the hierarchy operates, and the way that education is treated by political decision makers results in a system that is more likely to retain the status quo than to change" (p. 3).

Effecting change in this amorphous, fundamentally conservative "system," when educators seem fatalistic or defensive, and when parents indicate that their local schools are serving the community well and need not change, has been and will continue to be an incredibly complex, intractable problem.

Misplaced Focus

The good news is that there are strategies for school improvement that can make a difference in the effectiveness of schools. The bad news is that the excellence movement, the restructuring movement, and the NCLB reform effort failed to use these strategies. The top-down impetus of the excellence movement and sanction-ridden provisions of NCLB failed to build the internal capacity and internal accountability essential to continuous improvement. As Fullan (2006) contends, reforms based on sanctions and external pressure and control may help a school move from "awful" to "adequate," but they work on only a small part of the problem, violate everything known about change processes that lead to sustainable reform, cause the best teachers to abandon a "failing" school, and actually create conditions that guarantee the improvements will not be sustained. As he writes, "There is, in other words, virtually no chance the approach will result in good let alone great schools" (p. 29).

The laissez-faire approach of the restructuring movement was built on the faulty premise that simply encouraging schools to reform themselves would lead to educators in schools throughout America simultaneously discovering the strategies that would lead to higher levels of student achievement. There is, however, virtually no evidence to support that premise; in fact, there is considerable evidence educators in schools that have been left to their own devices are no more likely to engage in meaningful dialogue regarding matters essential to teaching and learning than their more rigidly supervised counterparts (Elmore, 2003; Kruse, Seashore Louis, & Bryk, 1995; Schlechty, 2005).

Lack of Clarity on Intended Results

Past reform efforts have been characterized by a lack of clarity on intended results. While there has been general agreement that schools should improve, consensus on the criteria that should be used to assess that improvement remains elusive. This inability to articulate the desired results in meaningful terms has led to initiatives that focused on methods and processes rather than on results.

No Child Left Behind attempted to address this issue by defining results as success on an annual test developed and administered by each of the 50 states. This definition has been attacked by educators and noneducators alike. Educators challenge the ability of a single test on a single day to assess the achievement of a student. Groups like the New Commission on the Skills of the American Workforce (2007) criticized NCLB's focus on basic skills and its inattention to determining whether or not students were "comfortable with ideas and abstractions, good at both analysis and synthesis, creative and innovative, self-disciplined and well organized, able to learn very quickly and work well as a member of a team and have the flexibility to adapt quickly to frequent changes in the labor market as the shifts in the economy become even faster and more dramatic" (p. 8).

Lack of Perseverance

Because schools have been unable to articulate the results they seek, they have become susceptible to following the educational fads du jour. As a result of the constant cycle of initiating and then abandoning innovative fads, educators rarely pursue ideas with the diligence and tenacity that is necessary to anchor a change within the school. Overwhelmed by disconnected, fragmented, incoherent change initiatives that seem to descend upon them one after another, teachers often respond to calls for change with jaded resignation. New proposals fail to generate either enthusiasm or overt opposition from teachers because experience has taught them that "this too shall pass." Phil Schlechty (2005) argues that nothing has been more destructive to the cause of school improvement than this inability to stay the course, and reforms will continue to fail unless systems are put in place to support and sustain improvement over time.

A Failure to Appreciate and Attend to the Change Process

Most educators have not been trained in initiating, implementing, and sustaining change. They have neglected the process of creating a "critical mass" of support or have failed to proceed because of the mistaken notion that they needed unanimous support before launching an initiative. They have regarded conflict as a problem to avoid rather than an inevitable and valuable byproduct of substantive change. They have failed to anchor the change within the culture of the school. They have considered a change initiative as a task to complete rather than an ongoing process. In short, school practitioners have not made a sufficient effort to become skillful in the complexities of the change process.

Can Public Education Be Saved?

It is far easier to critique past strategies for improving schools and districts than it is to identify and implement strategies that are more effective. There is, however, a prevailing consensus on what pathway offers the best hope for significant improvement. Researchers from a variety of fields—organizational development, leadership practices, school improvement, teacher preparation, professional development, effective schools, and change processes—have all offered remarkably similar models for school improvement.

The good news is that there is greater understanding and consensus regarding what must be done to help more students learn at higher levels than ever before in the history of public education. Simply put, if schools are to be significantly more effective, educators must break from the industrial model upon which they were created and embrace a new model that enables them to function as professional learning communities. The next chapter will make what we consider is a compelling case for that assertion.

Chapter 3

Making the Case for Professional Learning Communities

The use of professional learning communities is the best, least expensive, most professionally rewarding way to improve schools. . . . Such communities hold out immense, unprecedented hope for schools and the improvement of teaching.

—Mike Schmoker

Research demonstrates that the success of most interventions designed to improve organizational performance depends largely on implementing what is already known, rather than from adopting new or previously unknown ways of doing things.

—Jeffrey Pfeffer and Robert Sutton

What would it take to persuade educators that successfully implementing professional learning community practices is the most promising path for sustained and substantive improvement of our schools and districts? A leader facing this challenge could take some comfort in knowing that there is abundant research to support PLCs. That leader could present the following findings from researchers both inside and outside of education to convince those who find research persuasive.

Research Supporting Professional Learning Communities

- The most successful corporation of the future will be a learning organization. (Senge, 1990, p. 4)

- Every enterprise has to become a learning institution [and] a teaching institution. Organizations that build in continuous learning in jobs will dominate the twenty-first century. (Drucker, 1992, p. 108)

- Preferred organizations will be learning organizations.... It has been said that people who stop learning stop living. This is also true of organizations. (Handy, 1995, p. 55)

- Only the organizations that have a passion for learning will have an enduring influence. (Covey, Merrill, & Merrill, 1996, p. 149)

- The new problem of change . . . is what would it take to make the educational system a learning organization—expert at dealing with change as a normal part of its work, not just in relation to the latest policy, but as a way of life. (Fullan, 1993, p. 4)

- We have come to realize over the years that the development of a learning community of educators is itself a major cultural change that will spawn many others. (Joyce & Showers, 1995, p. 3)

- If schools want to enhance their organizational capacity to boost student learning, they should work on building a professional community that is characterized by shared purpose, collaborative activity, and collective responsibility among staff. (Newmann & Wehlage, 1995, p. 37)

- [We recommend that] schools be restructured to become genuine learning organizations for both students and teachers; organizations that respect learning, honor teaching, and teach for understanding. (Darling-Hammond, 1996, p. 198)

- We argue, however, that when schools attempt significant reform, efforts to form a schoolwide professional community are critical. (Louis, Kruse, & Raywid, 1996, p. 13)

- Louis and Marks (1998) found that when a school is organized into a professional community, the following occurs:

  1. Teachers set higher expectations for student achievement.

  2. Students can count on the help of their teachers and peers in achieving ambitious learning goals.

  3. The quality of classroom pedagogy is considerably higher.

  4. Achievement levels are significantly higher.

- We support and encourage the use of professional learning communities (PLCs) as a central element for effective professional development and a comprehensive reform initiative. In our experience, PLCs have the potential to enhance the professional culture within a school district. (Annenberg Institute for School Reform, 2004, p. 3)

- The framework of a professional learning community is inextricably linked to the effective integration of standards, assessment, and accountability . . . the leaders of professional learning communities balance the desire for professional autonomy with the fundamental principles and values that drive collaboration and mutual accountability. (Reeves, 2005, pp. 47–48)

- Well-implemented professional learning communities are a powerful means of seamlessly blending teaching and professional learning in ways that produce complex, intelligent behavior in all teachers. (Sparks, 2005, p. 156)

- [In the most successful schools] leadership ensures there are integrated communities of professional practice in the service of student academic and social learning. There is a healthy school environment in which student learning is the central focus. . . . Research has demonstrated that schools organized as communities, rather than bureaucracies, are more likely to exhibit academic success. (Goldring, Porter, Murphy, Elliott, & Cravens, 2007)

- Outcomes for both staff and students have been improved by organizing professional learning communities. For staff, the results include:

  - Reduction of isolation of teachers

  - Increased commitment to the mission and goals of the school and increased vigor in working to strengthen the mission

  - Shared responsibility for the total development of students and collective responsibility for students' success

  - Powerful learning that defines good teaching and classroom practice, that creates new knowledge and beliefs about teaching and learners

- Increased meaning and understanding of the content that teachers teach and the roles that they play in helping all students achieve expectations

- Higher likelihood that teachers will be well-informed, professionally renewed, and inspired to inspire students

- More satisfaction and higher morale, and lower rates of absenteeism

- Significant advances into making teaching adaptations for students, and changes for learners made more quickly than in traditional schools

- Commitment to making significant and lasting changes

- Higher likelihood of undertaking fundamental, systemic change

For students, the results include:

- Decreased dropout rate and fewer classes "cut"

- Lower rates of absenteeism

- Increased learning that is distributed more equitably in the smaller high schools

- Larger academic gains in math, science, history, and reading than in traditional schools

- Smaller achievement gaps between students from different backgrounds (Hord, 1997)

- A school-based professional community can offer support and motivation to teachers as they work to overcome the tight resources, isolation, time constraints and other obstacles they commonly encounter. . . . In schools where professional community is strong, teachers work together more effectively, and put more effort into creating and sustaining opportunities for student learning. (Kruse, Seashore Louis, & Bryk, 1994, p. 4)

- Such a tipping point—from reform to true collaboration—could represent the most dramatic shift in the history of educational practice. . . . We will know we have succeeded when the absence of a "strong professional learning community" in a school is an embarrassment. (Schmoker, 2004c, p. 431)

Organizations That Endorse Professional Learning Communities

Some educators, however, may not be persuaded by research. Leaders making the case for PLCs could point out to those who are skeptical of research that the organizations created for the specific purpose of making the profession more rewarding, satisfying, and effective have almost universally endorsed the PLC concept as a key strategy for accomplishing their objectives. Leaders could cite the following organizations and their recommendations.

The fundamental premise of the National Commission on Teaching and America's Future (NCTAF) is that school reform cannot succeed without creating conditions in which teachers teach well. The Commission has identified the creation of "Strong Learning Communities" as one of its three core strategies for improving both teaching and schools:

Quality teaching requires strong, professional learning communities. Collegial interchange, not isolation, must become the norm for teachers. Communities of learning can no longer be considered utopian; they must become the building blocks that establish a new foundation for America's schools. (2003, p. 17)

The National Board for Professional Teaching Standards (NBPTS) was formed to advance the quality of teaching and learning by developing professional standards for accomplished teaching. Its position statement includes the following:

> Five Core Propositions form the foundation and frame the rich amalgam of knowledge, skills, dispositions and beliefs that characterize National Board Certified Teachers (NBCTs). The fifth proposition calls upon teachers to be members of learning communities . . . to collaborate with others to improve student learning . . . to work with other professionals on instructional policy, curriculum development and staff development. (National Board for Professional Teaching Standards, 2007a)

The Interstate New Teacher Assessment and Support Consortium (INTASC) was created by the Council of Chief State School Officers to develop a common core of teaching proficiency that would clarify the knowledge, skills, and dispositions all teachers should demonstrate to be considered "professional." The standards included the following statements:

> Professional teachers assume roles that extend beyond the classroom and include responsibilities for developing the school as a learning organization. . . . Professional teachers are responsible for planning and pursuing their ongoing learning, for reflecting with colleagues on their practice, and for contributing to the profession's knowledge base. (Interstate New Teacher Assessment and Support Consortium, 1992, p. 13)

The National Council of Teachers of Mathematics (NCTM) called upon math leaders to do the following:

1. Ensure teachers work interdependently as a professional learning community to guarantee continuous improvement and gains in student achievement.

2. Create the support and structures necessary to implement a professional learning community.

3. Ensure a systemic implementation of a professional learning community throughout all aspects of the mathematics curriculum, instruction and assessment at the school, district, or regional level. (National Council of Teachers of Mathematics, in press)

The National Council of Teachers of English (NCTE) has created the Professional Learning Communities at Work Series—a topical resource kit to help teachers work as PLCs as they focus on key issues such as adolescent literacy, secondary writing, and teaching English language learners. An NCTE position paper argued that PLCs make teaching more rewarding and combat the problem of educators leaving the profession:

> Effective professional development fosters collegial relationships, creating professional communities where teachers share knowledge and treat each other with respect. Within such communities teacher inquiry and reflection can flourish, and research shows that teachers who engage in collaborative professional development feel confident and well prepared to meet the demands of teaching. (National Council of Teachers of English, 2006, p. 10)

The National Science Teachers Association (NSTA) issued a position paper (2006) in which it asserted that a key component of high-quality staff development would "facilitate the development of professional learning communities."

The Southwest Educational Development Laboratory (SEDL), particularly its professor emerita Shirley Hord, has been engaged in the ongoing exploration of the potential of PLCs. As SEDL reported in one of its publications on the topic:

> Professional learning communities offer an infrastructure to create the supportive cultures and conditions necessary for achieving significant gains in teaching and learning. Professional learning communities provide opportunities for professional staff to look deeply into the teaching and learning process and to learn how to become more effective in their work with students. (Morrissey, 2000)

The National Education Association (NEA), America's largest teaching organization with over 2.7 million members, is committed to making teaching more rewarding and satisfying. In pursuit of its long-term vision of "a great public school for every student," the NEA has created its own recommended school improvement model: The Keys to Excellence. The model is intended to help educators develop school improvement plans and to help them meet the challenges of the No Child Left Behind Act (NCLB). Although the model never uses the term professional learning community, its six keys to a quality school are consistent with PLC principles. The NEA keys and examples of some of the specific indicators the organization has identified for each follow:

1. Shared understanding and commitment to high goals

   - The staff has a collective commitment to and takes responsibility for implementing high standards for all students.

   - The school operates under the assumption that all students can learn.

2. Open communication and collaborative problem solving

   - Teachers and staff collaborate to remove barriers to student learning.

- Teachers communicate regularly with each other about effective teaching and learning strategies.

3. Continuous assessment for teaching and learning

    - Student assessment is used for decision making to improve learning.

    - A variety of assessment techniques are used.

4. Personal and professional learning

    - Teachers have regularly scheduled time to learn from one another.

    - Professional development has a direct, positive effect on teaching.

5. Resources to support teaching and learning

    - Computer hardware and software supplies are adequate for students and teachers.

    - Support services are adequate.

6. Curriculum and instruction

    - Instruction includes interventions for students who are not succeeding.

    - Teachers are open to new learnings and rethink their approaches to teaching and assessment practices based on teacher-directed action research and other classroom based inquiries. (National Education Association, 2003)

The president of the American Federation of Teachers (AFT), an organization representing 1.4 million members, called for those interested in improving schools to "make schools learning communities for teachers as well as students. Provide for master teachers, teacher centers, real professional development in the schools—with time for teachers to work with one another to overcome children's learning problems as they come up" (Feldman, 1998).

The National Middle School Association (NMSA) issued a position paper titled *This We Believe,* outlining its recommended strategies for improving schools. NMSA called for the following:

> Building a learning community that involves all teachers and places top priority on the education and healthy development of every student, teacher, and staff member . . . professional development should be integrated into the daily life of the school and directly linked to the school's goals for student and teacher success and growth. To meet these goals, people work together in study groups, focus on learning results, analyze student work, and carry out action research. (2003, p. 11)

Principals have also been urged by their professional organizations to focus their efforts on developing their schools as professional learning communities.

The National Association of Elementary School Principals (NAESP, 2001) has clarified the essential responsibilities of principals in its publication *Leading Learning Communities: Standards for What Principals Should Know and Be Able to Do* in which it states:

> If adults don't learn then students won't learn either. . . . The school operates as a learning community that uses its own experience and knowledge, and that of others, to improve the performance of students and teachers alike. . . . They must be a place where learning isn't isolated, where adults demonstrate they care about kids but also about each other. In such places, learning takes place in groups. A culture of shared responsibility is established, and everybody learns from one another. (p. 5)

The National Association of Secondary School Principals (NASSP) calls upon high schools to engage in an improvement process that will ensure success for every high school student. In *Breaking Ranks II* (2004), the NASSP urges principals to focus on the development of a professional learning community within each school as a primary improvement strategy. In *Breaking Ranks in the Middle* (2006), the NASSP organizes 30 recommendations for improving middle schools into three general areas, the first of which calls for "collaborative leadership and professional learning communities" (p. 23).

In citing its recommendations for effective professional development, the National Staff Development Council (NSDC) (2007) contends, "[Effective] staff development that improves the learning of all students organizes adults into learning communities whose goals are aligned with those of the school and district."

The North Central Association Commission on Accreditation and School Improvement (NCA) is responsible for the accreditation of more than 8,500 schools in 19 states. Concluding that its process works "hand in hand" with the PLC concept, the NCA reported:

> Working at complementary levels—the school and classroom—the NCA school improvement and PLC processes reinforce and strengthen one another. They are not mutually exclusive, but rather mutually supportive. If we want to ensure that no child is left behind, we must understand the important relationship between the NCA school improvement process and PLC. . . . The use of PLC at the classroom level has dramatically increased teachers' ability to implement a guaranteed and viable curriculum, monitor student progress with colleagues on school improvement goals and curriculum objectives, and improve the teaching and learning process. The strong link between school improvement goals and PLC at the classroom level allows all children to be successful. (Colliton, 2005, pp. 1–2)

If leaders need even more evidence to help them make the case for the PLC concept, they can go to the rich resource www.allthingsplc.info for a closer look at research findings supporting the concept, articles explaining it, tools and templates to assist with implementation, a blog for seeking answers to questions, and examples of schools that have implemented the concept successfully.

Bridging the Knowing-Doing Gap

In short, the case for PLCs is compelling, and we have discovered it is not difficult to persuade educators of the merits of the PLC concept. What is difficult, however, is to persuade them to implement the practices essential to the concept. The good news is that educators *know* how to improve schools and districts. The bad news is they have lacked the resolve to *do* what is necessary to convert their organizations into professional learning communities. In *The Knowing-Doing Gap,* Jeffrey Pfeffer and Robert Sutton (2000) describe this disconnect between knowledge and action as one of the great mysteries of organizational life. As they ask, "Why does knowledge of what needs to be done so frequently fail to result in action or behavior that is consistent with that knowledge?" (p. 4). We remain convinced that closing the knowing-doing gap will require purposeful action to alter not only the existing structures of schools and districts, but more importantly, the cultures that have created and sustained those traditional structures.

It has been said that the culture of any organization is found more in the unwritten and unexamined stories and mythology that drive it than in specific rules and regulations. For example, baseball, "America's pastime," has a well-established set of rules that have changed very little over the past century: three strikes and you are out, 90 feet between the bases, the infield fly rule, and so on. The rulebook identifies 23 different ways in which a batter can reach first base. Baseball also has an elaborate set of *unwritten* rules that have evolved over the last 100 years that all players are expected to observe. For example, a player who hits what he knows will be a home run must not stand in the batter's box to admire it because to do so insults the pitcher. A player should never steal a base late in a game when his team is far ahead because it is considered "showing up" one's opponent. If the star player of a team has been hit by a pitch, his pitcher is expected to retaliate by hitting a member of the offending team with a pitch because part of a pitcher's job is to protect teammates. In short, there are unwritten stipulations that some things simply are not done in baseball, and those who violate those norms can expect to pay a penalty—usually in some form of retaliation from the other team.

Education has developed its own stories, its own tradition of unwritten rules or norms that impact the day-to-day workings of schools across the United States. Like baseball, these norms are not only unwritten, they are largely unexamined. They simply represent "the way we do things here." Someone entering the profession as a new teacher in a traditional school will soon discover the unwritten rules, the way things are to be done. If those rules or norms were written, here is what they might say:

> A new teacher in our school has to earn his or her dues. You will be assigned to teach the most difficult students and will be expected to take a position in the extracurricular program, which will add to the demands on your time as you struggle to make the transition into the profession. We veterans teach the "good" kids—the highest achieving and most motivated students—and are assigned the best rooms as a perquisite for paying our dues.

> The cardinal rule here is "Mind your own business!" You will be given a textbook, state standards, and a district curriculum guide; but, in actuality, what we teach, how we pace the content, the priority we assign to different topics, how we assess students, how we grade their work—in short, virtually everything that happens in our classrooms—is left to our individual discretion. Never, ever question the practice of a colleague because to do so is considered a major affront. It is, however, perfectly permissible to comment on conditions or practices outside of the classroom. School policies, administrative decisions, the parents, state regulations, sports, and current events are examples of the many acceptable topics

you can discuss. You must, however, avoid probing into the practices of a colleague because it might be construed as criticism. Remember you are responsible for your own classroom and kids, and your colleagues are responsible for theirs. Respect the privacy and professionalism of your colleagues.

Our job is to teach, and the students' job is to learn. We do our jobs when we present clear and engaging lessons and provide students with an opportunity to demonstrate their learning. Focus on coverage—teach as much of the curriculum as possible—and understand that the degree to which students learn each year will depend on their ability and responsibility. Don't expect recognition. What little satisfaction and reinforcement you get will come from the occasional student who excels or who makes a point to express his or her appreciation to you. Savor those anecdotal triumphs.

You are responsible for your own professional development, which almost always occurs away from our campus. You will advance on the salary schedule if you take graduate courses, so you would be wise to find a program that is convenient, allows you to pursue your personal interests, and is not too rigorous. Staff development that occurs here on inservice days is typically not very meaningful, but occasionally they will bring in a speaker who is entertaining.

You are lucky to work in this school because you are generally left alone to focus on your own classroom without a lot of outside interference. You will be granted tenure as long as you don't refer too many kids to the office for discipline, generate a lot of parent complaints, miss deadlines, or have personality conflicts with the administration.

Then you will advance on the unofficial hierarchy of the faculty as senior members of the staff retire. Play your cards right, pay your dues, and someday you might get the good kids and the good room.

The Story That Drives a PLC

The unspoken assumptions that a new teacher would learn in a highly developed PLC would be quite different. If they were put in writing, they would look like this:

> In this school, you are expected to take an intense personal interest in the success of all of our students. You could never help all students learn if you work in isolation, so you will become a member of a collaborative team—colleagues who work interdependently to achieve a common goal for which they are mutually accountable. One of the most important responsibilities of every member of this staff is to make positive contributions to his or her team. You will be assigned a mentor from your team to assist with your transition to our school, but you will find the collaborative culture of your weekly team meeting to be a major source of support as you work your way through the daily questions and challenges confronting a teacher.
>
> Equity is an important issue in this school. You will find that teams work continuously to ensure all students in the same course have access to the same knowledge and skills and have their work assessed according to the same criteria regardless of the teacher to whom they are assigned. Your team has clarified the most essential learnings for each unit of your course, agreed on the general pacing of the content, and developed a series of common assessments that will be administered to all the students in your course. You will benefit greatly from

this clear understanding of what students are expected to learn and how they will be asked to demonstrate their learning for every unit you teach.

Your teammates will solicit your questions and recommendations regarding the curriculum and assessments and will encourage you to become an active participant in their decision-making process. Don't hesitate to do so. One of the reasons the team recommended you for this position is its members felt you could make a contribution to their work.

Our commitment to equity also means the issue of what happens when some students do not learn is not left to chance or to the discretion of individual teachers. We have created a systematic intervention process to monitor student learning on a timely basis and to ensure students receive additional time and support for learning in a consistent and directive way as soon as they experience difficulty. In order for that system to work, you must report student progress accurately and often and be as precise as possible regarding the skill or concept the student is struggling to master. Remember there is a structure in place to support your efforts to help all students learn, and you must make certain your students have access to that structure.

You and your teammates will analyze the results from every common assessment, not only to identify students who are having difficulty, but also to identify the strengths and weaknesses of each member's instruction. On every common assessment you will be given prompt feedback regarding the success of your students in achieving the team's agreed-upon standard of proficiency compared to all the other students who took the assessment. The information is presented in a very user-friendly format and is openly shared among teammates, so everyone has a wonderful opportunity to learn about the materials and methods of colleagues who are getting the best results for each skill or concept that is taught. Your team will have a designated leader, but you will discover that leadership in this school is a function of expertise rather than position. When the evidence demonstrates you have been extraordinarily effective in helping your students learn a particular skill or concept, you will be encouraged and expected to take the lead in helping colleagues develop new insights and strategies in those areas.

Building shared knowledge is the prerequisite homework for making a decision in our school. We attempt to resolve every important question and issue by engaging in collective inquiry, jointly examining both external and internal evidence of best practice, and honestly assessing our own practice in light of the evidence. We operate from the premise, "Without evidence, you are just another person with an opinion." We make our important decisions—what to teach, how to assess student learning, best instructional practices, how to assign grades, and so on—on the basis of evidence rather than opinions. Pilot projects are common and help us gather additional information before moving forward with a schoolwide initiative.

Every team is expected to develop and pursue SMART goals to drive the continuous improvement process of the school. The goal will be aligned with one of our school goals, will focus on results that require evidence of student learning, and will call for a significant contribution from every member of the team in order to be achieved.

One of the most powerful forms of professional development we experience is the ongoing, job-embedded learning that takes place among teammates as they work together to meet the needs of all their students. Days specifically set aside for professional development in the school calendar are typically reserved for teams. You and your teammates will be able to identify and pursue the topics you feel are most critical to achieving your SMART goals. We learn collectively, we stay focused on issues that have the most powerful impact on teaching and learning, and we move quickly to apply our new skills and insights. We value learning by doing, and you will see that working here is the best graduate program you could ever have.

It should be evident to you how serious we are about hiring people who fit our culture. Before you were offered a job here, the school principal and your team interviewed you at length, asked you to respond to a variety of different scenarios, probed your thinking, and observed you teach several classes. We have invested considerable effort to bring you to our campus, we expect you to be successful, and we are prepared to offer you extensive support to promote that success. To be recommended for tenure, however, you must prove your strong commitment to the learning of all students, become a positive contributing member to your team, and demonstrate a willingness to continue your own professional learning.

This is a wonderful place to work. Celebration is an important part of who we are. Every faculty meeting celebrates the efforts and achievements of a variety of individuals and teams. The team process fosters both appreciation and recognition as you make contributions to your colleagues and they recognize the improvement in your teaching. The achievement of SMART goals is another cause for collective celebration and builds a powerful sense of individual and collective self-efficacy. You will have a sense of belonging and connection because you will always have someone to turn to for help in meeting the challenges of this profession. All the systems that have been created to keep us focused on student learning will remind you of the significance of the work we do, and there is something very powerful about being part of a collective effort to achieve a mighty purpose. Finally, you will become the very best educator you can be by virtue of the fact that you work in this school, and there is a tremendous sense of satisfaction that comes with fulfilling your full potential as a professional and as a person.

Which of these two stories is at work in your school and district? If schools and districts are to engage in the substantive changes essential to raising student achievement, educational leaders must help create a new story regarding the purpose of their schools and the actions essential to achieving that purpose. Citing research, highlighting the endorsements of professional organizations, and arranging visits to successful schools can help make the case for PLCs. Ultimately, however, educational leaders must help establish new assumptions and new systems if schools are to help more students learn at higher levels.

Changing the Story Can Help Change the System

The aging of the current teaching force has caused national concern about the possibility of a teacher shortage in the coming years. The real problem in education, however, has never been the ability to attract people to teaching, but to retain them in the profession. As the National Commission on Teaching and America's Future reported, "Our inability to support high quality teaching in many of our schools is not driven by too few teachers entering the profession, but by too many leaving it for other jobs" (2003, p. 6).

Almost half of new teachers leave the profession within their first 5 years of teaching. The solution to this problem is not to pour more new teachers into schools, but to make schools more inviting and rewarding places for all of the educators who work there. W. Edwards Deming once observed, "Put a good person in a bad system and the system wins every time, no contest." For too long we have attempted to solve the problems of education by pouring more good people into a bad system. It is time to create better systems—to make schools more hospitable places for students and adults so that ordinary people can accomplish extraordinary things. We know some schools promote more good teaching in more classrooms more of the time. We know some schools provide educators with both the information and support essential to their continuous improvement. We know some schools are specifically designed to ensure a systematic and collective response to the challenges facing educators rather than leaving isolated individuals on their own to cope with complex problems. We know some schools create the conditions that help educators become more effective simply by virtue of the fact that they have the good fortune to work in those schools. It is time to apply what we know and make these conditions the norm rather than the exception. It is time to close the knowing-doing gap and to make every school a professional learning community.

Chapter 4

The Challenge of Cultural Change

The pathology of American schools is that they know how to change. They know how to change promiscuously and at the drop of a hat. What schools do not know how to do is to improve, to engage in sustained and continuous progress toward a performance goal over time.

—Richard Elmore

The difficulty lies not so much in developing new ideas as in escaping old ones.

—John Maynard Keynes

External efforts to improve schools invariably focus on structural changes—the changes that impact policies, procedures, rules, and relationships. When a state or province increases graduation requirements, mandates more minutes of instruction in a content area, adopts more rigorous standards for teacher certification, or creates a system of sanctions for low-performing schools, it is engaged in structural change. When a district moves its high schools to a block schedule, reorganizes its schools into smaller units, announces its junior high schools will now function as middle schools, or requires students to wear uniforms, it too is engaged in structural change.

Policymakers are particularly fond of structural changes because these modifications are immediate and visible. A structural change can be announced with a flourish, and a legislator, governor, education minister, or school superintendent can point to tangible evidence of his or her efforts to improve schools. Unfortunately, structural changes typically neither impact the practices of teachers in their classrooms nor the assumptions that drive those practices, and thus they are insufficient to improve schools.

The Importance of Cultural Change

Even a cursory review of literature on the change process indicates that meaningful, substantive, sustainable improvement can occur in an organization only if those improvements become anchored in the culture of the organization: *the assumptions, beliefs, values, expectations, and habits that constitute the norm for that organization.* As Roland Barth (2001) wrote:

> The school's culture dictates, in no uncertain terms, "the way we do things around here." Ultimately, a school's culture has far more influence on life and learning in the schoolhouse than the state department of education, the superintendent, the school board, or even the principal can ever have. . . . The culture is the historically transmitted pattern of meaning that wields astonishing power in shaping what people think and how they act. (pp. 7–8)

All schools have cultures. They may foster collaboration or isolation, promote self-efficacy or fatalism, be student-centered or teacher-centered, regard teaching as a craft that can be developed or as an innate art, assign primary responsibility for learning to teachers or students, view administrators and teachers as colleagues or adversaries, encourage continuous improvement or defense of the status quo, and so on.

And while it is true that educators shape their school cultures, it is probably more accurate to say that their school cultures shape them. Edgar Schein (1992) described culture as "the assumptions we don't see" (p. 21). Cultural norms exert a powerful influence on how people think, feel, and act, and because educators are so immersed in their cultures, they often find it difficult to step outside of their traditions and assumptions to examine their conventional practices from a critical perspective.

It is understandable that policymakers focus on structural changes in schools. While they can pronounce a change in policy or procedures for schools, they cannot legislate or mandate a change in the assumptions, beliefs, values, expectations, or habits of the educators within those schools. Cultural changes are less visible, more amorphous, and *much* more difficult to make; yet unless efforts to improve schools ultimately impact the culture, there is no reason to believe schools will produce better results. As Michael Fullan (2007) wrote:

> Most strategies for reform focus on structures, formal requirements, and events-based activities. . . . They do not struggle directly with the existing cultures within which new values and practices may be required. . . . Restructuring (which can be done by fiat) occurs time and time again whereas reculturing (how teachers come to question and change their beliefs and habits) is what is needed. (p. 25)

Ken Blanchard (2007) came to a similar conclusion about the need to focus on culture. He wrote, "If a change is introduced that is not aligned with the current culture, you must alter the existing culture to support the new initiative or accept that the change may not be sustainable in the long term" (p. 246).

So we come to a central premise of this book, a point to which we will return again and again: *It is impossible for a school or district to develop the capacity to function as a professional learning community without undergoing profound cultural shifts.* Those who cultivate PLCs must engage in an intentional process to impact the culture. Restructuring can certainly facilitate the process and is often a prerequisite for moving forward, but merely changing structures is never sufficient to create a

PLC. The work of developing PLCs is not the work of adopting new programs or implementing an innovative practice; it is the challenge of reculturing—the challenge of impacting the assumptions, beliefs, expectations, and habits that constitute the norm. When that work is done successfully, the school or district becomes a very different place. As Andy Hargreaves (2004) observed, "A professional learning community is an ethos that changes every single aspect of a school's operation. When a school becomes a professional learning community, everything in the school looks different than it did before" (p. 48).

In *Learning by Doing* (2006), we cited some of the cultural shifts schools undergo on the journey to become a PLC—shifts in purpose, the use of assessments, responses when students do not learn, the work of teachers, the focus of daily activities, and approaches to professional development. The chart on pages 93–95 provides an overview of these shifts.

Embracing the Difficulty of the Challenge

Bringing about cultural change in any organization is a complex and challenging task. Phil Schlechty (2005) refers to the challenge of reculturing as "disruptive change" because it "calls upon the system and those who work in it to do things they have never done" (p. 3). It has also been referred to as "second-order change"—innovation that represents a dramatic departure from the expected and familiar. Second-order change is perceived as a break from the past, is inconsistent with existing paradigms, may seem at conflict with prevailing practices and norms, and requires the acquisition of new knowledge and new skills (Marzano, Waters, & McNulty, 2005).

Cultural Shifts in a Professional Learning Community

A Shift in Fundamental Purpose

From a focus on teaching . . .	to a focus on learning
From emphasis on what was taught . . .	to a fixation on what students learned
From coverage of content . . .	to demonstration of proficiency
From providing individual teachers with curriculum documents such as state standards and curriculum guides . . .	to engaging collaborative teams in building shared knowledge regarding essential curriculum

A Shift in Use of Assessments

From infrequent summative assessments . . .	to frequent common formative assessments
From assessments to determine which students failed to learn by the deadline . . .	to assessments to identify students who need additional time and support
From assessments used to reward and punish students . . .	to assessments used to inform and motivate students
From assessing many things infrequently . . .	to assessing a few things frequently
From individual teacher assessments . . .	to assessments developed jointly by collaborative teams
From each teacher determining the criteria to be used in assessing student work . . .	to collaborative teams clarifying the criteria and ensuring consistency among team members when assessing student work
From an over-reliance on one kind of assessment . . .	to balanced assessments
From focusing on average scores . . .	to monitoring each student's proficiency in every essential skill

(continued)

Cultural Shifts in a PLC (continued)

A Shift in the Response When Students Don't Learn

From individual teachers determining the appropriate response . . .	to a systematic response that ensures support for every student
From fixed time and support for learning . . .	to time and support for learning as variables
From remediation . . .	to intervention
From invitational support outside of the school day . . .	to directed (that is, required) support occurring during the school day
From one opportunity to demonstrate learning . . .	to multiple opportunities to demonstrate learning

A Shift in the Work of Teachers

From isolation . . .	to collaboration
From each teacher clarifying what students must learn . . .	to collaborative teams building shared knowledge and understanding about essential learning
From each teacher assigning priority to different learning standards . . .	to collaborative teams establishing the priority of respective learning standards
From each teacher determining the pacing of the curriculum . . .	to collaborative teams of teachers agreeing on common pacing
From individual teachers attempting to discover ways to improve results . . .	to collaborative teams of teachers helping each other improve
From privatization of practice . . .	to open sharing of practice
From decisions made on the basis of individual preferences . . .	to decisions made collectively by building shared knowledge of best practice
From "collaboration lite" on matters unrelated to student achievement . . .	to collaboration explicitly focused on issues and questions that most impact student achievement
From an assumption that these are "my kids, those are your kids" . . .	to an assumption that these are "our kids"

Cultural Shifts in a PLC (continued)

A Shift in Focus

From an external focus on issues outside of the school . . .	to an internal focus on steps the staff can take to improve the school
From a focus on inputs . . .	to a focus on results
From goals related to completion of projects and activities . . .	to SMART goals demanding evidence of student learning
From teachers gathering data from their individually constructed tests in order to assign grades . . .	to collaborative teams acquiring information from common assessments in order to (1) inform their individual and collective practice, and (2) respond to students who need additional time and support
From independence . . .	to interdependence
From a language of complaint . . .	to a language of commitment
From long-term strategic planning . . .	to planning for short-term wins
From infrequent generic recognition . . .	to frequent specific recognition and a culture of celebration that creates many winners

A Shift in Professional Development

From external training (workshops and courses) . . .	to job-embedded learning
From the expectation that learning occurs infrequently (on the few days devoted to professional development) . . .	to an expectation that learning is ongoing and occurs as part of routine work practice
From presentations to entire faculties . . .	to team-based action research
From learning by listening . . .	to learning by doing
From learning individually through courses and workshops . . .	to learning collectively by working together
From assessing impact on the basis of teacher satisfaction ("Did you like it?") . . .	to assessing impact on the basis of evidence of improved student learning
From short-term exposure to multiple concepts and practices . . .	to sustained commitment to limited, focused initiatives

Those who hope to develop their schools and districts as PLCs must remember that every existing system has a well-entrenched structure and culture already in place. People working within that system will typically resist change and fight to preserve the status quo. In fact, in the midst of the change process, educators are likely to perceive that their school has been weakened, their opinions are not valued, and that the stability of the school has been undermined. Periods of frustration, and even anger, are not uncommon (Marzano, Waters, & McNulty, 2005), and it may become difficult to remember Fullan's (2007) assurance that "conflict and disagreements are not only inevitable but fundamental to successful change" (p. 21). In short, real change is real hard.

One of the most damaging myths about school leadership is that the change process, if managed well, will proceed smoothly. That myth often causes educators to view problems and conflict as evidence of mistakes or a mismanaged process rather than as the inevitable byproducts of serious reform. Seymour Sarason (1995) tried to expose that myth when he wrote:

> The decision to undertake change more often than not is accompanied by a kind of optimism and rosy view of the future that, temporarily at least, obscures the predictable turmoil ahead. But that turmoil cannot be avoided and how well it is coped with separates the boys from the men, the girls from the women. It is . . . rough stuff. . . . There are breakthroughs, but also brick walls. (p. vii)

Therefore, attempts to persuade educators to participate in substantive reform by assuring them that change will be easy are patently dishonest. Principals and teachers should be advised (and should acknowledge) from the outset that transforming their schools from the industrial model to PLCs will be difficult regardless of how carefully they plan and how skillfully they manage the process. Still, they can make their reculturing efforts more effective by becoming students of the process of improving organizations.

Leading the Improvement Process

We made a conscious decision to title this section "Leading the *Improvement* Process" rather than "Leading a *Change* Process," and we believe the distinction represents far more than semantics. While we are convinced that making the transition from a traditional school to a PLC will require substantive *changes* in both the structures and cultures of schools and districts, the effectiveness of those changes must ultimately be assessed by the extent to which they improve the ability of educators to fulfill the fundamental purpose of their organizations: helping all students learn at high levels. The challenge for school and district leaders is not merely to become skillful in the change process per se. Neither students nor educators are served by the successful implementation of the wrong changes. We are not proponents of change for change's sake, and we are convinced that many educators have jumped aboard the never-ending parade of bandwagons touting the latest change to *avoid* engaging in sustained, substantive reform. The challenge facing educational leaders is to become skillful in the *improvement* process—a challenge they can only meet if they can sustain a collective focus on a few issues that matter over an extended period of time. Any references we make to a "change process," therefore, should be considered in the context of improvement toward a particular end—helping more students learn at higher levels.

A review of the research for help on how to implement and sustain a successful improvement process is likely to create more confusion than clarity. Consider the following explanations that have been offered for the failure of school reform initiatives:

- The change moved too fast—people were overwhelmed.

- The change moved too slowly—people lost their enthusiasm.

- The change lacked strong leadership from the principal.

- The change relied too heavily on the leadership of a strong principal.

- The change was too big and attacked too much at once—people change incrementally, not holistically.

- The change was too small—organizations need a more aggressive, comprehensive shake-up if change is to be substantive.

- The change was top-down without buy-in from the faculty.

- The change was bottom-up without the support of the central office or administration.

- Gains were celebrated too soon, and the sense of urgency was lost.

- Gains were not recognized and celebrated, and the initiative lost momentum.

- Schools were unwilling to change—they were steadfastly committed to the status quo.

- Schools embraced every change that came along and careened from fad to fad.

- Leaders failed to develop a critical level of support before initiating change.

- Leaders mistakenly insisted on overwhelming support as a prerequisite for initiating change—a stipulation that ensured implementation would never occur.

Each of these observations can, of course, be a valid assessment of the failure of a change initiative. Yet the paradoxes they present fail to offer guidance on overcoming obstacles to substantive innovation. What is the answer then? What must educators understand about the improvement process if they are to transform their schools into learning communities?

Common Mistakes in the Change Process

John Kotter (1996) of the Harvard Business School identified the eight most common mistakes in the change process in his seminal work, *Leading Change*:

1. **Allowing too much complacency.** Kotter contends that the biggest mistake people make when trying to change organizations is to plunge ahead without establishing a sufficient sense of urgency. He argues that this is a fatal error because change efforts always fail when complacency levels are high.

2. **Failing to create a sufficiently powerful guiding coalition.** Individuals working alone, no matter how competent or charismatic they are, will never have everything that is needed to overcome the powerful forces of tradition and inertia. A key to successful change is creating first a guiding coalition and ultimately a critical mass of people within the organization who will champion the change process together.

3. **Underestimating the power of vision.** Vision helps to direct, align, and inspire the actions of the members of an organization. Without the clear sense of direction a shared vision provides, the only choices left to individuals within an organization are to "do their own thing," to check constantly with supervisors for assurance about the decisions they must make, or to debate every issue that arises.

4. **Undercommunicating the vision by a power of 10.** Without credible communication, and a lot of it, change efforts are doomed to fail. Three types of errors are common. In the first, leaders underestimate the importance of communicating the vision. They mistakenly believe sending a few memos, making a few speeches, or holding a few meetings will inform people in the organization of the change and recruit them to it. A second mistake is divided leadership. While the head of the organization

articulates the importance of the change, other leaders in the organization may tend to ignore it. The third mistake is incongruence between what key leaders say and how they behave. Strategies to communicate vision are always ineffective if highly visible people in the organization still behave in ways that are contrary to the vision.

5. **Permitting structural and cultural obstacles to block the change process.** Organizations often fail to address obstacles that block change. These obstacles typically include a) structures that make it difficult to act, b) insufficient training and support for people who are critical to the initiative's success, c) supervisors who do not endorse the change, and d) information and reward systems that are not aligned with the new vision. Simply declaring a new vision is not sufficient. The organization must make every effort to remove the structural and cultural barriers that threaten to impede the implementation of that vision.

6. **Failing to create short-term wins.** Change initiatives risk losing momentum if there are no short-term goals to reach and celebrate. Most people will not "go on the long march" unless they see compelling evidence within one year that the journey is producing desirable results. Creating short-term wins requires establishing goals, identifying performance criteria, achieving the goals, and then publicly celebrating the results.

7. **Declaring victory too soon.** There is also a difference between celebrating a win and declaring victory. Until change initiatives become anchored in the culture, they are fragile and subject to regression. Handled properly, the celebration of short-term wins can give the change initiative the credibility it needs to tackle bigger, more substantive problems. Handled improperly, this celebration can contribute to the complacency that is lethal to the change process.

8. **Neglecting to anchor changes firmly in the culture.** Change sticks only when it is firmly entrenched in the school or organization's culture, as part of "the way we do things around here." As Kotter (1996) concludes, "Until new behaviors are rooted in social norms and shared values, they are always subject to degradation as soon as the pressures associated with a change effort are removed" (p. 14).

Not content with a mere eight imposing obstacles, Ken Blanchard (2007, pp. 203–04) has compiled an even more extensive list of why change initiatives fail. His list includes the following reasons:

- Those leading the change think that announcing the change is the same as implementing it.

- People's concerns with the change are neither surfaced nor considered.

- Those being asked to change are not involved in planning the change.

- There is no urgent or compelling reason to change. The case for change is not communicated.

- A compelling vision about the future benefits of the change has not been developed or communicated.

- The leadership team does not include early adopters, resisters, or informal leaders.

- The change is not piloted, so the organization does not learn what is needed to support the change.

- Organizational systems are not aligned with the change.

- Leaders lose focus or fail to prioritize, causing "death by 1,000 initiatives."

- People are not enabled or encouraged to build new skills.

- Those leading the change are not credible—they undercommunicate, send mixed messages, and do not model the behaviors the change requires.

- Progress is not measured, and no one recognizes the changes that people have worked hard to make.

- People are not held accountable for implementing the change.

- People leading the change fail to respect the power of the culture to kill the change.

- Possibilities and options are not explored before a specific change is chosen.

Each of these mistakes represents a potential minefield for those attempting to traverse the perilous path of transforming a school from its industrial traditions into a PLC. Any one of them can destroy the change process. So, what is the most promising path for those well-intentioned educators who are willing to undertake this perilous journey?

Fear as a Catalyst for Change

Kotter's contention that significant change requires a sense of urgency would seem to validate the strategies of past school reform efforts. The rhetoric of *A Nation at Risk* was, after all, an explicit attempt to alert America to an alleged national crisis. Advocates of school choice, charter schools, and vouchers argued these reforms were needed to shake educators from their lethargy because unless principals and teachers felt the "spur of the market," they would never change. No Child Left Behind was an even more forceful effort to create a sense of urgency among educators, threatening them with a variety of sanctions up to and including the loss of their jobs and the closing of their schools. If these attempts could not generate a sufficient sense of crisis to prompt school improvement, what could?

But rather than seeking new and more effective initiatives to foster fear, perhaps better questions might be, "Does creating a sense of urgency actually motivate change," and, "Is a sense of urgency truly a prerequisite for change?" Alan Deutschman (2007) reviewed studies of medical patients who were given the option of "change or die" and then posed this question:

> What if you were given that choice? *For real.* . . . We're talking actual life and death now. Your own life and death. What if a well-informed, trusted authority figure said you had to make difficult and enduring changes in the way you think, feel, and act? If you didn't, your time would end soon—a lot sooner than it had to. Could you change when change really mattered? When it mattered the most?

Deutschman reported that studies consistently revealed 9 of 10 patients would be unable to make and sustain the changes necessary *to save their lives.*

Clearly, urgency alone is not sufficient to serve as a catalyst for change. Furthermore, it would seem impossible to create an adequate sense of crisis in a school with a good reputation where students are achieving reasonably well, parents are satisfied with the education their children receive, and the staff is content with the existing conditions. Yet even these schools must be improved if all students are to achieve at high levels.

So if fear is not an effective motivator for undergoing important change, what is? In our workshops, we often ask participants to think of a time in their life when they made the decision to undertake a significant change even though they knew the transition would be difficult, even painful. Invariably their responses speak of hope for a better future, a more satisfying and fulfilling life than what they were experiencing. It was not fear that drove them—it was hope.

When Deutschman found examples of people who were successful in their attempts to bring about dramatic changes in their lives despite seemingly overwhelming odds, he discovered that they had formed new relationships that inspired and sustained hope. In his study of school cultures, Evans (1996) came to a similar conclusion. He wrote, "Of all the factors vital to improving schools, none is more essential—and vulnerable—than hope" (p. 290). Kotter and Cohen (2002) might very well have been describing contemporary educators when they wrote:

> We fail at change efforts not because we are stupid, overconfident, and unemotional beings, although it can seem that way at times. We fail because we haven't sufficiently experienced highly successful change. Without that experience, we are too often left pessimistic, fearful, or without enough faith to act. So we not only behave in less effective ways, we don't even try. (p. 13)

It follows, then, that those who set out to transform their schools and districts must work both on strengthening relationships and building a collective sense of self-efficacy, a task so important John Gardner (1988) referred to it as a "leader's highest duty." Studies within and outside of education consistently report that those most effective in leading a change process convey a "contagious" or "infectious" passion, energy, enthusiasm, and conviction about the ability of the staff to accomplish great things collectively (Fullan, 2001; Goleman, 2002; Kanter, 2004; Marzano, Waters, & McNulty, 2005).

Hope, however, is not a strategy, and despite the popularity of Rhonda Byrne's self-help book *The Secret* (2006), we are convinced that leaders must do more than wish for good things to happen and immerse themselves in positive thoughts. As Kanter (2004) wrote, "The positive outlook that optimists project does not come from ignoring or denying problems. Optimists simply assume that problems are temporary and can be solved, so optimists naturally want more information about problems, because then they can get to work and do something" (p. 210).

Leadership Strategies for Changing Culture

But what is it exactly that effective leaders *do* when it comes to transforming the very culture of the organization? Do they resort to "tight leadership"—imposing a new regimen and demanding that employees adhere to the direction that has been established from the top? Or do effective leaders change the culture of their organizations by using a "loose" approach to leadership that encourages those within the organization to pursue their own independent interests and initiatives in the belief that such freedom and autonomy will spark the energy and enthusiasm necessary for significant change?

Michael Fullan (2007) argues that this question of loose versus tight leadership represents "the essential dilemma" of large-scale school reform, and after exploring that question throughout his distinguished career, he has concluded that *neither strategy works* (our emphasis). He writes, "Top-down change doesn't work because it fails to garner ownership, commitment, or even clarity about the nature of the reform. Bottom-up change—so-called let a thousand flowers bloom—does not produce success on any scale. A thousand flowers do not bloom and those that do are not perennial" (p. 11).

Other students of school reform have come to the same conclusion. In their review of a century of school reform in the United States, Tyack and Cuban (1995) concluded that while top-down reforms may impact educators, educators also impact reforms. Teachers and principals can respond to new mandates with passive compliance rather than actual commitment, and they have become adept at ignoring reforms when they close their school or classroom doors and continue doing what they have always done. As Tyack and Cuban warned (and NCLB has illustrated), simply delivering new regulations to the schoolhouse door will not improve schools.

There is, however, simply no evidence that loose strategies are any more effective in reculturing schools than the flawed tight strategies now in vogue in the United States. As we mentioned in chapter 2, educators in schools that enjoy the autonomy of site-based decision-making are no more likely to engage in serious professional dialogue about matters directly impacting teaching and learning than are their more rigidly supervised counterparts in highly centralized districts and schools. In fact, Schlechty (2005) argues that "much harm has been done to public education and to the ideas of equity and excellence" by poor implementation of site-based management (p. 9). Alas, merely empowering educators in every school to pursue their own version of improvement through site-based management does not guarantee teaching and learning will improve.

So, if neither top-down nor bottom-up strategies will improve schools, we return to the question, what is it exactly that effective leaders should *do* when it comes to initiating changes specifically intended to improve their schools and districts by transforming the very culture of the organization? Tyack and Cuban (1995) recommend leaders "seek a *middle course* [italics added] between the top-down mode of reform . . . and the random approach of letting a thousand flowers bloom" (p. 109).

We recommend a very different approach. In their study of highly effective organizations that were able to sustain greatness over an extended period of time, Collins and Porras (1997) found that ineffective organizations fell victim to the "Tyranny of Or," which they defined as "the rational view that cannot easily accept paradox, that cannot live with two seemingly contradictory forces at the same time" (p. 44). The Tyranny of Or would demand a district either be centralized *or* decentralized, value strong leaders *or* empowered teachers, promote organizational consistency *or* individual autonomy.

Collins and Porras found that great organizations rejected the Tyranny of Or and embraced the "Genius of And"—the ability to embrace both extremes at the same time. They stressed that the Genius of And was not just a question of balance because "balance implies going to the mid-point, fifty-fifty, half and half" (p. 44). The great organizations they studied did not seek the grey of balance, but instead sought to be distinctly both A and B at the same time. A district that embraced the Genius of And would not seek a middle ground; it would hope to have strong leaders *and* empowered teachers, insist on consistency in important elements of district practice *and* champion both school-based and individual autonomy.

The most fertile ground for cultivating PLCs is found in district and school cultures that are *simultaneously loose and tight.* Some elements of the culture are tight. These elements clarify shared purpose and priorities as well as the parameters within which all members are expected to operate on a day-to-day basis. Within those parameters, however, is tremendous latitude for individual and collective innovation, empowerment, and autonomy. In *Good to Great,* Jim Collins (2001) refers to this concept as "a culture of discipline" (tight) with an "ethic of entrepreneurship" (loose); it is "a culture built around the idea of freedom and responsibility within the framework of a highly developed system" (p. 124). We will return to this concept of loose-tight cultures throughout the book, but for now we want to assert our contention that those who are successful in building PLCs will become adept at creating and operating within cultures that are simultaneously loose and tight.

First Steps in Reculturing

In this chapter we have argued:

- The culture of an organization is found in the assumptions, beliefs, values, expectations, and habits that constitute the norm for that organization.

- Creating a PLC in a school or district requires—and, in fact, is synonymous with—changing the culture (that is, reculturing).

- Reculturing is extremely difficult, and neither top-down nor bottom-up strategies have proven effective in reculturing schools or districts.

- The most powerful concept for bringing about the necessary transformation to become a PLC is the concept of a simultaneously loose and tight culture.

This list still provides no real specifics regarding what leaders should *do* to impact culture, no step-by-step strategy for reshaping the assumptions, beliefs, values, expectations, and habits of the people in their organization. But the answer to the question, "How do we impact culture?" is simple: Effective leaders do not begin by focusing on changing assumptions and beliefs; they begin by focusing on changing *behaviors.*

The "central challenge" and "core problem" in every phase of any organization's improvement process is *"changing people's behavior,"* that is, "what people do, and the need for significant shifts in what people do" (Kotter & Cohen, 2002, p. 2). In their analysis of improving organizations, Pfeffer and Sutton (2000) wrote, "There is a large literature demonstrating that attitudes *follow* behavior. That means people accept new beliefs as a result of changing their behavior" (p. 65). Fullan (2007) insists "all successful change processes have a bias for action . . . behaviors and emotions change before beliefs—we need to act in a new way before we get insights and feelings related to new beliefs" (p. 41). Richard Elmore (2002) urged educational leaders to embrace and utilize this research when he advised, "Only a change in practice produces a genuine change in norms and values . . . grab people by their practice and their hearts and minds will follow."

Thus, it is essential to understand 1) the challenge of changing culture begins with the challenge of changing behavior, and therefore 2) actual changes in culture occur late in the process. Schools and districts can initiate new practices and processes to promote a new culture, stimulate dialogue to articulate and reexamine existing assumptions, and build shared knowledge and create new experiences to foster different beliefs and assumptions, but the culture will not really be transformed until new practices, processes, assumptions, and beliefs become the new norms, the new "how we do things around here." That transformation takes place at the end, rather than the beginning of a change process. Leaders do not first change the culture to get people to act in new ways, they first change how people act in an effort to change the culture (Kotter & Cohen, 2002).

A Different Metaphor

The question facing educational leaders is not "Will our school or district have a culture?" but rather, "Will we make a conscious effort to shape our culture?" Once again, every school and district has a culture, and the collective assumptions, habits, expectations, and beliefs that constitute the norm for the people in the organization exist as surely as the school buildings themselves.

And although leaders are sometimes told they must "build" a strong culture, cultures cannot be built. Architects and engineers construct a building using a linear, sequential model. Phase one must be addressed before moving to phase two. The building process is both visible and time-bound. Eventually, building ends and maintenance begins. The building is relatively permanent, specifically constructed to resist external pressures such as weather. Finally, a building is not constructed by accident. Unless there is a decision to erect the structure and purposeful steps taken to carry out that decision, the building will not exist.

None of this is true with culture. Tending to culture is nonlinear and requires rapid responses to unanticipated problems as they arise. Cultural norms are typically invisible, implicit, and unexamined, made up of scores of subtleties in the day-to-day workings of the school. Culture is ongoing. At no point can it be said that the culture is complete and permanent. In brief, school culture is organic rather than static.

The more accurate metaphor for the process of shaping culture is not erecting a building, but cultivating a garden. A garden is nonlinear, with some elements dying out as others are being born. A garden is influenced both by internal and external factors. Its most vital elements occur underground and are not readily visible. Most importantly, a garden is fragile and very high maintenance. Even the most flourishing garden will eventually become overgrown if it is not nurtured. Flowers left unattended eventually yield to weeds. The same can be said of school cultures. Unless educators carefully and constantly tend to their schools' cultures by shaping the assumptions, beliefs, values, expectations, and habits that constitute the norm within them, toxic weeds will eventually dominate (DuFour & Burnette, 2002).

Reason for Hope

We have stressed throughout this chapter that reculturing schools and districts to become PLCs is a difficult task; it is not, however, impossible. In fact, there is reason for optimism. Michael Fullan (1997), the most thoughtful observer of school reform over the past quarter century, sounded a pessimistic note when he wrote, "None of the current strategies being employed . . . result in widespread change. The first step toward liberation in my view is that we are facing a lost cause" (p. 220). Ten years later (2007), he was decidedly more optimistic when he wrote, "I believe we are closer than ever in knowing what must be done to engage all classrooms and schools in continuous reform" (p. 19) and "breakthrough forces for educational change now seem to be in our midst" (p. 229). One reason for his optimism is that "developing PLCs has turned out to be one of the leading strategies of reform and PLCs are becoming more prominent and more sharply defined" (p. 98). Much difficult work remains to be done, but, perhaps we are nearing the tipping point described by The National Commission on Teaching and America's Future (2003) when PLCs will no longer "be considered utopian" but will in fact "become the building blocks that establish a new foundation for America's schools" (p. 17).

In setting out to create PLCs, effective leaders will help create a shared sense of moral purpose about the work to be done. They will continually come back to the "why" of school improvement as they move forward with the "how." They will help to develop a shared sense of what the school or district might become, a clear and compelling future that is unarguably superior to the status quo. They will help shape the collective commitments that give people throughout the school or district clear parameters and priorities that guide their day-to-day decisions and enable them to exercise their professional judgment and autonomy. They will help establish widely understood indicators of progress that can be monitored on an ongoing basis both to provide staff with the feedback essential to continuous improvement and to provide a basis for celebration of progress. And they will effectively communicate the significance of this shared purpose, better future, collective commitments, and indicators of progress with clarity, consistency, and conviction. In short, they will lay the foundation of a PLC. In chapter 5, we will examine how they proceed in this challenge.

Chapter 5

Clear Mission and Shared Vision

Great schools "row as one"; they are quite clearly in the same boat, pulling in the same direction in unison. The best schools we visited were tightly aligned communities marked by a palpable sense of common purpose and shared identity among staff—a clear sense of "we."

—Thomas Lickona and Matthew Davidson

You can leave a lasting legacy only if you can imagine a brighter future, and the capacity to imagine exciting future possibilities is the defining competence of leaders.

—James Kouzes and Barry Posner

In *Professional Learning Communities at Work* (1998), we stressed the importance of a faculty developing a shared understanding of and commitment to the fundamental purpose of its school. We still do. After all, a 5-year study of more than 1,500 schools in 16 states conducted by the Center on Organization and Restructuring of Schools found the most successful schools function as professional communities "in which teachers pursue a clear shared purpose for all students' learning, engage in collaborative activity to achieve that purpose, and take collective responsibility for student learning" (Newmann & Wehlage, 1995, p. 30). Certainly clarity of purpose and a willingness to accept responsibility for achieving that purpose are critical to school improvement.

Unfortunately, however, many educators interpreted our advocacy for shared mission as a call to write a new mission statement. They engaged staff in painstaking wordsmithing to draft yet another variation of the standard commitment to help all students learn, celebrated the completion of their task, and then returned to business as usual.

There is an enormous difference between writing a mission and *living* a mission. In fact, Pfeffer and Sutton (2000) found that ineffective organizations often resort to writing a mission statement to create the illusion of action, substituting writing a mission statement for actually taking meaningful steps to bring that mission to life. They could find no evidence that merely crafting and displaying a new mission statement impacted how people in an organization act. We concur. We have found no correlation between the presence of a written mission statement—or even the wording of a mission statement—and the ability of a school to function as a PLC. As we wrote in *Learning by Doing* (2006), "The words of a mission statement are not worth the paper they are written on unless people begin to *do* differently" (p. 19). The mission of a school or district is not revealed by what people say, but rather, by what they do.

What if schools were subject to a "truth in advertising" law that required them to post their "real" mission statements—the candid statements based on actual actions and assumptions of those within the school? We suggest the following statements represent the candid missions of many schools in North America:

- "It is our mission to help all students learn *if* they are conscientious, responsible, attentive, developmentally ready, fluent in English, and come from homes with concerned parents who take an interest in their education."

- "Our mission is to create a school with an unrelenting focus on learning; failure is not an option. But ultimately it will be the responsibility of the student and his or her parents to take advantage of the opportunities for learning."

- "Our mission is to take credit for the accomplishments of our highest-achieving students and to assign blame for low performance to others."

- "Our mission is to ensure success for all our students. We will do *whatever it takes* to ensure their success—provided we don't have to change the schedule, modify any of our existing practices, or adopt any new practices."

- "It is our mission to ensure the comfort and convenience of the adults in our organization. In order to promote this mission, we place a higher value on individual autonomy than we do on ensuring that all students learn. We will avoid any change or conversation that might create anxiety or discomfort or infringe on individual autonomy."

A New Mission Requires New Actions

It is time for educators to move beyond the rhetoric of "learning for all" and to embrace that sentiment as the core purpose of their schools. To do so, they again must understand the historical origins of the schools in which they work. America's schools have never operated under the premise that educators were to help all students learn. The greatest advocates of public education in this country, the Thomas Jeffersons and Horace Manns, always assumed that one of the functions of universal elementary schooling was to sort and select students—to identify the gifted and to weed out the less capable as students advanced along the educational system. High schools were created with the specific purpose of offering very different programs to students based on their perceived aptitudes and assumed positions in society. In 1920, university presidents complained that schools were sending too many students on to higher education when only 3% of the population had earned a degree (DuFour, DuFour, Eaker, & Karhanek, 2004). Thus, contemporary educators are being called upon to fulfill a new purpose—high levels of learning for all students—in institutions specifically designed to reflect very different assumptions and to serve an entirely different purpose. To meet that challenge, educators must do more than write catchy mission statements; they must align the structures and cultures of their institutions to support their new mission. They must act in new ways.

So allow us to offer some specific advice on this topic. You already know how to articulate your mission, and if you harbored any doubts regarding the fundamental purpose of your schools, No Child Left Behind removed them when it codified the mission of public schools. The purpose of schooling is to help all students learn—to ensure that in every grade, every course, and every unit of instruction, all students acquire the intended knowledge, skills, and dispositions deemed most essential to their success. Assuming your current mission pays homage to "learning for all," it is perfectly serviceable. Do not waste another minute writing a mission statement, but instead begin the hard work of aligning all the practices, policies, and procedures of your school with that mission.

Our colleague Janel Keating helped move educators in her district from rhetoric to action when she pressed her staff to answer the questions, "What would it look like in our schools *if we really meant it* when we said our fundamental purpose is to ensure all students learn? What would people see us doing?" Those are powerful questions. We offer the following answers.

If we really mean it when we say we want all students to learn, certainly we would create systems to ensure . . .

1. Every teacher is engaged in a process to clarify exactly what each student is to learn in each grade level, each course, and each unit of instruction.

2. Every teacher is engaged in a process to clarify consistent criteria by which to assess the quality of student work.

3. Every teacher is engaged in a process to assess student learning on a timely and frequent basis through the use of teacher-developed common formative assessments.

4. Every school has a specific plan to ensure that students who experience initial difficulty in learning are provided with additional time and support for learning during the school day in a timely and directive way that does not cause the student to miss any new direct instruction.

5. Every school has a specific plan to enrich and extend the learning of students who are not challenged by the required curriculum.

6. All professionals are organized into collaborative teams and are given the time and structure during their regular workday to collaborate with colleagues on specific issues that directly impact student learning.

7. Every collaborative team of teachers is called upon to work interdependently to achieve a common SMART goal for which members of the team are mutually accountable.

8. Every teacher receives frequent and timely information regarding the success of his or her students in learning the essential curriculum and then uses that information to identify strengths and weaknesses as part of a process of continuous improvement.

9. Building shared knowledge of best practice is part of the process of shared decision-making at both the school and team level.

10. Every practice and procedure in place in the school has been examined to assess its impact on learning.

11. School leaders are held accountable for ensuring all of the above happen.

We will elaborate on these points and cite the research base to support them in subsequent chapters. We contend, however, that none of the points is counterintuitive. It makes sense that if we are passionate about all our students learning, we would clarify what we want them to learn, monitor each student's learning on a timely basis, respond with additional time and support when students struggle, and enrich and extend learning for those who are not challenged. It makes sense that we would work together collaboratively rather than in isolation, and that our collaborative teams have goals, because without a goal they would not be teams. It makes sense that we would be hungry for evidence of our effectiveness and use that evidence in an ongoing process to strengthen our skills, insights, and understandings of our craft. It makes sense that as a *learning* community, we would build learning into our decision-making processes, and we would be willing to examine all of our practices and discard those that discourage student learning. It makes sense that school leaders would be held accountable for focusing on the fundamental purpose of their schools.

This assertion—that the fundamental purpose of the school is to help all students learn the knowledge, skills, and dispositions most essential to their success—is the biggest of the big ideas that drive the work of PLCs. When educators embrace that idea and act upon it, all the other elements of PLCs begin to fall into place. If they reject the premise or merely pay lip service to it, they will never fully develop their capacity to create a PLC. Therefore, we assert that this is an area where leaders must be tight; they must insist that their schools and districts will be organized and will operate in accordance with a commitment to learning for all students.

There are strategies and processes to engage staff in the consideration of the issues listed here, and plenty of latitude in terms of how those issues might be addressed in individual schools and classrooms. In other words, within the tight parameter of a commitment to learning for all, there are many opportunities to be loose—to provide staff with the autonomy and freedom to move forward in different ways—and we will again offer examples in subsequent chapters. The bottom line, however, is this: If educational leaders are not prepared to be tight regarding the core purpose of their organizations, if they are not prepared to communicate that purpose clearly and consistently, if they are not prepared to insist that their schools and districts align their practices with that purpose, then they will not create PLCs, regardless of what else they are tight about.

The Second Building Block: Shared Vision

People often use the terms mission and vision interchangeably: "Oh sure, we have a mission/vision." We contend that in applying the terms to the foundation of a PLC, they represent distinctly different issues. Whereas mission addresses the question of *why* an organization exists by clarifying its essential purpose, vision asks, "*What* must we become to fulfill our purpose, what future do we hope to create for this organization?" When colleagues address the question of vision, they are attempting to describe a realistic, credible, attractive future for the organization—a future that is better and more desirable in significant ways than existing conditions. A shared vision offers a target that beckons (Bennis & Nanus, 1985).

It is difficult to overstate the importance of shared vision in the establishment of a PLC. Researchers within and outside of education routinely reference its significance both in the improvement process and as an essential element of an effective organization (Blanchard, 2007; Eastwood & Seashore Louis, 1992; Fullan, 2007; Kouzes & Posner, 2006; Newmann & Wehlage, 1996; Schlechty, 2005). It has been described as essential to a successful change process (Kotter, 1996), and an absolute requisite for any learning organization (Senge, 1990). The ability to craft and communicate a shared vision has been cited as a critical element of effective leadership (Bennis, 2003; Interstate School Leaders Licensure Consortium, 1996; Kanter, 2004; Leithwood, Seashore Louis, Anderson, & Wahlstom, 2004; Tichy, 1997). The assertion of Burt Nanus (1992) reflects the conclusion of many researchers who have explored how to improve organizations: "There is no more powerful engine driving an organization toward excellence and long-range success than an attractive, worthwhile and achievable vision of the future, widely shared" (p. 3).

But the development of shared vision has been particularly troublesome for educators. Reformers and critics of education have bombarded teachers and principals with countless (and often conflicting) images and ideas about how schools should function and the purposes they should serve. Inundated by this cacophony of mixed signals and anxious to be all things to all people, educators have often resorted to vision statements filled with sweeping generalities.

So the lack of a compelling vision for public schools continues to be a major obstacle in any effort to improve schools. Those who hope to develop a school's capacity to function as a PLC cannot overlook the importance of this critical building block in achieving that goal. Until educators can describe the ideal school they are trying to create, it is impossible to develop policies, procedures, or programs that will help make that ideal a reality. In the indisputable logic of the great Yankee philosopher Yogi Berra, "If you don't know where you are going, you probably aren't going to get there."

Creating a Vision of a Professional Learning Community

Ken Blanchard (2007) warns, "The process you use to develop a vision is as important as the vision itself" (p. 233). It is not by chance that we repeatedly refer to this building block as *shared* vision. When a group has a collective sense of ownership in and commitment to the future they are working together to create, vision can exert a powerful influence on their organization. If the vision represents the proclamation of a single leader or the words on a paper drafted at a Board of Education summer retreat, it will have little impact.

Bryan Smith (in Senge, Kleiner, Roberts, Ross, & Smith, 1994) offers five scenarios for implementing a vision within an organization (p. 314):

1. **Telling.** The boss assumes that he or she knows what the vision should be and announces it to the organization in the grand dictatorial tradition: "It's my way or the highway."

2. **Selling.** The boss assumes that he or she knows what the vision should be and attempts to persuade members of the organization before proceeding.

3. **Testing.** The boss has an idea about what the vision should be, but seeks reactions from those in the organization to help him or her refine and redesign the vision before proceeding.

4. **Consulting.** The boss puts together a representative committee of members of the organization and encourages it to develop a vision for his or her review and approval. The boss then reserves the right to accept or ignore the recommendations.

5. **Co-creating.** The boss and members of the organization, through a collaborative process, build a shared vision together.

This co-creating strategy is certainly not the most efficient way to develop a written vision statement, but it is the strategy most likely to result in the shared vision critical to a learning community. A vision will have little impact until it is understood, accepted, and connects with the personal visions of those within the school or district. The key to developing a *shared* vision is not to impose a new direction on an unwilling faculty, but rather to build consensus regarding common causes, interests, goals, aspirations, and direction. Thus, creating a shared vision requires engagement and dialogue rather than a monologue (Axelrod, 2002). As Blanchard (2007) writes, "The best way to initiate, implement, and sustain change is to increase the level of influence and involvement from the people being asked to change, surfacing and resolving concerns along the way. Without this strategy, you cannot achieve the cooperation and buy-in you need from those responsible for making the changes you've proposed" (p. 225).

Leaders who are the most skillful in building consensus need not resort to saying, "Listen to me, I have decided what we must become," but will instead be able to say, "I have listened to you, and this is what I heard you say you want for yourselves and for our students."

Building Consensus in a Professional Learning Community

The best-intentioned leaders often fall victim to common mistakes as they attempt to help a staff develop a shared direction and desired future for their schools and districts.

Mistake #1: Leaders Attempt to "Go It Alone"

One of the most consistent cautions of those who have studied the improvement process both inside and outside of education is that significant and complex change requires dispersed leadership. Consider the following samples of their advice:

- No one individual is ever able to develop the right vision, communicate it to large numbers of people, eliminate all obstacles, generate short-term wins, lead and manage dozens of change projects and anchor new approaches deep in an organization's culture. A strong, guiding coalition is always needed. . . . Building such a team is always an essential part of the early stages of any effort to restructure a set of strategies. (Kotter, 1996, p. 52)

- We expected to find that the first step in taking a company from good to great would be set a new direction, a new vision and strategy for the company, and then to get people committed and aligned behind that direction. We found something quite the opposite. The leaders who ignited the transformation from good to great, first got the right people on the bus. . . . They built a superior leadership team. (Collins, 2001, p. 41)

- The first step a school leader should take to enhance the achievement of students in schools is to create a strong leadership team. (Marzano, Waters, & McNulty, 2005, p. 98)

- Rather than focusing on the character traits and actions of individual leaders—in the heroic American tradition of charismatic leadership—we will increasingly have to focus on the distribution of leadership. (Elmore, 2004, p. 42)

A "guiding coalition," the "right people on the bus," "leadership team," "dispersed leadership"—while the terminology may vary, the underlying premise does not: Individual leaders must have allies if they are going to establish and pursue a new direction for their organizations. This group could take a variety of forms—the school improvement committee, a task force created to lead the investigation into a specific improvement initiative, a representative from each of the grade-level teams, people who have volunteered to work on an issue because of their interest in the topic, staff who are recognized to have particular expertise or influence—but it is a mistake to move forward with substantive change without a group to guide the process. A leader who is unable to persuade a small cadre of key people to champion the journey has no chance of winning the support of the entire group. One of the first questions a leader should ask in considering the challenge of co-creating a vision is, "Who is our guiding coalition?" Failure to attend to coalition building is "probably the most neglected step in the change process" (Kanter, 1999).

Mistake #2: Leaders Use a Forum That Is Ill-Suited to the Dialogue Necessary for Consensus

Principals or superintendents who convene an entire faculty in an effort to build consensus make two mistakes. First, they give the impression they are going it alone, trying to sell the group on their idea. Second, they use a format designed for presentations rather than conversation. If people are going to consent to a new vision—a significant departure from their past practices—they will need to have their questions answered. Often, these questions are personal—"How will this impact me?" Large-group presentations provide little opportunity to ensure these questions are asked and answered. Kouzes and Posner (2006) contend it is impossible for a leader to create a compelling image of the future unless he or she knows what people within the organization want and need. That knowledge can only be acquired through small-group dialogues, through first seeking to understand before seeking to be understood (Covey, 1989).

Mistake #3: Leaders Pool Opinions Rather Than Build Shared Knowledge

A professional *learning* community makes important decisions by *learning* together, by building shared knowledge, rather than by merely pooling opinions. Effective leaders realize that if they ask uniformed people to make decisions, the end result will be uninformed decisions. Therefore, they are vigilant about ensuring people have ready access to the most relevant information and that the group has collectively studied the information before it is called upon to make a decision. The assumption here is that when people of good faith have access to the same information, the likelihood of their arriving at similar conclusions increases exponentially. Access to information is the lifeblood of empowered groups.

The two areas most essential for a group to review in a discussion of the future of the school or district are 1) the current reality and 2) evidence of best practice. More than 20 years ago, Naisbitt and Aburdene (1985) offered the common-sense conclusion that people find it much easier to move from point A to point B if they know where point B is and how to recognize it when they arrive. We contend, however, that in many schools and districts there is confusion regarding point A—the starting point or current reality. Therefore, a key step in the process of clarifying the future is an honest assessment of the present, a diligent effort to confront the brutal facts (Collins, 2001).

The chart on pages 125–127 is a useful tool for gathering this crucial information.

A Data Picture of Our School

Student Achievement Results

Indicator	Year 20___ –20___	Year 20___ –20___	Year 20___ –20___	Facts About Our Data
Based on Our School Assessment Data				
Based on Our District Assessment Data				
Based on Our State Assessment Data				
Based on Our National Assessment Data				

Student Engagement Data

Average Daily Attendance				
Percentage of Students in Extracurricular Activities				
Percentage of Students Using School's Tutoring Services				
Percentage of Students Enrolled in Most Rigorous Courses Offered				
Percentage of Students Graduating Without Retention				
Percentage of Students Who Drop Out of School				
Other Areas in Which We Hope to Engage Students, Such as Community Service				

(continued)

A Data Picture of Our School (continued)

Discipline Data

Indicator	Year 20__ –20__	Year 20__ –20__	Year 20__ –20__	Facts About Our Data
Number of Referrals/Top Three Reasons for Referrals				
Number of Parent Conferences Regarding Discipline				
Number of In-School Suspensions				
Number of Detentions/Saturday School				
Number of Out-of-School Suspensions				
Expulsions/Other				

Survey Data

Indicator	Year 20__ –20__	Year 20__ –20__	Year 20__ –20__	Facts About Our Data
Student Satisfaction or Perception Assessment				
Alumni Satisfaction or Perception Assessment				
Parent Satisfaction or Perception Assessment				
Teacher Satisfaction or Perception Assessment				
Administration Satisfaction or Perception Assessment				
Community Satisfaction or Perception Assessment				

A Data Picture of Our School (continued)

Demographic Data

Indicator	Year 20___-20___	Year 20___-20___	Year 20___-20___	Facts About Our Data
Free and Reduced Lunch				
Percent Mobility				
Percent Special Education				
Percent English as a Second Language				
Ethnicity				
Other				

One important point about data that we will return to in later chapters is that without a basis of comparison, data do not inform. Therefore, if a school or district hopes its staff members will make *informed* decisions, leaders must present data in ways that provide meaningful bases of comparison in a very user-friendly way. The objective is not to train teachers and principals to become statisticians who can explain the nuances of a z-score. The objective is to give people the information they need in a clear and concise format to help them develop the shared knowledge and understanding that lead to good decisions.

Data analysis can become even more revealing when achievement data are disaggregated by gender, race, socioeconomic status, students with disabilities, and students with limited English proficiency. When it comes to painting a data picture of a school or district, the precision of pointillism is preferable to the broad-brushed strokes of impressionism. The goal in assessing the current reality is collective clarity rather than a general impression. Finally, all staff members should be invited to identify other sources of data they feel may be relevant to clarifying the current conditions in their schools.

There is also a rich literature describing the practices and characteristics of high-performing organizations, effective schools, and quality school districts. Educators who are being called upon to determine the future direction of their schools and districts should build shared knowledge regarding this research and become students of its findings. Once again, the distribution of this research should be accompanied by guiding questions and an invitation to all staff members to identify and submit additional pertinent research. Staff members should also be cautioned that different researchers often use slightly different terminology to describe the same practice or principle, and that understanding common principles is more important than identifying consistent vocabulary.

So, at the risk of redundancy, let us stress that those who lead the improvement process must do more than pool opinions. They must help to create professional *learning* communities; they must build shared knowledge and ensure that people are *learning* together by providing access to the same relevant and user-friendly information *before* asking them to make important decisions. They must demonstrate "an unrelenting commitment to gather the facts and information necessary to make more informed and intelligent decisions, and to keep pace with new evidence and use the new facts to update practices" (Pfeffer & Sutton, 2006, p. 14).

Mistake #4: Leaders Allow for Ambiguity Regarding the Standard for Moving Forward

Leaders can do everything right in the process to create a shared vision—create a guiding coalition, engage in meaningful dialogue, gather and disseminate the information people need in order to make a good decision—only to encounter difficulty because of confusion about the level of support needed to move forward. In our work with schools, we frequently ask a straightforward question: "How do you define *consensus* when your staff considers a proposal?" Individual responses from members of the same staff vary greatly. Responses range from, "We all must agree to support the proposal," to "We all must agree not to sabotage the proposal," to "Majority rules." One candid superintendent told us that in his district they have arrived at consensus "when everyone agrees with my position."

It is extremely difficult for an organization to make a decision by consensus if members do not have a common understanding of the meaning of the term *consensus*; nevertheless, most of the schools and districts in which we have worked have no working definition of the term. As a result, people who have participated in the same decision-making process can come to very different conclusions about whether or not the group has agreed to move forward. This lack of clarity can create confusion, mistrust, and cynicism regarding both the process and those who lead it, all of which constitute major barriers to building shared vision.

Mistake #5: Leaders Set an Unrealistic Standard for Moving Forward

When leaders assume the school or district cannot move forward with an initiative until "all of us agree to support it" or "all of us agree we can live with it," or set any standard that begins with "all of us . . . ," they mistake unanimity for consensus. In the real world of schools, if all of us must agree before we can act, we will be subjected to constant inaction, a state of perpetual status quo. If the school-improvement train must wait until every member of the staff is on board, it will never leave the station. Any organization that hopes to develop the action orientation and the "learning by doing" philosophy of a PLC must avoid establishing a standard for action that makes moving forward almost impossible.

The definition of consensus we prefer (DuFour, DuFour, Eaker, & Many, 2006, p. 214) establishes two simple standards that must be met in order to move forward if a decision is made by consensus.

We have achieved at consensus when . . .

1. All points of view have been heard.

2. The will of the group is evident even to those who most oppose it.

This definition not only can help eliminate ambiguity by establishing a specific standard for action, but the standard it sets allows for action despite reservations, or even opposition, on the part of some staff members.

The following story illustrates an effective process for avoiding these five common mistakes when building consensus.

A Story of Shared Vision

Principal Ken Williams knew his school was what Susan Rosenholtz (1989) refers to as "stuck." Although thus far it had met the requirement of Adequate Yearly Progress stipulated by No Child Left Behind, student achievement was not improving. He realized his staff members were well-intentioned and working hard, but he was less certain they were working smart. He was concerned that if the school continued with its current practices in the coming year, there was no reason to believe student learning would improve. Ken was convinced it was time he and the staff engaged in a process to reflect on the current status of student achievement and to examine the research regarding schools that have a positive impact on student learning.

Ken decided to bring his concerns and his proposal to the school improvement team to solicit their reactions and advice. In his first year as principal, he had worked with Tom Johannsen, the representative of the teachers' association, to recruit members to the school improvement team and to ensure that it included both representatives from every department and staff with a wide range of experience. He had personally asked Sara Ritchie, one of the most respected and influential teachers in the school, to chair the team. He, Sara, and Tom had promised each other that there would be "no surprises"—that none of them would bring an issue, proposal, or concern to the school improvement team for deliberation until the three of them had discussed it first. After asking a few clarifying questions, Sara and Tom agreed that proposing an idea to study how the school might be improved was an appropriate topic for the school improvement team to consider.

Ken and Sara then met with the team to propose that the entire staff engage in a process to examine the current levels of student achievement in the school as well as the research on best practices for improving schools. Although members of the team were not opposed to the proposal, their initial concerns, as usual, focused on time: They wondered if teachers had the time to read through volumes of research and wade through reams of data on student achievement. They wondered if it would just be easier for the principal to report his conclusions about student achievement for the group to consider. Ken stressed the importance of the entire staff learning together rather than reacting to the conclusions and recommendations of the principal. He assured the team he understood their concerns about time, and he would present both the data and research to staff in a concise and user-friendly way that honored teachers' time. With this assurance that their concerns had been addressed, the improvement team agreed to facilitate the process.

During the next few days, Ken and the team compiled information for their indicators of student achievement chart and distributed them to the entire staff. All staff members were asked to review the information and to identify any other data they felt would be relevant to assessing the current levels of student achievement. (See pages 432–437 in the Appendix for the complete research data by Ken and his team.) They were also asked to keep several key questions in mind as they reviewed the information:

1. What factual statements can we make about our current reality? For example, the statement, "The percentage of students achieving the grade of A has increased each of the past 2 years" is a fact, not an interpretation.

2. What do you feel we can be particularly proud of regarding our current reality?

3. What trends do you see in the data?

4. What are some areas of concern you identified as you reviewed the data?

5. What inferences can we draw from the data regarding our improvement in achieving our fundamental purpose of learning for all?

Finally, staff members were asked to prepare to respond to these questions in small-group dialogues to be conducted by representatives of the school improvement team during the following week. The dialogues represented a joint agreement between Ken and the teachers' association. The tradition in the school had been for all staff members to attend two after-school meetings per month. Ken felt these mandatory meetings at the end of the day accomplished little and were better suited to presentations than dialogue. He preferred having conversations with small groups of staff members to hear their concerns and thoughts and respond personally to their questions. He proposed abolishing the after-school faculty meetings if the staff agreed to meet once each month with him in small-group dialogues scheduled before school, after school, and during every period of the day. Most teachers preferred coming to these conversations during their preparation periods and were delighted to forgo one preparation period in exchange for the elimination of after-school faculty meetings.

When the day of the small-group dialogues arrived, faculty members reported very consistent findings regarding their interpretations of the information they were given. Those findings included:

1. Our students are experiencing more success in math than other areas of the curriculum.

2. The percentage of students receiving the grade of A has increased slightly over the past 2 years, but so has the percentage of students receiving Ds and Fs.

3. Our students do not perform well on state and national assessments compared to similar schools in our area, except in math.

4. We were slightly ahead of the state averages on most areas of the state achievement test in 2006, but we have fallen behind the state average in all areas except math in 2008.

5. The percentage of students pursuing our most rigorous curriculum has declined slightly in each of the past 2 years.

6. The percentage of students receiving Ds and Fs each year seems to correspond with the percentage of students not meeting the standards on the state assessments in most subject areas.

7. Our student achievement indicators have remained essentially the same over the past 3 years.

8. Despite the hard work we are doing, we seem to be stuck. What we are doing now is not leading to more students achieving at higher levels.

Some teachers reacted defensively to the data, arguing they should not be held responsible for students who refused to apply themselves. Others challenged the validity of the state and national assessments. The school improvement committee anticipated these reactions and discussed in advance how they should respond. They explained that no one was assigning blame for the results:

> At this point, the data reveal all students are not learning at high levels as our mission statement proclaims; however, they do not tell us why. We do know there is little evidence we will achieve better results next year if we continue to do what we have done. Everyone acknowledges we are working hard, but it is time to explore steps we might take to improve upon these results. Furthermore, if we dismiss these results as invalid, we have an obligation to offer alternative evidence that our students are learning. At this point, we are not sure what evidence that might be, but we would welcome your thoughts as to what evidence we could explore.

Although this response did not satisfy all staff, it was clear that most faculty members agreed the school should at least consider the possibility of changing some of its practices. The improvement team members promised to explore research-based strategies for raising student achievement and report their findings back to the staff.

In the following weeks, Ken gathered several syntheses of research on the characteristics of schools with improving student achievement. He presented his findings first to Sara and Tom, and then to the improvement committee for their reactions and suggestions. The improvement team then agreed to submit the research summary to the staff and to invite all their colleagues to identify other research findings on factors that impacted student achievement. They asked every member of the faculty to be prepared to address seven questions at the small group dialogue scheduled for the next month:

1. Which characteristics occur on at least two of the seven studies we have considered?

2. What do you find more striking about the lists—their similarities or their differences?

3. Which findings resonate with you? Which three characteristics from the lists are most important to you?

4. In what area have we excelled or made significant progress?

5. What area requires our attention?

6. Do you reject any of these research findings as invalid?

7. Can you describe the school you would like to help create here?

When the small-group dialogues were held to discuss the research, once again staff members offered very consistent responses to the questions, "Which indicators occur in at least two of the studies?" and "Can you describe the school you would like to help create?" Those responses included the following:

1. High expectations for student achievement

2. Clarity regarding purpose and the intended results for each course and unit of instruction

3. Frequent monitoring of student learning and use of the results to inform and improve teacher practice

4. Structures to provide students with additional time and support for learning when they struggle

5. Widely dispersed leadership

6. A collaborative culture with collective responsibility for student learning

7. A Board of Education, administration, parents, and community that value and respect educators as professionals and support the work of the school

8. A school environment conducive to learning that supports and nurtures both students and adults

9. Efforts and accomplishments of students and adults that are appreciated and celebrated

Members of the school improvement team promised to develop a description of their school that would incorporate these characteristics and present it to the faculty for consideration during the next round of small-group dialogues. The team appointed its most skillful writer to develop the first draft and spent one team meeting critiquing and revising that draft. By the end of the meeting, they agreed to submit the statement shown on page 137 to the staff.

The statement was distributed to all staff and, once again, members of the improvement team led a series of small-group dialogues to answer questions, address concerns, and solicit reactions. As part of that process, they asked half of each group to generate a comprehensive list of reasons to *oppose* the statement, while the other half generated reasons to *support* it. Participants were told to set aside their personal feelings at this stage of the process and attend to the task of listing reasons to support or oppose the statements. After the groups listed all the pros and cons they could envision, the representatives of the improvement teams asked if participants felt comfortable that all points of view on the matter had been generated to the best of the group's ability. When participants concurred, the team members called their attention to the next standard for reaching consensus: Is the will of the group evident even to those who most oppose it?

Each member of the staff was asked to demonstrate his or her level of support for the statement by using the "fist-to-five" technique that was standard practice in the school. It called for all participants to raise

A Shared Vision of the School We Strive to Create

In order to fulfill the fundamental purpose of helping all our students learn at high levels, we are dedicated to creating a school in which . . .

1. Every teacher, parent, and student is clear on the knowledge, skills, and dispositions students are expected to acquire in each course, grade level, and unit of instruction.

2. The learning of each student is monitored on a timely basis. When students experience difficulty, the school has structures in place to ensure they receive additional time and support for learning.

3. There is a climate of high expectations for student success, and staff members communicate their high expectations to students, parents, and one another.

4. A collaborative culture ensures staff members work together interdependently to better meet the needs of their students and to analyze and improve their professional practice.

5. Frequent reporting of student progress toward explicit learning outcomes helps staff members and parents take collective responsibility for student learning.

6. Structures are created to promote widely dispersed leadership throughout the school.

7. Staff members enjoy considerable professional autonomy within specific and clearly understood parameters.

8. All staff members continually grow in their professional expertise because structures to support their ongoing, job-embedded learning and continuous improvement are built into the school day and school year.

9. Students and adults alike believe their efforts, improvements, and achievements will be recognized and celebrated.

10. There is a safe and orderly environment.

their hands simultaneously and demonstrate their level of support by raising the appropriate number of fingers according to the following scale:

Five Fingers—I love this statement, and I am willing to be a champion for its ideas in our school.

Four Fingers—I strongly agree with this statement and hope we can become this school.

Three Fingers—This statement is okay with me.

Two Fingers—I have reservations about this statement and cannot support it.

One Finger—I disagree with this statement and cannot support it.

Fist—I am adamantly opposed to this statement and, if I had the power, I would veto moving forward with it.

Participants were advised that no one had veto power, but a fist was a way to indicate a strong opposition to the statement. Participants were also given the option of filling out a form to indicate their level of support if they preferred not to raise their hands. Results were presented to the entire group before the meeting adjourned. All but one of the small groups endorsed the proposed statement, and the school improvement team reported that the will of the group was to support the description and begin working to align practices with that description.

Several points in this scenario warrant emphasis. First, notice that the presentation of data included several comparisons: How does the achievement of our current students compare with other schools in our state, the nation, schools in our area that are similar to us, and with the performance of our students in the past? Without that basis of comparison, it would be impossible to get a sense of the level of effectiveness of the school. Second, neither the principal nor the school improvement team analyzed the data or the research and *reported* findings to the staff. Although that tactic may be more efficient, it is far less effective in building a *shared* understanding of the current reality and best practices for school improvement because it makes staff members passive recipients of the conclusions drawn by someone else, rather than active participants engaged in a process to build shared knowledge. Third, notice that the entire staff was invited to propose additional sources of data and research for examination. There was no effort to screen or withhold information, and every member of the staff was able to present additional information for consideration by the entire group. Fourth, the process used to consider all points of view resulted in a comprehensive list of pros and cons without the ac-rimony that often accompanies conflicting opinions in immature orga-nizations. And fifth, members of the school improvement team led the small-group dialogues instead of the principal dominating the process.

We have used this process in workshops or in our work with schools and districts hundreds of times, and the will of the group was imme-diately clear even to those most vehemently opposed to the proposal. While it does not result in unanimity, it does result in consensus, and at that point, the school or district should move forward—beyond dia-logue to action.

The Struggle of Consensus

Creating a shared vision is a constant challenge of building con-sensus and unity without paying the price of compromises that di-minish either the substance or the clarity of the vision statement. Disagreements should not be glossed over, nor opposing perspectives squelched. Participants should be encouraged to honor all perspectives, to articulate the reasoning behind their positions, to explore strategies to resolve differences, and to find common ground. But differences of opinion should not be used as an excuse for inaction. Once again, con-sensus does not mean unanimity, and schools that believe every staff member must be an enthusiastic proponent of a new vision statement may be setting a standard that is impossible to meet. When everyone has had the opportunity to express his or her ideas, and the will of the group has become evident to all (even to those who might oppose it), the faculty *has* reached a consensus and should be prepared to move forward with everyone's support. If the vision results in recognizable improvements, even those who were initially skeptical will be inclined to support it in time.

If the will of the group is not easily evident, and the decision was to be made by consensus, the school or district should not move forward. Instead, the effort to build shared knowledge should continue through more shared research, site visits to other schools, or hearing from educators who are already engaged in the initiative. Another powerful way of building shared knowledge is conducting a pilot of the initiative before attempting to implement it across the school or district. A few schools may be willing to test the impact of an improvement initiative within a district. A department, grade-level team, or several course-specific teams may engage in this action research within their school. A well-conducted pilot can help identify unforeseen problems with implementation, build shared knowledge about benefits, create more advocates, and increase the likelihood of successful implementation across the larger organization (Blanchard, 2007). It is important, however, that the pilot be viewed as a short-term action-research project for the benefit of the entire school or district, rather than as an ongoing experiment that separates it from the rest of the organization. Schools and districts are adept at first isolating and then killing alternative programs that are considered outside the mainstream of the organization.

A District- or School-Level Vision?

Should the vision be written at the district or school level? This question relates to an issue we addressed earlier—the dilemma of too-tight versus too-loose leadership. A vision crafted at the district level and presented to the schools with an expectation of compliance neither allows leaders to hear and connect with the hopes and dreams of people throughout the organization nor provides the necessary level of engagement and learning for all staff to feel a sense of ownership and commitment to the stipulated direction. If, on the other hand, staff members at each school are merely encouraged to create their own unique vision of the school they seek to create without any overarching sense of shared purpose, priorities, or guiding principles, the district has reinforced the notion that each school is its own kingdom.

We would, once again, urge schools and districts to reject the Tyranny of Or and embrace the Genius of And. District leaders have an obligation to create and clarify shared purpose, priorities, and guiding principles that should be evident in every school in the district. A vision statement for the district can contribute to that clarity. In creating that statement, district leaders should engage staff to the greatest degree possible. We recommend, however, that the staff members of each school should then study that district statement and use it as part of the process we have described for creating a shared understanding of the school they are working together to create. In other words, the staff members of each school should engage in the process of creating and clarifying a vision for their school that aligns with the district vision for all of its schools. We will return to this issue in chapter 13 in our discussion of the role of the central office in creating PLCs.

Questions to Guide the Process

Roberts and Smith (in Senge, Kleiner, Roberts, Ross, & Smith, 1994, p. 208) suggest the following questions to guide the development of a shared vision:

1. What would you like to see our school become?

2. What reputation would it have?

3. What contribution would it make to our students and community?

4. What values would it embody?

5. How would people work together?

In *Learning by Doing* (2006), we proposed the following questions to clarify the intended future direction of the school or district:

1. Can you describe the school we are trying to create?

2. What would our school look like if it were a great place for students? What would it look like if it were a great place for teachers?

3. It is 5 years from now, and we have achieved our vision as a school. In what ways are we different? Describe what is going on in terms of practices, procedures, relationships, results, and climate.

4. Imagine we have been given 60 seconds on the nightly news to clarify the vision of our school or our district to the community. What do we want to say?

Evaluating the Vision Statement

Kotter (1996, p. 72) contends that effective visions have the following characteristics:

They are . . .

- Imaginable—they convey a picture of what the future will look like.

- Desirable—they appeal to the long-term interests of stake-holders.

- Feasible—they comprise realistic, attainable goals.

- Focused—they are clear enough to provide guidance in decision making.

- Flexible—they are general enough to allow for individual initiative and changing responses in light of changing conditions.

- Communicable—they are easy to communicate and explain.

Our criteria are more succinct:

1. Does the vision result in people throughout the organization acting in new ways that are aligned with the intended direction that

has been established? The effectiveness of a vision statement is not determined by its eloquence, but rather by its ability to promote new behaviors for people throughout the organization.

2. Do people at all levels use the statement to guide their day-to-day decisions?

3. Is the statement used to modify structures, processes, and procedures to better align with the intended direction of the school or district?

The Benefits of a Clear, Shared Vision

Educators who work to develop a clear, shared vision of the school or district they are attempting to create benefit in a number of ways.

Shared Vision Motivates and Energizes People

When people can connect their daily tasks with larger goals and collective purposes, they are more likely to think their work is meaningful. Commitment and meaning will help sustain the effort and energy needed for the difficult work of implementing change.

Shared Vision Creates a Proactive Orientation

Schools and districts tend to be reactive, problem-driven organizations. If a problem arises, the standard response is to seek to restore the status quo. Shared vision enables organizations to move from this reactive orientation to a proactive outlook that is focused on creating a new future.

Shared Vision Gives Direction to People Within the Organization

When educators have a clear sense of the purpose, direction, and the ideal future state of their school or district, they are better able to understand their ongoing roles within the organization. This clarity simplifies the decision-making process and empowers all members of the staff to act with greater confidence. Rather than constantly checking with their bosses for approval, employees can simply ask, "Is this decision or action in line with the vision?" and then act on their own.

Shared Vision Establishes Specific Standards of Excellence

A shared vision articulates standards of excellence, benchmarks by which individuals can measure their work.

Shared Vision Creates a Clear Agenda for Action

Most important, a shared vision can create an agenda for action. A vision statement enables educators to assess current policies, practices, programs, and performance indicators, and then identify discrepancies between the existing conditions in the school or district and those described in the vision statement. Until an organization has clarified what it is trying to become, attempts to improve it will be futile. A vision statement provides the essential bridge between the current reality and what the school or district hopes to become in the future.

A Final Caution

Throughout this chapter we have described a process to engage educators in clarifying the future they desire for their schools and districts. That process is intended to develop a concise written statement that describes the school or district they hope to create. We believe there is benefit to committing this shared sense of direction to writing because the clarity and precision of good writing can help eliminate ambiguity. It is important, however, for educators to recognize the difference between developing a vision statement and actually having a shared vision. Written statements never change anything. It is the dialogue about hopes and aspirations that engages people and allows them to find meaning in the statement (Axelrod, 2002). Furthermore, Fullan (2007) has consistently warned that shared vision comes later in the change process, that it is an outgrowth of people taking action together and learning through common experiences, rather than a prerequisite for action. He writes, "Shared vision or ownership (which is unquestionably necessary for success) is more an *outcome* of a quality change process than a *precondition* for success" (p. 41). Educators can clarify a general sense of direction at the outset of an improvement initiative, but a shared vision emerges over time as a result of action, reflection, and collective meaning based on collective experiences.

Chapter 6

Shared Values
(Collective Commitments)
and Common Goals

Values provide guidelines on how you should proceed as you pursue your purpose and picture of the future. They answer the question . . . "How?" They need to be clearly described so that you know exactly what behaviors demonstrate that the value is being lived. Values need to be consistently acted on, or they are only good intentions.

—Ken Blanchard

Abundant research and school evidence suggest that setting [common] goals may be the most significant act in the entire school improvement process, greatly increasing the odds of success.

—Mike Schmoker

Once educators have clarified the fundamental purpose or mission of their school or district and described the future they are trying to create through developing a shared vision statement, they should turn their attention to the third building block of a professional learning community: shared values, or collective commitments. Whereas the mission building block addresses the issue of *why* our organization exists, and the vision building block establishes *what* we hope it will become, values address *how* we will fulfill our purpose and make our desired future a reality. When educators clarify and commit to certain shared values, they are engaged in the essential ABCs of school improvement— identifying the actions, behaviors, and commitments necessary to bring mission and vision to life.

The literature on organizational effectiveness typically refers to this concept as "values," but we believe the term "collective commitments" is a more accurate description of what transpires in effective schools and districts. People make a conscious and deliberate effort to identify the specific ways they will act to improve their organizations, and then they commit to one another to act accordingly.

If we use the vision statement from chapter 5 as an example, a staff would examine the statement's various components and ask, "What must we commit to do to create such a school?" Commitments would flow from dialogue generating a series of "if/then" statements such as these:

- *If* we are to be a school where teachers and students are clear on the knowledge, skills, and dispositions students must acquire in each course, grade level, and unit of instruction, *then* we must agree to develop a guaranteed curriculum and commit to implement that curriculum in our classrooms.

- *If* we are to be a school that ensures high levels of learning for all students, *then* we must monitor each student's learning on a very timely basis using a variety of assessment strategies and create systems to ensure they receive additional time and support as soon as they experience difficulty in their learning.

- *If* we are to create a collaborative culture, *then* we must be positive, contributing members to our collaborative teams and accept collective responsibility for the success of our colleagues and our students.

An administrative team looking at the same vision statement might identify commitments such as these:

- *If* we are to be a school that provides a guaranteed curriculum and frequently monitors student learning through a wide variety of assessments, *then* we must provide each collaborative team with the resources, time, and training to create the curriculum and assessments.

- *If* we are to become a school that supports the ongoing, job-embedded learning of staff to promote continuous improvement, *then* we must provide staff with time to learn with and from one another, and develop the parameters and processes to ensure their shared learning is in areas that impact student achievement.

- *If* we are to be a school with widely dispersed leadership, *then* we must create structures to promote multiple leadership opportunities and define our job, in part, as developing the leadership potential in others.

Adlai Stevenson High School in Lincolnshire, Illinois, has been described as the most recognized and celebrated school in the United States. It is one of the few schools in the country to receive the United States Department of Education's Blue Ribbon Award on four occasions, an accomplishment that required the school to reach a high standard of excellence—and then continue to improve each year for the next 15 years under five different principals and four different superintendents. It was one of the first comprehensive high schools in the country designated as a New American School, a model of successful school reform. It continues to attract almost 3,000 visitors each year to its campus as educators from around the world come to observe its practices. One of the many factors that has contributed to Stevenson's success is the willingness of its various constituencies to articulate the collective commitments their group is prepared to make to create the extraordinary school described in its vision statement. Board members, administrators, teachers, support staff, parents, and students—all have convened to study the vision statement and clarify their commitments. (See page 448 in the Appendix for Stevenson's complete vision statement.)

These statements of collective commitments are not just words on a paper—they drive the day-to-day work of the school. Every candidate for a teaching or administrative position is asked to review them before applying, and the statements are referenced repeatedly as part of the interview process. The commitments are studied and discussed during new staff orientation as veteran representatives of the group review each commitment and stress its significance. Experienced teachers tell new staff members, "This is what it means to join this faculty. These are the promises we make to each other and to our students. These are the promises that have made us who we are, and we ask you to honor them." Upperclassmen mentors review the student commitments with incoming freshmen during the first week of school and stress, "These are the commitments the students who have gone before you have made to make Stevenson the school it is today. If you honor these commitments, you can be assured you will be successful here, and you will make an important contribution to our school's tradition of excellence."

Stevenson begins each school year by sharing the collective commitments of each group—not only with every student, but with every parent as well. Parents receive a letter clarifying that "these are the promises we, the administrators and teachers, make to you and your students. We take these promises very seriously, and if ever you feel we are not living up to them, please contact us." The letter also explains what is asked of parents by reviewing the collective commitments created by a parent task force. The message is very explicit: "We have made promises to you, and these are the promises we ask you to honor so together we can create the school that will best meet the needs of your sons and daughters." As Tom Sergiovanni (2005) wrote about this aspect of Stevenson, "The commitment of each of the constituent groups represents promises, and public promises at that. Teachers for example are telling students, administrators, and everyone else what they intend to do to implement the school's vision. Since promises made must be promises kept, Stevenson is not only developing an accountability system that is public, but a covenant of obligations that unites its various groups as a community of responsibility" (p. 60).

In our work with schools, we have found it is commonplace for schools and districts to present written mission statements. Vision statements are not as ubiquitous, but they are also the norm. Most schools and districts, however, have not clarified the specific commitments people are prepared to make in order to fulfill the mission (why we exist) and achieve the vision (what we hope to become). Yet we contend that attention to and articulation of the commitments the adults in a school are willing to make to students and to one another can represent an important step on the journey to becoming a PLC for the following reasons.

Collective Commitments Contribute to the Action Orientation of a Professional Learning Community

Articulating specific collective commitments helps people move from aspirations to actions. When educators discuss mission, they can wax philosophic. When they consider vision, they have a future orientation—"Wouldn't it be nice if someday we could look like this?" But when they clarify collective commitments, they make promises about what they are prepared to do *now* to create the school or district that represents their shared hopes for themselves and their students. The conversation about school improvement takes on a sense of specificity, immediacy, and action. Knowing the school you want to create is different from taking action to create it, but when members of the staff promise to act in certain ways, they take an important step in closing the knowing-doing gap.

Collective Commitments Clarify How Each Member Can Contribute to the Common Purpose and Shared Vision of the School or District

Mission and vision focus on the organization—this is why our organization exists, and this is what we hope it will become. Collective commitments focus on *people* and how each person can contribute to the collective effort. When teachers and administrators are guided by collective commitments that are widely understood and honored, each member of the organization recognizes he or she can play an important role in shaping a new future for the school or district. This awareness can be very empowering.

Collective Commitments Can Help Create an Internal Focus

A few years ago, Rick began working with a high school faculty only to be told by several teachers that they saw little reason to explore strategies to improve their school because they were already aware of what needed to be done to raise student achievement. He invited the staff to work in small groups to generate ideas for improving their school. After a short time, the teachers presented the following list:

1. More funding from the state

2. Smaller class size

3. Higher salaries

4. More support staff

5. Abolition of state testing

6. More supportive and involved parents

7. Better preparation in the middle school

8. Students who are more motivated and responsible

9. Less interference from the central office

Rick wished them well in the pursuit of these improvement strategies, but asked them to consider a second list of ideas for improving their school:

1. Working in high-performing collaborative teams whose members work interdependently to improve both adult and student learning

2. Committing to a guaranteed and viable curriculum with clearly defined essential knowledge, skills, and dispositions for every unit

3. Participating in close, frequent monitoring of each student's learning through a variety of assessment strategies including team-developed common, formative assessments

4. Creating and implementing a systematic plan to ensure students who struggle to learn a concept are provided additional time and support for learning

5. Providing each teacher with frequent information regarding the proficiency of his or her students in acquiring the essential outcomes in comparison to similar students working to achieve the same outcomes

When we ask participants in our workshops to reflect on the differences between the two lists, they have no difficulty seeing that the first list has an external focus and requires actions and commitments from other people to improve the school. This staff was simply hoping someone else would solve their school's problems. In this case, however, hope is neither a virtue nor a strategy: It is an abdication of responsibility.

The second list includes all those things that a staff could commit to do to help students learn at higher levels. Furthermore, the factors presented on the second list have a more powerful impact on student achievement than the "wish list" generated by the faculty.

People who have succumbed to "learned helplessness" are not doomed to a life of resignation. They can learn to develop a strong sense of self-efficacy (Seligman, 2006). When educators shift their dialogue from common complaints to collective commitments, they move from a focus on "them" to a focus on "we," from a focus on what others must do to improve the situation to a focus on what we can do to make the school or district a better place. They move from a focus on what we can't stand to a focus on what we stand for. Collective commitments can help educators concentrate on what is within their sphere of influence, which is not only more effective in terms of improving their organizations, but is also far better for their emotional health and well-being (Goleman, 1995).

Collective Commitments Provide a More Effective System of Accountability

Traditional hierarchies operate from the premise that people will do what needs to be done to advance the organization *if* rewards and incentives encourage desirable behavior and sanctions and punishments are applied for counterproductive behavior. The challenge in such a system is first to establish the right incentives and proper sanctions, and then to provide sufficient supervision to ensure they are dispersed appropriately. Tom Sergiovanni (2005) contends school leaders should base their efforts less on the traditional management premise that "what is rewarded gets done" and more on the idea that "what is rewarding gets done" (p. 10). He writes, "When something is rewarding, it gets done even when no one is looking; it gets done even when extrinsic awards and incentives are scarce or non-existent" (p. 11).

When educators are united in a common endeavor, when they feel they are contributing to creating a better future for their schools and districts, they are far more likely to see their work as rewarding than the isolated teachers and principals whose interests never extend beyond their individual classrooms or schools. And when they clarify and commit to the specific responsibilities they will assume in the collective improvement effort, they are more likely to fulfill those responsibilities than colleagues whose behavior is shaped by administrative rewards and sanctions. As Pfeffer and Sutton (2006) wrote, "One of the most persistent and powerful social psychological processes is that of commitment—we are more likely to carry through on decisions we have made and are therefore committed to" (p. 199).

When members of an organization understand its purpose, know where it is headed, and then pledge to act in certain ways to move it in the right direction, they do not need prescriptive rules and regulations to guide their daily work. When people have made promises to each other, they are more likely to honor those promises and hold each other accountable.

We do not mean to suggest that the presence of articulated collective commitments will inspire every person on a staff to live by those commitments on a daily basis. Discrepancies between what people say and what people do will continue to exist. Mutual accountability and peer pressure will not always prevail. In those instances, leaders must be willing to address the problem. The presence of collective commitments, however, allows principals, central office members, and teacher leaders to assume a new role—the role of promoter and protector of the shared vision the staff has created and the pledges staff members have made to one another to make that vision a reality. When leaders must address a concern with a staff member, they can reference the commitments ("Here are the promises we have made to one another, and we need you to honor them"), rather than the chain of command ("I'm the boss") or the policy manual ("The district policy says you must do this"). In so doing, they operate with the full weight of the moral authority of the group behind them, as protectors of mutual pledges rather than keepers of the rules.

Of course in the real world of schools there will still be a need for written policies and faculty manuals. Policy manuals and contracts serve a purpose. But what we are calling for here goes beyond policies and contracts. We are advocating clearly defined *covenants* that unite people in a common cause, create interdependent relationships, foster participation, and help educators find shared meaning in their work.

Collective Commitments Help to Change the Culture of Organizations

As collective commitments articulate new expectations and establish new norms, they help to reshape the culture of schools and districts. As Richard Elmore (2004) wrote, "Cultures do not change by mandate; they change by the specific displacement of existing norms, structures and processes by others; the process of cultural change depends fundamentally on modeling the new values and behaviors that you expect to displace the existing ones" (p. 11). Put another way, people are more likely to change the culture of their organizations—the assumptions, beliefs, values, expectations, and habits that constitute the norm—as a result of acting in new ways, and the very purpose of articulating collective commitments is to clarify the new behaviors and to solicit support for them. If, as we suggested in chapter 5, the central challenge of every organization's improvement process is changing people's behavior, addressing the issue of collective commitments is one of the most powerful tools we know of for meeting that challenge.

When we work with schools and districts, adults inevitably seek assurances—commitments, if you will—from their supervisors before they will agree to proceed with an improvement initiative. For example, they ask leaders to pledge that they will not be called upon to work beyond their contractual day, or that the results from common assessments will not be used in the evaluation process in a punitive way, or that working in collaborative teams does not mean they must teach in a prescribed, lockstep manner. These are legitimate concerns, and we support the idea that promises should be made to address them. But rarely do educators take the next step beyond promises to discuss the commitments they are prepared to make to their colleagues. Even more rare is the school in which educators have clarified the commitments they make to their students. We believe these crucial conversations can accelerate a school's progress on the PLC journey, and we urge educators to move beyond the assurances they seek for themselves to explore the commitments they are prepared to make to their colleagues and to every student who walks through the doors of their school.

Consider the following suggestions when developing collective commitments.

Limit the Commitment Statements to a Reasonable Number

We worked with a group of aspiring principals who were engaged in an intensive 6-week summer training program. In the first few days of their training, they established 28 commitment statements regarding how they would work together. When we arrived during their final week of training, we saw all 28 commitments proudly displayed on chart paper around the room (it took all four walls to hold them). We soon realized that these future leaders were not observing a single one of those commitments as their individual and collective behavior consistently violated the pledges they had made to one another. It is far better to have a few, specific agreements and to honor them than to create a laundry list of assurances that are ignored. If your list of commitments has reached double digits, you should consider consolidating it.

Be Explicit and Direct Rather Than Vague and Ethereal

Remember that statements of collective commitments are intended to clarify the very specific actions we have pledged to take on behalf of others. Ambiguity is the antithesis of meaningful collective commitments. Avoid vague statements that allow for a wide range of actions. For example, "We will make our decisions based on the best interest of the student" offers no direction to a high school algebra teacher with a student who is struggling academically. One teacher may decide it is in the student's best interest to remove him from the course and place him in a class better suited to his ability so the student will not become frustrated. Another may conclude the student's difficulty is caused by lack of effort, and in the student's best interest, the teacher may decide to let him suffer the consequences of failure as an important life lesson. Another teacher allows the student to earn sufficient extra credit for projects unrelated to the essential skills of the class so that, in the student's best interest, he will not fall behind in credits. Another insists the student come in after school for individualized help so that, in the student's best interest, he can master the content. Another opposes requiring the student to seek help after school because he is on an athletic team, and, in his best interest, he needs this venue where he can experience success. Yet another teacher suggests that, in the student's best interest, he should be transferred to another instructor who might be a better fit for his learning style. A "student's best interest" is likely to lie in the eye of the beholder, and thus it makes for an ineffective commitment statement.

Schools should also avoid writing statements as beliefs. Once again, collective commitments are intended to clarify what we intend to *do*, not what we believe. For example, a staff could heartily endorse the premise, "We believe in a safe and orderly environment," and assume it is exclusively the job of the administration to ensure such an environment. Furthermore, beliefs are much more difficult to monitor. A teacher who consistently fails half of her class could continue to say she "believes in the potential" of her students and assign blame to the students themselves for failing to strive to achieve that potential. The action orientation that collective commitments are intended to promote is more likely to occur when those commitments are described as behaviors instead of beliefs (Senge, Kleiner, Roberts, Ross, & Smith, 1994).

Finally, even the most morally impeccable statements are ineffective as collective commitments if they do not establish clear expectations about what each person is expected to *do* to fulfill the commitments. "We promise to help our students become lifelong learners" is a wonderful sentiment, but a staff will have difficulty assessing its effectiveness in fulfilling that promise. When educators articulate collective commitments, they should get down to the nitty-gritty details: What do we promise to do, today, to support our colleagues and our students?

Common Goals

The final essential pillar in the foundation of a PLC requires clear *goals* that guide the ongoing work of educators on a day-to-day basis. While vision establishes what the school or district is working to become and collective commitments specify what educators will start doing today to move their organization in the intended direction, goals establish clear benchmarks of progress and milestones on the improvement journey. As James Champy (1995) wrote, "Vision is the rhetoric of inspiration . . . while goals are the rhetoric of accountancy" (p. 54).

Effective goals also contribute to the action orientation of a PLC. Clearly understood goals motivate and energize people to take purposeful action, particularly when they are accompanied by ongoing feedback regarding progress (Csikszentmihalyi, 1997; Kouzes & Posner, 1999). When people understand the goals of their organization and how their jobs can contribute to the achievement of those goals, they enjoy not only more positive feelings regarding their work, but also a stronger sense of self-worth and self-efficacy (Amabile & Kramer, 2007). In fact, Blanchard (2007) contends, "Goal setting is the single most powerful motivational tool in a leader's toolkit" (p. 150).

But in order for goals to have a positive impact on any organization, they must be specific enough to help people in the organization gauge their progress and remain focused on the right priorities. Since the priority in schools should be higher levels of student learning, goals should have a direct and observable impact on student achievement. The SMART goal acronym (Conzemius & O'Neill, 2005) serves as a useful tool in the goal-setting process, calling for goals that are:

- **Strategic and Specific**—The goal is linked to the organization's purpose and vision and sufficiently specific to avoid ambiguity or confusion.

- **Measurable**—The organization has established baseline measures from which to assess progress.

- **Attainable**—People in the organization believe that with collective effort they can accomplish the goal.

- **Results-Oriented**—The goal focuses on outcomes rather than inputs and results rather than intentions. Once again, because the purpose and priority in schools and districts should be higher levels of student learning, a SMART goal will call for evidence of improved student achievement, and it will be student-centered rather than project-centered or teacher-centered.

- **Timebound**—The goal should include a timeframe for when specific action will be taken and when it is anticipated that the goal will be accomplished.

School District 54 in Schaumburg, Illinois, is a good example of a district approach to meaningful goals. Schaumburg has established only three goals:

1. Students who have attended District 54 schools for at least 1 year will read at grade level upon entering third grade.

2. Each school will close the achievement gap for all students in reading and math as measured by both district and state assessments.

3. At least 90% of all students will meet or exceed standards in reading and math as measured by both district and state assessments.

Each of these goals focuses on the priority of the district—student learning—and provides measurable indicators to monitor progress. In addition to the goals, the district has identified "initiatives," which are intended to help achieve the goals, but are not to be confused with goals themselves. Initiatives represent the means to the end, strategies to achieve the goal. For example, initiatives for Schaumburg in 2007–2008 included such important activities as implementing a core literacy program, developing the capacity of staff to work as members of a PLC, supporting the development and implementation of common formative assessments in each school, and establishing timely and flexible intervention and enrichment strategies in each school. Note that these initiatives, while important, are not goals, and that the effectiveness of the initiatives will ultimately be assessed by their impact on student learning.

Compare the Schaumburg approach to the following goals established by other districts:

1. We will train all K–6 teachers in cooperative learning during the first semester.

2. Principals will conduct at least two classroom walkthroughs each day throughout the school year.

3. All high schools will move to a block schedule by the fall of 2008.

4. We will prepare our students to be lifelong learners who are equipped with the skills necessary to succeed in the 21st century.

The first three goals are certainly measurable, attainable, and time-bound, but they focus on training, tactics, and projects rather than on results. Each of these goals could be achieved, and student learning could actually decline. They focus on means rather than ends. The fourth goal is the kind of politically correct bromide that often passes for a district goal, but has the comforting advantage of holding no one accountable for anything.

Other Keys to Effective Goals

Doug Reeves (2006) has found a negative correlation between the number of pages in a district's strategic plan and its gains in student achievement—the thicker the plan, the less likely students are learning. One of the most consistent recommendations of organizational theorists and educational researchers alike is that leaders should limit the number of goals the people in their organizations are asked to pursue (Blanchard, 2007; Drucker, 1992; Lencioni, 2005; Schmoker, 2003;

Senge, Kleiner, Roberts, Ross, & Smith, 1994). Districts would be far better served if they resisted the temptation to develop a litany of goals and instead heeded Michael Fullan's (2007) advice to begin each year with a single overriding priority of helping more students learn at higher levels and eliminating gaps in achievement based on race, gender, or socioeconomic status. Fullan's proposal for an ongoing goal of "raising the bar and closing the gap" reinforces and reiterates the fundamental purpose of the district and asks people to assess their efforts on the basis of improving their collective capacity to fulfill that purpose. When it comes to district goals, the adage "less is more" should prevail.

A district's sustained commitment to a few key goals over an extended period of time can also help foster a culture of continuous improvement. The students, teachers, and administrators in the Schaumburg district are far better served by an ongoing, focused concentration on their three SMART goals than by annual pronouncements of new goals. Schaumburg's educators will, in all likelihood, require years to achieve the ambitious goals they have established, but every year can mark progress toward the intended outcomes, progress that can be noted, celebrated, and used to establish new baseline data for the coming school year. Ongoing organizational commitment to a few focused goals, even as key players come and go, can provide the continuity of purpose and direction educators are craving.

Finally, school leaders must remember that districts and schools do not have goals, people do—or they do not. District goals will impact what happens in schools only if steps are taken to ensure each school aligns its SMART goals with those of the district and understands how it must contribute to the larger organization. School goals will impact what happens in courses and grade levels only if the collaborative teams of teachers within the school have aligned their SMART goals with those of the school and understand how they can contribute to the success of the school. Team goals will impact what happens in an individual teacher's classroom only if teachers commit to one another that they will work together interdependently to achieve goals for which they have agreed to be mutually accountable. In later chapters, we will have much more to say about the vital importance of SMART goals in building the capacity of teachers to work together as members of collaborative teams, but for now we will simply reiterate the significance of goals in establishing the foundation of a strong PLC.

The Pursuit of Nonmeasurable Goals

Albert Einstein once observed, "Everything that is measurable is not important, and everything that is important is not measurable." There are certainly many *important* goals that educators hope to achieve on behalf of their students that are not readily conducive to measurement—issues of character, citizenship, self-efficacy, emotional intelligence, and resilience, to name just a few. These issues are indeed difficult to measure and typically will not be addressed on high-stakes assessments, but that does not diminish their importance, and we believe educators should be vigilant in seeking more effective ways to instill these important characteristics in the students they serve.

We contend, however, that educators are prone to making two errors when it comes to these issues. First, they fall victim to the Tyranny of Or and suggest that schools can either educate for intellect *or* character. Second, they fail to make any effort to assess their impact as teachers on matters they contend are important to them. Education is not a zero-sum game where success in one area inevitably diminishes the possibility of success in others. Thomas Lickona and Matthew Davidson (2005) found the best schools do not fall victim to the Tyranny of Or, but instead are "committed to helping students become *smart* (in the multi-dimensional sense of intelligence) *and* to helping them become *good* (in the multi-dimensional sense of moral maturity). They foster excellence and ethics" (p. v). We have seen no evidence that schools with high expectations for student achievement produce students who are less ethical, less responsible, or less civic-minded than low-performing schools.

Furthermore, schools and districts have typically made little effort to gather evidence of their effectiveness in instilling the virtues they often claim are so important to them. As Peter Senge and his coauthors (1994) observed, "Many of the most important results may not be quantifiable, but that doesn't mean they are unknowable" (p. 46). It is incongruous for any organization to proclaim the vital importance of a particular outcome and then make no effort to monitor the attainment of that outcome. Ongoing monitoring is one of the most powerful ways organizations communicate what is truly important and valued. Schools may not be able to measure the specific degree to which a student has learned emotional intelligence any more than a wife can measure the extent to which her husband's love for her has increased or decreased over the course of the year, but in both instances, certain indicators could be identified to clarify expectations and assess improvement. When educators claim traditional assessments offer no insights into the most important goals for their students, and then do nothing to create their own strategies for monitoring what they claim is important, they absolve themselves of all responsibility and hold themselves accountable for nothing.

A Solid Foundation Is Just the Start

Imagine that clear mission (purpose), shared vision, collective commitments (values), and SMART goals represent four pillars that constitute the very foundation of a PLC (see page 166). Each pillar asks a question of the people in the school or district: Why do we exist? What do we hope to become? What commitments must we make to create the school or district that will improve our ability to fulfill our purpose? And what goals will we use to monitor our progress?

In *Learning by Doing* (2006), we wrote the following:

> When teachers and administrators have worked together to consider those questions and reach consensus regarding their collective positions on each question, they have built a solid foundation for a PLC. Much work remains

to be done, for these are just a few of the steps in the thousands of steps that must be taken in the never-ending process of continuous improvement. But addressing these questions increases the likelihood that all subsequent work will have the benefit of firm underpinnings. If staff members have not considered these questions, have done so only superficially, or are unable to establish common ground regarding their positions on the questions, any and all future efforts to improve the school will stand on shaky ground. (p. 23)

Put another way, the most effective leaders continually refer not only to the "how" of school improvement—this is how we will assign teachers into teams, how we will provide them with time to collaborate, how we will assess student learning, how we will respond when students do not learn—but also to the "why" people are engaged in these important actions. Consistent and clear references to the foundation return people throughout the organization to the question of "Why?" and therefore help educators assign much-needed purpose and meaning to their day-to-day actions.

More commonly, however, educators fail to build upon the foundation. They mistake writing a mission statement for living a mission, substitute crafting a vision statement for taking purposeful steps to create a more powerful school or district, settle for identifying collective commitments rather than honoring them, or confuse the announcement of joint projects with the collective pursuit of results-oriented goals that foster interdependence and mutual accountability. Written documents will never improve an organization unless they serve as a catalyst for action.

One area of our deepest learning over the years regarding what it takes to improve schools is the importance of an action orientation. Even educators who *know* the schools they hope to create, the commitments they agree to honor, and the goals that they will pursue,

The Four Pillars of a Professional Learning Community

Mission

Why do we exist?

Vision

What do we hope to become?

Values

What commitments must we make to create the school or district that will improve our ability to fulfill our purpose?

Goals

What goals will we use to monitor our progress?

face the continuing challenge of turning their knowledge into *action* consistent with that knowledge. They must close the gap between *knowing and doing* (Pfeffer & Sutton, 2000). Talking is not doing. Writing statements is not doing. Developing improvement plans is not doing. Only doing is doing, and in the next chapters we will attempt to provide a detailed explanation of what educators *do* when they are members of a PLC.

Chapter 7

Teaching in a Professional Learning Community

The most persistent norm that stands in the way of 21st-century learning is isolated teaching in stand-alone classrooms. Transforming schools into 21st-century learning communities means recognizing that teachers must become members of a growing network of shared expertise.

—Kathleen Fulton, Irene Yoon, and Christine Lee

Confidence blossoms when people feel connected rather than isolated, when they are willing to engage and commit to one another, when they can act together to solve problems and produce results, ignoring boundaries between them. . . . Bonds grow from working together on real and important tasks that achieve success.

—Rosabeth Moss Kanter

During one of our workshops, a panel made up of teachers from highly effective professional learning communities was fielding questions from the audience. When asked how teaching in a PLC is different from teaching in a traditional school, one of the panelists answered, "Working in a PLC means you never again have to face the challenges of teaching alone." We think that concise answer captures the most significant distinction between working in a PLC and a more traditional school. The collaborative culture and systematic supports embedded in a PLC have significant benefits for teachers:

- Everyone has someone to turn to and talk to when confronted with the difficulties of teaching.

- Everyone has colleagues with whom and from whom they can learn.

- Everyone has teammates who are helping them achieve their goals.

- Everyone benefits from processes specifically aligned to promote the learning of their students.

- Very importantly, everyone operates within a built-in system of accountability because they are expected to contribute to the continuous improvement of their team and their school.

It is this shift—from a culture of isolation to a culture of collaboration, from working independently to working interdependently, from the pursuit of individual goals and interests to mutual accountability for fulfilling collective purpose and achieving common goals—that generates the strongest appeal for some teachers and, to be candid, elicits the greatest opposition from others.

For more than 30 years, any serious study of the culture of teaching has reached the same conclusion: Teachers work in isolation. Overcoming this traditional norm of teacher isolation is one of the most formidable barriers to creating a PLC. Educators themselves support the conclusions of the research; they acknowledge that they work alone. We have asked more than a thousand different groups of educators, "Do you believe that researchers are correct when they report that teachers typically work in isolation?" We cannot recall a single instance when a group—or even individuals within the group—challenged the conclusion. We regularly ask the question, "How many of you can complete this sentence because you have said it or heard it: 'I wish they would just give me my kids, give me my books, give me my room, and. . . ." We never fail to get a booming response of "Leave me alone!"

Richard Elmore (2003) argues that the existing structure of schools not only allows for, but actually fosters teacher isolation and serves to "buffer" teachers from accountability from what takes place in their classrooms. Educator evaluations are almost invariably perfunctory, and teachers are rarely called upon to provide concrete evidence of what they are teaching, how they are assessing, the criteria they use in determining the quality of student work, the instructional strategies and materials they utilize in the classroom, the factors they consider in determining a student's grade, and most importantly, the degree to which their students are acquiring the intended knowledge, skills, and dispositions.

Even worse, educators can spend an entire career in the profession and never know how well they teach a particular concept in comparison to their colleague teaching the same concept in the classroom across the hall. The scant indicators of learning that do exist are often dismissed as irrelevant. For example, anyone who has been in this profession for any length of time has witnessed teachers justify a significantly higher failure rate than their peers in the same school with the explanation that they have "higher standards." Those same teachers routinely either expect the administration to resist the pleading of students and their parents for transfers to another classroom, or they are indifferent to the exodus that occurs on an annual basis. They are indeed protected or "buffered" from inspection of or interference in their classrooms. As a result, classroom teachers are far too often immersed in a "culture of privacy and non-interference [that] is the best friend of the status quo" (Schmoker, 2006, p. 14).

The Knowing-Doing Gap at Work

Those seeking evidence of a classic case of the knowing-doing gap need look no further than this issue of teacher isolation versus teacher collaboration. Research has repeatedly concluded that teacher isolation has adverse consequences for students, for teachers, and for any effort to improve schools. In 1971, psychologist Seymour Sarason reported that because teachers rarely had contact with one another, they *"are psychologically alone even though they are in a densely populated setting"* (1996, p. 133). Sarason suggested teachers adapt to being alone by creating a culture of *individuals* concerned about himself or herself rather than a culture of *group* concerned with the pursuit of the profession's best practices. In 1975, Dan Lortie described how the isolation of classroom teachers prevented them from developing and sharing knowledge of their craft. The 1980s brought John Goodlad's (1984) analysis of the work of teachers, which led to his conclusion that teacher autonomy and isolation caused them to make decisions on curriculum, assessment, and instruction without the benefit of input from colleagues. In her research, Susan Rosenholtz (1986) discovered two distinctly different school cultures: one in which collaboration, continuous improvement, and shared learning was the norm, and the other in which autonomy and privatization left the question of quality teaching up to individual teachers to pursue according to their very different perspectives of quality. In the 1990s came Judith Warren Little's critique of school cultures entitled *The Persistence of Privacy* (1990), Ann Lieberman's finding (1995) that the most powerful impediment to school improvement was teacher isolation, and the work of the National Commission on Teaching and America's Future (1996), which concluded that the norm of teachers working in isolation prevented the teacher collaboration and shared learning essential to improving student achievement.

The turn of the century brought Elmore's critiques (2002, 2003, 2006) of perverse teacher isolation. Little and her colleagues (2003) re-emerged with the lament that the culture of isolation, privacy, and non-interference and the unwillingness of teachers to work together to examine evidence of student learning continued to prevent teachers from getting around to the hard work of improving instruction. Yet another study concluded, "The most persistent norm that stands in the way of 21st-century learning is isolated teaching in stand-alone classrooms"

(Fulton, Yoon, & Lee, 2005). Elmore (2006) was merely repeating more than 30 years of consistent findings when he wrote:

> The design of work in schools is fundamentally incompatible with the practice of improvement. Teachers spend most of their time working in isolation from each other in self-contained classrooms. . . . The problem with this design is that it provides almost no opportunity for teachers to engage in continuous and sustained learning about their practice in the setting in which they actually work. . . . This disconnect between the requirements of learning to teach well and the structure of teachers' work life is fatal to any sustained process of instructional improvement. (p. 127)

Educators have also known for quite some time that building a collaborative culture in which people work together interdependently to fulfill their shared purpose and achieve their common goals is an essential strategy for sustained school improvement. Consider the following findings:

- The single most important factor for successful school restructuring and the first order of business for those interested in increasing the capacity of their schools is building a collaborative internal environment that fosters cooperative problem-solving and conflict resolution. (Eastwood & Seashore Louis, 1992, p. 215)

- The ability to collaborate—on both a small and large scale—is becoming one of the core requisites of postmodern society. . . . In short, without collaborative skills and relationships it is not possible to learn and to continue to learn as much as you need in order to be an agent for social improvement. (Fullan, 1993, pp. 17–18)

- An interdependent work structure strengthens professional community. When teachers work in groups that require coordination, this, by definition, requires collaboration. When groups, rather than individuals, are seen as the main units for implementing curriculum, instruction, and assessment, they facilitate development of shared purpose for student learning and collective responsibility to achieve it. (Newmann & Wehlage, 1995, p. 37–38)

- The key to ensuring that every child has a quality teacher is finding a way for school systems to organize the work of qualified teachers so they can collaborate with their colleagues in developing strong learning communities that will sustain them as they become more accomplished teachers. (National Commission on Teaching and America's Future, 2003, p. 7)

- Collaboration and the ability to engage in collaborative action are becoming increasingly important to the survival of the public schools. Indeed, without the ability to collaborate with others the prospect of truly repositioning schools in the constellation of community forces is not likely. (Schlechty, 2005, p. 22)

- A precondition for doing *anything* to strengthen our practice and improve a school is the existence of a collegial culture in which professionals talk about practice, share their craft knowledge, and observe and root for the success of one another. Without these in place, no meaningful improvement—no staff or curriculum development, no teacher leadership, no student appraisal, no team teaching, no parent involvement, and no sustained change—is possible. (Barth, 2006, p. 13)

Professional organizations for educators have certainly endorsed the premise that educators should work together collaboratively. Consider the conclusions of the following organizations:

- Some of the most important forms of professional learning and problem solving occur in group settings within schools and school districts. Organized groups provide the social interaction that often deepens learning and the interpersonal support and synergy necessary for creatively solving the complex problems of teaching and learning. And because many of the recommendations contained in these standards advocate for increased teamwork among teachers and administrators in designing lessons, critiquing student work, and analyzing various types of data, among other tasks, it is imperative that professional learning be directed at improving the quality of collaborative work. (National Staff Development Council, 2001)

- High performing schools tend to promote collaborative cultures, support professional communities and exchanges among all staff and cultivate strong ties among the school, parents, and community. . . . Teachers and staff collaborate to remove barriers to student learning. . . . Teachers communicate regularly with each other about effective teaching and learning strategies. (National Education Association, 2007)

- It is time to end the practice of solo teaching in isolated classrooms. Teacher induction and professional development in 21st century schools must move beyond honing one's craft and personal repertoire of skills. Today's teachers must transform their personal knowledge into a collectively built, widely shared, and cohesive professional knowledge base. (National

Commission on Teaching and America's Future, 2005, p. 4)

- Accomplished teachers collaborate with others to improve student learning. . . . They work with other professionals on instructional policy, curriculum development and staff development. (National Board for Professional Teaching Standards, 2007a)

- Successful middle level teacher preparation programs place a high premium on teaching prospective and practicing middle level teachers about the importance of collaboration with colleagues and other stakeholders. One of the unique characteristics of middle level schools for teachers is the heavy emphasis on collaboration. . . . Teachers are not operating in isolation. This permits insights and understandings about young adolescent students to be shared with others and therefore maximized. (National Middle School Association, 2006)

- Isolation is the enemy of learning. Principals who support the learning of adults in their school organize teachers' schedules to provide opportunities for teachers to work, plan, and think together. For instance, teams of teachers who share responsibility for the learning of all students meet regularly to plan lessons, critique student work and the assignments that led to it, and solve common instructional or classroom management problems. (National Association of Elementary School Principals, 2001, p. 45)

- A high school will regard itself as a *community* in which members of the staff collaborate to develop and implement the school's learning goals. Teachers will provide the leadership essential to the success of reform, collaborating with others in the educational community to redefine the role of the teacher and to identify sources of support for that redefined role. (National Association of Secondary School Principals, 2004, p. 4)

At some point, those of us in education must acknowledge we cannot claim confusion regarding this issue. The research has been clear and consistent, professional organizations for teachers and administrators at all grade levels have advised us, and our direct observations in our schools and districts confirm it: Isolation is the enemy of school improvement. In fact, it is difficult to find either supporting research or advocates for the position that educators best serve their children, themselves, or the profession by working in isolation. We *know* this. Yet, we have been reluctant to *do* anything to correct the situation.

In fact, educators have been willing accomplices in fostering this professional isolation. Roland Barth (1991) challenged teachers and principals to admit they had contributed to the problems of public schooling and that the solution to those problems would require them to change some of their assumptions and practices. He wrote, "God didn't create self contained classrooms, 50 minute periods, subjects taught in isolation. *We* did—because we find working alone safer than and preferable to working together. We *can* work to change the embedded structures so that our schools become more hospitable places for student and adult learning. But little will really change unless we change *ourselves*" (p. 125).

Fifteen years later, Barth (2006) bemoaned the fact that the structure and culture of most schools continued to foster "parallel play" rather than meaningful collaboration when he wrote the following:

Parallel play, a wonderful concept from the preschool literature, is thought to be a primitive stage of human development through which 2- and 3-year-olds soon pass on their way to more sophisticated forms of interaction.

> To illustrate, imagine two 3-year-olds busily engaged in opposite corners of a sandbox. One has a shovel and a bucket; the other has a rake and a hoe. At no time do they share their tools, let alone collaborate to build a sandcastle. They may inadvertently throw sand in each other's face from time to time, but they seldom interact intentionally. Although in close proximity for a long period of time, each is so self-absorbed, so totally engrossed in what he or she is doing, that the two of them will go on for hours working in isolation. Parallel play offers, of course, a perfect description of how teachers interact at many elementary, middle, and high schools. (p. 10)

For 35 years, educators have been advised that this tradition of teacher isolation is one of the most formidable barriers to school improvement, and that professional collaboration is essential to building the capacity to meet the needs of students; nevertheless, they have proven reluctant to acknowledge and address this detrimental tradition. Unless educators confront this challenge directly, the critique of public education (or what is left of it) in 2050 will begin with the lament that educators work in isolation.

A New Image for the Profession

The main obstacle in closing this knowing-doing gap is the continuing image of the school organized into a series of independent classrooms, each led by a virtually autonomous teacher who bears only partial responsibility for the learning of his or her students and none for students assigned to other classrooms. School structures have reinforced this image at every turn. The layout of the buildings, the incentives for professional development, and the teacher supervision and evaluation process all contribute to the notion that the school is nothing more than a series of individual classroom kingdoms overseen by independent subcontractors.

We believe that the first step in breaking free of the traditional norm of educators working in isolation is to establish a new image of the fundamental structure of the school, one that is based on a communal gathering of high-performing collaborative teams that share collective responsibility for the learning of their students.

The collaborative team has been described as follows:

- "The basic building block of any intelligent organization" (Pinchot & Pinchot, 1993, p. 66)

- "A critical component of every enterprise—the predominant unit for decision making and getting things done. . . . Working in teams is the norm in a learning organization." (Senge, Kleiner, Roberts, Ross, & Smith, 1994, p. 51)

- "The best way to achieve challenging goals. . . . Teams nurture, support, and inspire each other." (Tichy, 1997, p. 143)

- "Far more productive than any other form of organizing. There is a clear correlation between participation and productivity." (Wheatley, 1999, p. 152)

- "The strategic vehicle for getting work accomplished . . . the vehicle for moving organizations into the future. . . . They make better decisions, solve more complex problems, and do more to enhance creativity and build skills than individuals working alone." (Blanchard, 2007, p. 172)

If the team structure is so essential to creating the collaborative culture of a PLC, it is important that educators come to a common understanding of the meaning of the word *team*. Bringing a group of teachers together on a regular basis does not make them a team. Asking them to work on the same task does not make them a team. Even working toward the same goal may not make them a team.

When we call upon educators to embrace the image of collaborative teams to drive the new structure and culture of their schools and districts, we ask them to envision *a group of people working together interdependently to achieve a common goal for which they are mutually accountable.* It is only when educators need each other, rely on each other, and depend on each other to achieve the shared goal of helping more students learn at higher levels that they are operating as a team. At that point, the success of every member of the team, and equally important, the success of every student served by the team, become the concern of the entire team.

Consider this analogy: Every fall 40,000 runners participate in the Chicago marathon. They are a group of people working together in close proximity, all striving to achieve a common goal—completing the race in a good personal time. Despite the fact that they share the same goal and are working very hard in close proximity to one another, they are not a team. An individual runner can achieve his or her goal regardless of what happens to rest of the participants. The same is true of most educators. Teachers can be working together in close proximity in rooms adjacent to one another. They can be working very hard in pursuit of the same goals—helping all students learn their math facts in third grade or write a persuasive essay in ninth grade. Nevertheless, they are not a team. In both instances the missing element is *interdependence.* The success or failure of a teacher in one classroom has no impact on the others.

Contrast that with the most successful professional basketball team in the history of the National Basketball Association—the 1995–1996 Chicago Bulls, who won 72 of their 82 games during the regular season and swept to the championship in the playoffs. Michael Jordan was arguably the greatest basketball player of all time, but for 6 years he was unable to lead the Bulls to the championship despite his individual brilliance. It was not until Phil Jackson became the coach that the Bulls became champions. He installed a new system that relied less on Jordan's individual talent and more on the coordination of an interdependent team. Jordan remained the leading scorer, but other members of the team were given important supporting roles. In the 1995–1996 season, Dennis Rodman was not asked to score points, but was given the primary responsibility for rebounding. Ron Harper was assigned to defend the leading scorer on the opposition. Toni Kukoc was the first substitute off of the bench and was responsible for bringing energy and scoring when he stepped on the floor. The team lacked a dominant center, so three different players divided their time in the position, and each was expected to play defense, rebound, and wear down the opposition with their allotted 18 fouls per game. Steve Kerr was the 3-point shot specialist. Scottie Pippen was the do-everything player who was called upon to score, defend, and rebound.

In order for Michael Jordan to score, the team would have to defend and rebound, a center would set screens at the high post for him to use, and Kerr and Pippen would move to an open spot on the court to deter defenders from double- or triple-teaming him. Even Jordan, the greatest player ever, *needed* the support of his teammates. Pippen was never able to lead a team to a championship without Jordan. The Bulls would have never been world champions if they had to rely on Rodman for offense or on Kerr to penetrate a defense. Like all great teams, they worked together *interdependently* to achieve their common goal (the championship), and they were mutually accountable to one another for achieving that goal. Each member contributed his strengths to the effort and relied on his teammates to help overcome his weaknesses.

Thus, a critical element in establishing effective collaborative teams in a PLC is creating *interdependent* relationships. As Pfeffer and Sutton (2000) wrote, "Interdependence is what organizations are about. The willingness of individuals to cooperate with other members of an organization is one of the major determinants of organizational effectiveness and efficiency" (p. 197). It is only when schools and districts create interdependent relationships among educators that they can expect to create the collective capacity to impact student achievement in a profoundly positive way (Elmore, 2006; Kruse, Seashore Louis, & Bryk, 1995; McLaughlin & Talbert, 2006; Newmann & Wehlage, 1996; Sergiovanni, 2005).

Time for a New Story

All organizations and the people within them create stories about themselves that help make sense of their world. The process of changing an organization is the process of changing its story (Gardner & Laskin, 1996). For too long the story that has guided the work of educators is the story of the individual teacher responsible only for his or her students. This image has been perpetuated in contemporary society as well. Think of the messages of the films *Dead Poets Society, Stand and Deliver, Freedom Writers, Dangerous Minds,* or *Mr. Holland's Opus.* A heroic teacher, working in isolation, fights the entrenched bureaucracy of the system and the low expectations of colleagues to make a difference in the lives of his or her students. The key to improving schools, according to this mythology, is finding more of these heroic individuals to lead their isolated classrooms.

It is time to embrace a new story, a new image of teaching, one that celebrates professionals who work together interdependently to accomplish collectively what they could never accomplish alone.

Converting a Hard Fact Into Dangerous Half-Truths

Gradually, educators throughout North America have come to acknowledge that working collaboratively offers a better hope of helping all students learn than working in isolation. Grudgingly, they are beginning to acknowledge that they can play a role in tearing down the walls of isolation and building a collaborative culture. Once again, however, a hard fact regarding the importance of a collaborative culture has often been diluted into dangerous half-truths. First, educators often substitute congeniality for collaboration (Barth, 2006; Sergiovanni, 2005). If the members of a group get along with one another or perhaps read and discuss the same book, they are satisfied they are a collaborative team. They are not—just as good friends or the members of Oprah's Book Club are not collaborative teams.

Collaboration—or co-laboring—in a PLC entails working together interdependently in systematic processes to analyze and impact professional practice to improve individual and collective results.

The second half-truth asserts that "collaboration is good." But there is nothing inherently "good" about collaboration (Fullan, 2007; Little, 1990). It represents a means to an end rather than the end itself. Collaboration can serve to perpetuate the status quo rather than improve it, to reinforce the negative aspects of the culture rather than resolve them, to reiterate faulty assumptions rather than subject them to collective inquiry. Collaboration can, and sometimes does, dissolve into grouping by griping, a forum for petty grievances, and a reaffirmation of resignation and helplessness. A collaborative culture can be powerful, but as Fullan (2001) warns, unless people "are focusing on the right things they may end up being powerfully wrong" (p. 67).

W. Edwards Deming observed, "It is not enough to do your best; you must know what to do and then do your best" (2000, p. 19). We are convinced that teachers typically do their best; however, they have not always known what to do. If the key to improving schools is "*learning to do the right things* in the setting where you work" (Elmore, 2006, p. 73), then the key to effective collaboration is to ensure that educators collaborate, or co-labor, on the "right" things—the things that actually impact student learning. Therefore, we argue that effective collaborative teams will engage in collective inquiry into the four critical questions of learning. We address the first of these questions in some detail in this chapter, and the other three questions in the next chapter.

1. What is it we want our students to learn? What knowledge, skills, and dispositions do we expect them to acquire as a result of this course, grade level, or unit of instruction?

2. How will we know if each student is learning each of the essential skills, concepts, and dispositions we have deemed most essential?

3. How will we respond when some of our students do not learn? What process will we put in place to ensure students receive additional time and support for learning in a timely, directive, and systematic way?

4. How will we enrich and extend the learning for students who are already proficient?

1. What is it we want our students to learn? What knowledge, skills, and dispositions do we expect them to acquire as a result of this course, grade level, or unit of instruction?

An absolute priority of every team in a PLC is to clarify what students must learn. In doing so, members of the team will be called upon to identify both the most essential skills and concepts students must acquire, as well as curriculum content that should be eliminated to provide more instructional time for what is deemed essential. A common criticism of virtually all state standards is that there are far too many of them (Popham, 2005; Reeves, 2002). W. James Popham (2005) contends that the typical process used to create state standards—convening subject-matter experts to ask them what is important and significant about their subjects—inevitably results in the conclusion that *everything* is important. As he writes, "These committees seem bent on identifying skills that they fervently wish students would possess. Regrettably, the resultant litanies of committee-chosen content standards tend to resemble curricular wish lists rather than realistic targets." Marzano (2003) estimates if schools attempted to teach all the standards that have been identified in the 49 states that have adopted standards, as well as the standards recommended by national organizations that have weighed in on the subject, it would require 23 years of schooling. He concludes, not surprisingly, that the American curriculum is not viable; that is, it cannot be taught in the amount of time available for schooling.

We are unaware of any movement to convert the American educational system from K–12 to K–22, and therefore, teachers will continue to grapple with the endemic curriculum overload of public education in this country. That overload has resulted in two significant barriers to student achievement. First, too many teachers make *coverage* of the curriculum a priority. The ability to say, "I taught it" becomes the primary objective, and student learning becomes a secondary consideration. Second, the overload forces teachers to make decisions about what they will teach and what they will exclude. As individual teachers make those decisions independently, what students learn becomes a function of the teacher to whom they are assigned, rather than a function of a common curriculum experience. A sixth-grade teacher who is assigned students from four different fifth-grade teachers in her same school cannot be certain of what those students were taught, much less what they learned. There is no "guaranteed curriculum" to assure all students have access to the same knowledge, skills, and dispositions (Marzano, 2003).

Doug Reeves (2002) offers the most insightful recommendations as to how educators should respond to the plethora of standards they are called upon to teach. Reeves makes the common sense argument (one which he then supports by research) that not all standards are created equal; some are simply more important, or powerful, than others. For example, a state may include "identifying the main idea of a reading passage" and "naming the capital of each of the 50 states" among their standards for fifth-grade students. Few people, however, would argue that the ability to recall state capitals is as significant to a student's success as his or her ability to read a passage and understand its meaning.

Reeves (2002) offers a three-part test for teachers to use to identify the most significant or powerful standards: endurance, leverage, and readiness for the next level of learning. As he explains:

- **Endurance.** "Standards that meet the criterion of endurance give students skills or knowledge that remains with them long after a test is completed. Standards on research skills, reading comprehension, writing, map reading, and hypotheses testing are all examples of enduring knowledge" (p. 49–50).

- **Leverage.** "The criterion of leverage helps the leader and teachers identify those standards applicable to many academic disciplines. Two examples that one can find in every set of academic standards are nonfiction writing and interpretation of tables, charts, and graphs. The evidence is quite clear that if students engage in more frequent nonfiction writing, their performance in other academic disciplines improves" (p. 50).

- **Readiness for the next level of learning.** To address this criterion, a collaborative team of teachers would ask the team of colleagues in the grade level above them to identify the essential knowledge and skills students must acquire to be successful in their class next year.

A school committed to helping all students learn at high levels must have a process in place to ensure that every teacher is clear on the question, "Learn what?" for each course, grade level, and unit of instruction. Reeves may refer to power standards, Marzano to a guaranteed and viable curriculum, and Lezotte to clear and focused academic goals, but they all are advocating the same principle: Schools are more effective when the teachers within them have worked together to establish a clear and consistent understanding of what students must learn.

2. How will we know if each student is learning each of the essential skills, concepts, and dispositions we have deemed most essential?

This question serves as a linchpin of the collaborative team process. Before team members can answer it, they must back up to clarify what students must learn. And after attempting to answer it through a variety of assessments, they will confront the challenge of responding to students who had difficulty at the same time they extend and enrich the learning for students who demonstrated proficiency. Thus, the work of the collaborative team flows up and down from the challenge of assessing student learning in the most authentic and beneficial ways. We will explore that challenge in chapters 8 and 9.

3. **How will we respond when some of our students do not learn? What process will we put in place to ensure students receive additional time and support for learning in a timely, directive, and systematic way?**

We submit that what typically happens when a student does not learn will depend on the practices of his or her individual teacher rather than on any coordinated, collective response. Furthermore, in traditional schools teachers bear no responsibility for the learning of students who are not specifically assigned to their classroom. This traditional structure has contributed to the norm of teacher isolation and to uneven and inequitable support for students. We will explore how teams and schools address the challenge of this question in chapter 10.

4. **How will we enrich and extend the learning for students who are already proficient?**

One of the concerns expressed about the PLC concept is that its attention to the learning of *all* students will divert resources and attention to students who are struggling to the detriment of students whose learning could be enriched. We will explore how teams and schools address this challenge in a PLC in chapter 10.

PLCs Build Shared Knowledge Rather Than Pool Opinions

As the *professionals* within a PLC, teachers must constantly seek the best strategies for helping their students learn at the highest possible levels. Their search must move beyond pooling opinions—"This is how I like to teach this concept," "I have always done it this way," or "This seems to work for me." Professionals will seek to discover and implement the best practices in teaching. They will become students of the research base on teaching. Although it is beyond the scope of this book to provide a detailed analysis of effective teaching strategies, powerful resources are available to teachers and teams committed to the study of their craft. For example, Robert Marzano's synthesis of the research (2003) identifies 34 specific teaching behaviors under 9 different instructional strategies that have proven to be effective in helping students learn at higher levels. Jonathon Saphier (2008) and his colleagues at Research for Better Teaching have synthesized the knowledge base on teaching to focus on 17 critical areas of classroom performance. More importantly, they offer powerful insights as to how specific strategies can be matched to student needs. The third edition of the *Handbook of Research on Improving Student Achievement* (Educational Research Services, 2004), offers insights into effective strategies for teaching specific subject areas as well as the most powerful general instructional practices.

It is imperative to stress, however, that members of a collaborative team in a PLC will not limit their study of effective practices to the research of others, but they will also conduct their own action research with each unit they teach. After the team has reached agreement on what students must learn and on the strategies for assessing their learning, each member of the team has the autonomy to select and implement the instructional strategies he or she believes will yield the best results. *How* skills and concepts are taught is left to the discretion of individual teachers, and variability of strategies is valued as an important tool in the team's action research. Once the common assessment is administered, the team examines the results together to identify the strategies that led to the highest levels of learning. Members then teach one another, using their individual strengths to enhance the overall effectiveness of the team.

Effective teaching requires considerable autonomy and discretion in the day-to-day, moment-to-moment decisions teachers make in their individual classrooms. Members of PLCs support that autonomy because they recognize scripted lessons and lockstep pacing will not develop the capacity of teachers to improve either their instruction or their schools. When, however, teachers are presented with clear evidence that particular instructional strategies consistently yield better results for students, they are expected to develop their ability to use those strategies in their classrooms. This typically is not a problem, since we have found that evidence of student learning is the most powerful motivator for teachers to change their practice.

Some of our colleagues have suggested that we should include the question, "What are the most effective strategies for teaching these skills?" among the critical questions a team would discuss *prior* to initiating instruction or creating and administering a common assessment. We certainly are not opposed to teachers having this conversation early in the process; we caution, however, that until they have concrete evidence of the effectiveness of different strategies, they are engaged in conjecture. The more powerful conversations regarding best practice occur when people have shared access to the evidence of effectiveness of various instructional strategies. Those conversations become the kind of professional dialogue that contributes to teacher growth; they are concrete, specific, precise, and grounded in evidence.

We cannot stress emphatically enough that the only reason the members of a collaborative team of teachers explore these four critical questions together is to improve student achievement by identifying students who need intervention and enrichment and by using their collective analysis of evidence to inform and improve their professional practice. If teams merely generate data from assessments and then continue with business as usual, there will be no gains in student achievement. In other words, *teams engage in the process of addressing the four critical questions in order to address the ultimate issue: How can we use this evidence of student learning to respond to our students and improve our individual and collective teaching?*

A Collaborative Team at Work

The following story of the second-grade team at Westlawn Elementary School in Fairfax County, Virginia, offers insight into the workings of a collaborative team within a PLC.

Diana, Se, Marie, and Amy, the second-grade team at Westlawn Elementary, began their collaborative process for improving math proficiency for their students by engaging in collective inquiry regarding the current results and practices in second-grade math. Their math achievement data from the previous year's summative district assessment indicated 78% of second graders met or exceeded the district's proficiency target in math. They agreed to establish a team SMART goal to improve upon last year's results by at least 10% on that same summative district assessment. The goal was strategic in that it was aligned with the school's goal to increase the percentage of students meeting or exceeding proficiency in math as measured on local, county, state, and national indicators. The team goal was measurable because it asked for a 10% increase over the previous year. The team believed the goal was attainable—that is, they felt they could accomplish it. It was results-oriented because improved results (higher levels of student learning) were required to achieve the goal. It was time-bound because the goal was to be accomplished within the course of the school year.

Prior to developing strategies to achieve their goal, Diana, Se, Marie, and Amy had a candid conversation about how they had approached the math curriculum in the previous year. They acknowledged they had followed the same 4-step pattern for each unit:

- **Step 1.** Administer the pre-assessment from the textbook.

- **Step 2.** Teach the unit.

- **Step 3.** Administer the post-assessment from the textbook.

- **Step 4.** Move on to the next unit, repeating steps 1 through 3.

They recognized they would only improve student performance in math across second grade by seeking out and implementing new and better practices. They committed to each other to use the team learning process of a PLC to guide their teamwork throughout that year.

What Did They Do?

1. They clarified the 8 to 10 most essential student learning outcomes (skills, concepts, dispositions) in math for each semester by doing the following:

   - Talking with the third-grade team to determine the skills and concepts most essential to student success in math for entering third graders

   - Analyzing and clarifying their state and division second-grade math standards

   - Consulting with school and division math specialists to clarify multiple interpretations of the same standards

   - Analyzing the district assessment, and identifying where their students had struggled in the previous year

   - Developing a math curriculum map and common pacing guide they all agreed to follow

2. They created a series of common formative assessments aligned to the essential math outcomes by doing the following:

   - Studying the language and format of the district's summative assessment of second-grade math

   - Selecting appropriate items aligned to the essential math skills from math textbooks, individual teacher assessments, and state and national websites providing released math items

   - Creating new items deemed by the members of the team to be valid ways of assessing the essential skills

   - Including at least five items per skill on each common assessment to provide students an adequate opportunity to demonstrate their proficiency

   - Increasing the number and frequency of assessments so that only two or three skills were considered on each assessment

3. They established a proficiency target of 80% for each skill on each assessment. For example, if they used five items to assess a particular skill, students needed to solve four of the five problems correctly to be deemed proficient.

4. They collectively analyzed the results from each common formative assessment, identifying, skill by skill, the individual students throughout second grade whose scores exceeded, met, or fell below the team's proficiency target.

Through this collaborative analysis of common formative assessment data, the team was quickly able to do the following:

- Identify individual students who were experiencing difficulty on any skill.

- Identify individual students who were already highly proficient.

- Create flexible groups of students across the grade level for the intervention/enrichment period each day based on skill-by-skill proficiency.

- Establish a protected block of time each day for the team, resource specialists, and instructional assistants to provide students with coordinated and precise intervention and enrichment based on students' personal needs.

- Identify the teachers whose students were experiencing the greatest success on each skill.

- Assign students who were struggling with a particular skill to work with the teachers experiencing the best results in that skill on the common assessments during their intervention/enrichment period.

- Explore and discuss the strategies being used in individual classrooms.

The team also engaged students in the process of monitoring their own learning by requiring each student to maintain simple bar graphs indicating his or her proficiency on each essential math skill. Items on the assessment were arranged by skill, and each item was assigned its own box on the graph. After every common assessment, students would color in the box for each item they answered correctly. As individual students discovered they had not met the proficiency target on a particular essential math skill or concept, they knew to report to the corresponding small-group tutorial during the intervention/enrichment period to receive additional support for their learning.

At the completion of this skill-driven intervention cycle, the team administered another form of the common assessment to students who had experienced difficulty on any of the essential skills. At that point, new student learning groups were formed. Students who demonstrated proficiency were moved to enrichment groups, while students who continued to struggle were moved to smaller, more intensive group interventions.

This intervention/enrichment process ensured that any student in second grade who was having difficulty understanding a skill would receive intensive, small-group instruction from the most effective teacher on the team for that particular skill. The process allowed the team to continue with new direct instruction during the regular math period each day, so the difficulties of a few did not adversely impact the opportunity for all students to learn new material. Meanwhile, the team continued to build shared knowledge of the best way to help young students acquire math skills through a collective study of the research on the topic. At the same time, however, members were conducting their own action research on effective math instruction and learning from one another.

What Did They Learn?

As the members of the second-grade team and the school-based support team collectively responded to the individual and small-group learning needs of their students, skill by skill throughout the first semester, they discovered dramatic gains in the number of students achieving

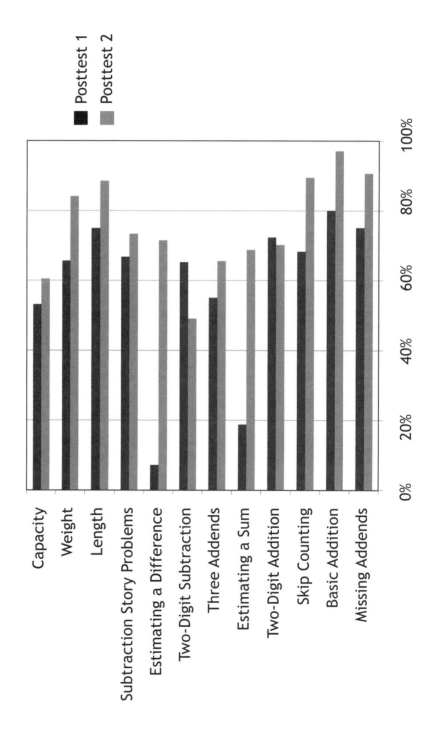

Final Data: Results of Posttest 1 and Posttest 2 for Second-Grade Math

or exceeding proficiency—*except* in two skill areas: two-digit addition and two-digit subtraction (see the graph on page 194).

Of course, they celebrated both the growth of individual students and the team's progress toward achieving its math SMART goal, but they were puzzled as to why students continued to struggle with the two skills, even after intervention. As they probed deeper, they learned the two distinct skills had something in common—both required the students to regroup numbers to solve two-digit addition and subtraction problems. They also discovered each member of the team had utilized all of the various strategies and "tricks" for teaching regrouping to students, and no member had been able to help students overcome their difficulties with the skill. At that point, Diana, Se, Marie, and Amy recognized *they* needed to learn new ways of teaching regrouping before they could help all students learn to apply the skill. The teachers were working hard and doing their best, but now they needed some time and support from an external source to strengthen their own capacity to meet the needs of their students. Doing their best was not enough. They had to heed Deming's advice and first learn what to do, and then do their best.

The team shared its concern with the principal, Kim Dockery, who made arrangements for a math professor from a local university to help them develop additional strategies for helping young "concrete" learners understand the "abstract" concept of regrouping numbers. Team members then engaged in learning by doing—applying the new practices in their classrooms, reflecting on what worked and what did not, and supporting one another as they strengthened and stretched their own learning and developed new skills.

This team learning process had several positive consequences. First, the team achieved its goal: More second-grade students achieved proficiency in math than ever before. Second, the teachers enhanced their professional expertise and became more skillful in teaching mathematics. Third, the teachers felt a greater sense of self-efficacy, more confident that their collective efforts have a powerful effect on student learning. Fourth, students who in the past might have concluded at age 7 that "I'm not good in math" were spared the attendant short-term and long-term implications of that perception, and instead entered third grade confident of their ability. Fifth, parent requests for teacher changes were diminished because parents recognized that the entire team was working together to ensure all students became proficient in the same essential skills.

This success story is not an aberration. In fact, it has been replicated not only by other teams at Westlawn Elementary School, but also by teams throughout North America in schools at all grade levels, serving students across all socioeconomic levels. The same common elements appear in those success stories:

1. A shared commitment to helping all students learn at high levels

2. Clarity among teachers regarding the essential knowledge, skills, and dispositions students must acquire as a result of each course, grade level, and unit of instruction

3. Clarity and consistency among teachers regarding the criteria to be used in assessing the quality of student work

4. Frequent common formative assessments to monitor each student's learning on a timely basis

5. Systematic interventions to provide additional time and support for students who experience difficulty, and additional opportunities for them to demonstrate that they have learned

6. Teachers working interdependently in collaborative teams to achieve results-oriented goals for which they are mutually accountable, and taking collective responsibility for the learning of all students

7. Individual teachers as well as teams using results from a variety of assessments to respond to the learning needs of individual students and to inform and improve their professional practice

8. Teams engaged in collective inquiry and building shared knowledge of effective practices by examining both internal and external sources of information

9. Ongoing, job-embedded learning for teachers as part of their routine work practice in recognition of the power of learning by doing

10. Clear parameters regarding what is tight about the school's culture and where individuals and teams can exercise professional autonomy

Creating these conditions is difficult but doable, more a question of will than skill, of "want to" than "know how." We *know* how to improve student achievement, but the question remains, "Will we break from the constraints of traditional school cultures and begin the process of closing the knowing-doing gap?" If educators are to help more students learn at higher levels, they must break free from the restraints of their traditional structures and cultures and embrace what Michael Fullan (2007) has called "the new professionalism," which is "collaborative, not autonomous; open rather than closed; outward looking rather than insular. . . . The teaching profession must become a better learning profession" (p. 297).

Chapter 8

Assessment in a Professional Learning Community

Control and improvement come from measures that pro-vide information about processes, measures that give people immediate and understandable information about how they need to act.

—Jeffrey Pfeffer and Robert Sutton

When both the creation of assessments and the evaluation of student work are the result of collaborative processes, teachers and school leaders can quickly evaluate the effec-tiveness of strategies, make mid-course corrections, express some new hypotheses about what actions they might take to improve student learning, and within days or weeks, have additional evidence with which the new hypotheses can be tested. Their model of teaching professionalism is . . . a commitment to a continuous cycle of "try it, test it, improve it."

—Doug Reeves

Consider, once again, the origins of public education in the United States. If elementary schools were created to sort and select students ac-cording to their aptitude, to sift the "boy of best genius" from the rubble each year, and if high schools were created to classify and then edu-cate students according to "differences among children as to aptitudes, interests, economic resources, and prospective careers" (National Education Association, cited in Lazerson & Grubb, 1974), then educators needed tools to assist them in the sorting and classifying process. Assessments of various forms became the instruments for addressing that need.

One of the first formal assessments specifically designed for this rating and ranking was the intelligence quotient, or IQ test, which was based on the premise that intelligence is a function of innate ability, something a student is born with, not something he or she acquires. When IQ tests were administered to hundreds of thousands of American soldiers as the United States entered World War I, the results suggested that the average mental age of Americans was 14. Based on this finding, many concluded that most Americans were uneducable beyond high school. This led concerned university presidents to seek an assessment instrument to establish which students had the aptitude for higher education. James Conant of Harvard University was one of those presidents, and he assigned one of his deans, Henry Chauncey, to find a test to identify students who had the natural ability to meet the academic challenges of college. Chauncey turned to Carl Brigham, a Princeton psychologist who had tweaked the intelligence test administered to army recruits to create a test purporting to determine the academic potential of students—the Scholastic Aptitude Test (SAT). Chauncey began using the test to select scholarship recipients for Harvard. Soon other universities began administering the test as well, and by the 1940s, it had become the basic admission test for hundreds of colleges. In 1948, Educational Testing Service was chartered, and Chauncey became its president ("Secrets," 2007).

Chauncey was very explicit in his goal: He hoped to create a new meritocracy by using SAT scores to categorize, sort, and route students to their roles in society (Lemann, 2000). Ironically, Brigham, the author of the SAT test, came to debunk the entire concept of an "aptitude test." He concluded the movement to test for intelligence or aptitude was based on "one of the most glorious fallacies in the history of science, namely that the tests measured native intelligence purely and simply without regard to training or schooling. The test scores very definitely are a composite including schooling, family background, familiarity with English and everything else" (in Pacenza, 2007).

Educators have not, however, relied solely on commercial assessments to facilitate the sorting and selecting process. They have been willing accomplices in and contributors to the process of ranking and labeling students and have used their own varied classroom assessments to help achieve that objective. Elementary schools might create groups of bluebirds, redbirds, robins, sparrows, and crows, while high schools might create honors, accelerated, regular, modified, and remedial groups; but, both have operated under the assumption that high achievement is limited to a select number of students who have won the genetic lottery and therefore possess the innate aptitude to learn at high levels. A student entering a school system in kindergarten and remaining in the system for 13 years would graduate with a number certifying his or her rank—for example, number 112 in a class of 181. Placement of one student above another is often determined by a hundredth of a percentage point. This very precise ranking is, of course, based on the disjointed and dissimilar criteria used by dozens of teachers who are not required, expected, or even encouraged to come to a common understanding of how students should be assessed, the rigor of their classroom assessments, the criteria to be used in determining the quality of student work, or the factors to be used in deciding student grades. Hundreds of subjective judgments by disconnected teachers contribute to the establishment of a final class rank that is then presented under the pretext of objectivity.

If the fundamental purpose of schooling is to sort and select students, using assessments in this way makes sense because this assessment *practice* aligns with the *purpose* of the enterprise—sorting and selecting. If, however, a school or district hopes to operate as a professional learning community, it embraces a very different purpose of schooling—high levels of learning for *all* students—and it *must* use assessments in a very different way to align with that purpose.

Summative Versus Formative Assessment

One of the most promising developments in contemporary education is a new and deeper understanding of the potential of assessment to be a powerful tool for informing and improving the teaching and learning process. Educators today are more attuned to the distinction between summative and formative assessment. They understand a summative assessment is an assessment *of* learning, a tool to answer the question, "Did the student learn by the deadline?" with a "yes" or "no," "pass" or "fail," "proficient" or "not proficient."

They have learned a formative assessment is an assessment *for* learning, a tool used to inform both the teacher and the student about the student's current level of achievement, to guide the teacher's instructional practice, to help the student understand what steps must be taken to further his or her learning, and to motivate the student to take those steps (Wiliam & Thompson, 2007). They have been told that while a summative assessment is designed for accountability, a formative assessment supports learning (Stiggins, 2007) because the evidence from the assessment is used to adapt teaching strategies to meet student needs (Black & Wiliam, 1998). Doug Reeves' vivid analogy (2000)—a formative test is to a summative test as a physical examination is to an autopsy—has helped educators sharpen the distinction between these two very different types of assessment.

Most educators understand that the high-stakes state and provincial tests taken by their students are summative assessments, and while these tests may attempt to hold schools (and sometimes students) accountable for learning, they do very little to inform or improve professional practice. Invariably, state and provincial tests assess too many skills and concepts infrequently rather than a few essential skills and concepts often. Teachers typically wait months to get the results instead of receiving timely feedback regarding student learning, and the results are often reported in general terms rather than with precise information about the strengths and weaknesses of individual students.

There is abundant evidence that an emphasis on such summative or "end-of-process" measures without formative or "in-process" feedback on what is working and what is not creates stress and frustration for people throughout an organization but does little to build capacity to improve upon the results (Pfeffer & Sutton, 2000). When we share this research finding with educators, they nod knowingly and chant, "Amen!" They recognize from experience that the high-stakes summative tests administered by their states and provinces are not very helpful in improving their classroom instruction.

Educators are less likely to recognize, however, that the assessments they create for their individual classrooms are almost always summative assessments as well, assessments of learning rather than assessments for learning, autopsies rather than physical examinations. How have teachers at all levels typically created and used their classroom assessments? An individual teacher works in isolation to create the test for his or her students, administers the test, grades the results for each student, records the score in the grade book, returns the test to the students, and reviews the answers with them. The class then moves on to the new content of the next unit, despite the fact that some students were unable to demonstrate proficiency on the skills and concepts just assessed. This failure to learn is irrelevant for teachers and students alike because the test has signaled the unit is *over*—regardless of whether or not all students learned. Analysis of the test results may help a teacher understand why the students failed on an assessment in the same way the results of an autopsy can shed light on the cause of death. If, however, the results from the test have merely been certified and recorded without any effort to diagnose the problem and prescribe an antidote to help students who are struggling, the test is as beneficial to the teaching and learning process as the results of an autopsy are to the cadaver.

Continuing to use assessments for the sole or primary purpose of rating student learning at the end of a unit or course fails to take advantage of one of the most powerful tools available for promoting the learning of both students and adults. Formative assessment has tremendous potential to improve rather than merely rate and record student learning, and it is imperative that educators begin to tap into that potential. Consider the following:

> There is strong and rigorous evidence that improving formative assessment can raise standards of pupils' performance. There have been few initiatives in education with such a strong body of evidence to support a claim to raise standards. (Black & Wiliam, 2004, p. 20)

> Assessment for learning . . . when done well, is one of the most powerful, high-leverage strategies for improving student learning that we know of. Educators collectively at the district and school levels become more skilled and focused at assessing, disaggregating, and using student achievement as a tool for ongoing improvement. (Fullan, 2004, p. 71)

> Assessment for learning rivals one-on-one tutoring in its effectiveness and . . . particularly benefits low-achieving students. (Stiggins, 2004, p. 27)

> Formative assessments are one of the most powerful weapons in a teacher's arsenal. An effective standards-based, formative assessment program can help to dramatically enhance student achievement throughout the K–12 system. (Marzano, 2006, back cover)

But if educators are to realize the potential of this powerful tool for learning, they must come to a clearer understanding of formative assessment and the different forms it might take.

Formative Assessment in the Classroom

One of the most consistent findings from the research on effective schools and effective teaching is the power of frequent monitoring of student learning. Good teachers are assessing *all* the time, using a variety of strategies to check for student understanding during every class period. They then use the information to provide specific and precise feedback to students and to adjust their teaching. In this sense, the ongoing, minute-by-minute assessments teachers use in their classrooms each day represent an important example of assessment for learning. The work of Rick Stiggins has been particularly powerful in helping teachers understand the significance of ongoing classroom assessment and the importance of engaging the individual student in the process of monitoring his or her own learning. Stiggins (2002) contends teachers can use assessment to "advance and not merely check on student learning" by doing the following (pp. 761–762):

- Understanding and articulating *in advance of teaching* the achievement targets that their students are to hit

- Informing their students about those learning goals, *in terms that students understand*, from the very beginning of the teaching and learning process

- Becoming assessment literate and thus able to transform their expectations into assessment exercises and scoring procedures that *accurately reflect student achievement*

- Using classroom assessments to *build students' confidence* in themselves as learners and help them take responsibility for their own learning, so as to lay a foundation for lifelong learning

- Translating classroom assessment results into frequent *descriptive feedback* (versus judgmental feedback) for students, providing them with specific insights on how to improve

- Continuously *adjusting instruction* based on the results of classroom assessments

- Engaging students in *regular self-assessment*, with standards held constant so that students can watch themselves grow over time and feel in charge of their own success

- Actively involving students in *communicating* with their teachers and their families about their achievement status and improvement.

Dylan Wiliam and Marnie Thompson (2007) have also examined the power of formative classroom assessment. They offer their own five key strategies teachers should use to support formative assessment in their classrooms:

1. Clarify and share learning intentions and criteria for success. Make clear to students what they should know and be able to do and the criteria they should use to assess the quality of their work until it meets the intended standard.

2. Engineer effective classroom discussions, questions, and learning tasks.

3. Provide specific feedback that moves learners forward.

4. Activate students as instructional resources for one another. Train students to help each other assess and improve their work according to the criteria for success.

5. Activate students as the owners of their own learning. Ensure students have a clear understanding of what they are to learn and what "good" work looks like, so they will be able to monitor their own progress and identify the steps they must take to move forward, rather than relying solely on the judgment of the teacher.

Of course, at some point, every teacher goes beyond daily checks for understanding and makes use of a more formal assessment of student learning. Results from these assessments may be used in a variety of ways. Most often, these assessments do not serve a formative purpose, but are merely given to monitor the learning of students and to assign a grade. Conscientious teachers may analyze the results of their formal assessments in an effort to identify areas where students may be experiencing difficulty; however, even this analysis does not ensure the assessment is formative. Wiliam and Thompson (2007) offer the following helpful distinctions:

> An assessment *monitors* learning to the extent that it provides information about whether the student, class, school or system is learning or not; it is *diagnostic* to the extent that it provides information about what is going wrong; and it is *formative* to the extent that it provides information about what to do about it. (p. 62)

For example, Rick taught Becky to play tennis. He carefully monitored her progress and offered suggestions and encouragement. At one point, he was able to provide her with very specific feedback regarding one element of her game that was impeding her progress and preventing her from learning how to play at a proficient level. He could show her that 88% of her unforced errors had come from her backhand, and that on more than 90% of those errors, she had hit the ball into the net. This was excellent *diagnostic* feedback—precise, accurate, and based on solid data. What he could not do was actually teach her how to hit a better backhand. He could make her aware of the problem, but he was clueless as to how to resolve it other than by hitting her thousands of backhands and having her repeat the error of her stroke over and over. Becky then took a single lesson from a tennis professional who suggested she abandon the one-handed backhand Rick had tried to teach her (the only strategy he knew), and instead use a two-handed backhand. In 15 minutes Becky was cracking backhands with authority. Rick monitored and diagnosed, but it was the tennis professional who gave Becky *formative* feedback, providing her with specific and precise information regarding how to achieve the intended outcome.

This same scenario is played out in schools on a regular basis. Individual teachers create an assessment to monitor student learning.

Often they merely record the results and move on to new content, making it a summative assessment. Sometimes, however, they use the assessment to diagnose the problem, to identify where the students are experiencing difficulty. If, however, they have already used all of their available instructional strategies to teach the concept or skill, and they do not know what else to try, the assessment will not be formative. To be formative, the teacher and/or student must know how to resolve the problem that is impeding the student's learning. If, however, teachers work together to create *common* assessments to administer to all of their students, those assessments are more likely to be formative because a team of teachers is in a better position to identify strategies to resolve difficulties in student learning than a teacher who is working alone.

Common Formative Assessments

Imagine a different approach to assessment—an approach that brings teams of teachers together to create and use formative assessment across their classrooms. Instead of an individual teacher developing and administering a summative test at the end of a unit, a collaborative team of teachers responsible for the same course or grade level creates a *common* formative assessment before teaching a unit. Members of the team agree on the standard students must achieve to be deemed proficient and establish when they will give the assessment. They discuss different ways to help students understand what they must learn; different ways to teach the essential skills, concepts, and strategies; and different ways to check for student understanding in their individual classrooms throughout the unit. On each day of instruction, teachers benefit from having complete clarity regarding what students must learn and an understanding of how students will be called upon to demonstrate their learning. Immediately after administering the assessment, the team analyzes the results. If those results indicate an individual teacher's students are having difficulty with a concept, other members of the team can offer alternative strategies to teach the concept, thereby helping each other expand their repertoire of teaching techniques and skills. This team dialogue and sharing of ideas means the assessment is far more likely to be formative ("This is how we can solve the problem") rather than merely diagnostic ("This is the problem students are experiencing"). If, as we illustrated in the previous chapter, the team discovers none of its members are able to help students learn an important concept, the team can then turn its attention to the very specific professional development and adult learning that will help resolve the difficulty.

Once again, while effective, ongoing, minute-by-minute assessment by individual classroom teachers is essential to good teaching, frequent common formative assessments created by teams of teachers also play a vital role in monitoring student learning. After studying schools that were most effective in helping all students learn, Doug Reeves (2006) concluded, "Common formative assessments are essential for all schools" (p. ix). He is not alone in reaching that conclusion. Once again, educators are hearing very consistent advice:

- Evidence from numerous schools, as well as broad concurrence of the research community, point to proven structures and practices that make an immediate difference in achievement. They begin when a group of teachers meets regularly as a team to identify essential and valued learning, develop common formative assessments, analyze current levels of achievement, set achievement goals, and then share and create lessons and strategies to improve upon those results. (Schmoker, 2004b, pp. 48–49)

- To the extent that teachers work together in teams to 1) analyze, understand and deconstruct standards, 2) transform standards into high quality classroom assessments, and 3) share and interpret the results together, they benefit from the union of their wisdom about how to help students continue to grow as learners. (Stiggins, 2005, p. 82)

- Common formative assessments [provide] regular and timely feedback regarding student attainment of the most critical standards . . . [and] also foster consistent expectations and priorities within a grade level, course, and department regarding standards, instruction, and assessment. . . . Most importantly, common formative assessment results enable educators to diagnose student learning needs accurately *in time to make instructional modifications.* In addition, common formative assessments provide students with timely feedback regarding their current level of understanding so that they can identify for themselves what they already know and what they have yet to learn. (Ainsworth, 2007, pp. 95-96)

- This team effort [to develop common formative assessments] does more than produce great assessments. It provides teachers with interdependent support for one another. . . .The group process—organized properly—provides a safe and restorative place for the sharing of best practices, for requesting professional help or advice, and for creating a sense of community that cannot help but carry over into the classroom to positively impact student learning. (Ainsworth & Viegut, 2006, p. 39)

- Collaborative assessment holds high promise for promoting genuine change in how teachers regard student work and use that assessment for learning. When teachers work together to establish criteria for judging their students' work, set standards, and make group decisions, the collaboration has many spin-offs. . . . They tend to enhance one another's understanding of instruction and curriculum, develop agreement about

> the nature and quality of the instruments and approaches for assessing their students' work, challenge and question their own expectations for students, and develop more confidence in their decisions and in their accountability to the outside community. (Earl & LeMahieu, 1997, p. 166)

Wiliam and Thompson (2007) offer several reasons to support their contention that formative assessments created by collaborative teams (or *teacher learning communities*, the term they use) offer the largest gains in student learning.

First, it takes strong subject matter expertise to create powerful assessments, to identify the specific problems students are experiencing based on the results, and to generate solutions to those problems. Teachers working collectively are more likely to possess that expertise than teachers working in isolation.

Second, the fact that evidence of student learning is gathered by the team from within the school eliminates the familiar lament, "That may work in those schools, but it won't work for our kids." The real-life stories and testimonials of peers typically carry more weight with teachers than a researcher's findings. So when they see compelling evidence of students taught by their colleagues who are achieving at higher levels, they are more motivated to investigate alternative instructional strategies.

Third, there is discomfort involved in implementing new strategies, and teachers are more likely to assume those risks if they have the support of their collaborative team. Teachers repeatedly reported the commitments they had made to teammates kept them moving forward with implementation of new strategies.

Fourth, when teachers develop common formative assessments they are engaged in the most powerful form of professional development—learning that is job-embedded and sustained over time rather than episodic and fleeting.

Fifth, common formative assessments help educators make the transition from a focus on teaching to a focus on learning. They begin to think in terms of "What learning should result from this unit?" and "How will students demonstrate their learning?" rather than focusing on the series of activities they will orchestrate as part of the instructional process.

The fourth and fifth points are particularly important in promoting PLCs. We have argued that the biggest big idea of a PLC is a shift from a focus on teaching to a focus on learning, and that when collaborative teams of teachers work together to clarify what students must learn and how they will demonstrate their learning, they are engaged in powerful professional development that facilitates that shift. Effective teachers know exactly what their students should know and be able to do as a result of the learning experience. They also know exactly how their students will be called upon to demonstrate their learning (Brophy, 2004; Marzano, 2007; Popham, 2001a; Saphier, Haley-Speca, & Gower, 2008). This clarity benefits teachers and students alike. Schools that create systems to ensure teachers work together, prior to teaching a unit, to clarify essential outcomes and to identify the specific strategies and instruments to be used in monitoring student learning, increase the likelihood of more effective teaching in more classrooms.

We offer our own arguments as to why assessments created by a team of teachers should be included in every school's process for monitoring student learning.

Team-Developed Common Assessments Are More Efficient

If five teachers teaching the same course or grade level are responsible for ensuring all students acquire the same knowledge and skills, it makes sense those teachers would work together to determine the best methods to assess student learning. A team of teachers could divide responsibilities for creating a unit and developing assessments. Teachers working in isolation replicate and duplicate effort. They work hard, but they do not work smart.

Team-Developed Common Assessments Promote Equity

The use of common assessments increases the likelihood that students will have access to the same curriculum, acquire the same essential knowledge and skills, take assessments of the same rigor, and have their work judged according to the same criteria. We have witnessed repeated examples of teachers who were *emphatic* about the need for consistency, equity, and fairness in terms of how they were dealt with as adults, but were completely unconcerned about the inconsistency, inequity, and lack of fairness that characterized the assessment of student learning in their school. If every teacher has license to assess whatever and however he or she wishes, according to criteria unique to and often known only by that teacher, schools will never be institutions that truly model a commitment to equity.

Team-Developed Common Formative Assessments Help Monitor and Improve Student Learning

We have cited several researchers who have concluded that team-developed common formative assessments are one of the most powerful strategies available to educators for improving student achievement.

Team-Developed Common Formative Assessments Can Inform and Improve the Practice of Both Individual Teachers and Teams of Teachers

Teachers do not suffer from a lack of data. Virtually every time a teacher gives an assessment of any kind, the teacher is able to generate data—mean, mode, median, standard deviation, percentage failing, percentage passing, and so on. As Robert Waterman (1987) advised, however, data alone do not inform practice. Data cannot help educators identify the strengths and weaknesses of their strategies. Data inform only when they are presented in context, which almost always requires *a basis of comparison.*

Most educators can teach for their entire careers and not know if they teach a particular concept more or less effectively than the teacher next door because the assessments they generate for their isolated classrooms never provide them with a basis of comparison. Most educators can assess their students year after year, get consistently low results in a particular area, and not be certain if those results reflect their teaching strategies, a weakness in the curriculum, a failure on the part of teachers in earlier grades to ensure students develop prerequisite skills, or any other cause. In short, most educators operate within the confines of data, which means they operate in the dark. But in a PLC, collaborative teams create a series of *common* assessments, and therefore every teacher receives ongoing feedback regarding the proficiency of his or her students in achieving a standard the team has agreed is essential, on an assessment the team has agreed represents a valid way to assess what members intend for all students to learn, *in comparison to other students attempting to achieve the same standard.* That basis of comparison transforms data into information.

Furthermore, as Richard Elmore (2006) wrote, "Teachers have to feel that there is some compelling reason for them to practice differently, with the best direct evidence being that students learn better" (p. 38). When teachers are presented with clear evidence their students are not becoming proficient in skills they agreed were essential, as measured on an assessment they helped to create, and that similar students taught by their colleagues have demonstrated proficiency on the same assessment, they are open to exploring new practices. When the performance of their students consistently prevents their team from achieving its goals, they are typically willing to address the problem. In fact, we consider team-developed common formative assessments one of the most powerful motivators for stimulating teachers to consider changes in their practice. As Fullan (2008) has concluded, this openness or "transparency," when correctly implemented, is a powerful tool for change because it creates the positive pressure essential to improvement efforts.

If every teacher in North America received this information on a regular and timely basis, *and* had the ongoing support of his or her colleagues through the collaborative team process, our schools would experience gains in student achievement. It has been said that gathering data is the beginning of wisdom, but sharing data is the beginning of community. When data are easily accessible and openly shared among members of a collaborative team, schools foster a professional learning *community*.

Team-Developed Common Formative Assessments Can Build the Capacity of the Team to Achieve at Higher Levels

As Wiliam and Thompson (2007) found, the conversations surrounding the creation of formative assessments are a powerful tool for professional development. When schools ensure every teacher has been engaged in a process to clarify what students are to learn and how their learning will be assessed, they promote the clarity essential to effective teaching. When teachers have access to each other's ideas, methods, and materials, they can expand their repertoire of skills. When a team discovers the current curriculum and their existing instructional strategies are ineffective in helping students acquire essential skills, its members are able to pursue the most powerful professional development because it is specific, job-embedded, and relevant to the context of their content, their strategies, their team, and their students. Very importantly, when a team works together to create assessments to answer the question, "How will we know our students are learning?" members are developing their own assessment literacy. Schools can raise student achievement if teachers become more skillful in the use of assessment. Our friend and colleague Cassie Erkens, who has helped educators across North America enhance their assessment skills, has found a team's collective inquiry and collaborative dialogue regarding what constitutes a valid assessment to be extremely effective in helping build those skills.

Team-Developed Common Formative Assessments Are Essential to Systematic Interventions When Students Do Not Learn

We argue that if educators were truly committed to high levels of learning for all students, they would not leave the question, "What happens when some students do not learn?" to chance. They would instead work together to create systems of interventions to ensure any student who struggles receives additional time and support for learning in a timely and directive way. Team-developed common formative assessments are a critical element of that system of intervention. We will elaborate on this point in chapter 10.

Not every assessment should be a common assessment. There is still a place for individual teachers to create their own formal assessments. Team-developed common assessments will never eliminate the need for individual teachers to monitor student learning each day through a wide variety of strategies that check for understanding. But if schools are ever to take full advantage of the power of assessment to impact student learning in a positive way, they must include common formative assessments in their arsenal. Professional learning communities will make team-developed common formative assessments a cornerstone of their work.

Creating and Using Common Formative Assessments

But schools must be certain the assessments created by teams are assessments *for* learning rather than assessments *of* learning. The fact that a collaborative team creates an assessment certainly does not make it formative. Teams regularly create series of summative assessments. The frequency of these assessments will not make them formative. Weekly assessments are summative if all teachers do is record the grades and move on. The questions that appear on a test or when the test is administered will not determine if it is formative. It is what happens *after* students are assessed that makes a test or project formative. We contend that three things must happen to make an assessment formative:

1. The assessment is used to identify students who are experiencing difficulty in their learning.

2. A system of intervention is in place to ensure students experiencing difficulty devote additional time to and receive additional support for their learning.

3. Those students are provided with another opportunity to demonstrate their learning and are not penalized for their earlier difficulty.

These criteria might be applied differently depending on the nature of the assignment. For example, a seventh-grade team of teachers is helping students learn to write a persuasive essay. The team agrees on the elements of an effective essay, creates a rubric for evaluating the writing, and gathers anchor papers to illustrate the progression of an essay from unsatisfactory to exemplary. Teachers share this information with their students and help them learn to apply the rubric to several examples of writing. The team then assigns students to write a draft of a persuasive essay. Teachers ask students to review each other's writing according to the criteria they have learned and then offer feedback to a classmate. Teachers then collect the revised drafts, but do not assign a grade. Instead, each teacher reviews the writing of his or her students and offers specific and precise written advice on each paper regarding what the author can do to improve the writing. One teacher discovers her students consistently struggle with writing an effective thesis statement and solicits ideas from her colleagues on effective ways to help students learn the skill. She focuses on that skill while teaching the next few lessons, and implements the suggestions of her colleagues. All students are directed to create another revised draft that incorporates the feedback they received on their first attempt. This process of feedback and revision for individual students continues until each student demonstrates proficiency. Ultimately, students come to understand the adage "There is no such thing as good writing, only good rewriting," and they become confident in their ability to write.

In another scenario, a freshman algebra team creates a common formative assessment to be administered at the conclusion of the 3-week unit they are about to teach. When the team analyzes the results from that assessment, they discover students are having difficulty with one skill, and they explore new strategies for teaching that skill in the next unit. They also discover, however, that 12 of their 100 students are floundering in algebra and have failed the test. The students remain in the algebra class each day and continue with new direct instruction, but they are also required to receive additional, focused instruction on the specific skills they have not yet mastered in the tutorial center during each school day. They work with adult and student tutors in small groups, complete additional problems, and get ongoing and precise feedback. After 2 weeks of this intensive tutoring, they are required to take another version of the earlier assessment to demonstrate they have become proficient. Some earn Cs and Bs on this assessment, and these new grades replace their earlier failing grades. Those who are still not proficient are required to continue with the tutorial sessions.

We contend both of these scenarios represent formative assessment. Black, Harrison, Lee, Marshall, and Wiliam (2004) advise an assessment activity can be an assessment for learning and thereby enhance student achievement "if it provides information that teachers and their students can use as feedback in assessing themselves and one another and in modifying the teaching and learning activities in which they are engaged. Such assessment becomes 'formative assessment' when the evidence is actually used to adapt the teaching work to meet learning needs" (p. 10).

In each of the scenarios we described, the assessment helps to identify students experiencing difficulty. These students are given specific feedback, and they are encouraged, and, in fact, required to keep working until they achieve the standard. They are not penalized because of their initial difficulty. The message their school sends them is, "All of you can and will acquire this essential skill, and we will continue to support your learning until you are successful." This is very different from the message attached to assessments in traditional schools: "This unit is over regardless of how you performed." Teachers in both scenarios also use the information from the assessments to give direction to their next instructional topics and strategies. The assessments inform and shape their practice, and therefore, we contend, are formative.

Our position has been challenged in several ways. Some have argued students should not be given a second opportunity to learn, or, at the very least, their initial failure should be included in calculating the grade. They claim it would be unfair to allow low-performing students the opportunity to earn a grade similar to those of students who were proficient on the initial assessment. Our response is that every school mission statement we have read asserts the school is committed to helping *all students learn*. We have yet to find a mission statement that says, "They must all learn fast or the first time we teach it." If some students must work longer and harder to succeed, but they become proficient, their grade should reflect their ultimate proficiency, not their early difficulty.

We are then often challenged to clarify how we would respond to students who demonstrate proficiency, and then ask to keep working and striving so they can be given another opportunity to demonstrate they have learned at higher levels and thus improve their grade. We find the question puzzling. Any school committed to high levels of learning for all students would encourage rather than impede students who are determined to continue learning, and grading practices should promote that extra effort by supporting students who hope to move from proficient to advanced learning.

There are those who argue that an assessment can neither be formative nor an assessment for learning if any grade is given. We do not subscribe to that position. We have found in the real world of schools, some assessments in some subject areas are, in fact, tests rather than projects or papers. If educators give those tests to monitor student learning, and then advise students that performance on the test has no impact or bearing, those educators often will get less than the best effort of many students. This, in turn, calls the validity of the results into question. We contend common formative assessments are used for important reasons—to inform teacher practice and respond to students who are not learning—and, therefore, educators have a legitimate reason to create conditions that promote the best efforts of their students on those assessments. If, however, the assessments are truly *for* learning, students who struggle should receive additional time and support *and* should be provided another opportunity to demonstrate learning without an adverse effect on their grade.

Building Shared Knowledge of Quality Assessments

Recently, we worked with a state department of education, encouraging it to promote frequent common formative assessments developed by collaborative teams of teachers as a key element of its initiative to improve student learning. A senior member of the state department responded that teachers are incapable of writing quality assessments, so if the state commits to the use of common formative assessments, the department of education would need to contract with a private company to write the assessments. We were stunned by this comment that teachers cannot be trusted to create valid assessments, and we immediately asked this question: If teachers cannot be trusted to work together to create assessments, then why are they trusted to create their own in their individual classrooms?

Imagine the following scenario: A parent in that state brings a lawsuit against his child's school because the child failed a course (or was retained in elementary school, denied a high school diploma, did not meet a graduation requirement, and so on—the possibilities are endless). The suit argues the adverse consequence suffered by the student was the result of the subjective judgment of the classroom teacher who based her decision on the varied assessments she created and administered throughout the year. The parent argues the punishment is unwarranted because teachers are incapable of creating fair and accurate assessments of student learning. Thus, punishing his child on the basis of those assessments is arbitrary and capricious. The parent calls as a star witness this senior member of the state department and asks him to testify in court what he has already publicly stated: Teachers cannot be trusted to create valid assessments.

Here is the hard fact: If teachers do not work together to create assessments, then individual teachers create their own. Which assessment is likely to be of higher quality—one written by a teacher working in isolation or one developed by a team working together to clarify what students must know and be able to do, studying and discussing the best strategies for gathering evidence of student learning, developing common criteria for judging the quality of student work, and critiquing, challenging, and expanding upon one another's suggestions for assessing their students? We are convinced that the first attempt at a common formal assessment by a collaborative team of teachers who make a collective effort to gather evidence of their students' learning will be superior to the formal assessments those same teachers have developed working in isolation. We are also convinced this process of building common assessments is far more likely to enhance the assessment literacy of teachers over time than the process of each teacher developing his or her own formal assessments.

Of course teachers in a PLC should attempt to build shared knowledge about effective assessment strategies. They would seek the advice and insights of some of the nation's leading experts in the field. For example, *Ahead of the Curve: The Power of Assessment to Transform Teaching and Learning* (2007), edited by Douglas Reeves, offers excellent information from leaders in the field of assessment. W. James Popham (2001a) suggests his third edition of *Classroom Assessment: What Teachers Need to Know* and Rick Stiggins' (2001) third edition of *Student-Involved Classroom Assessment* as examples of helpful texts that provide teachers with everything they need to develop better assessments.

There are certainly general principles regarding good assessments teachers should consider when they seek evidence of student learning. These principles include the following:

1. It is better to assess a few essential skills of undisputed importance frequently than many skills infrequently (Popham, 2001; Reeves, 2002).

2. Teachers must be able to have a clear, concise picture of what students must know and be able to do in order to write a good assessment, and they must be able to explain the intended learning to students in terms the students can understand (Stiggins, 2007; Wiliam & Thompson, 2007).

3. Assessments should be balanced, providing a wide variety of opportunities for students to demonstrate learning in different ways (National Education Association, 2005). Any single assessment tool is inherently flawed, and therefore different strategies should be used to gather evidence of students' acquisition of essential knowledge and skills. Popham (2001a) makes the point succinctly: "Assessment diversity is dandy; one-type testing is troubling" (p. 117).

4. Assessments should be authentic when possible. According to Perkins (1992), authentic assessments have the following characteristics:

    •   They are open-ended rather than one-right-answer problems.

    •   They are not solvable by applying a routine method.

    •   They require substantive understanding of meaning.

    •   They demand more time than conventional problems.

    •   They call for pulling together a number of different ideas from the subject matter and often involve writing or oral explanation as well as formal manipulations such as computation.

5. Teams should use other assessments as external validators of the rigor and relevance of their own assessments. They should align their classroom assessments with state standards and be able to establish a strong correlation between success on their assessments and other high-stakes tests their students will be required to take (National Education Association, 2007).

6. Assessments should be useful to both teachers and students (Black, Harrison, Lee, Marshall, & Wiliam, 2004; Popham, 2001a; Stiggins, 2007).

7. Assessments should help students clarify the discrepancy between their level of achievement and the intended standard of learning, and offer direction and encouragement as to what steps students can take to close the gap (Stiggins, 2007). There is abundant evidence that monitoring learning and providing feedback to students can either encourage or discourage continued student effort. Black, Harrison, Lee, Marshall, and Wiliam (2004, p. 18) reported the following:

    • A comprehensive review of research studies of feedback found that feedback improved performance in 60% of the studies. In the cases where feedback was not helpful, the feedback turned out to be merely a judgment or grade with no indication of how to improve.

    • Students who are told that feedback "will help you learn" learn more than those who are told that "how you do tells us how smart you are and what grades you'll get." The difference is greatest for low achievers. . . .

    • In a competitive system, low achievers attribute their performance to lack of ability; high achievers, to their effort. In a task-oriented system, all attribute performance to effort, and learning is improved, particularly among low achievers.

Jere Brophy (2004), who has examined the issue of student motivation as much as anyone in North America, advises teachers to "*emphasize the role of assessment in providing informative feedback about progress*. . . Portray tests as opportunities to find out how 'we' are doing. . . . Express confidence that students will succeed if they apply themselves to lessons and learning activities. Portray yourself as a helper and resource person who assists your students in preparing for assessments, not as a remote evaluator" (p. 79).

Teachers should examine, review, discuss, and apply these indicators of effectiveness when creating their common formative assessments. In the final analysis, however, we agree with Popham (2001a), who concluded that classroom assessment is not rocket science, that what educators need to know about assessment is quite straightforward rather than mysterious or esoteric, and that reading a good introductory text on assessment for a night or two will provide an educator with everything he or she really needs to know about the topic. We also concur with Doug Reeves who argues the goal is not to turn teachers into psychometricians and statisticians, but rather to help them gather useful information regarding student learning so they can adjust their instruction and ensure individual students benefit from systematic interventions. As Reeves (2007) writes, "Practical utility takes precedence over psychometric perfection" (p. 235).

Finally, we agree with Pfeffer and Sutton (2000) who found that the deepest and most meaningful learning occurs when people *do* the work rather than train to do the work or plan to do the work. This learning by doing is enhanced when it occurs within the collective and social interaction of a team as opposed to when it occurs in isolation (Fullan, 2001). Rick Stiggins (1999) got it right when he concluded the best strategy for enhancing the assessment literacy of teachers is to have a team of colleagues study the topic together, immediately apply their new knowledge in their classrooms, and then share their experience with colleagues. As he wrote, "This strategy is affordable, effective, and essential if we seek to create more effective schools. . . . The result will be greater academic success" (p. 198).

So the state official who claimed that teachers could not be trusted to create common formative assessments was exactly wrong. Assessment, when done well, represents one of the most powerful weapons in an educator's arsenal for enhancing professional practice and improving student learning. Leaving the issue of assessment to commercial testing companies, the central office, or textbook publishers deprives classroom teachers of this powerful weapon and is akin to sending a soldier into battle unarmed. Common formative assessments created by collaborative teams represent the "best practice in assessment" (Reeves, 2004, p. 71) and the "gold standard in educational accountability" (p. 114). No district or school should allow educators to abdicate their responsibility to utilize this important resource for student and adult learning. A district that is serious about developing its collective capacity to improve student achievement would be tight on ensuring common formative assessments created by collaborative teams would be in place in all of its schools. The creation and analysis of those assessments are crucial to the collective inquiry, commitment to continuous improvement, and results orientation of a PLC.

Chapter 9 demonstrates the crucial importance of team-developed assessments to the PLC process through the power of a story Rick first published in *Ahead of the Curve: The Power of Assessment to Transform Teaching and Learning* (2007).

Chapter 9

A Tale of Excellence in Assessment

In the previous chapter, we examined the technical aspects of assessment in a professional learning community. In this chapter, we illustrate the potential power of effective assessment practices through the oldest teaching vehicle known to man—a story.

This story proposes a model of excellence in assessment in a PLC. The protagonist of the story is a high-school teacher, but the message applies equally and with little revision to middle and elementary schools as well. "Once Upon a Time: A Tale of Excellence in Assessment" first appeared as Rick's contribution to *Ahead of the Curve* (DuFour, 2007).

After 10 years as a high-school social studies teacher, Peter Miller was convinced that kids were kids and schools were schools. So when his wife suggested they move across the country to be closer to her family, he willingly agreed. He applied at several schools and was offered an interview at Russell Burnette High School.

The interview process at Burnette intrigued Peter. At every stage of the process, the selection committee stressed that the school had created a collaborative culture in which teachers worked together to help all students learn. Teacher teams had created a "guaranteed and viable curriculum" that specified the knowledge, skills, and dispositions all students were to acquire in each course. Peter was asked to review the "Essential Learnings" established by the U.S. history team and was struck by the fact that the curriculum stressed only 10 key concepts each semester, rather than the long list of discrete facts he had been expected to teach at his former school.

The selection committee also gave Peter copies of the curriculum pacing guide, the common assessment calendar, examples of preassessments for several units, examples of common assessments, and the rubrics for evaluating student essays and term papers—all of which had been created by the U.S. history team. The committee asked Peter to critique each document and to express his concerns as well as suggestions for improvement. Peter was impressed by the active role the other history teachers played in the interview process, and equally impressed that he had been required to spend a day at the school teaching prior to being offered the job. He gladly accepted the offer to join the staff at Burnette and looked forward to establishing himself in his new school. He had none of the trepidation and self-doubt that had characterized his first year as a teacher. He was a veteran who knew how schools worked.

The school year at Burnette began with 3 full days for teachers to work prior to students arriving on campus. Peter was delighted; he would have plenty of time to get his room ready and to prepare his first unit. His enthusiasm diminished when he learned that mornings were reserved for teachers to meet in their collaborative teams. Peter had had little use for the faculty and department meetings in his previous school, and he quietly resented that team meetings at Burnette would intrude upon his personal time at such a busy point in the school year.

The first U.S. history team meeting, however, was nothing like the meetings at Peter's old school. Each member of the team studied the school's results from both the state assessment and the national ACT exam in social studies. The team also reviewed an analysis of the very strong correlation between results on their common assessments with the results of the high-stakes state and national exams.

"We know we are on the right track," Ambrose, the team leader, observed. "If we can help every student be successful on our ongoing common assessments, we can be very confident they will be successful on state and national assessments as well. We can continue to assess students in other concepts we deem important, but we have an obligation to help our students be successful on the high-stakes tests they must take." The team devoted the remainder of the morning meeting to identifying the areas where students had experienced difficulty on the two external exams and brainstorming instructional, curricular, and assessment strategies to address those areas.

The second U.S. history team meeting was devoted to reviewing the results of the common assessment students had taken at the end of the first unit in the previous school year. The team had analyzed the results at the end of that unit, and now they reviewed their findings and their ideas for addressing the concepts and skills where students had performed least well. Peter was puzzled. The results looked quite good to him.

"I think you should congratulate yourselves," Peter told his teammates. "Why are you taking time to review this exam? I don't see any evidence here of serious problems in student learning."

"It's just what we do here," his teammate Miriam explained. "We are always looking to get better, and even on a test where students did well, there's always a concept or a few items where they do least well. If our team can identify effective strategies for addressing those areas, we can become even more effective and help more students achieve at higher levels every year."

It was evident that the team did not merely consider student performance on the overall test. Members had identified the specific skills and concepts students were to learn and had established the score a student must obtain on each to be deemed proficient. This shift of emphasis from general performance to skill-by-skill analysis helped Peter to see that on one area of the test, many students failed to demonstrate proficiency. The team spent the rest of the meeting reviewing each component of the test and offering ideas for teaching and assessing the concepts and skills of the unit. Ambrose asked Peter to develop test items for the unit and to present them to the team for possible inclusion in the common assessment.

The third team meeting was devoted to a discussion of the prerequisite knowledge students would need to be successful in the first unit and how the team would determine which students lacked that knowledge. The team had reviewed key terms and concepts recommended by the National Center for History in the Schools and the National Council for the Social Studies, had selected the terms they felt were most essential to their curriculum, and then had assigned the terms to different units of instruction. The key vocabulary terms for the first unit included:

assimilation	expansionism	neutrality
autonomy	federal	protective tariff
cartography	imperialism	republicanism
colonization	inalienable	salutary neglect
constitutionalism	mercantilism	sovereign
culture	monarchy	sphere of influence
dissent	nationalism	

Miriam explained to Peter that at the start of every unit, teachers administered a brief preassessment of those terms to their students. Because there were at least two sections of history taught each hour, and because the history classrooms were next to one another, teachers were able to divide students into two different groups based on their proficiency with the vocabulary.

"So in my case, students who lacked the prerequisite vocabulary went with Frank," Miriam explained. "He introduced key terms with brief explanations, then asked students to define the term in their own words in the section of their history notebook devoted to terms and concepts. He helped them create graphic organizers and put them into pairs to review the terms."

"Meanwhile," Frank said, "students who were already proficient went with Miriam. She presented them with a high-interest article on the major themes of the unit and then led a discussion of the article."

The team then reviewed examples of some of the graphic organizers students had used in the past and discussed different strategies for presenting key vocabulary in terms students could understand. They also discussed questions they could use to stimulate discussion of the article to be presented to the second group of students.

By the end of this third day of preparation, Peter was growing uneasy. He had always enjoyed virtually unfettered autonomy in his teaching. He had been free to teach what he wanted, when he wanted, how he wanted, and to assess students in whatever manner he saw fit. Now he was part of a team that made those decisions collectively. Peter was not convinced that all this teaming and collective decision-making was in the best interests of teachers or students. On the eve of his first day of classes, he was less confident of his ability to fit in at his new school, and he questioned whether he had made the right choice in accepting the position there.

At Last: The Familiar Territory of the Classroom

Once the students arrived, however, Peter felt far more comfortable. He discovered that he still enjoyed great autonomy in how he conducted his classroom and how he taught his content on a day-to-day basis. His concern that his instruction and daily pacing would be prescribed proved to be unfounded. His team had helped clarify what students were to learn in the unit, and he knew that each U.S. history teacher would present, review, and discuss those same essential learnings with students in the first few days of class. He also knew that all U.S. history students would take the team's common assessment on the same day at the end of the third week of class. In the meantime, however, Peter was free to make decisions each day regarding how to teach and how to check for student understanding.

Peter's team continued to meet for 1 hour each week. On Monday mornings, teachers reported to work 15 minutes earlier than usual, and the start of classes was delayed 30 minutes in order to create this collaborative time. Teachers were then allowed to leave 15 minutes earlier than usual on Mondays, so they were not required to work longer hours or to sacrifice personal time in order to collaborate with their colleagues.

The first few minutes of each meeting were spent debriefing members of the team on how they felt the unit was going. Members were encouraged to express any concerns. The team then turned its attention to the five-point rubric that had been created to score student responses to essay questions. Members reviewed the criteria they had established for assessing the quality of student essays and then examined different anchor essays that reflected each score. At subsequent meetings, they individually scored the same student essay and then shared their conclusions.

"We're willing to accept a difference of one point on the five-point scale," Ambrose explained, "but if two members present scores with a variance of more than one point, we'll discuss the variance, review our rubric and the anchor essays, and then determine an appropriate score." Peter was somewhat chagrined when he was the only team member whose score deviated from the rest of the team the first two times they practiced applying the rubric. His colleagues, however, were very supportive. They explained the thought process they used in scoring the sample and encouraged him to articulate his reasoning. The dialogue was helpful, and on the third attempt to review a sample essay, his score was consistent with his colleagues.

The ability to write a well-reasoned, persuasive essay that incorporated historical evidence was one of the essential outcomes all history students were expected to achieve. So Peter followed the lead of his teammates and taught his students the rubric to ensure they understood the criteria they should use in judging the quality of their own work. He devoted class time to reviewing the rubric with his students, providing them with sample essays from the past, and leading the class in scoring essays of different quality.

Peter had already discovered the importance of checking for student understanding on an ongoing basis. He felt he was proficient in using classroom questions and dialogues for that purpose. He directed questions to students randomly, rather than relying primarily upon volunteers. He extended wait time whenever students struggled and refused to let any student simply declare he or she did not know the answer. He would prod, rephrase, ask them to explain their thought process, and insist they clarify exactly what they did understand and exactly where they were confused. Students soon learned that a simple shrug would not suffice for Mr. Miller. They also learned that he rarely affirmed or corrected an answer immediately. Instead, he would provide more wait time and then direct a student's response to several other students for analysis and comment. He encouraged debate and insisted that students explain their thought process.

Peter did not limit his strategies for checking student understanding to questioning during class. He would typically begin each class by directing students to write in their notes, "At the end of today's class, I will be able to . . . " and asking them to explain how that day's lesson was linked to the essential learnings of the course. At the conclusion of the class he would pose a question, ask students to write a response in their notes, and quickly check each student's response to see if there was confusion. He frequently called upon students to identify similarities and differences between historical events and eras or to develop analogies between historical situations and contemporary events. He often presented a statement, challenged students to explain whether or not they agreed, and then used disagreements or confusion as an opportunity to clarify. He did not believe in giving homework every day, but when he did assign homework, he made a point of providing specific feedback to students. In short, Peter was confident his students were well-prepared when they took the team's first common assessment.

The First Common Assessment

The assessment was in two parts. The first section included multiple choice and matching items, while the second presented an essay question. Peter presented the results from the first part of the assessment to his department chairman and received two printouts the next day. The first showed how his students had performed on each skill and concept the team had assessed, compared to the performance of all the students who completed the assessment. The second printout presented an item analysis that compared the results of his students to all students on each item on the assessment.

The night before the next team meeting, Peter's wife asked how his classes were going. "Well, I'm generally pleased," Peter told her, "but on our common assessment, my students struggled with one concept—distinguishing between different forms of government. Their scores prevented our team from achieving its target for that concept." He grimaced. "I'm not looking forward to admitting that tomorrow." Privately, he hoped he would be able to avoid saying anything.

The next team meeting was a revelation to Peter. Although each teacher had received only the analysis for his or her own students compared to the total group, teachers were extremely open with their results. "My students obviously didn't get the concept of republicanism," Miriam said. "How did the rest of you teach that?" Various team members shared their strategies, then brought up the weak spots in their own students' performance.

Encouraged by their openness, Peter shared his concerns about his students' understanding of different forms of government. The team's response could not have been more positive. Frank and Miriam suggested instructional strategies. Ambrose offered a graphic organizer he had developed that had helped students use comparison and contrast to understand the concept. Skill by skill, concept by concept, the team reviewed student performance, identified whose students had excelled and whose students had struggled, and engaged in lively dialogue about strategies for teaching concepts more effectively.

The team then turned its attention to the item analysis and identified three items on the 30-item test that warranted review. The team quickly discovered that all three items assessed the same skill and that one of the items had been poorly written. They also discovered that the skill had been the last one taught in the unit. The team decided to rewrite the poorly written item and to change the pacing of the unit so members could devote more time to the skill prior to giving the next assessment.

Following the meeting, Peter asked Miriam, "What happens if we use all these strategies and student performance on that skill reaches proficiency?'"

"Why, we'll celebrate our success, of course," she said. "And then we'll look for the next items where students did less well. There will always be 'the lowest 10 percent' of items on any assessment we give. We attack those items, implement improvement strategies, celebrate our success, and then look for the next items. That is the beauty of continuous improvement. You never really arrive, but there is always a lot to celebrate."

Peter was perplexed by the team's policy regarding the essay portion of the assessment. Teachers were expected to provide specific feedback to each student regarding how he or she could improve the essay according to the team rubric, but they did not assign a specific grade to the essay. Students were then required to prepare a second draft of the essay that incorporated the recommendations before they would receive a grade.

"I don't understand the rationale behind this process," Peter said. "Why not grade the first essay and average the scores?"

"Well," Frank said, "we just don't think it's reasonable to assign a grade to skills students are attempting to use for the first time. We want our kids to have the benefit of specific feedback before we grade their efforts."

"We think giving feedback tells students that we expect them to achieve a standard," Miriam chimed in, "and that we'll ask them to re-fine and improve their work until they reach it. Later in the year, they won't have this chance, but for now, early in the learning process, we feel it's imperative that students benefit from practice and specific feedback before we assign grades to their work."

This feedback was part of a systematic structure to ensure learning. Shortly after the team administered the common assessment, teachers were required to complete progress reports sent to counselors, advisors, and parents. Students in danger of failing were required to report to the tutoring center, where they devoted extra time to their studies and received small-group and individualized tutoring—during the school day. Burnette High had created a schedule that ensured each student had one period available each day to receive this additional time and support for learning. Upperclassmen who did not require this interven-tion were given the privilege of unstructured time, while freshmen and sophomores were assigned to study halls.

Two weeks later, the students who had completed this first interven-tion were given another opportunity to demonstrate they had learned the key concepts of the previous unit by taking another form of the assessment. If they performed well, their failing grade was dropped and replaced with the higher grade for students. Miriam explained, "We say we want them all to learn; we don't say that we want them all to learn *fast* or the *first time*. If some students have to work harder and take lon-ger before they demonstrate proficiency, so be it. In the final analysis, if they demonstrate proficiency, we give them a grade that reflects that."

Peter was still a little skeptical. He thought that an opportunity to take a second assessment would cause students to "blow off" the first test. Afterwards, however, he had to admit that he was wrong. His juniors truly valued their unstructured time. They knew that poor performance on the first assessment would mean not only the loss of that privilege, but also an extra commitment of time and effort to learning what they should have learned in the first place. Peter could see no evidence that students were indifferent to the results of their first test. In fact, there was a palpable sense of academic press—a clear expectation that students must demonstrate they had actually acquired the essential knowledge and skills of the unit—that he had never before experienced.

Toto, I Don't Think We Are in Kansas Anymore

By the end of his first month at Burnette, Peter had come to realize this school was very different from those in which he had worked in the past. He had never experienced practices like working in teams, developing common assessments, aligning those assessments with state and national tests, using the results from previous assessments to guide instruction, identifying prerequisite knowledge for success in the unit, regrouping and sharing students, providing students with specific feedback rather than grades, providing systematic interventions when students were unsuccessful, and allowing students additional opportunities to demonstrate proficiency.

The difference in the use of assessments was one of the most striking contrasts between Peter's past practice and his new school environment. In his former school, individual teachers had either developed their own assessments or simply used the assessments provided in the textbook and teacher's manual. There, administering a test signaled the end of a unit, and the purpose of the test was to assign grades. Students who did not do well were exhorted to do better and try harder, but they rarely received specific feedback on how to improve—and almost never were given a second chance to demonstrate their learning. Students and teachers alike understood that taking a test meant the unit was over, and the class would move forward.

At Burnette, however, assessments were used to determine if students needed assistance in acquiring prerequisite skills prior to teaching each unit, to inform individual teachers of the strengths and weaknesses in their instruction, to help teams identify areas of concern in the curriculum, to identify students who needed additional time and support for learning, and to give students additional opportunities to demonstrate that they had learned. Assessment seemed to represent the most critical component of the collaborative culture that characterized the school, and the way teachers used assessments sent students a clear message that they were required, rather than invited, to learn.

By the end of his first semester, Peter considered Burnette's practices so powerful and practical that he questioned why he and his colleagues had not implemented them in his former schools. If certain background knowledge was an essential prerequisite for success in a unit, it just made sense to identify students who did not have that knowledge and to intervene on their behalf at the outset of the unit. If all the teachers of a course were expected to teach the same concept, it was certainly more efficient to work collaboratively in planning the unit, gathering materials, and developing assessments than to work in isolation and duplicate each other's efforts.

"In my old school," Peter told the U.S. history team one day, "what students learned, the rigor of their assessments, and the criteria used to judge the quality of their work depended on who their teacher was. We each worked in isolation. Here, however, our approach is so much more equitable. Students have access to the same curriculum and assessments of equal rigor, and we judge their work according to the same standard. At Burnette, I know all students are receiving the best education possible, in every classroom."

Peter had come to recognize the power of assessments in the service of learning—for students and teachers alike. The common assessments provided him with timely feedback on the success of his students in meeting an agreed-upon standard, on a valid assessment, in comparison to other similar students attempting to achieve the same standard. For the first time in his career, he was able to identify areas of strengths and weaknesses in his teaching and to use that insight in his dialogue with teammates to improve his instruction. Assessments had become a powerful tool in informing his practice.

More importantly, however, Peter had discovered the potential of assessments to enhance the learning of his students. By administering common assessments at the end of each unit, the members of his team were able to identify students who needed additional time and support for learning. Burnette's systematic intervention process required those students to continue to work on acquiring the essential skills in the tutoring center. Tutors then used the assessments to identify the specific skills and concepts a student had been unable to master and to provide precise instruction and feedback in a small-group setting to assist the student. It certainly made sense to Peter to use assessments not only to point out that a student had not learned, but also to provide the student with the specific feedback and information to improve upon the learning. Because assessments in his former school had been regarded as the conclusion of a unit rather than a critical element in the learning process, poor performance on an assessment sometimes had a devastating effect on a student's motivation. A series of bad test scores early in the semester could doom a student to a failing grade. Burnette's practice of allowing additional opportunities to demonstrate learning never deprived students of hope.

It had been a semester of growth for Peter. He had reexamined not only his practices, but also some of his fundamental assumptions. Not all schools were alike. Some school cultures and structures are far more effective in helping students learn. Even a veteran teacher like himself could learn to approach his profession from a new perspective. He had made the right choice in coming to Burnette, because this school had taken the assertion, "All Kids Can Learn," and added an even bolder proposition: School can be a place where even the adults could learn.

Unleashing the Potential of Effective Assessment

Burnette High School's assessment story is not a utopian ideal. It takes place in real schools with real teachers and real students. It does not require a windfall of new resources. It does, however, require something even more rare—the willingness to change the fundamental assumptions and practices that have characterized public education for decades.

Attention to this vital area must be a cornerstone of any school improvement effort. Schools simply cannot meet the challenges they face unless educators unleash the potential of effective assessment. To limit the use of this powerful instrument to ranking, sorting, and selecting students is analogous to using a computer as paperweight. When done well, however, assessment can help build a collaborative culture, monitor the learning of each student on a timely basis, provide information essential to an effective system of academic intervention, inform the practice of individual teachers and teams, provide feedback to students on their progress in meeting standards, motivate students by demonstrating next steps in their learning, fuel continuous improvement processes—and serve as the driving engine for transforming a school.

Chapter 10

Intervention and Enrichment in a Professional Learning Community

When you start with an honest and diligent effort to deter-
mine the truth of the situation, the right decisions often be-
come self-evident. . . . You absolutely cannot make a series
of good decisions without first confronting the brutal facts.

—Jim Collins

. . . Schools that have made great strides in achievement
and equity [employ] immediate and decisive intervention.

—Doug Reeves

Imagine parents who are visiting a number of different schools to determine where they will enroll their children. They visit with the principals to ask questions about each school and its policies, practices, and procedures. The following conversation ensues:

Parents: "We are impressed by your school's mission statement, which is very emphatic about your commitment to helping *all* students be successful here."

Principal: "Yes, in fact, our school motto is 'success for every child.' We do whatever it takes to help every student learn at the highest levels and to ensure we leave no child behind because failure is not an option, a mind is a terrible thing to waste, and the children are our future!"

Parents: "Sounds wonderful! So what happens in this school when a student is not learning?"

Principal: "If students experience difficulty, we encourage the teacher to reteach the concept."

Parents: "But if the teacher knew of a better way to teach the concept, wouldn't he have used that strategy the first time? Don't your teachers use the best strategies they know?

Principal: "Well, yes. But sometimes students who didn't understand a concept the first time it is taught will be more successful if they hear it again."

Parents: "Perhaps, but will a teacher really reteach a concept or unit if only one or two students are struggling? Wouldn't the teacher be more likely to move forward with new content?"

Principal: "Of course. We don't want to hold our capable students back. There are many learning standards we must address in our state, and so the curriculum must move along at a good pace."

Parents: "But what about the one or two students who are still struggling? We thought you were committed to their learning as well. What happens when just a few students don't learn?"

Principal: "Well, our teachers work very hard to encourage those students. Most teachers will contact parents and let them know of their child's difficulty. Some may even offer to work with the student before or after school."

> Parents: "We understand that teachers work hard, but can you tell us what specifically happens when a student does not learn?"

At this point in the conversation, if the principal were to heed Jim Collins' advice and "confront the brutal facts," he would be forced to say, "What happens when a student does not learn in our school will depend to a large extent on the teacher to whom he or she is assigned." This troubling fact does not come as a shock to those familiar with the workings of schools. Educators generally acknowledge there is no uniform or consistent strategy for responding to students who do not learn, and so the issue is left to each teacher to resolve on his or her own.

Some teachers challenge a student's placement in their classroom and recommend the student be assigned to less rigorous curriculum or special education. In *Whatever It Takes* (2004), we refer to these teachers as the "Charles Darwin" teachers—educators who believe their task is to assist in the sorting and selecting process. Charles Darwin teachers do not feel it is their responsibility to *create* winners, but rather it is there job to *identify* the winners based on students' innate ability.

Other teachers contend it is their job to teach, and it is the students' job to learn. These teachers argue school should prepare students for life, and since in life those who do not do their jobs well are likely to suffer consequences, students who do not do what is necessary to learn should suffer consequences. Irresponsible students should be allowed to fail so they learn an important life lesson. We refer to these teachers as "Pontius Pilate" teachers—they attempt to provide clear and engaging lessons, and then they wash their hands of students who do not learn.

Some teachers will dramatically lower their expectations within the classroom. They look for ways to help move students along to the next class or grade level even though the students have not become proficient in the most essential skills. They provide extra credit for work unrelated to the curriculum, allow students to substitute disconnected activities for essential learning, or assign grades on the basis of cooperation, participation, or perceived effort instead of on the basis of demonstrated proficiency. We call these teachers the "Chicago Cub fan" teachers because, like fans of the Cubs (the most futile franchise in the history of professional sports in America), they have no expectation of competence and focus instead on fostering warm feelings.

And then there are the teachers who monitor each student's learning on an individual basis and will devote additional time and support to those students, working with them before school, after school, and during recess or their lunch periods. They make personal sacrifices and insist students continue to put in the extra time until they are proficient. We refer to them as "Henry Higgins" teachers because, like Professor Henry Higgins in *My Fair Lady*, they devote the necessary time and individual attention to ensure a student is successful.

In most schools, what happens when students experience difficulty in learning will almost invariably depend on the teacher to whom they are assigned. Parents recognize this, and the more involved they are, the more they will do to ensure their child is assigned to the "right" teacher. Older students recognize this, and they will invent very creative stories in an effort to justify a schedule change from one teacher's class to another. And, worst of all, educators recognize this randomness in response to students who do not learn. Principals continue to place students in classrooms with teachers whose failure rate is three times higher than their colleagues, or teachers who are twice as likely to refer students for special education, or those who are consistently unable to help students demonstrate proficiency on high-stakes tests. School mission statements continue to pledge to help all students learn and staff continue to urge students to embrace fairness and equity as core values of a just society, and then those same schools resort to educational roulette when students experience difficulty.

This disjointed response can be attributed, in part, to the tradition of teacher isolation and the deeply ingrained image of individual teachers assuming sole responsibility for their own classrooms. If each classroom represents its own individual kingdom, and each teacher serves as sovereign ruler, what happens when students do not learn is just one more of the many issues left to the discretion of each teacher.

We believe, however, the bigger reason the question of what happens when students do not learn is left to each teacher is because schools have abdicated their responsibility to create a systematic response that ensures students receive additional time and support for learning in a rational and equitable way. Teachers throughout North America make the same discovery every year: Some of their students are not learning despite their very best instructional strategies. If those teachers turn to their school leaders to ask, "What do I do now? I have done all I know how to do and some students continue to struggle," they will be told, in effect, "It's up to you because we have no plan for dealing with students who do not learn."

This lack of a coordinated response when some students do not learn ranks near the top of the list of the many illogical and incomprehensible practices that occur in schooling. If certain conditions are absolutely essential to the ability of an enterprise to fulfill its fundamental purpose, people would expect the enterprise to monitor those conditions and to have a plan in place to ensure a timely response if they were compromised. We expect Starbucks to have a plan for monitoring coffee levels and for responding when coffee runs low. We expect Burger King to have a plan in place to ensure customers could purchase a burger, or that Red Lobster could, in fact, provide lobster to a hungry diner. We would find it odd indeed if those companies could not provide a basic service so essential to their fundamental purpose. We expect those running a nuclear power plant to monitor the conditions that allow it to provide safe nuclear power and to know what they will do if those conditions are compromised. If they failed to do so, we would charge negligence and threaten punitive damage. We expect an organization created for the specific purpose of responding to emergencies to have a coordinated plan for dealing with natural disasters in a timely manner, and we are outraged when we discover they do not. Yet educators, who claim the fundamental purpose of their schools is to ensure all students learn, seem not only unconcerned, but also unaware of the fact that their schools have no coordinated plan for addressing students who are not learning. Does this not seem odd? Where is the outrage at what could be argued is educational negligence? It is time for educators to confront some brutal facts and align their practices with their stated missions.

Schools That Do Not Leave Learning to Chance

There are schools at all grade levels that do not leave learning to chance. These schools have created coordinated plans to ensure any student who struggles in core classes receives additional time and support for learning in a directive, timely, and systematic way. Their plans do not require additional resources; however, they do require educators to use time differently and to assume new roles and responsibilities. The systematic plans of intervention of these schools depend on the willingness of staff members to examine and change their long-standing practices to help more students learn at higher levels.

Elementary School Examples

More than half of the students who attend Snow Creek Elementary School in rural Virginia are eligible for free and reduced lunch. In 2004, Snow Creek's third-grade students scored well below the state average on every subject on the state assessment. In reading, for example, only 40% of third graders met the proficiency standard, compared to 71% of students across the state.

When Bernice Cobbs came to the school as principal, she worked with the staff to implement professional learning community concepts, including systematic intervention for students who were struggling. Each grade-level team designated 30 minutes each day for differentiated instruction based on the results of the team's common formative assessments. During that intervention period, classroom teachers were joined by special education teachers and assistants, a Title I specialist, two part-time tutors hired using state remedial funds, and often, Cobbs herself. All students of a particular grade level were divided among this army of professionals. Students experiencing difficulty were assigned to work with the teacher whose students had demonstrated the best results on the common assessment. Another staff member would lead students who had demonstrated high proficiency in an enrichment activity. Yet another might supervise a different group of students during teacher read aloud or silent sustained reading, and still another might supervise students at independent learning centers. Groups were fluid, with students moving from group to group as they demonstrated proficiency.

In less than 2 years, Snow Creek had become a Title I Distinguished School. Students surpassed the state performance in every subject area and every grade level. The same group of students of which only 40% qualified as proficient in third-grade reading had 96% of those students achieve proficient status by fifth grade. Math proficiency for the same cohort jumped from 70% to 100%.

On the other side of the country, R.H. Dana Elementary School in Dana Point, California, serves a student population with 77.7% of students eligible for free and reduced lunch and 59.2% designated as Limited English Proficiency. In 2004, Dana students scored below the state average in all subject areas. The school set out to improve student achievement by asking teachers to work in collaborative teams and develop common formative assessments. Principal Chris Weber and the staff then created a system of interventions to support teachers—the Diagnostic, Explicit, and Systematic Student Support Program (DE-S3P). The system was specifically designed to provide students with additional time and support for learning, during the school day, in order to meet the needs of individual students prior to their academic failure. Teachers monitored student learning every 2 weeks. Time was set aside in each grade level's daily schedule for direct intervention, and the reading specialist, the resource teacher, the resource instructional aide, and five additional instructional aides were available to assist the team as students were divided into fluid groups based on their needs. Students who were more than 2 years behind their grade level also "double dipped"—they were assigned to two language arts or two math classes each day. By 2006, Dana students had surpassed the state average in every subject area. Dana had the highest gains in student achievement among the 55 schools in its district, cut the gap between white and Latino students nearly in half, and scored in the top 10% of the state among schools with similar student populations.

Kildeer Countryside School District 96, an elementary school district in suburban Chicago, faced the problem of how to go from good to great. In 2001, its students scored well above the state average on achievement tests, but the staff recognized that not all students were learning at high levels. Each of the schools in the district began to implement PLC concepts, including a plan for systematic interventions for students experiencing difficulty. Each school was free to create its own unique plan of intervention, but superintendent Tom Many asked all schools to ensure the plan was consistent with the SPEED intervention criteria (DuFour, DuFour, Eaker, & Many, 2006, p. 84):

- **Systematic:** The intervention plan is schoolwide, independent of the individual teacher, and communicated in writing (who, why, how, where, and when) to everyone: staff, parents, and students.

- **Practical:** The intervention plan is affordable within the school's available resources (time, space, staff, and materials). The plan must be sustainable and replicable so that its programs and strategies can be used in other schools.

- **Effective:** The intervention plan must be effective, available, and operational early enough in the school year to make a difference for students. It should have flexible entrance and exit criteria designed to respond to the ever-changing needs of students.

- **Essential:** The intervention plan should focus on agreed-upon standards and the essential outcomes of the district's curriculum and be targeted to a student's specific learning needs as determined by formative and summative assessments.

- **Directive:** The intervention plan should be directive. It should be mandatory—not by invitation—and a part of students' regular school day. Students cannot opt out, and parents and teachers cannot waive the student's participation in the intervention program.

With SPEED in place, student achievement on the state assessment began to rise, and it has continued to improve annually. More than 95% of the district's students are now meeting state standards, and Kildeer Countryside School District 96 has moved to the top 2% of all school districts in Illinois in terms of student achievement on the state assessment.

Middle School Examples

In 2002, students at Levey Middle School, a Title I school in suburban Detroit, were lagging far behind other Michigan students on the Michigan Educational Assessment Program. Only 30% of Levey students were proficient in reading and 31% in math, compared to state averages of 68% and 54%. Their scores were, however, comparable to the results of Michigan's African-American students, and since more than 90% of Levey students are African-American, some in the community attributed the low achievement to the racial composition of the students. Principal Anthony Muhammad was unwilling to accept that explanation and began the implementation of PLC concepts—teachers working in teams to clarify essential outcomes, write common assessments, and create a system of interventions for students who were struggling. An academic enrichment class was created at every grade level, and students were assigned to the class each day when grade-level common assessments indicated a problem in their learning. Mandatory tutoring sessions were created for students whose cumulative math grade dropped to D or F. Students who did not complete homework were required to report to the homework lunch program. If students continued to struggle, they were pulled from elective courses for additional tutoring in the core curriculum, and then allowed to return to the elective without academic penalty when they were passing all of their courses. The counseling staff developed an intervention program to assist students whose social needs were interfering with their academic success. Within 3 years, the number of students failing one or more classes dropped from 150 to 6. Within that same 3-year period, the percentage of Levey students demonstrating proficiency on the state test in reading rose from 30% to 88% and from 31% to 78% in math—far exceeding the state averages.

Three of every four students who attend Freeport Intermediate School in Brazosport, Texas, are eligible for free and reduced lunch, but they have the good fortune of attending one of the most highly recognized middle schools in the nation under the leadership of Clara Sale-Davis. Sale-Davis and her staff have created a schedule that offers an hour every day for intervention and enrichment. Freeport teachers assess student proficiency at the conclusion of short instructional units, and then they group and regroup students for the intervention/enrichment period on a very fluid basis. Students who are experiencing difficulty receive small-group instruction and tutorials, while students who are proficient pursue a variety of enrichment options. The entire team takes responsibility for each student's learning, and other staff members are available to assist to ensure students hear a variety of voices encouraging their learning. Failure rates have plummeted, and student achievement on the state assessment has soared. When the National Forum to Accelerate Middle-Grades Reform set out to identify model schools as part of its Schools to Watch program, it selected Freeport as one of four schools in the nation for that honor. When the National Association of Secondary School Principals created a process to find highly effective middle schools, it too selected Freeport as one of six schools in the nation for that recognition.

Pioneer Middle School in Tustin, California, serves a much more affluent community, but students there have also benefited from a school-wide plan to provide them with additional time and support for learning.

This plan—the "Pyramid of Interventions"—created by principal Mike Mattos and the staff, calls upon teachers every 3 weeks to identify students who are struggling. The administration and counselors then meet with the identified students on a weekly basis to monitor their progress and offer support and encouragement. The pyramid is tiered so that students who continue to struggle receive increasing amounts of time and support until they are successful. The school also changed some course offerings to provide some students with a double block of instruction each day. Students in those courses pursue the same curriculum as their classmates, but are given twice as much time to learn the content. Prior to these initiatives, Pioneer had increased less than 20 points on the state's Academic Performance Index during a 6-year period. With the interventions in place, achievement has soared by more than 50 points in 2 years. Pioneer now ranks among the top three middle schools in all of Orange County, California, the top 5% of middle schools in the state, and is recognized as a California Distinguished School.

High School Examples

Granby Memorial High School serves about 755 students in Granby, Connecticut, and Principal Alan Addley and his staff ensure each of those students will receive additional time and support for learning when they struggle. Granby has created a learning center where teachers from each discipline and student tutors are available during every period of the day to provide students with academic help. The center is open to any student, but those who are not being successful are assigned to the center and must devote extra time to their studies until their grades improve. Other elements of the Granby pyramid of interventions to support students include homework club, Saturday classes, mentoring, reading classes, a student assistance team, and a freshman team. As a result, over the past 5 years, Granby students have improved their achievement scores on every area of the state test and improved their composite score on the SAT exam by 38 points. The school has increased the percentage of its graduates taking Advanced Placement (AP) exams by 165% at the same time that the percentage of honor scores (rated 3 or higher) jumped from 51% to 81%. Granby Memorial became the first high school in Connecticut to be presented the state's Vanguard Award for demonstrating best practices in education.

Eastview High School in Apple Valley, Minnesota, serves more than 2,000 students and is consistently one of the highest performing schools in the state. The staff's attention to monitoring each student's achievement and responding to students who experience difficulty in a timely and systematic way has been a key factor in the school's success. Eastview devotes intensive attention to helping students make the transition to high school—working with middle schools to identify students who will need support, offering the Jump Start summer program in the summer prior to ninth grade for students who need assistance in becoming more structured, recruiting more than 200 upperclassmen to serve as mentors for incoming freshmen, and so on. The school then offers the Academic Coaching at Eastview (or ACE) program to provide prompt intervention when students struggle. The program includes four levels. In the first level, ACE Peer Tutoring, academically strong students tutor students who are struggling with their course work. In ACE Plus Level Two, students meet with their guidance counselor each week to review their academic progress, establish goals, and develop strategies for achieving those goals. In ACE Plus Level Three, students are assigned to a structured study hall, and the school's success coordinator meets with students each day to review their daily planner. ACE Plus Level Four students receive all of the support of the previous levels and are also assigned to a year-long course to monitor their daily work and provide individualized support in study skills, goal setting, reading and writing strategies, and using technology.

Eastview consistently ranks among the highest achieving schools in Minnesota, earning the state's highest academic recognition, the Ten Star Award, every year the school has been in existence. *Newsweek* magazine has included Eastview among "America's Best High Schools" on five occasions based on an academic challenge index that attempts to assess the degree to which schools include all students in rigorous curriculum.

Adlai Stevenson High School has grown from 1,600 students in the 1980s to its current size of 4,500 students, yet it continues to improve upon every local, state, and national indicator of student achievement. Every student who enrolls at Stevenson High School is guaranteed a foundational level of support. Students know with certainty that as freshmen they will meet four times each week with a faculty advisor whose sole responsibility is to ensure they have a successful first year of high school. They know an upperclassman mentor will function as their big brother or big sister throughout the year. They know their counselor will visit their advisory period each week to check on their progress. They know their teachers have created the same guaranteed and viable curriculum for each course, and their learning will be closely monitored through daily checks for understanding and frequent common assessments. They know their teachers will provide either a progress report or report card to their parents, advisor, and counselor every 3 weeks. They know if they are not passing their classes, they will be required to participate in an increasingly directive system of interventions, including mandatory study halls and visits to the tutoring center, guided study to monitor their completion of homework, study-skills classes, and support groups. They know the school has created a schedule that ensures they have time during their day to receive additional support for learning. They know that passing their courses means they will be given greater privileges and increasing autonomy as they advance through school, but keeping those privileges requires them to maintain passing grades. In brief, they know that their learning is not left to chance because their school has created a pyramid of interventions, a plan to monitor their learning on a regular and timely basis and to respond at the first sign they are experiencing difficulty.

A Common Theme in Uncommon Schools

The nine schools we described range in size from less than 200 students to 4,500 students. They are located in rural, suburban, and urban settings and serve students representing the full range of socioeconomic conditions in this country. At first glance, they look nothing alike; however, their practices are strikingly similar. Teachers work collaboratively to ensure students have access to the same knowledge and skills, regardless of the teacher to whom they are assigned. Teachers use frequent common formative assessments as part of the school's process to monitor student learning, and they use the results to inform and improve their classroom practice. And, very importantly, each school has created a plan to respond to students who are not learning with action taken *during the school day in a timely, directive, and systematic way.* What happens when students do not learn in these schools does not depend solely on their classroom teacher, but rather is part of a consistent, collective, school-wide response.

One of the most consistent messages from the research regarding both effective teachers and effective schools is the significance of high expectations for student achievement. But what does that mean? How are high expectations manifested in a classroom or school? How do students come to recognize their teachers and schools expect them to be successful?

After devoting his distinguished career to examining the practices of effective schools, Larry Lezotte (1991) concluded the following:

> [Initially] expectations were described in terms of attitudes and beliefs that suggested how the teacher should behave in the teaching-learning situation. . . . Unfortunately, this . . . proved to be insufficient to assure mastery for many learners. Teachers found themselves in the difficult position of having had high expectations and having acted upon them—yet some students still did not learn. . . . Implementing this expanded concept of high expectations will require the school as an organization to reflect high expectations. Most of the useful strategies will require the cooperation of the school as a whole; teachers cannot implement most of these strategies working alone

in isolated classrooms. Today, high expectations for success will be judged, not only by the initial staff beliefs and behaviors, but also by *the organization's response when some students do not learn.* (p. 2, italics added)

We argue educators who hope to create and communicate a culture of high expectations should respond collectively when some students do not learn by doing the following:

- Assuring students who experience difficulty are given extra time and additional support for learning

- Providing timely intervention at the first indication of difficulty in a way that does not remove students from the classroom during new direct instruction

- Becoming increasingly directive, requiring rather than inviting students to continue working until they are successful

- Being fluid, moving students in and out of various levels of intervention depending on their demonstrated proficiency

- Most importantly, being *systematic—ensuring* students receive support regardless of the individual teacher to whom they are assigned because procedures are in place to guarantee the *school* responds

Words of Caution About Systematic Interventions

Educators who attempt to create systematic interventions in their schools to support student learning should be mindful of the following cautions.

No System of Interventions Will Compensate for Ineffective Teaching

Educators must fight the war to raise student achievement on two fronts—providing time and support for teachers at the same time they are providing time and support for students. Teachers will need assistance to build their collective capacity to work in collaborative teams, clarify essential learning, develop high-quality assessments, and use data to inform and improve individual and team practice. No matter how effective they become in this process, however, they will continue to find that some students do not acquire the essential knowledge and skills despite their best efforts. If all students are to learn, there will always be a need to provide some of them with additional time and support.

On the other hand, although a system of interventions is a necessary condition for high levels of learning, it is not sufficient alone. No plan to provide students with additional time and help for learning can compensate for ongoing ineffective instruction. There is abundant research confirming that what teachers do in their individual classrooms matters a lot (Haycock, 1998; Marzano, 2003; Wright, Horn, & Sanders, 1997). Thus, while a staff is working to answer the question, "What will we do to provide intervention when our students do not learn?" it is also imperative members grapple with the question, "What represents best practice in teaching and assessing the essential knowledge, skills, and dispositions our student must acquire?" It would be a huge mistake to assume a system of interventions can solve the problems created by poor instruction occurring on a wide-scale basis. Schools need both skillful teachers and a system of interventions.

A System of Interventions Works Most Effectively in Schools Where Collaborative Teams of Teachers Have Established Essential Learning, Common Pacing, and Common Assessments

The complexity of supporting student learning is multiplied exponentially if the system of interventions is attempting to respond to isolated classrooms where teachers pursue their individual curricula, according to their own pacing, while using their own personal assessments. An elementary school has a far better chance of creating interventions that respond to 6 coordinated teams (one per grade level) instead of 24 independent kingdoms. A tutoring center for middle- or high-school students will find it extremely difficult to support student learning if the concepts students are learning and when they are expected to learn them vary throughout a department. A successful system of interventions will require not only a collective effort, but also a coordinated one.

A System of Interventions Should Fit the Context of Your School

Although we have proposed the parameters of an effective system of interventions, we are not advocating a particular model of intervention. The responses of the nine schools we have described in this chapter varied in execution, but were grounded in the same principles. Educators should not simply adopt the system of interventions of another school; they should create their own. We have great confidence in the ability of educators to create a serviceable plan of intervention if an entire faculty focuses its collective attention on the issue. Furthermore, the plan should not require a windfall of new resources, provided educators are willing to change some traditional practices and assume some new roles and responsibilities.

Do Not Fall in Love With a Tree—Embrace the Forest

We have witnessed educators become excited about a particular program within another school's system of interventions, and then replicate that program rather than the system. They become enchanted with the advisory program, swoon over the idea of upperclassmen mentors, or gush with enthusiasm over the concept of a homework club. All of these programs may be worthwhile, but none represent a school-transforming idea. They may constitute a small part of an intervention plan, but they will not provide students with the support they need to be successful. Asking the question, "Should we have an advisory program?" will not have a significant impact on either the culture of a school or the achievement of its students. But the question, "How can we give students in our school additional time and support for learning in a timely, directive, fluid, and systematic way that does not deprive them of any new direct instruction?" has the potential to transform a school.

Objections to Creating a System of Interventions

We have come to anticipate a predictable set of objections when we propose schools should ensure a collective, systematic response when students do not learn.

Objection 1: Attention Is Given to Students Who Are Not Learning at the Expense of Average and Gifted Students

The assumption behind this argument is that if some students who have struggled to learn become more successful, it is at the expense of other students. We find no evidence to support this assumption. The new higher level of learning for traditionally low-performing students is not subtracted from the learning of their classmates. In fact, all of the nine schools highlighted in this chapter not only helped low-achieving students become proficient as a result of their attention to student learning, but they also helped more students demonstrate the highest levels of proficiency. At the same time they built systems of interventions, each school addressed the fourth critical question driving the work of PLCs: What will we do to enrich and extend the learning for our students who are already proficient?

Between 2003 and 2006, Kildeer Countryside School District 96 increased the percentage of students scoring with advanced proficiency (the highest level in Illinois) in every subject in every grade on the state assessment, and the percentage of its eighth-grade students qualifying for advanced programs at their high school jumped from 20% to 42% in English and from 44% to 72% in math. Pioneer Middle School also increased the percentage of students achieving at the highest level on the state test in every grade level, for every subject, and for every subgroup in the school's population. Pioneer almost doubled the percentage of its eighth-grade students meeting the "advanced proficiency" standard in language arts between 2003 and 2007, and now almost half of the students in the school meet that highest standard for that subject area. Math results are even more impressive, with the number of students in seventh and eighth grade taking advanced math increasing from 144 in 2004 to 346 in 2007. In 2003, only eighth-grade students completed the state algebra exam in California, and only 3% of Pioneer's students achieved the "highly proficient" standard on the state test. By 2007, one third of seventh graders were enrolled in algebra, 99% of them scored proficient or higher, and 46% achieved the advanced proficiency level on the state exam. In 2003, one fourth of eighth graders enrolled in geometry, and 48% of those enrolled achieved advanced proficiency. In 2007, one third of eighth graders were enrolled in geometry, and 72% of those students scored at the advanced proficiency level. Clearly, Pioneer's attention to helping all students learn resulted in more students learning at the highest levels.

In 2006, one in four graduating seniors in the United States had taken an AP examination—the highest percentage in the history of the nation—but less than 15% of graduates were able to achieve an honors score of 3 or higher (College Board, 2007). Stevenson High School had almost 70% of its 2006 graduates taking an AP exam. Stevenson students far outpaced the national average on every AP exam (see examples in the chart on page 261)—despite the fact that Stevenson students, many of whom were ranked in the bottom third of their class, were competing against the top quarter of the nation's high-school students. Eighty-eight percent of exams written by Stevenson students qualified for honor grades, and the mode (or most frequent score) was a 5, the highest possible score on the exam.

Stevenson also scores among the top schools in the nation on the ACT examination, despite the fact that 100% of Stevenson students take the exam compared to 42% of the students in the rest of nation, virtually all of whom are college bound (ACT, 2006). Stevenson's focus on responding to students who are not learning clearly has benefited all of its students.

Giving attention to students who are not learning does not—and must not—mean that educators overlook the importance of challenging and stretching all students. One of the most common complaints from students regarding their schooling experience is that they are not challenged. Results from an extensive poll of high school students revealed two thirds of them were willing to work harder if their schools demanded more of them. Most respondents reported they felt ill-prepared for college. Only one in nine who had dropped out or were considering leaving high school did so because they felt the work was too difficult. The majority left because they were "not learning anything" or because they "hated school" (Janofsky, 2005). If educators are to address this problem, they must be committed to helping all students learn at high levels, and they must focus on stretching students and raising the academic bar, not lowering it.

A commitment to helping all students learn at high levels is beneficial to all students. As we wrote in *Whatever It Takes* (DuFour, DuFour, Eaker, & Karhanek, 2004):

> When teachers work together to become so skillful in teaching a particular concept that even students who typically have difficulty can understand that concept, all students benefit. When students of all abilities have a place to turn to for extra time and support if they experience initial difficulty in learning, all students benefit. The adage, "A rising tide lifts all boats" applies to the PLC concept. (p. 159–160)

Objection 2: Systems of Support Put the Burden for Learning on Educators Rather Than on Students; Interventions Will Only Enable Students, Encouraging Them to Be Irresponsible

This year, in districts throughout North America, elementary teachers will advise their students to be responsible for their own learning because "middle school teachers expect you to be independent learners." Middle school teachers will warn their students they are responsible for their own learning because "high school teachers won't cut you any slack." And high school teachers will advise students they are responsible

Advanced Placement Course	Percent Scoring 3 or Higher (Nation)	Percent Scoring 3 or Higher (Stevenson)
Biology	61%	98.5%
Calculus AB	61%	92.4%
Calculus BC	81%	100%
Chemistry	58%	93.4%
English Language	51%	94.8%
English Literature	62%	95.8%
European History	70%	90%
Government	55%	77.8%
Physics B	60%	98%
Physics C	71%	95%
Psychology	68%	94%
Studio Art	66%	100%
U.S. History	53%	80%

for their own learning because "no one will hold your hand in college or in the workplace." Students who do not heed this advice will suffer the consequences of failure, and educators will justify that failure as a part of teaching students to be "responsible."

This long-standing tradition will continue despite a century of evidence showing that allowing students to fail does nothing to teach them responsibility. Teachers will advise students if they do not complete all their homework, meet deadlines, and study diligently they will fail. Students who follow this advice will probably be successful, but inevitably other students will choose not to do what is necessary to succeed, will fail, and are perfectly willing to accept failure. It is time for educators to acknowledge the obvious: allowing students to act irresponsibly does nothing to teach them responsibility, and it is disingenuous to pretend it does. A school truly committed to teaching responsibility will convey a consistent message that learning is required rather than optional, and it will create policies and procedures that direct rather than invite students to do what is necessary to learn.

Inherent in the term responsible is the assumption one is "able to respond." Some students are not able to respond effectively when their teachers invite them to learn. Some do not have the study skills, dispositions, work ethic, capacity, or attitudes essential to academic success. So why not acknowledge this reality and intervene with strategies to provide students with these tools for success?

Here again the research on change is instructive: to change attitudes, focus first on changing behavior. Responsible people do the work; they do what is expected and required. When students in the schools highlighted in this chapter fail to act in ways that lead to success, the school takes steps to change their behavior by directing them to act in new ways. They will require students to attend tutoring sessions, insist students continue working on a project until it meets standards, and monitor the completion of their homework each day. When these new behaviors lead students to a new experience—academic success— and the success is acknowledged and celebrated, attitudes can begin to change. The behavior is more likely to be repeated until, eventually, it becomes habit and the need for monitoring is diminished as students develop a sense of self-efficacy.

For example, the staff of Papillion-LaVista High School in Papillion, Nebraska, witnessed a noticeable improvement in student work habits and saw the failure rate plummet when they adopted the position that "not doing your work is no longer an option in our school." Once students learned there were benefits to completing their work promptly and maintaining passing grades, and there were consequences that required them to complete late work or devote additional time to their studies if they were unsuccessful, they decided it would be in their best interests to do what responsible people do—that is, do the work.

When Stevenson High School began its system of interventions, some staff members raised sincere concerns that this support would foster irresponsibility and would have an adverse effect on the ability of students to be successful in college. Rather than merely debate their diverse opinions, the staff agreed to gather evidence to assess the impact of the school's practices on student responsibility. For more than a decade, the school has administered a student survey to each student in the school and to a random sample of former students 1 year and 5 years after their graduation from high school. For example, each senior is asked to indicate his or her personal level of agreement to the statement, "I became more responsible for my own learning as I advanced through high school." Year after year, roughly 90% of the students agree with that statement, and the majority of students "strongly agree." They are invited to respond to an open-ended question on the topic. An analysis of their responses from the most recent survey led to the following observation: "Once again, respondents praised Stevenson's effective blend of freedom and limits along with its challenging, yet supportive, academic environment where time-management skills were developed and personal initiative was rewarded."

When asked to identify the best part of their high school experience, these seniors did not indicate their school activities, athletics, or even their friendships as their most frequent response. Overwhelmingly they indicated the Stevenson staff was the best part of their experience as they described the adults in their schools as "lovable, caring, compassionate, supportive, attentive, passionate, intriguing, intelligent, brilliant, honest, sincere, empathetic, inspirational, encouraging, enjoyable, wonderful, talented, kind, funny, energetic, genuine, influential, helpful, committed, gifted, and memorable." As the report of the survey summarized, "Seniors have articulated the sentiment that Stevenson's staff members have enabled them to feel better about themselves and to achieve at a level of success many had never believed to be obtainable." Contrast that sentiment to Fullan's (2007) finding that a consistent and pervasive complaint of students is their teachers and administrators "don't care" about them. A focused system of interventions can address that complaint and demonstrate to students in a very tangible way that people throughout the school are invested in their success.

The structured phone interviews of a random sampling of students 1 year after their graduation from Stevenson also revealed very consistent findings. In the most recent survey, 78% of respondents reported they were *better* prepared for college than the other students attending their schools, 22% said their preparation was as good as their fellow students, and none indicated they were not as prepared. Eighty percent of the students had earned a grade point average of 3.0 or higher in college, and 99% had earned a 2.0 or higher.

But perhaps the most telling statistic in terms of the school's impact on the ability of its graduates to be successful in college comes in the phone survey of a random sample of alumni 5 years after their graduation. Consistently, almost 90% of respondents report they have earned a degree. Nationally, less than 40% of students who enter a 4-year college will earn a degree within 5 years, and less than 30% of those who enter a 2-year college will earn an associate degree in 3 years or less (ACT, 2006).

There will be those who will argue that Stevenson's experience is irrelevant because their school is not like Stevenson. We certainly acknowledge the danger in attempting to generalize based on the experience of a single school or even 100 schools. We suggest, however, the experience of thousands of schools over more than a century has demonstrated beyond any question that allowing students to choose to fail does not teach them responsibility. Perhaps it is time educators embrace a different strategy for responding to irresponsible behavior. If educators continue to assert they are committed to ensuring all students must learn, and they acknowledge there are certain steps students must take in order to learn, they will create systems to ensure those steps are taken.

Objection 3: The Schedule Won't Allow It

This pronouncement, "The schedule won't allow it," is the single most proffered explanation as to why a school has not created a systematic plan of intervention when students do not learn. It has the benefit of demonstrating our good intentions—"We would love to intervene when kids do not learn"—at the same time it absolves us of responsibility—"Alas, it is simply impossible given our schedule." Blame is assigned to an inanimate, abstract concept (the schedule) while people are exonerated for failure to act. We find this argument puzzling, and we offer these rhetorical questions to educators across North America:

- Did you mean it when you said the purpose of your school or district is to help all students learn? Was that a sincere declaration of intent and priority or politically correct hyperbole?

- Do you recognize that some students will require more time and support for their learning than others, that no research has concluded all students can learn if time and support are constants rather than variables in the learning process?

- Do you agree a school's schedule should reflect its purpose and priorities?

- Have you created a schedule that ensures you have access to all students who experience difficulty in order to provide them with additional time and support for learning?

When we pose these questions, one at a time, to educators, it is disheartening to hear them say, "Yes, we are committed to helping all students learn; yes, we recognize some will need more time and support if they are to learn; yes, a school's schedule should reflect its purpose and priorities; but, no, we do not have a system of interventions in place because the schedule won't let us." A school's schedule should be regarded as a tool to further priorities, not an impediment to change. Our advice to educators is simple: Your schedule is not a sacred document. If your current schedule does not allow you to provide students with something as essential to their academic success as extra time and support for learning, you should change it.

Consider a typical high school on a 4-by-4 block schedule that assigns every entering freshman to four 90-minute classes and one 30-minute lunch period per day. Students continue to be assigned to this same schedule every semester throughout their high school careers. In most states, those who pass all of their courses will have essentially completed all of their graduation requirements by the end of their seventh semester. Therefore, many will lighten their academic load in their final year of high school, enroll in college courses, or suffer from acute senioritis as they attend courses they know they will not need to graduate.

The freshman year is the crucial year for high school students. Students who struggle in the freshman year are the most likely to drop out of school prior to graduation, and those who have a successful year are likely to sustain that success. So how logical is it that educators would require their youngest, most vulnerable students to carry the heaviest academic load they will ever experience, during their most crucial year of school, while offering the oldest, most successful, and presumably most mature students in the school the lightest schedules?

We have asked thousands of educators to reflect on the advice they offered their own sons and daughters as they left for their freshman year of college. We ask, "How many of you urged your child to enroll in an academic overload for their first semester of college, pressing them to take 18 or 21 semester hours rather than 12 or 15 hours?" The question evokes a lot of laughter, because as educators we understand the significance of the first year of college. After all, more than 30% of college freshmen do not return to their schools for sophomore year. If we are advising our own sons and daughters to lighten their academic load in their first year so they do not become overwhelmed, then why do we require the children of others to carry a schedule that makes it impossible for them to seek or receive help in their most critical year of high school?

Imagine a high school assigns its entering freshman students to three standard 90-minute block courses each semester, along with one sequential course (for example, a math class) that meets for 45 minutes throughout the year. The remaining 45 minutes of that period is devoted to the pyramid of interventions. For example, all students may begin with an advisory/study hall period in which a faculty member meets with students individually to monitor their transition to high school while other students are completing their homework. Upperclassmen mentors might assist the advisor. After 3 weeks, any student who is failing or in danger of failing a class will be moved out of study hall to a tutoring center where teachers and members of the National Honor Society could provide small-group and one-on-one instruction. If, after 6 weeks of tutoring, the student is still in danger of failing, the counselor will coordinate a conference between the student, the parents, and the teacher to create a coordinated plan for resolving the problem, complete with the commitments each party is prepared to make to the other. If the problems persist, the student could be moved from the tutoring center to a guided study center where a staff member assists the student in completing homework assignments, helps him or her develop organizational and time-management skills, and provides ongoing encouragement and support.

This scenario is far more likely to help students experience a successful freshman year and develop the skills and habits critical to their success; it also conveys a sense of high expectations to students. Furthermore, it has no adverse impact on a student's ability to graduate within 4 years. Students who continue to struggle despite this support in their freshman year could be enrolled in only three classes in the first semester of their second year, in order to provide the student with even more time for support during the day.

We offer this scenario as only one example of how a school might adjust its schedule to create additional time and support for learning—it is not offered as a recommendation. Stevenson has an 8-period day, with one of the periods reserved for lunch. Eastview offers a similar schedule with 7 periods, one of which is extended an extra 40 minutes for lunch. Granby operates a modified schedule with an 8-period day on Monday, Tuesday, and Friday, and a block schedule on Wednesday and Thursday. Schedules can differ, but schedules should ensure educators are able to provide students with additional time and support for learning during the school day in ways that do not require students to miss new direct instruction.

Sadly, state legislatures are typically moving in the wrong direction on this issue. They cling to the assumption that if they merely demand more of students—more courses in particular subject areas, more minutes of instruction, more credits required for graduation—learning will increase. This is tantamount to a manufacturing company attempting to resolve quality issues by running the assembly line faster for more hours a day instead of examining the manufacturing process to identify and resolve problems.

The state legislature of Oklahoma was persuaded to reconsider its policy on this issue. Putnam City High School created a "flexible Friday" schedule that allowed students who were passing all of their classes an early release on Friday afternoons, while students who were failing a course, who were in danger of failing, who had not completed all of their work, or who needed to make up work due to absence remained on campus for intensive tutoring, advising, and to complete their work. When the state department of education advised school officials they were violating state policy because the early dismissal did not provide the number of minutes required of a school day, Principal Don Wentroth, teachers, and students took their case to the state legislature. After hearing students explain the benefits of their school's system of interventions and the positive impact it was having on their achievement, the Oklahoma House and Senate passed legislation allowing Putnam City to continue its practice. The percentage of Putnam City students failing a course dropped from 23% to 6%, and the percentage of students demonstrating proficiency on the state assessment in algebra jumped from 6% to 83% in a single year.

We urge other educators in North America to make direct appeals to their legislatures and departments of education to support a focus on learning rather than a focus on minutes of instruction. We urge them to support scheduling that allows for intervention when students struggle, rather than scheduling that ensures students are inaccessible for additional time and support during their school day. Educators must become advocates for the policies and procedures that support, rather than interfere, with student learning.

Is a System of Interventions the Same as Response to Intervention?

Astute readers may recognize that this idea of creating a system to monitor each student's learning and then providing a system of tiered supports of increasing intensity for students who struggle mirrors the Early Intervention Services stipulated in the federal Response to Intervention (RTI) initiative. Those astute readers are correct. In fact, the diagram of the RTI model replicates the illustration of the pyramid of interventions we have advocated for years (see page 270). Both models are based on the premise that special education should serve as a last resort, rather than as a first response when students experience academic difficulty.

As psychologist Abraham Maslow observed, "To the man whose only tool is a hammer, the whole world looks like a nail." If a school has no tool for responding to struggling students other than special education, it is inevitable the staff will come to rely on that tool too frequently. Special education plays an important role in contemporary education, but it should be reserved for those students who require its services to address a disabling condition, not as a catchall for every student experiencing difficulty.

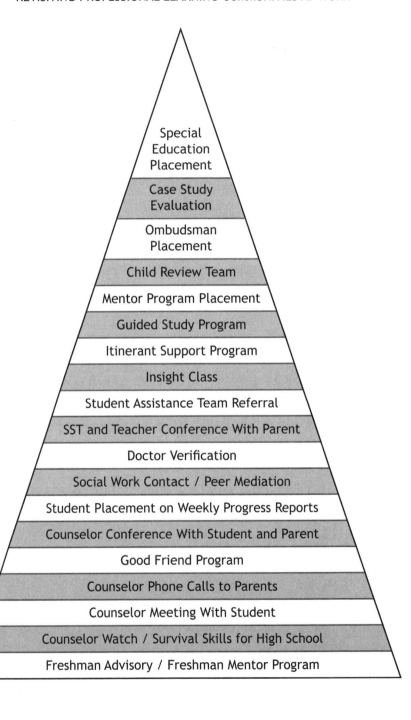

Special
Education
Placement

Case Study
Evaluation

Ombudsman
Placement

Child Review Team

Mentor Program Placement

Guided Study Program

Itinerant Support Program

Insight Class

Student Assistance Team Referral

SST and Teacher Conference With Parent

Doctor Verification

Social Work Contact / Peer Mediation

Student Placement on Weekly Progress Reports

Counselor Conference With Student and Parent

Good Friend Program

Counselor Phone Calls to Parents

Counselor Meeting With Student

Counselor Watch / Survival Skills for High School

Freshman Advisory / Freshman Mentor Program

The RTI model holds potential for having a positive impact on student learning, but only if 1) it leads educators to engage in serious collective inquiry into the question, "How will we respond when *any* student does not learn?" and 2) the dialogue leads to the creation of *systematic* interventions that ensure *all* students receive additional time and support for learning in a timely and directive way.

If, on the other hand, educators merely add RTI as an appendage to traditional school cultures or consider it a special education issue, they will neither become more successful in their efforts to help all students learn nor eliminate the unhealthy and unnecessary distinction between general education and special education students and the staff who serve them. For the best analysis of how schools might use RTI in ways that advance their capacity to function as PLCs, we highly recommend *Pyramid of Response to Intervention: RTI, PLCs, and How to Respond When Kids Don't Learn* by Buffum, Mattos, and Weber (2008).

A System of Interventions in Action

The following story illustrates a system of interventions at work in an elementary school.

As the end of her third year of teaching was drawing to a close, Hannah Lyn started to question whether she would remain in the profession. She began her career with high hopes and a determination to make a difference in the lives of her students. She quickly discovered, however, that teaching was more complex and difficult than she had imagined. After 3 years in the classroom, she continued to harbor doubts about her ability to inspire unmotivated students or to meet the needs of students who continued to struggle no matter what strategies she used. She decided to request a transfer to another school in the district to give herself one final chance to find satisfaction and fulfillment in her chosen profession.

Hannah was delighted to be offered a position teaching fourth grade at Helen Harvey Elementary School. She was even more delighted when she discovered the school operated exactly how the principal had described it during her interview. She was assigned to a collaborative team comprised of three other fourth-grade teachers and a special education teacher. Her team was provided time to meet every week and began every unit in language arts and math with a review of the essential learning all students were expected to acquire, the proposed pacing for the unit, and the common assessment they would administer at the conclusion of the unit. Questions that she had grappled with on her own at her other school were considered and resolved as a team at Harvey.

What impressed her the most, however, was the school's approach to intervention for students who experienced difficulty in their learning and enrichment for those who did not. At her previous school, she felt torn at the end of every unit. Some of her students had performed at very high levels and were ready for enrichment, while others clearly had not reached minimum proficiency and needed intervention. She was never quite sure what to do. Should she move forward with students who were ready for new learning, or should she reteach concepts to students not yet proficient? At Harvey, she discovered the staff had grappled with these questions collectively and then developed a highly coordinated systematic approach designed to meet the needs of all learners.

The daily schedule for every grade-level team included at least one 30-minute period for intervention and enrichment. This designated period was in addition to the new direct instruction continuing in every area of the content each day. Every team had been asked to adhere to the following tight parameters regarding this important block of time:

1. The block could be no less than 30 minutes each day.

2. The block had to be provided at the same time each day for every classroom in the grade level.

3. The block could not interfere with a student's recess or specials. Teachers were to avoid doing anything that might cause students to perceive intervention and enrichment as punishment.

4. The block must be fluid, with students moving easily between groups as their new levels of proficiency became apparent.

5. The block could not be offered at the same time as the block of any other grade level.

Using these tight parameters, the principal and grade-level team leaders created the following schedule for intervention/enrichment:

8:45–9:25	Second Grade
9:30–10:30	First Grade
10:35–11:35	Kindergarten
11:40–12:15	Third Grade
12:45–1:15	Fourth Grade
1:20–1:50	Fifth Grade
2:00–2:30	Additional Time K–5 by Request

Based on these designated times for intervention and enrichment and the times their grade levels were assigned to specials classes and lunch, Hannah and her colleagues created the following daily schedule to comply with the district's guidelines regarding the allocation of time for each content area:

Fourth-Grade Master Schedule for Daily Instruction

8:00–8:15	Instructional Staff Planning
8:15–8:40	Students Arrive; Breakfast, Fourth-Grade/First-Grade Reading Buddies
8:40–8:45	Tardy Bell, Attendance, Morning Announcements
8:45–9:30	Specials (Music, Art, Physical Education, and so on)
9:30–11:00	Language Arts

11:00–11:45	Social Studies
11:45–12:35	Lunch/Recess
12:45–1:15	Intervention and Enrichment
1:15–2:15	Math
2:15–3:00	Science
3:00–3:10	Afternoon Announcements/Dismissal
3:10–3:30	Instructional Staff Planning

Each time her team administered a common assessment, Hannah and her colleagues would examine the results together. For each skill or concept, they would identify all of the students who had not met the team's intended proficiency target, those who had met the target, and those who had excelled. Using this information, the team created student groups so that all fourth-grade students, not just those needing more time and support to reach proficiency on each skill, could benefit from the daily block of protected intervention and enrichment time. The team knew they could easily divide the students into as many as eight groups because the reading specialist and two floating tutors joined the five-member team each day. They also knew they could cluster students for team teaching whenever they deemed that the most promising structure for intervention and/or enrichment.

Planning for and Facilitating Intervention and Enrichment

The fourth-grade team always ensured that students who needed the most support to learn an essential skill or concept would be assigned to the teacher(s) on the team who had the best results for that skill on the common assessment. As they provided intervention for those students, the remaining members of the team—the reading specialist and tutors—divided the other fourth-grade students among them for enrichment and extension. Students typically remained with the same group for at least 2 weeks, at which point the students receiving intervention were reassessed using a second version of the team's common assessment. The team then used the new data to determine how to regroup students to better meet their learning needs.

In addition to the eight adults assigned to the fourth-grade intervention and enrichment block each day, a part-time literacy coach and a part-time gifted and talented coordinator joined the team 1 day each week. The team also benefited from the support of a very active adult volunteer program coordinated by the school's parent association, a partnership with a local company that had adopted their grade level and sent staff to mentor students at the school 1 day each week, and local college students who came to the school as part of their internship program. Although students who were struggling academically were always assigned to a teacher on the team, the ongoing presence of the other adults enabled the team to provide other students with very personal attention.

Hannah learned this block of time was not intended for new direct instruction, but was reserved for enrichment and intervention. She also learned each team had great autonomy regarding how they would utilize this protected period each day. Hannah and one of her teammates created and led a Junior Great Books group for the students who had excelled, the floating tutors monitored proficient students as they applied their newly learned reading skills to partner reading of grade-level trade books, while the other two fourth-grade teachers, the reading specialist, and the special education teacher provided intervention for the students who needed more time and support. As the year went on, the team rotated new groups of students through the enrichment activities, created independent study projects, computerized learning units, math team competitions, and a variety of instructional games and activities as options for students. Hannah and her teammates each worked with all groups of students at one time or another, always basing the student-placement decisions on the most current assessment data. They made a concerted effort to make both the intervention and enrichment activities for each group highly engaging, high interest, and very fluid. As soon as an individual student in the intervention group demonstrated proficiency, the student was moved to another group, thereby allowing teachers to provide even more personalized attention to students who still required intervention. Hannah discovered the collective and systematic plan for responding to each student in fourth grade was differentiation at its best.

Teams also had autonomy regarding the subject area they would focus on during intervention and enrichment. Hannah's team typically devoted 2 weeks to language arts and then 1 week to math, but they were free to deviate from that schedule when the assessment results suggested students needed more intensive work in one area. The team also integrated social studies and science content into the language arts intervention and enrichment block to strengthen student knowledge in those areas at the same time they addressed reading and writing skills.

Hannah learned the funding for the floating tutors had come from the faculty's decision to redirect money from the remediation program that had traditionally been offered after school. Her previous school had also offered after-school remediation, but it seemed the students who needed support most were the least likely to stay for help. Even students who were willing to stay often could not because the school was unable to provide busing. Therefore, the Harvey faculty had elected to divert their state remedial funds from an optional after-school program that was proving to be ineffective to a required program that could be integrated into each school day. The two floating tutors were not certified teachers, but they were college graduates who had served as substitute teachers in the district. They had demonstrated their ability to work with and relate to students and staff, and they were pleased to accept a position that allowed them to work in one school every day to assist with the program.

The special education teacher assigned to the team also played an important role in this process to meet the needs of all students. In Hannah's former school, it was generally understood that special education teachers were responsible for the learning of special education students. At Harvey, either the special education teacher or assistant was available to help the team during every intervention and enrichment block. Equally important, however, was that teacher's contribution to the team's instructional and assessment process. Grade-level teachers worked with special education teachers to clarify the knowledge and skills all fourth-grade students were to acquire and what students would be asked to do to demonstrate proficiency on local, district, and state assessments. The special education teacher then became the consultant to the team concerning instructional strategies to support the learning of students with special needs and alternative methods of assessing their skills.

Involving Parents as Partners

Hannah also appreciated Harvey's approach to parent involvement. At her former school, parents were invited to meet with their children's teacher at Back-to-School Night at the beginning of the first semester, and each teacher used his or her time with parents differently. At Harvey, parents met with all the teachers of the grade-level team on an evening designated for that specific grade level, and each team used the time to conduct grade-level parent workshops. The workshops included an overview of key concepts of the curriculum, sample assessments for essential skills, an explanation of the team's strategy for enrichment and intervention, and a description of special projects and events students would experience that semester. Most importantly, the team provided parents with practice/tutorial packets aligned with essential outcomes in language arts and math. The packet included a pacing calendar so parents were aware of the skills and concepts their students were learning each month. It also included materials parents could use at home to reinforce those essential skills and concepts, along with quick assessment tools so parents could check their children's learning. Members of the team then demonstrated how parents might use the materials at home with their own children by working with a few students from the grade level. Finally, the team explained how parents could use a weekly communication form to indicate if, from the parents' perspective, their student was having difficulty with a skill or concept.

Parents unable to attend the workshops were sent the tutorial packets with a cover letter from the team explaining the contents. A few days later, the homeroom teacher contacted those parents to discuss the packet and answer any questions the parent might have.

Hannah was truly impressed by this approach to helping parents become partners in the learning of their children. Not only were parents made aware of the expectations for learning for their children, but, more importantly, they were given tools and materials to help monitor and support that learning. Furthermore, the parent workshops helped parents to understand that their child was part of a clearly defined program of studies that was not solely dependent on the classroom teacher to whom he or she was assigned. Parents appreciated a system that ensured every student had access to the experience and expertise of the entire collaborative team.

Integrating Specials Areas

Students at Harvey also had the benefit of learning from specialist teachers each week—teachers who had expertise, training, and passion in areas such as art, music, physical education, guidance counseling, computers/technology, and library science/media studies. Specialists at Harvey were considered important allies in the collective effort to help all students learn.

At the beginning of the school year, each grade-level team provided the specialists and resource teachers with the list of essential skills and the pacing guide for their grade. Faculty meeting time was then set aside to explore ways the specialists and resource teachers could connect their content to essential grade-level standards. For example, the music teacher helped the fourth-grade students learn songs that reinforced essential science vocabulary and concepts, the physical education teacher practiced and reinforced math facts during fitness exercises, the art teacher connected an art history lesson and project to the first unit in fourth-grade social studies, and the librarian helped students become familiar with resources they could use when conducting research for a project the team had developed.

As the year progressed, the grade-level teams provided the specialists and resource teachers with copies of their biweekly grade-level newsletter to parents, a tool designed to keep parents and staff alike informed of the essential skills students were learning. Each team also provided specialists and support staff with a monthly "scoop sheet" listing specific essential concepts and skills to be introduced at that grade level in the coming month. This coordinated approach to curriculum and instruction helped the students to recognize that every adult in the building was part of a big team striving to help them learn at very high levels.

Using the Child Study Team in a New Way

Hannah discovered yet another major difference between her former school and Harvey Elementary: the use of the child study team. At her former school, the team served one purpose—to facilitate the placement of students into special education. Those who served on the team knew it would make few demands on their time until spring when they would be very busy reviewing the status of students who had been recommended for special education by their classroom teachers.

Harvey's child study team—which included the principal, the counselor, a representative from special education, classroom teachers, and parents—met throughout the year and was responsible for creating a structured system of more intensive interventions for students in the regular education program who were experiencing difficulty. Members of the grade-level team were responsible for presenting evidence of a student's achievement and explaining their concerns. The child study team would then create a plan for meeting the needs of that student. Typically the plan included adjustments in the student's schedule to provide more individualized and extended time for learning. Meetings always concluded by establishing a date 4 to 6 weeks in the future when the team would reconvene to assess the student's progress. Hannah considered this approach much more proactive than what she was accustomed to, and noticed her former school had assigned many more students to special education.

Hannah's experience at Harvey Elementary revitalized her. No longer did she have to tackle the complexities of teaching alone. Now crucial issues such as the content to teach, the pacing of instruction, effective instructional strategies and materials, and the different ways to monitor student learning were addressed and resolved by a team of colleagues working and learning together, with each member contributing to the shared purpose and goals of the team. At her former school, if students in her classroom were struggling to learn, she was the only one in the school who knew, and she was the only one responsible for doing something about it. At Harvey, the school's system of interventions meant her teammates and other members of the staff were available to support the learning of her students, and she could contribute to the learning of students outside of her classroom. At Harvey, students were not divided into "your kids" and "my kids"; they were "our kids," and every student could benefit from the expertise of any member of the team.

Hannah had expected teaching to be difficult, but prior to coming to Harvey, she was beginning to think it was *impossible* for teachers to meet the needs of their students. Now she concluded that a collective, collaborative, systematic approach to meeting the needs of students could help her realize her hope of making a significant and positive difference in the lives of students.

We began this chapter with a hypothetical conversation between parents and a principal, and we would like to conclude it with an appeal to the parent perspective. We have asked educators throughout North America to recall the day they took their first-born child to school for the first time—a vivid memory for most parents. We then ask them to imagine they are given a choice. In School A, their child will be assigned to a single classroom teacher each year for their first 5 or 6 years of schooling. That teacher will be solely responsible for their child's learning, and thus the extent of the learning will depend almost exclusively on the strengths and weaknesses of that teacher in different subject areas. In School B, their child will be assigned to a collaborative team of teachers each year, and the entire team will take an interest in and be responsible for his or her learning. At the first evidence the child is experiencing difficulty in learning, the teacher on the team most effective in teaching that skill or concept will work with the child in intensive, small-group tutoring until he or she becomes proficient. Furthermore, the members of the team will constantly gather evidence of all students' learning and use that evidence to inform and improve their individual practice as part of the continuous-improvement process that drives the work of the school. When we ask which school educators would choose for their own child, the answer, invariably and unanimously, is "School B." We contend, then, if School B is what we want for our own children, we have an ethical obligation to provide such schools for all children.

Chapter 11

The Classroom as a Learning Community

I've come to the frightening conclusion that I am the decisive element in the classroom. It's my daily mood that makes the weather. As a teacher, I possess a tremendous power to make a child's life miserable or joyous. I can be a tool of torture or an instrument of inspiration. I can humiliate or humor, hurt or heal. In all situations, it is my response that decides whether a crisis will be escalated or de-escalated and a child humanized or de-humanized.

—Haim Ginott

Running a school where the students all succeed, even if some students have to help others to make the grade, is good preparation for democracy.

—William Glasser

Although the emphasis of this book is the importance of educators working together to create schools and districts that function as professional learning communities, individual teachers can apply the same principles and concepts to create learning communities in their classrooms. Just as schools benefit from a focus on learning, a collaborative culture, and the use of evidence of results to inform and improve practice, so do the classrooms within those schools.

If the traditional image of schools is a series of individual classrooms staffed by relatively autonomous teachers, the traditional image of the classroom is individual students competing with one another for the limited recognition and honors offered by their schools. Classrooms can and should, however, function as communities where individual students support one another, draw strength from one other, and "acknowledge the possibility of doing together what is impossible to do alone" (Some, 1996, p. 25). The best schools and classrooms foster a sense of community that can "bind students and teachers together in special ways . . . [that] lift both teachers and students to higher levels of self-understanding, commitment, and performance. . . . Community can help teachers and students be transformed from a collection of 'I's' to a collective 'we,' thus providing them with a unique and enduring sense of identity, belonging, and place" (Sergiovanni, 1994, p. xiii). There are specific steps teachers can take to transform their individual classrooms into learning communities.

Collaboratively Developed Classroom Norms

One of the first challenges we ask teachers to address when they are organized into collaborative teams is to establish the agreed-upon norms that will guide their work together. All groups will eventually develop norms—standard patterns of behaviors and attitudes. In a PLC, rather than simply allowing norms to emerge, teachers reflect upon the norms that will make their collective experience more satisfying and fulfilling, and then they commit to acting in accordance with those norms. Initially, teachers often equate norms with rules; however, in the context of collaborative teams, norms represent the collective commitments individuals make to one another so their work will be more rewarding. Explicitly stated, norms allow members of a team to clarify expectations of one another and to express their hopes about the experience they are about to share. Norms play an important role in transforming a group into a high-performing team (Druskat & Wolf, 2001).

Norms can also have a significant impact on the environment of an individual classroom, and we recommend teachers engage students in a collaborative process that leads the class to establish a few specific promises that each student understands, owns, and therefore agrees to honor. Students also benefit from clear expectations. Engaging students in dialogue about their hopes for the class, their teacher, and most importantly, one another is an excellent way to begin community building in the classroom.

Students are accustomed to the teacher clarifying rules on the first day of school—procedures to promote the smooth operation of the classroom. Some examples include the following:

- You must be in your seat when the bell rings.

- You must raise your hand and wait to be called upon before speaking.

- You must be given permission before . . .

    - Getting out of your seat

    - Going to the bathroom

    - Speaking to a classmate, and so on

The classroom as a learning community would certainly ask students to identify the rules they feel are necessary to promote learning for all (Marzano, 2007). Teachers should also, however, ask students to consider the commitments they will make to one another to help each other enjoy a successful and satisfying school year.

For example, imagine a classroom teacher who asks students to think of a time when they were members of a group or team and enjoyed a wonderful experience, as well as any instances when their membership was unsatisfying, disappointing, or even hurtful. Students typically generate answers such as these:

- I liked it when we all supported each other and cheered for each other.

- I liked it when I knew my teammates were committed to doing their best.

- I didn't like being on my team because there were too many cliques.

- I didn't like it when people would put each other down or criticize each other.

Once the lists are complete, students are asked to consider the commitments they could make to one another that would promote the conditions on the positive list and avoid those on the negative list. The resulting norms typically include such commitments as these:

1. We will support each other's learning and encourage each other.

2. We will act respectfully toward one another, always treating each other as we would like to be treated.

3. We will contribute to our cooperative learning teams and help each other achieve the essential outcomes of each unit.

Of course, the nature and extent of student collaboration to establish norms will depend to some extent on the age of the students. Even in primary grades, however, students can be engaged in the process of establishing an agreed-upon way of doing things and articulating expectations for both behavior and learning.

There is compelling evidence that developing classroom norms "is a worthwhile investment not only for building a sense of community within the classrooms but also in terms of individual and group achievement, classroom management, and emotional stability for students and the teacher" (Levine, 2003, p. 10). Norms can also serve as a powerful tool for teachers and students to use when addressing someone who fails to honor the commitments of the group. Thus, the teacher who applies learning community concepts in the classroom will not limit his or her dialogue with students to rules, which tend to focus on efficiency. They will also address the collective commitments students can make to one another to promote positive relationships, academic success, and a sense of community.

Tips for Effective Classroom Norms

The work of William Glasser, Harry Wong, and Lee Canter could serve as valuable resources for teachers who are looking for a deeper exploration of classroom norms than we are able to provide in this book. We do, however, offer the following suggestions for teachers considering using norms to create a learning community in their classrooms.

Align Classroom Norms With School-Wide Expectations

Help students build shared knowledge on documents such as the school-wide code of conduct, key components of the character-education curriculum, report card standards for citizenship and work habits, and so on, so that students align their classroom norms to the school's expectations for students.

Keep the List of Norms Few in Number

It is much better to ask the class to agree on a few (four to six) essential commitments rather than a long list of rules. The shorter list increases the likelihood that students will remember the norms and put them into practice.

Allow Each Classroom to Establish Its Own Norms

The collaborative process of developing norms is more important than the actual list of norms. Norms should reflect the commitments of the members of the classroom community, and every student in the class should be engaged in making those commitments.

State Norms as Commitments to Act in Certain Ways Rather Than as Beliefs

The power of classroom norms lies in the fact that the group, through a collaborative process, commits to behave in certain, specific ways. For example, "We will treat one another with consideration and respect" is more powerful than "We believe in courtesy."

Review and Refer to Norms on a Regular Basis

For the first few months of school, it will be helpful to begin and end every class period or school day with a review of the agreed-upon norms. For example, ask each student to engage in a written or verbal reflection of how well he or she feels the class is living up to the norms, and then ask each student to report on his or her own observance of the norms.

Model and Celebrate the Classroom Commitments

Students learn what their teacher truly values by the way their teacher behaves. Teachers who model the established norms of their classroom and celebrate evidence of the norms at work in the classroom send the message that the norms are important, which increases the likelihood that students will act in accordance with them. Norms also are a powerful tool for addressing inappropriate behavior, providing teachers with a basis for confronting behavior that is incongruent with the classroom commitments (Marzano, 2007). Over time, students will become more adept at monitoring their own behavior and applying gentle peer pressure if others are violating classroom norms.

Strategies for Creating a Learning Community in the Classroom

Once the classroom norms have been developed to help promote a positive environment for learning, teachers can help students turn their attention to the question, "What is it I am expected to learn?"

Present Clearly Defined Learning Outcomes in Terms Students Understand

We have stressed repeatedly that any school committed to helping all students learn will take steps to ensure every teacher can answer the question, "What are students expected to learn?" for every course, grade level, and unit of instruction. One of the main differences between effective and ineffective teachers is that the former know exactly what they want to accomplish, and so they are able to monitor student learning on a continuous basis. But if classrooms are to function as learning communities, teachers will be certain to review the "Learn what?" question with students and answer it in terms each student can understand. The power of clearly defined outcomes is magnified significantly when students themselves understand the learning targets that have been established for them. Therefore, teachers whose classrooms function as learning communities make a conscious effort to adopt the students' frame of reference, using vocabulary, examples, metaphors, and stories specifically designed to clarify targets in terms students can understand. It is only when students become clear regarding intended outcomes that they can play an important role in monitoring their own learning.

Rick Stiggins (2001) has been a forceful and effective advocate of the need for teachers to establish specific learning targets that define student success in "kid friendly language so those we expect to hit the target know precisely what we expect of them" (p. 58). It is of little value, for example, for a teacher to tell students, "This semester you will learn to write a good persuasive essay," unless he or she can provide students with samples of student work that demonstrate "good" writing in a way that distinguishes it from "fair" or "great" writing. This strategy helps students see the differences.

Therefore, as teachers in a PLC approach each unit, they begin with the end in mind. They make certain their students understand 1) what they will know and be able to do as a result of the unit, 2) why it is important, 3) how they will demonstrate their knowledge and skills, and 4) what specific criteria are being used to assess the quality of their knowledge and skills. A *good* teacher has reflected upon each of these questions and is able to answer them. A *great* teacher ensures his or her *students* have considered and can answer each of these questions.

Encourage Student Participation in Assessment of Their Learning

Providing students with feedback regarding their learning is one of the most powerful factors impacting student achievement. In fact, after reviewing over 8,000 studies, one researcher concluded, "The most powerful single modification that enhances student achievement is feedback. The simplest prescription for improving education must be dollops of feedback" (Hattie, 1992, p. 9). The feedback is most powerful, however, when it is *timely, specific* to established criterion, and *corrective* in nature. In other words, feedback should be provided promptly, it should help students recognize the level of their performance relative to a specific target of knowledge or skill, and it should go beyond stipulating whether a response is right or wrong and instead provide an explanation of what is right and what is wrong to encourage the student to keep working (Marzano, Pickering, & Pollock, 2001).

Even the best-intentioned teacher will have difficulty meeting these standards if he or she is the only person to provide feedback in the classroom. For example, a high school English teacher responsible for 100 students who hopes to devote 15 minutes per week to providing each student with feedback on his or her writing will need 25 hours per week to complete this task. This would be a daunting task to say the least. If, however, students are clear on the learning targets they are expected to achieve, and if they understand the criteria being used to assess the quality of their writing, they can provide their peers with timely, specific, and corrective feedback. This student feedback can both enhance student learning and contribute to a sense of community (Marzano, Pickering, & Pollock, 2001).

Students who understand the specific learning targets they are expected to achieve can also monitor their own learning through charts that help them track their own progress (Marzano, 2007). Consider again the second-grade team from Westlawn Elementary School in Fairfax County, Virginia, from chapter 7. Once the teachers on that team clarified the most essential second-grade math outcomes, they shared those outcomes with the students and parents in the fall and then referenced them constantly throughout the school year during each unit and each lesson. For example, when they started the unit on addition, team members presented each student with this very specific list of essential outcomes:

In this unit on addition, I will learn how to . . .

- Add numbers to the sum of 18.
- Solve the missing addend.
- Find a related addition sentence.
- Use correct addition vocabulary.
- Use a graph to solve problems.
- Solve story problems.

Immediately after each formative assessment, each student completed a summary sheet similar to the sample shown on page 292.

This quick review enabled students to identify where they were having difficulty. Students then assigned themselves to the appropriate group or learning center during the intervention and enrichment block in their daily schedule. For example, if a student got only one out of four story problems correct on the assessment, he or she worked with a teacher and the other second-grade students who needed more practice with that skill during intervention period for several days. The teacher then asked each student to think aloud as he or she worked on a problem and then immediately identified and clarified any errors. Ultimately, the students were reassessed, they plotted their results once again, celebrated their improvements with their teacher, and determined where to go next in their learning process.

Use Cooperative Learning

Cooperative learning strategies, when implemented well, not only have a significant positive impact on student achievement, but they also require students and teachers to create classrooms that function as

Name: _____ Date: _____

Directions: Use your green crayon to complete each bar graph, showing the problems you solved correctly on this assessment by marking the box above it.

My Math Concepts

I am learning how to . . .

Add numbers to the sum of 18: ☐ ☐ ☐ ☐ ☐ ☐ ☐ ☐
                                  1   4   7   9 11 16 26 28

Solve the missing addend: ☐ ☐ ☐ ☐ ☐
                        2   3   5   8 10

Find a related addition sentence: ☐ ☐ ☐ ☐ ☐
                              6 12 13 14 27

Use correct addition vocabulary: ☐ ☐ ☐ ☐
                            15 17 18 29

Use a graph to solve problems: ☐ ☐ ☐ ☐
                        19 21 22 25

Solve story problems: ☐ ☐ ☐ ☐
                20 23 24 30

learning communities. Johnson and Johnson (1994) contend there are three basic ways students can interact with each other as they learn:

1. They can compete to see who is best.

2. They can work individualistically toward a goal without paying attention to other students.

3. They can work cooperatively with a vested interest in each other's learning as well as their own.

There is substantial evidence that cooperative learning groups are far more powerful than either of the other two approaches (Johnson, Johnson, & Stanne, 2000; Marzano, Pickering, & Pollock, 2001). Recent research regarding group processes indicates the interaction that occurs during cooperative learning develops understanding and awareness in students that is extremely difficult to achieve without such interaction (McVee, Dunsmore, & Gavalek, 2005). Furthermore, the small (three or four member) team structure recommended for cooperative learning provides a learning environment better suited to address certain fundamental human needs. As William Glasser (1998) notes, "Learning together as a member of a small learning team is much more need-satisfying, especially to the needs for power and belonging, than learning individually" (p. 48).

Cooperative learning, by definition, requires students to work together to accomplish shared learning goals, meaning an individual student can accomplish his or her learning goal only if the other members of the group achieve theirs (Johnson & Johnson, 1994). Therefore, a teacher who utilizes the cooperative learning strategy designs lessons to include five basic components advocated by Johnson and Johnson:

1. Clearly Perceived Positive Interdependence

The teacher structures the lesson so students recognize they will "sink or swim" together. Every student has two basic responsibilities: learn the assigned material, and ensure that all members of the group learn the assigned material. Contributions from each member are indispensable for success, and every member has a unique contribution to make to the group effort.

2. Face-to-Face Promotive Interaction

Students encourage and facilitate each other's efforts to achieve, complete tasks, and produce in order to reach the group's goals. They help each other, share resources, provide each other with feedback to improve performance, push each other to put forth the effort essential to achieve their mutual goal, and applaud the improvement of their teammates.

3. Individual Accountability/Personal Responsibility

Individual students are held accountable by teammates and the teacher for contributing their fair share to the team's success. The team must be aware of who needs assistance, support, and encouragement, and each individual must be responsible for his or her own learning in order to help the team achieve its goals. Academic freeloading is not permitted, and teachers closely monitor the work of the teams to ensure each member is contributing.

4. Appropriate Use of Interpersonal and Small-Group Skills

To coordinate efforts to achieve their mutual goals, students must do the following:

1. Get to know and trust each other.

2. Communicate accurately and unambiguously.

3. Accept and support each other.

4. Resolve conflict constructively.

Therefore, teachers make a conscious effort to teach, recognize, and reward these skills.

5. Group Processing

In a classroom learning community, the teacher helps students reflect on the effectiveness of their cooperative teams. Students are asked to describe what actions by group members were helpful and unhelpful, and they must then make decisions about what actions to continue or change. According to Johnson and Johnson (1994), such processing does the following:

- Enables learning groups to focus on maintaining good working relationships among members

- Facilitates the learning of cooperative skills

- Ensures that members receive feedback on their participation

- Ensures that students think on the metacognitive as well as the cognitive level

- Provides the means to celebrate the success of the group and reinforce the positive behaviors of group members

Astute readers will recognize that the cooperative learning classroom described here mirrors the process of teachers working in collaborative teams within a PLC. Both call for a fundamental reorganization that fosters working in teams rather than working alone. Both call upon members of the team to establish interdependent relationships, to pursue SMART goals (strategic and specific, measurable, attainable, results-oriented, and timebound) for which members are mutually accountable, to take an interest in and promote the success of their teammates, to identify problems any member of the team may be experiencing, to share their knowledge and insights to help members resolve their problems, to develop open and trusting relationships, to encourage teammates, to acknowledge and celebrate improvement, to reflect on the effectiveness of their team, and to consider ways to improve it. In brief, both call for cooperation and collaboration rather than competition and isolation.

The Partnership for 21st Century Skills (2007) has attempted to identify the skills students must acquire to be effective in the contemporary workplace. Among those skills are the following:

- The ability to work effectively with diverse teams

- Flexibility and willingness to be helpful in making necessary compromises to accomplish a common goal

- The ability to assume shared responsibility for collaborative work

The likelihood of students acquiring these essential skills will increase significantly when teachers both model them in their professional relationships with colleagues and organize their classrooms into learning communities that call upon students to demonstrate these skills each day.

A Word of Caution for Creating Classroom Learning Communities

Educators sometimes lose sight of the classic advice, "All things in moderation." Marzano, Pickering, and Pollock's (2001) review of effective classroom practice led them to assert that cooperative learning may be the most powerful of classroom grouping strategies, a strategy that can have a very positive effect on learning. They also warn, however, that it can be overdone. Not every lesson should be designed for cooperative learning any more than every teaching decision or task should fall to a collaborative team of teachers to resolve. People also need time to learn on their own. Students can and do benefit from other instructional strategies, and best practice in teaching will always include multiple and varied strategies that do not rely solely on one technique.

A Classroom Learning Community in Action

The example of the classroom as a learning community presented earlier in this chapter referenced the work of a collaborative team of second-grade teachers; however, the concept can have a powerful impact on student learning at all grade levels. Math teachers at Adlai Stevenson High School have created one of the most successful Advanced Placement Calculus BC programs in the nation by using the team metaphor to help students create a learning community within their classrooms.

On the first day of class, calculus students are told they are pre-paring for the "championship game" to be held in May (the AP exam). Every unit and every lesson will be designed to prepare them to win the championship. They will "practice" and "scrimmage" every day as they are arranged into four-member teams to work together on problems the "coaches" (that is, teachers) have developed to prepare them for success. The purpose of every practice and scrimmage is to involve members of the team in helping one another improve. If a teammate is having diffi-culty, the members of the team are responsible for assisting that person in resolving the problem.

Of course all teams must have a goal, and for Calculus BC students, their SMART goal is explicitly stated on the first day of class and then repeated throughout the year: *Every student will achieve a score of 3 or higher on the AP exam in May.* Students are reminded over and over again that in order to achieve the goal, each of them must be dedicated not only to his or her own achievement, but also to the learning and understanding of his or her teammates.

The coaches present each student with the commitments they have made to prepare their students for success, as well as the commitments they have made to their colleagues as coaches. They then ask each four-member team of students to generate the commitments they are pre-pared to make to one another. All teams report their agreements to the entire class, and any team can then modify and adjust its commitments if its members hear ideas from others they think might benefit them.

Every common assessment the calculus coaches prepare and ad-minister throughout the year represents a regular season game, and students are called upon to help one another prepare to be successful on those game days so they have momentum going into the champi-onship. The coaches review the "stat sheets" (assessment results) with the team after each game to identify problem areas. Students are then provided some time during "practice" (class) to help each other work on those problem areas so the mistakes are not repeated in the next game. Individual students set short-term goals, such as "On the next assessment, I will be able to solve problems dealing with cosine," and team members help prepare each other to achieve those goals. If the team is unable to resolve issues that may interfere with attaining goals, members solicit the help of other teams, and finally seek the guidance of their coaches.

On the day before the big game (the AP exam), the coaches present every student with a brightly colored t-shirt with a distinctive slogan for that year's team. For example, one year the t-shirts borrowed from late night television host and comedian David Letterman to list the top 10 reasons a student should pass the AP calculus exam:

10. Because you are smart enough!

9. Stevenson teachers make calculus understandable and fun!

8. Graphing calculators can be used at Stevenson.

7. You will receive college credit.

6. Your parents will save money.

5. A calculus class in college could be very theoretical.

4. Review and cumulative exams do not exist in college.

3. You can earn money by tutoring calculus in college.

2. Classes at Stevenson are small.

1. Stevenson teachers do not use the "bell curve" for grading.

On game day, all students wear their t-shirt (and their game face) as they take their exam. In the past 3 years, 361 Stevenson students have taken the AP exam for Calculus BC, and *every one of them has earned an honor grade of 3 or higher.*

Certainly, many things have contributed to this incredible result at Stevenson. The clear and focused academic goals presented in terms students can understand, the frequent monitoring of their learning, the precise feedback regarding areas of difficulty students experience, the system of interventions that occurs within the classroom and across the course, and the commitment of the teachers to improve their own instructional effectiveness have all played a role in this remarkable story of the realization of high expectations for student learning. But the ability of the teachers to create classroom communities where students are organized into teams in which members work interdependently to achieve shared goals for which they are mutually accountable has been a major factor in the extraordinary success of this program.

Chapter 12

The Role of the Principal in a Professional Learning Community

Throughout the years, leaders from all professions, from all economic sectors, and from around the globe continue to tell us, "You can't do it alone." Leadership is not a solo act; it's a team performance . . . the winning strategies will be based on the "we not I" philosophy.

—James Kouzes and Barry Posner

Sharing leadership is a fundamental principle and dynamic of learning communities. We encountered no instances to support the "great leader theory," charismatic people who create extraordinary contexts for teaching by virtue of their unique vision. Strong principals empower and support teacher leadership to improve teaching practice.

—Milbrey McLaughlin and Joan Talbert

When the first studies of effective schools were conducted in the 1970s, researchers concluded the correlates of effective schools—high expectations, clear and focused academic goals, a safe and orderly environment, and frequent monitoring of student learning—could neither be brought together nor kept together without strong administrative leadership from the principal (Brookover & Lezotte, 1979; Edmonds,

1979; Lezotte, 1991). This finding regarding the critical role of the principal in creating the conditions for school improvement has been replicated repeatedly for 30 years. Consider the following findings:

- Teachers' relationship with the principal and their perceptions of the principal as a leader have a major impact on school climate and teacher satisfaction. Most schools lack the capacity for improvement and renewal because their principals lack the prerequisite skills of group leadership. Principals typically lack the capacity to lead in the solution to school-wide problems. (Goodlad, 1984)

- The role that principals play as they interact with teachers makes a profound impact on teacher behavior and student learning. . . . The leadership of the school principal is critical to improving the workplace for teachers. (Smith & Andrews, 1989, p. viii)

- How can schools become professional communities? Success depends largely upon human resources and leadership. The effectiveness of a school staff depends much on the quality of leadership. (Newmann & Wehlage, 1995, p. 37)

- The principal plays a critical role in the development of professional learning communities, forging the conditions that give rise to the growth of learning communities in schools. (Louis, Kruse, & Raywid, 1996, p. 19)

- Principals are widely seen as indispensable to innovation. No reform effort, however worthy, survives a principal's indifference or opposition. (Evans, 2001, p. 202)

- It turns out that leadership not only matters: it is second only to teaching among school-related factors in its impact on student learning. . . . Indeed, there are virtually no documented instances of troubled schools being turned around without intervention by a powerful leader. Many other factors may contribute to such turnarounds, but leadership is the catalyst. (Leithwood, Seashore Louis, Anderson, & Wahlstom, 2004, p. 3, 5)

- If you take the principal and other key building leaders out of the picture as a committed and skillful force for these qualities, then no successful professional learning community will form. The possibilities of all other forces combined (state education law and policy, standardized testing and accountability, central office, staff development, parent and community pressure) to raise student achievement are fatally weakened. (Saphier, 2005, p. 38)

- Research over the last 35 years provides strong guidance on specific leadership behaviors for school administrators and those behaviors have well-documented effects on student achievement. . . . A highly effective school leader can have a dramatic influence on the overall academic achievement of students. (Marzano, Waters, & McNulty, 2005, p. 7, 10)

- Because of their positional authority and control over school resources, principals are in a strategic position to promote or inhibit the development of a teacher learning community in their school. . . . School administrators set the stage and conditions for starting and sustaining the community development process. (McLaughlin & Talbert, 2006, p. 56)

- It should be clear, then, that school improvement is an organizational phenomenon, and therefore the principal, as leader, is key. (Fullan, 2007, p. 167)

Given the vital importance of the principalship, it is not surprising that many authors and organizations have offered advice regarding the position and keys to fulfilling its responsibilities. Principals have been urged to be "instructional leaders" who function as "forceful and dynamic professionals through a variety of personal characteristics, including high energy, assertiveness, ability to assume the initiative, openness to new ideas, tolerance for ambiguity, a sense of humor, analytic ability, and a practical stance toward life" (Smith & Andrews, 1989, p. 8). The same study identified 10 different behavioral descriptors that call upon principals to assume four roles: "principal as resource provider, principal as instructional resource, principal as communicator, and principal as visible presence" (p. 9).

Philip Hallinger and Joseph Murphy's (1985) conceptual model of the principalship offered three leadership dimensions for the role along with specific leadership practices for each dimension:

1. Defining the school's mission

   - Framing school goals
   - Communicating school goals

2. Managing the instructional program

   - Supervising and evaluating instruction
   - Coordinating the curriculum
   - Monitoring student progress

3. Promoting a positive learning climate

   - Protecting instructional time
   - Promoting professional development
   - Maintaining high visibility

- Providing incentives for teachers
- Enforcing academic standards
- Providing incentives for students

Leithwood, Seashore Louis, Anderson, and Wahlstom (2004, p. 3) offered these three keys to effectiveness for principals:

1. Setting directions—charting a clear course that everyone understands, establishing high expectations, and using data to track progress and performance

2. Developing people—providing teachers and others in the system with the necessary support and training to succeed

3. Making the organization work—ensuring that the entire range of conditions and incentives in the school fully supports rather than inhibits teaching and learning

Yet another team of researchers (Goldring, Murphy, Elliott, & Cravens, 2007) created a model for school leaders consisting of six core components and six key processes. Core components, which they defined as "characteristics of schools that support the learning of students and enhance the ability of teachers to teach," included high standards for student learning, rigorous curriculum, quality instruction, a culture of learning and professional behavior, connections to external communities, and systemic performance accountability that utilizes both internal and external accountability measures. Key processes, which they defined as "leadership behaviors that raise organizational members' level of commitment and shape organizational culture," included planning, implementing, supporting, advocating, communicating, and monitoring.

The Interstate School Leaders Licensure Consortium (1996) has decreed that quality school leaders promote the success of all students by doing the following:

- Developing a vision of learning shared and supported by the school community

- Advocating, nurturing, and sustaining a school culture and instructional program conducive to student learning and professional growth

- Ensuring effective and efficient management of the learning environment

- Responding to the diverse community interests and needs and mobilizing community resources

- Acting with integrity, fairness, and in an ethical manner

- Understanding and responding to the larger political, social, economic, and cultural context

Principals at all levels receive specific recommendations for their leadership roles. Elementary school principals have been urged to embrace specified standards for what they should know and be able to do to lead learning communities (National Association of Elementary School Principals, 2001, p. 6–7). Those standards include the following:

- Lead schools in a way that places student and adult learning at the center.

- Set high expectations and standards for the academic and social development of all students and the performance of adults.

- Demand content and instruction that ensure student achievement of agreed-upon standards.

- Create a culture of continuous learning for adults tied to student learning and other school goals.

- Use multiple sources of data as diagnostic tools to assess, identify, and apply instructional improvement.

- Actively engage the community to create shared responsibility for student and school success.

The National Association of Secondary School Principals has presented nine cornerstone strategies and 30 recommendations that middle school principals should implement to create the collaborative leadership, professional learning community, personalized school environment, and aligned curriculum, instruction, and assessment that are essential to improving student learning (2006).

In *Breaking Ranks* (1996), high school principals received 80 recommendations for leading their schools. Eight years later, *Breaking Ranks II* gave principals a different framework that included 31 recommendations and seven cornerstone strategies to address three core areas of school improvement: developing a professional learning community, providing students with meaningful adult relationships to support their learning, and developing personalized, relevant, and rigorous learning experiences for students to prepare them for success beyond high school (National Association of Secondary School Principals, 2004).

Kathleen Cotton's (2003) review of the research led her to identify no less than 25 principal behaviors that affect student achievement. Two years later, Marzano, Waters, and McNulty (2005) conducted a meta-analysis of the research on school leadership to identify 21 different responsibilities school leaders must fulfill.

It could be argued the primary task of the principal is leadership; however, even on this seemingly unassailable responsibility, principals have received mixed messages. Do those who sit in the principal's chair function most effectively when they act as instructional leaders, transformational leaders, servant leaders, strategic leaders, learning leaders, empowering leaders, or moral leaders? Even the most diligent principal, one who is willing to explore the numerous recommendations regarding how he or she could be most effective in the role, is likely to be overwhelmed by the avalanche of advice and the ever-expanding lists of responsibilities. Principals are now called upon to do far more than "run a tight ship," provide an orderly environment, and ensure the happiness of the adults in the building. In fact, Michael Fullan (2007) claims the increasingly unreasonable demands of the job have put the principalship in an "impossible position" (p. 168).

The Principal in a Professional Learning Community

The most effective organizations have the ability to "reduce all the challenges and dilemmas to simple ideas" by focusing on what is essential and using the simple ideas as a frame of reference for all their decisions (Collins, 2001, p. 91). The best leaders respond to the complex and competing demands of their position by identifying "the few crucial things that matter most right now and relentlessly communicating about those few things" (Pfeffer & Sutton, 2006, p. 206). In short, effective organizations and those who lead them "keep the main thing the main thing."

We believe principals benefit from embracing a few key ideas to help them create a meaningful and manageable conceptual framework for addressing the complexities of the position. We assert principals of PLCs must:

1. Be clear about their primary responsibility.

2. Disperse leadership throughout the school.

3. Bring coherence to the complexities of schooling by aligning the structure *and* culture of the school with its core purpose.

Principals of PLCs Are Clear About Their Primary Responsibility

Peter Drucker (1992) has urged leaders to define and clarify their essential task by considering the question, "What is the one thing that I, and only I, can do that if done well will make a difference in this organization?" (p. 345). Clarity and specificity about the essence of their main task are the hallmarks of effective leaders. When working with principal groups, we often ask participants to imagine they are being visited by extraterrestrials who have been sent to clarify the role of the person earthlings call "the principal." Participants typically struggle to respond. This is problematic because the way in which people define their job has a significant impact on how they approach their work each day.

We urge those who hope to serve as the principal of a PLC to define their job as follows:

> My responsibility is to create the conditions that help the adults in this building continually improve upon their collective capacity to ensure all students acquire the knowledge, skills, and dispositions essential to their success.

If principals approach their work each day with an understanding of and commitment to this fundamental responsibility, they increase the likelihood that their day-to-day decisions will be aligned with the big ideas that drive PLCs.

Principals of PLCs Disperse Leadership

Philip Hallinger (2007) found that views of the principalship have evolved during the 3 decades he has studied the position. The 1980s was the era of strong *instructional leaders*, and the research offered tales of aggressive, dynamic, assertive, and highly directive men and women who were determined to bring their personal vision of effective schooling to life. Although these strong leaders could serve as catalysts for school improvement, the improvement was difficult to sustain beyond the tenure of the principal.

The 1990s brought the idea of *transformational leadership* to the position. Principals were now called upon to reduce their control of staff and to instead empower individuals to make their own decisions, fulfill their personal visions of schooling, and help teachers become the best they could be. Just as school sites were given greater autonomy during this era, principals extended greater autonomy to classroom teachers. As we have seen in earlier chapters, however, merely providing educators with more autonomy does not ensure they will focus on matters that have a positive impact on student learning, and individual development does not guarantee organizational improvement.

With the turn of the century, principals were urged to embrace *shared leadership* as the model best suited to the new image of the school as a community of learners. This concept is based on the premise that expertise is widely distributed throughout a school rather than vested in an individual person or position. A principal, therefore, should develop the capacity of people throughout the school to assume leadership roles and view himself or herself as a leader of leaders.

Each of these images has something to offer the contemporary principal. Principals of a PLC will certainly need to be directive instructional leaders on occasion. They should be committed to empowering teachers and encouraging both the collective autonomy of teams as well as latitude for individuals within well-defined parameters. If, however, principals are to create the conditions that help the adults in their schools continually improve upon their collective capacity to ensure all students acquire the knowledge, skills, and dispositions essential to their success, they must embrace the concept of widely shared leadership for both research-based and practical reasons.

In chapter 5, we offered quotes from researchers both inside and outside of education who arrived at the same conclusion: No single person has the expertise, influence, and energy to initiate and sustain a substantive change process. Researchers who have focused on the role of principals in building PLCs concur. McLaughlin and Talbert (2006) found that "strong learning communities develop when principals learn to relinquish a measure of control and help others participate in building leadership throughout the school" (p. 81). Their synthesis of the research on the principalship led Marzano, Waters, and McNulty (2005) to urge principals to disperse responsibilities throughout a leadership team to create a "purposeful community . . . with the collective efficacy and capacity . . . to accomplish goals that matter to all community members through agreed upon processes" (p. 99). Lieberman (1995) concluded effective principals must "act as partners with teachers, involved in a collaborative quest to examine practices and improve school" (p. 9). Louis, Kruse, and Marks (1996) found schools with strong PLCs were led by principals who "delegated authority, developed collaborative decision-making processes, and stepped back from being the central problem solver" (p. 193). Senge and Kofman (1995) concluded "leadership in a learning community is inevitably collective" (p. 34). Once again, creating a PLC means shaping a new school culture, and that Herculean task will require more than one leader.

Furthermore, no single person could address all the responsibilities principals have been asked to shoulder. Marzano, Waters, and McNulty (2005) acknowledged it would be rare indeed to find an individual capable of mastering the 21 different responsibilities required of contemporary school leaders. They assert the only practical solution to this challenge is to develop a strong leadership team that assumes collective responsibility for creating conditions that enhance student and adult learning.

The opportunity to lead in a PLC should not, however, be limited to a designated team. Principals should work with staff to create structures to foster widely dispersed leadership. For example, in addition to a school leadership team, a leader could be designated for every grade-level, interdisciplinary, or course-specific team. Individual staff members could lead task forces to examine some aspect of the school and develop recommendations to improve it. Most importantly, the collaborative-team learning process creates the opportunity for situational leadership based on expertise. Every teacher in a PLC can assume the lead in the team's collective inquiry into best practice when results from common assessments indicate an individual has developed particular expertise in teaching a concept or skill. Membership on a team gives everyone "a chance to shine, a way to demonstrate leadership" (Kanter, 2004, p. 225). As Sergiovanni (2005) writes, "Viewing leadership as a group activity linked to practice rather than just an individual activity linked to a person helps match the expertise we have in a school with the problems and situations we face" (p. 45).

The best way principals can help others learn to lead is to put them in a position where they are called upon to lead, and then provide them with feedback and support as they move forward. As a study conducted by the Center for Creative Leadership (Hernez-Broome & Hughes, 2004) concluded, "The goal of leadership development ultimately involves action not knowledge . . . [helping people] to learn from their work rather than taking them away from their work to learn. . . . State of the art leadership development now occurs in the context of ongoing work initiatives that are tied to organizational imperatives" (p. 27).

Reciprocal Accountability

But building capacity requires more than assigning new responsibilities to people and allowing them to flourish or flounder, to sink or swim. When principals ask teachers to lead, they are asking them to take responsibility for something beyond their classroom. Therefore, principals of PLCs recognize they have an obligation to provide staff with the resources, training, mentoring, and support to help them successfully accomplish what they have been asked to do. Elmore (2006) refers to this relationship as *reciprocal accountability*—"for every increment of performance I demand of you, I have an equal responsibility to provide you with the capacity to meet that expectation" (p. 93).

For example, if teachers are being asked to collaborate, principals have an obligation to create structures that make collaboration meaningful rather than artificial, to guarantee time for collaboration during the contractual day, to establish clear priorities and parameters so that teachers focus on the right topics, to help teams make informed decisions by making the essential knowledge base easily accessible to them, to provide meaningful and timely training based on the specific needs of each team, to offer templates and models to guide their work, and to specify clear expectations and standards to help teachers assess the quality of their work. Principals will need the support and assistance of other leaders in these endeavors, but they have a responsibility to provide their staff members with everything they need to be successful in this important work.

The "Critical Issues for Team Consideration" handout on pages 314–315 is a useful tool to help principals, team leaders, and members of collaborative teams stay focused on the "right work" and to clarify their reciprocal accountability. A principal could meet with team leaders prior to initiating each issue with the teams to explore the question, "What resources and support will you need to accomplish this task successfully?"

For example, when considering the first issue, developing team norms, team leaders might ask the principal the following questions:

- What is a team norm? How are we defining the term?
- Why is it important to have norms? What is the significance of a team having explicitly stated norms?
- What are some examples of norms?
- What are the norms of high-performing teams?
- Can we provide a template and/or process for writing norms?
- What suggestions or tips can we offer to guide the work as teams write norms?
- How can we assess the quality of team norms?
- What happens if the team balks at writing norms? How should we respond?
- What happens if a team member does not honor norms?

Critical Issues for Team Consideration

Team Name: _____

Team Members: _____

Use the following rating scale to indicate the extent to which each statement is true of your team.

1	2	3	4	5	6	7	8	9	10
Not True of Our Team				**Our Team Is Addressing This**					**True of Our Team**

1. ___ We have identified team norms and protocols to guide us in working together.

2. ___ We have analyzed student achievement data and established SMART goals to improve upon this level of achievement we are working interdependently to attain. (SMART goals are Strategic and Specific, Measurable, Attainable, Results-Oriented, and Timebound.)

3. ___ Each member of our team is clear on the knowledge, skills, and dispositions (that is, the essential learning) that students will acquire as a result of (1) our course or grade level and (2) each unit within the course or grade level.

4. ___ We have aligned the essential learning with state and district standards and the high-stakes assessments required of our students.

5. ___ We have identified course content and topics that can be eliminated so we can devote more time to the essential curriculum.

6. ___ We have agreed on how to best sequence the content of the course and have established pacing guides to help students achieve the intended essential learning.

7. ___ We have identified the prerequisite knowledge and skills students need in order to master the essential learning of each unit of instruction.

8. ___ We have identified strategies and created instruments to assess whether students have the prerequisite knowledge and skills.

9. ___ We have developed strategies and systems to assist students in acquiring prerequisite knowledge and skills when they are lacking in those areas.

10. ___ We have developed frequent common formative assessments that help us to determine each student's mastery of essential learning.

11. ___ We have established the proficiency standard we want each student to achieve on each skill and concept examined with our common assessments.

12. ___ We use the results of our common assessments to assist each other in building on strengths and addressing weaknesses as part of an ongoing process of continuous improvement designed to help students achieve at higher levels.

13. ___ We use the results of our common assessments to identify students who need additional time and support to master essential learning, and we work within the systems and processes of the school to ensure they receive that support.

14. ___ We have agreed on the criteria we will use in judging the quality of student work related to the essential learning of our course, and we continually practice applying those criteria to ensure we are consistent.

15. ___ We have taught students the criteria we will use in judging the quality of their work and provided them with examples.

16. ___ We have developed or utilized common summative assessments that help us assess the strengths and weaknesses of our program.

17. ___ We have established the proficiency standard we want each student to achieve on each skill and concept examined with our summative assessments.

18. ___ We formally evaluate our adherence to team norms and the effectiveness of our team at least twice each year.

When considering the third issue on the list of critical issues—clarity regarding the knowledge, skills, and dispositions students must acquire for the course or grade level and every unit of instruction—the principal and team leaders would work together to ensure they could answer questions such as these:

- Why should we ask teachers to engage in this activity? What are the benefits of addressing this issue?

- What do the state standards stipulate students must learn? Are we providing each teacher with ready access to the state standards?

- What does the district curriculum guide stipulate students must learn? Are we providing every teacher with ready access to the curriculum guide?

- What skills and knowledge have been identified as most essential by national organizations as well as by the teachers in the grade level or course above ours?

- How will we provide teams with time to complete this task?

- What criteria can we use in determining the significance of a recommended standard?

- What knowledge, skills, and concepts are emphasized on district, state, and national assessments that will be administered to our students? What format will those assessments use? How will students be asked to demonstrate their proficiency on the assessments?

- What is a reasonable number of anticipated essential learnings for each grade level or course?

- How will we respond if teachers suggest we can skip this step because the state, district, or textbook has already specified what students must learn?

- How will we respond if teachers suggest we are attempting to take away their autonomy?

- What is the timeline for completing this task?

- What happens if the team cannot reach consensus on this question of what students must learn?

By reviewing each issue and activity with team leaders prior to their leading the collective inquiry process with their colleagues, a principal can identify and then gather the resources to help leaders facilitate the process, rehearse the questions and issues likely to arise, and help boost the confidence of the team leaders. In this sense, the principal functions as a servant leader by giving the people in the organization the tools and skills to ensure their eventual success as they undertake a challenge. The principal of a PLC will have high expectations for the adults in the organization, but those expectations are always accompanied by the question, "What can I do to help you?"

When Kouzes and Posner (1987) examined how effective leaders get things done in their organizations, they identified five core practices common to successful leaders. The most significant of those practices was that leaders empowered others, which they described as "the process of turning followers into leaders themselves" (p. 179). Two decades later, they reiterated this idea that leaders who leave the most lasting legacy are those who see their role as teaching, serving, and developing others to function as leaders (Kouzes & Posner, 2006).

Principals of PLCs Bring Coherence to the Complexities of Schooling by Aligning the Structure and Culture of the School With Its Core Purpose

Establishing clarity and coherence in schools is particularly challenging for educators who suffer from the "projectitis" and "initiative fatigue" caused by the relentless ebb and flow of new programs and projects washing upon them constantly from the federal, state, and district level. But the "coherent integration of cultural and structural conditions" is essential to the success of educators who hope to create PLCs and raise student achievement (Newmann & Associates, 1996, p. 14).

Elmore (2006) asserts coherence on basic goals and values is a "precondition for the exercise of any effective leadership around instructional improvement" (p. 63). We urge principals to reverse the logic of Elmore's assertion and to recognize their effective leadership is a prerequisite for establishing the coherent sense of purpose, direction, and goals essential to an improving school.

Principals of PLCs provide clarity and coherence when they remain focused on the purpose of their schools and their responsibilities as principals. They know the school exists to help all students learn at high levels, and they know if that purpose is to be accomplished, they must create the conditions that help the adults in the building continually improve upon their collective capacity to ensure all students acquire the knowledge, skills, and dispositions essential to their success.

The certainty of purpose that characterizes principals of PLCs does not mean they possess all the answers. It does mean, however, that they are skillful at asking the right questions and engaging people throughout the school in the consideration of those questions. Getting the questions right has been described as essential to effective leadership because engaging people in the right questions can help determine the focus and future of the organization (Block, 2003).

We suggest principals of PLCs use the three big ideas presented in chapter 1 to keep the following questions at the forefront of their schools:

1. Because we are committed to helping all students acquire the knowledge, skills, and dispositions essential to their success, our collective inquiry should explore the following questions:

   • Have we helped each collaborative team of teachers build shared knowledge regarding state standards, district curriculum guides, trends in student achievement, and expectations for the next course or grade level?

- Has our collective inquiry enabled each team to identify the *essential* knowledge, skills, and dispositions for every unit of their course or grade level?

- Can this curriculum be taught in the amount of time we have available to teach?

- How can we ensure each teacher is aware of and committed to teaching the agreed-upon guaranteed and viable curriculum?

- What evidence are we gathering to assess the learning of our students? Is there additional evidence that would provide us with useful information?

- Have the members of every collaborative team clarified the criteria they will use in judging the quality of student work, and can they apply those criteria consistently?

- What systems are in place to monitor the learning of every student on a frequent and timely basis?

- Do we use assessments to identify students who are experiencing difficulty?

- Do we provide students who experience difficulty with additional time and support for learning in a timely, directive, and systematic way?

- Do we provide students who experience difficulty with multiple opportunities to demonstrate their learning?

- What strategies have we put in place to enrich and extend the learning of students who are proficient?

- Have we examined all of our practices and procedures to ensure they encourage student learning rather than discourage it?

- Do our day-to-day actions convey the message to our students and each other that we expect all students to learn at high levels?

2. Because we understand we cannot help all students learn without a collaborative and collective effort, our collective inquiry should explore the following questions:

   - Are all staff members assigned to a collaborative team whose members are working interdependently to achieve a common SMART goal for which they are mutually accountable?

   - Have we provided teams with adequate time to meet? What strategies could we explore for providing more time for collaboration?

   - What evidence do we have that teams are focusing on the right things—the issues that can have the greatest impact on student learning?

   - What resources and support do our collaborative teams need to develop their capacity to improve student achievement?

   - Have we provided parents with the resources, tools, and timely information that enable them to be partners in the education of their children?

3. Because we recognize our collective efforts must be assessed on the basis of results rather than activities, our collective inquiry should explore the following questions:

   - What evidence do we have that our curriculum, instruction, and assessments are preparing all our students for success on the high-stakes tests they are expected to take?

   - What evidence do we have that our curriculum, instruction, and assessments have prepared all our students for success at the next level, even after they have left our school?

- Is every member of the staff aware of last year's results on local, state, and national indicators of student achievement for his or her team and for the school in general?

- Are the members of every team aware of our school goals and clear on how their team is contributing to achieving those goals?

- Are we providing every teacher and every team with ongoing and timely information about results, and are they able to use that information to improve their individual and collective practice? How do we know?

- What evidence do we have that we are more effective in helping students learn today than we have been in the past?

- Are we making decisions based on evidence rather than on conjecture or appeals to mindless precedent?

Research on the principalship has consistently described the most effective principals as instructional leaders—an image that has the principal "hip-deep in curriculum and instruction" (Hallinger, 2007). We advocate for a new image. Schools do not need instructional leaders; they need *learning leaders*—leaders fixated on evidence of learning. When principals use the questions presented here to drive a school, they move the conversation from "What was taught?" or "How was it taught?" to the far more important questions of "Was it learned?" and "How can we use evidence of learning to strengthen our professional practice?"

This shift in focus will impact the day-to-day work of the principal in significant ways. For example, the formal teacher supervision and evaluation process used in most school districts is grounded in the assumptions of traditional bureaucracy—supervisors must monitor and inspect the work of subordinates to ensure it meets standards. In this traditional model, it is assumed that teachers only have "regular" vision; therefore, we need principals with *"super"* vision to monitor and improve their practice. Thus, principals should conduct both frequent walkthroughs of classrooms as well as lengthier classroom observations to gather information to be used in the formal evaluations of teachers. A second assumption that drives this process is the notion that principals should improve their schools one teacher at a time because, once again, a school is nothing more than a series of independent classrooms.

We believe principals should devote considerable time observing the classrooms of teachers new to the building to provide those teachers with support, assist in their orientation to the school, and communicate what is valued. We recognize there are benefits to principals meeting with individual teachers to discuss curriculum and instruction, and the classroom supervision process provides a venue for that discussion. We understand most districts and states require some form of formal classroom observations of teachers on a periodic basis, and we think the clinical supervision model provides the best format for that task. We have high regard for the work of Charlotte Danielson (2007) and believe she provides an important framework for analysis of and dialogue about teaching. Nevertheless, we submit the following hard facts that we contend represent the norm for most formal teacher-evaluation processes:

- Although one of the stated purposes of teacher evaluation is to identify and remediate unsatisfactory performance, it is an *extremely* rare occurrence for a teacher to be designated as unsatisfactory because of his or her classroom teaching. For example, the state of Illinois has over 130,000 full-time teachers in its public schools, but only two teachers per year, on average, are dismissed for incompetence ("Protecting Mediocre Teachers," 2005). The odds are far greater that a tenured teacher would be struck by lightning during his or her lifetime than found to be an ineffective teacher.

- Teachers who do receive an evaluation they consider to be negative are unlikely to be receptive to the feedback. They are far more likely to attribute a poor evaluation to personality conflicts with the principal or the principal's subjectivity or lack of understanding than to weaknesses in their instruction. After all, previous principals found them to be satisfactory, if not exemplary.

- Middle and high school principals could not possibly have sufficient content expertise in all the different subject areas to provide a valid assessment of a teacher's instruction. Although they may focus on general teaching strategies, they would be hard pressed to determine the rigor, relevance, or clarity of the content being taught in courses ranging from foreign languages, to advanced calculus, to construction trades.

- Even if a principal is able to help an individual teacher develop or improve an instructional strategy, the improvement does not necessarily improve the school because, once again, individual development does not guarantee organizational improvement.

- The hours principals devote to formal teacher evaluation contribute little to the overall improvement of a school. Principal evaluation of teachers is a low-leverage strategy for improving schools, particularly in terms of the time it requires of principals.

Assume a well-intentioned principal devotes 120 hours per year to classroom walkthroughs, pre-observation conferences, formal observations, post-observation conferences, write-ups, and conversations associated with teacher evaluation. This is a conservative figure requiring the principal to devote less than 4 hours per week to the task. Now assume that same principal dedicates those 120 hours to working with staff members to develop their capacity to contribute to their collaborative teams, to removing obstacles from their collaboration, to ensuring they have the training and support they need to become high-performing teams. As a result of this process, each teacher becomes more certain regarding what students must learn and how students will demonstrate their learning. Each teacher receives evidence of his or her students' learning multiple times throughout the year and is able to consider the extent of their learning compared to the other students attempting to achieve the same standard. Each week teachers are provided with time to meet with colleagues who teach the same content and solicit their help in addressing areas of concern. Which of these strategies—individual teacher evaluation or building the capacity of collaborative teams—is more aligned with the ideas that our school is committed to learning rather than teaching, that we must work collaboratively and collectively to help all students learn, and that we must be hungry for evidence of student learning and use it as part of a continuous improvement cycle? Which of these strategies is more likely to be effective in persuading a teacher to reexamine his or her practice—a judgment about instruction following a single classroom observation or clear evidence his or her students did not learn compared to similar students who did? Which strategy is more likely to result in content-based, instructionally focused discourse? Which strategy reflects more of a commitment to widely dispersed leadership based on expertise rather than authoritarian leadership based on position? Most importantly, which of these strategies is more likely to have a positive impact on student and adult learning?

Fullan (2007) argues that although the demands upon and expectations for principals have increased dramatically, little has been removed from their plates. We concur, and suggest it is time to remove low-leverage/high-time tasks from the principalship. Teacher supervision and evaluation is one of those tasks. If principals cannot be relieved of the task, they should fulfill their state's and district's minimum requirement and devote their efforts and energy to more high-leverage strategies for improving their schools.

A New Image of Leadership

The idea of the charismatic individual principal who personally transforms a school must give way to a new image of leadership. Collins (2001) found a negative correlation between charismatic leadership and sustained greatness in the organizations he studied. The most effective leaders focused on building the capacity of their organizations to improve continuously, on developing the next generations of leaders, and on ensuring the organization would continue to thrive long after they were gone (Collins, 2001). Pfeffer and Sutton (2006) arrived at a similar conclusion, asserting leaders have the most positive impact when they focus on developing systems, teams, and cultures to ensure the ongoing success of the organization. These leaders viewed their jobs as establishing the conditions and preconditions for others to succeed.

Principals who hope to leave a positive legacy in their schools must recognize their effectiveness as leaders will be determined *after* they have left their schools. Educators have come to equate changes in leadership with changes in direction. As a result, they approach every initiative by every new principal with an air of resignation—a "this too shall pass" mentality. But a change in leadership need not result in a change in direction if 1) the initiative has been grounded in effective improvement processes and systems rather than on a charismatic individual, and 2) leaders have been developed throughout the organization to sustain those processes. Michael Fullan (2004) put it best when he said, "The main mark of an effective principal is not just his or her impact on the bottom line of student achievement but also *how many leaders he or she leaves behind who can go even further*" (p. 31).

Engaging people in the pursuit of the right questions is a powerful way for principals to reveal their priorities and give direction to people throughout the school. We will offer additional strategies in chapter 13 for the central office, where leaders also face the challenge of clarifying and communicating priorities. We close this chapter, however, with advice from the field. We have asked principals who are developing some of the most effective PLCs in the nation to share their insights on keys to the principalship.

Mike Mattos, Principal of Pioneer Middle School, Tustin, California

Oscar Wilde once wrote, "Experience is simply the name we give our mistakes." If this is the case, then during the past 7 years, I have gained a lot of "experience" as the principal of a PLC school. Based on these experiences, I share the following advice.

Don't Skip Mission

When you begin to implement PLC practices, you might fall victim to the tendency to disregard the reculturing that must take place and focus instead on restructuring your school. While it is important to address site programs and procedures, at the foundation of all PLC practices are two fundamental assumptions about the culture of your school: You must believe that *all* students can learn at high levels, and you must assume responsibility to make this outcome a reality for every child. Unfortunately, many schools embrace an entirely opposite cultural outlook, believing instead that the socioeconomic factors of poverty, race, and language are the strongest determining factors of student success. If a majority of your school staff does not believe that they or their students have the ability to overcome these outside factors, there are no structural changes that can overcome this defeatist attitude. If you implement structural changes before building consensus for a mission of learning for all, it is like building the roof before building the house.

It's Not "Buy-In," It's "Ownership"

The most common obstacle I hear from administrators who are starting down the road to becoming a PLC is a lack of staff "buy-in." I dislike the term *buy-in* because it suggests that you must offer your faculty incentives to help students learn. It is not a question of buy-in, but empowerment and ownership. People invest themselves in what they help create, so if you want buy-in, engage your staff as equal partners in creating the collective mission, vision, and practices of your school.

Essential Means Essential

There are six essential characteristics to being a PLC:

1. Shared mission, vision, collective commitments, and goals

2. Collaborative teams focused on learning

3. Collective inquiry into the current reality of the school and best school practices

4. An action orientation

5. A commitment to continuous improvement with continuous-improvement processes embedded into the routine practices of the school

6. A focus on results

These characteristics are called essential for a reason: Failure to address even one will ultimately halt the success of the whole. Additionally, do not fall into the trap of viewing these characteristics as an implementation checklist; that is, do not think that by creating a new school mission statement or putting teachers into collaborative teams, you can check off a task on your PLC to-do list. This managerial approach to PLC implementation lacks a deep understanding of the essential characteristics and how they work interdependently to create an ongoing *process* to improve student learning. The characteristics are not singular actions to be accomplished, but ongoing goals that must be continually reconsidered and embedded within all the school's beliefs and procedures.

Finally, do not confuse "simple" with "easy." One of the compelling attributes of a PLC is the simplicity of its practices—or as many people say, "It just makes sense." Unfortunately, many people associate simplicity with ease, and being a PLC is not easy—if it was, everyone would be doing it. But despite this, I could not imagine a more worthwhile or professionally rewarding pursuit.

Ken Williams, Principal of E.J. Swint Elementary School—The Learning Academy, Jonesboro, Georgia

Those familiar with the PLC concept typically think, "This just makes sense." Principals who attempt to bring the concept to life in their schools, however, must prepare for and embrace what I call PLC "*diple-mentation.*" Some phases of PLC implementation may indeed proceed very smoothly, coming together almost poetically, as you reculture your school to this far more effective way of teaching and learning. Invariably, however, other elements of the process will be wrought with false starts, errors, challenges, and frustration—that is, *implementation dips.* It is during those times that steadfast leadership from the principal is most critical.

Early in my career, I thought of myself as a failure when encountering implementation dips. I soon realized, however, these setbacks represent a valuable part of the PLC process, the essence of learning by doing. Every initiative that does not proceed as planned provides an opportunity for reflection, building shared knowledge, collective insights, refinement, and the chance to begin again more intelligently.

Through all of the diplementation challenges, I remained committed to our school becoming a PLC. The message never changed. Our mission never changed. We made the necessary adjustments within the context of our shared vision of improving student learning by becoming a PLC. This constancy and resolve provided the reassurance and encouragement our staff needed during the low points of diplementation.

So, I offer this advice: First, anticipate diplementation, and continue to support the hard work of your staff as it moves forward. Second, demonstrate flexibility and a willingness to modify the details of implementation while staying committed to the fundamentals of PLCs—a commitment to the learning of all students, a determination to create a collaborative culture, and an intense focus on results to guide your efforts and decisions. If you stay the course, you can accomplish something tremendously significant—you can make a positive difference in the lives of the students and staff you serve.

Bernice Cobbs, Former Principal of Snow Creek Elementary School, Penhook, Virginia; Current Principal of Boones Mill Elementary School, Boones Mill, Virginia

As I reflect on the principal's role in a PLC, three words come to mind: relevance, rigor, and relationships. These three words go hand in hand with the PLC process. As I began my journey as the principal of

Snow Creek Elementary School, it was important to me to understand the overall culture of the school, and the only way to do that was to build a professional relationship with the individuals I was appointed to lead. I did not fly through the door wearing my PLC cape and tights, attempting to save the school from evil forces. How did I start? I started slowly because Snow Creek School, like all schools, had established policies, practices, procedures, and rituals.

The summer before I began my first school year at Snow Creek, I met with the staff to ask crucial questions that would guide our work together:

1. What are three things that are important for people to know about our school?

2. What are the indicators that Snow Creek is a high-achieving school?

3. What are our schoolwide goals and benchmarks?

4. How do we monitor student achievement?

We then organized our staff into teams to ensure every teacher was implementing a guaranteed curriculum that was rigorous and relevant. Teams were also asked to establish strategies to monitor student learning on a frequent basis, and to work to achieve specific goals related to student learning in every grade level. Early in the process, I made a point to visit team meetings on a regular basis to monitor their progress and to provide the support they needed to become effective teams. We also devoted our faculty meetings to supporting PLC processes. For example, analyzing data was an area identified for ongoing staff development, and many faculty meetings focused on analyzing data and developing a system of interventions based on that analysis.

I offer the following suggestions to principals who hope to create PLCs in their own schools:

1. You will need widely dispersed leadership throughout the faculty. If you succeed, it will be because of the staff, not in spite of the staff, so engage teachers in ongoing dialogue about what needs to be done and what you can do to help them.

2. Team meetings and staff meetings must be purposeful and specifically designed to focus on what the staff can do to raise student achievement.

3. You must become a student of the PLC process and model the concepts and ideas for your staff.

4. Create systems to monitor student learning that are doable, teacher-friendly, and that provide teachers and teams with the timely information vital to improved instruction and intervention.

5. Keep accountability in the forefront. Every practice in the school should reflect a commitment to helping all students learn.

Clara Sale-Davis, Former Principal of Freeport Intermediate School, Freeport, Texas

Every principal eventually will leave his or her school, and therefore principals who lead PLCs must ensure they have developed other leaders to continue the journey after their inevitable departure. John C. Maxwell, author of *The 21 Irrefutable Laws of Leadership* (1998), refers to this as "The Law of Legacy," contending a leader's "lasting value is measured by succession" (p. 224)—that is, what occurs *after* the leader has left.

The Law of Legacy is not the norm in education. In my experiences as a public school educator, the arrival of each new principal or superintendent signals the winds of change. Cultures and philosophies swing like a pendulum, and apple carts are overturned to ensure everyone understands there is a new sheriff in town. Sometimes the change is needed, but often the new agenda represents change for the sake of change.

But when a school functions as a PLC, it generates many leaders who are guided by a shared vision, and thus it is able to stay the course regardless of a change in leadership. If the PLC concept has been firmly planted and has strong roots, those leaders remain committed to the journey.

An example I often share with other principals is my personal story of simultaneously battling cancer and running a school. When I learned my diagnosis would lead to radiation and chemotherapy, I contemplated a leave of absence. My grade level leaders, department chairs, cadre leaders, and assistant principals assured me that a formal leave would not be necessary and urged me to manage the school from home via phone and email.

My medical journey began. Even in my chemo fog, I realized the school continued to flourish because of its many leaders—leaders in every grade, department, and cadre who had been trained and groomed to carry out our shared vision. Our school not only survived without a principal, but became one of the highest performing schools in the district despite the fact that it served the highest percentage of students in poverty.

I returned to Freeport as a cancer survivor and began training five interns who eventually became principals at other schools. Freeport has become the training ground for leaders because it demonstrates the power of dispersed leadership and committed people working interdependently to make a difference in the lives of students. More importantly, its students have benefited from being immersed in a culture where adults have modeled self-efficacy and a willingness to accept responsibility for results.

So I offer the same advice to you that I offered these future principals. First, you must see yourself as a leader of leaders, and you must develop the leadership capacity of others. Second, demonstrate your commitment to the fundamental purpose of helping all of your students learn by doing "whatever it takes" to ensure their learning. There will be days when the pyramid of interventions seems more like a mountain of obstacles, but keep climbing and others will follow. Third, constantly remind staff members of the significance of the work they do. In shaping the lives of their students, they are shaping the future because, as Henry Adams observed, "A teacher affects eternity; he can never tell where his influence ends." Finally, remember the Law of Legacy. The ultimate test of your leadership will be your ability to generate other leaders who are capable of taking the school even further after you have gone.

Lillie Jessie, Principal of Elizabeth Vaughan Elementary School, Woodbridge, Virginia

About 10 years ago, I began to generate a list of my roles and responsibilities as a principal. I was convinced that I, like other principals, had at least 100 things to do. I was right, of course. Today there are more than 300 items on that list. Implementing a PLC, however, requires you to focus with laser-like accuracy on what matters, which is *learning*. Unfortunately, you will still have the other 299 items on your list. I offer the following three time-management keys for successful PLC implementation.

1. **Focus on learning instead of teaching.** A lot of valuable time can be lost monitoring what teachers plan to do, or by observing instructional strategies rather than monitoring the learning that results from instruction. This is a balancing act. Thursday is my data discussion day with teachers. This weekly time for discussion is engraved in stone, barring emergencies. Public, faculty-wide data sharing celebrations are built into the schedule three times a year. Deprivatization of practices, focusing on evidence of student learning, and confronting the current reality will help you avoid wasting valuable time working on what does not contribute to student and adult learning.

2. **Avoid becoming a "Whatever you say—I *hope* it will work" principal.** Implement practices that are best for children instead of those that please the adults and boost your popularity. Once you open the Pandora's box of collaboration, be ready for the natural tendency of staff to seek shortcuts around the process. Implementing a PLC is not synonymous with open-

ended experimentation. For example, several times teachers have wanted me to sign off on the panacea of departmentalization in our elementary school to reduce the burden of planning. This structure, however, was not conducive to collaboration or common assessments, and neither the data nor the physical layout of the building supported it. When I explained why I could not support the proposal, one teacher said to me, "Thanks. Most principals would have given in and said, 'Okay' instead of making us rethink this." Teachers admire principals who have principles.

3. **Avoid initiative and project overload.** Although limiting initiatives and projects is difficult because of the new accountability demands on school systems, principals must keep their staffs focused on the "main thing," and then rechannel the collective effort and energy into what matters. Somehow you have to *balance* all of the plates on your table, but it is critical that you determine what should be on the big center platter. Your school mission has to be at the center. It cannot be a beautifully written statement that has no impact on your daily practice. Our PLC mission of "Excellence for All...Whatever It Takes" will have no impact on the school unless it drives our daily actions and decisions. As the poster in my office reminds me each day, "Make the Main Thing the Main Thing . . . LEARNING!"

Dick Dewey, Former Principal of Eastview High School, Apple Valley, Minnesota

Effective leaders use the power of stories as an essential tool in the challenging work of shaping culture. As Sergiovanni (2001) writes, it is through important stories that "the school's culture is strengthened and its center of values becomes more public and pervasive" (p. 349). Be mindful of the maxim, "The people who tell the stories determine the culture," and embrace your responsibility to be the chief storyteller for your school.

For example, in the early stages of transformation, your quest to build capacity to function as a PLC will likely involve a small coalition of collaborators. Empower these pioneers with the prioritized and embedded time, space, resources, opportunity, support, and training necessary to focus their attention and help them experience success one step at a time. Then tell their evolving stories to persuade others. Keep the spotlight on their work. Publicly celebrate their successes and use the inevitable mistakes as instructive opportunities to build trust, a risk orientation, and flexibility into the culture.

Continue to share accounts of success while also respectfully and consistently shedding light on those aspects of your current reality that need to change. Use every opportunity to weave a story of an unfolding crusade toward educational excellence and equity. Infuse your stories with community values that are prized to remind staff not only where the organization is going and how to mark its progress, but even more importantly, why it is going there in the first place.

Your stories are not merely meant to entertain, but to teach and inform. As Kouzes and Posner (1999) write, "Stories make standards come alive. They move us and touch us. By telling a story in detail, leaders illustrate what everyone needs to do to live by the organization's standards. They communicate the specific and proper actions to be taken" (p. 106). When your daily conversations as well as the school's rituals and ceremonies consistently articulate the desired moral image of your PLC and celebrate the progress being made in moving toward that image, you contribute to greater clarity and coherence for every constituency comprising your school community. Furthermore, you increase the likelihood of continued progress because success becomes a very irresistible story.

Clarifying Priorities

Although these principals offer different perspectives on the position, they are united by several common characteristics. They define the purpose of their school as ensuring learning for all students, and they insist that the practices of the school are aligned with that purpose. They recognize that it takes a collective effort to ensure all students learn, and thus they foster both a collaborative culture and widely dispersed leadership. Finally, their intense focus on student learning and insistence that the school gather and act upon evidence of that learning contribute to clarity and coherence for their staffs. There is no ambiguity about priorities in their schools.

Chapter 13

The Role of the Central Office in a Professional Learning Community

> *Major change almost never wells up from the bottom. It begins near the top (and if not, it almost never takes hold without strong backing from the top). It typically starts with a key leader and a small core of people who care strongly about a particular solution to a problem. It spreads out from there. As the process unfolds, the need for pressure and support requires the assertion of executive influence. . . . Authentic leaders develop and maintain their capacity to apply top-down influence.*
>
> —Robert Evans

The Effective Schools researchers of the 1980s argued that the individual school should serve as the primary unit of change in school improvement (Lezotte, 2001). After his extensive study of schooling in America, John Goodlad arrived at the same conclusion, arguing that school improvement should "shift from the district level to the school site" (1983, p. 556). Consequently, the role of the central office in improving student learning went largely unexamined. Eventually, however, "it became clear that school improvement resulting in increased student achievement could only be sustained with strong district support"

(Lezotte, 2001). Recent research has revealed "a statistically significant relationship between district leadership and student achievement" (Waters & Marzano, 2006, p. 3). Considerable attention is now being paid to the important role the central office can play in school improvement, and recommendations regarding how central office leaders can best fulfill that role have become more explicit.

One review of research studies conducted since 1990 (Shannon & Bylsma, 2004) identified common themes in the recommendations for district leaders, clustering them into four broad categories:

1. Ensure quality teaching and learning through coordinated and aligned curriculum and assessment, coordinated and embedded professional development, and quality classroom instruction.

2. Provide effective leadership by establishing high expectations focused on learning goals and eliminating distractions and competing programs. Provide stable leadership to sustain improvement programs until they are institutionalized.

3. Develop support for system-wide improvement through timely use of data from a variety of sources. Provide the technological infrastructure, the training, and the time for teachers to delve into the data to inform their practice.

4. Promote clear, collaborative relationships by ensuring understanding of school and district roles with a balance between autonomy and control. Nurture a professional culture and collaborative relationships. Manage the impact of the external environment on schools.

The National Clearinghouse for Comprehensive School Reform conducted its own review of the research (Appelbaum, 2002) and concluded that districts should do the following six things to support school improvement:

1. Remove competing programs and requirements.

2. Empower schools to make decisions.

3. Build links between state standards and accountability measures, the district curriculum, and the improvement initiative at the school level.

4. Create a network of schools engaged in the improvement initiative so they can learn from one another.

5. Assist schools in gathering and using data.

6. Provide each school with a district-level liaison who understands the improvement model.

In 2006, Steve Anderson reported research that identified 12 keys to district support for school improvement (in Fullan, 2007, pp. 214–215):

1. A district-wide sense of efficacy

2. A district-wide focus on student achievement and the quality of instruction

3. Adoption of and commitment to district-wide performance standards

4. Development and adoption of district-wide curricula and approaches to instruction

5. Alignment of curriculum, teaching and learning materials, and assessment to relevant standards

6. Multimeasure accountability systems and system-wide use of data to inform practice, hold school and district leaders accountable for results, and monitor progress

7. Use of targets and phased-in focuses of improvement

8. Investment in instructional leadership development at the school and district levels

9. A focus on district-wide, job-embedded professional development and support for teachers

10. A district-wide and school-level emphasis on teamwork and professional community (including, in several cases, positive partnerships with unions)

11. New approaches to board-district relations and in-district relations

12. Strategic relations with state reform policies and resources

Waters and Marzano's (2006) meta-analysis of the research led them to conclude superintendents have a significant impact on student achievement when they focus their efforts on creating goal-oriented districts using the following strategies:

1. Using collaborative goal-setting that engages multiple constituencies in establishing student-achievement goals for the district and for each school

2. Identifying non-negotiable goals (that is, goals all staff members must act on) in at least two areas: specific student achievement targets for each school and use of research-based instructional strategies for each classroom. The authors clarified that the instructional goal did "not mean a single instructional model that all teachers were required to employ. It did, however, mean that the district adopted a broad but common framework for classroom instructional design and planning, common instructional language or vocabulary, and consistent use of research-based instructional strategies in each school" (p. 13).

3. Securing the support of the Board of Education for district goals

4. Monitoring district goals on an ongoing basis

5. Providing resources—time, money, training, personnel, and materials—to support the goals

But despite all this advice, district-level leaders still often lack a clear understanding of how to provide the systematic support to implement and sustain professional learning communities (Annenberg Institute for

School Reform, 2004). The appropriate delivery of central office support for improvement at the local school site remains a matter of considerable confusion and contention.

Is There a Place for Top-Down Leadership?

We have noticed an interesting phenomenon when we work with educators on strategies to improve student achievement in their buildings. They sometimes confide in us that the central office has issued a "top-down mandate" requiring all schools to embrace and model certain key concepts and practices. The term *top-down* is uttered with disdain, a pejorative term used in much the same way Rush Limbaugh would use the word *liberal,* with the assumption that we will be appalled by this affront to the autonomy of educators. After all, as we pointed out in chapter 4, is there not ample evidence that top-down improvement does not work (Fullan, 2007; Tyack & Cuban, 1995)? Is it not clear that improvement initiatives will fail unless there is buy-in, a willingness of those engaged in the initiative to rally around it? Have researchers not warned that without this buy-in, leaders will only generate resentful compliance that dooms the initiative to failure (Hargreaves & Fink, 2006; McLaughlin & Talbert, 2006)? Should not the people closest to the action, those at the school site, decide the direction of their schools?

In the ongoing debate of the efficacy of strategies to improve school districts—top-down versus bottom-up—it is apparent that top down is losing. We have encountered many district leaders who are reluctant to champion improvement for fear of being labeled with the epithet "top-down leader"—the unkindest cut of all.

The glib advice given to superintendents who actually hope to improve their schools is they must simply build widespread consensus for a concept or initiative before proceeding. But what happens when a well-intentioned leader does everything right—engages staff members in the consideration of a change initiative and presents a compelling case for moving forward—and the staff still prefers the status quo? And what if the initiative clearly and unquestionably represents a better way of operating than what currently is in place? Is the laissez-faire leadership of simply allowing people to do as they wish really the only alternative when collective inquiry, persuasion, and attempts at building consensus fail to stir people to act in new ways?

The tension regarding "who decides who decides" how (or even if) a school will be improved ignores a more central issue: Does professional autonomy extend to the freedom to disregard what is widely considered to be best practice in one's field? We suggest educators have danced around this question rather than addressing it, and their inattention to the issue has fostered an unhealthy and unrealistic sense of what constitutes professional autonomy. District leaders have contributed to this peculiar view of professionalism because they have allowed teachers and principals the discretion to ignore even the most widely recognized best practices of the profession.

As we have pointed out in earlier chapters, there is considerable evidence that leaving the issue of school improvement to each school to resolve on its own does not result in more effective schools (Elmore, 2003; Fullan, 2007; Schlechty, 2005). Therefore, leaders who create schools and districts capable of sustained substantive improvement are not laissez-faire in their approach to education. They are skillful at using the concept we introduced in chapter 4—simultaneous loose and tight leadership—and thus are able to foster autonomy and creativity (loose) within a systematic framework that stipulates clear, nondiscretionary priorities and parameters (tight). Waters and Marzano (2006) refer to this concept as "defined autonomy" and found that superintendents who had a positive impact on student achievement were very directive in specifying achievement goals and expectations at the same time they provided school leadership teams with autonomy and authority for determining how to meet those goals.

Tight About What?

Of course, the key to effective loose-tight leadership is getting tight about the right things. The standard must rest on compelling evidence of best practice, instead of on personal preference. Loose-tight leadership calls upon leaders to exercise wisdom, which Pfeffer and Sutton (2006) describe as "knowing what you know and knowing what you don't know . . . striking a balance between arrogance (assuming you know more than you do) and insecurity (believing that you know too little to act)" (p. 52). Wisdom enables people to act on current knowledge while they remain open to new knowledge, ideas, and insights. Wisdom "means they can do things now and keep learning along the way" (p. 53).

There is compelling evidence that some practices in education are more effective than others for improving student learning (see the feature box below and on the following page). When education leaders are aware of this evidence, they must act on what they know at the same time they remain open to promising new ideas. They must close the knowing-doing gap.

Conditions That Promote Student Learning at Higher Levels	Conditions That Have an Adverse Impact on Student Learning
• Teachers focus on learning rather than on teaching.	• Teachers define their role as teaching, regardless of whether or not students learn.
• Teachers are so clear about the essential knowledge, skills, and dispositions students must acquire that they have created a guaranteed and viable curriculum aligned with district and state standards.	• What students learn in a given course or grade level depends on the teacher to whom they are assigned.
• Student learning is monitored both through ongoing and varied checks for understanding each day in individual classrooms as well as through frequent common formative assessments.	• Teachers and administrators use only summative assessments to measure student learning.
• Students understand the learning targets they are expected to achieve and the criteria used to monitor the quality of their work.	• Students are unclear regarding what they are to learn and guess about how their learning will be assessed.

(continued)

Conditions That Promote Student Learning at Higher Levels (continued)	Conditions That Have an Adverse Impact on Student Learning (continued)
• Schools create and implement plans to provide students with additional time and support for learning in a timely, directive, and systematic way when students have difficulty in mastering essential learning.	• What happens when students do not learn depends on the teacher to whom they are assigned.
• Schools have systems in place to extend and enrich the learning for students who are proficient.	• Curriculum moves at a lockstep pace regardless of the degree of student proficiency.
• Teachers work together collaboratively on matters directly related to quality teaching and learning.	• Teachers work in isolation.
• Teachers use evidence of student learning to establish SMART goals as part of an embedded continuous improvement process.	• School improvement focuses on completion of projects rather than evidence of student learning.
• Teachers receive timely information about the learning of their students in comparison to other similar students, and then they work with their colleagues to build on their strengths and address their weaknesses.	• Teachers receive data that do not inform their practice.
• Teachers communicate high expectations for student achievement, conveying both their conviction that students will be successful if they work hard and their willingness to help students until they are successful.	• Students believe their learning depends on their innate ability rather than their willingness to work at learning.
• The staff makes a concerted and continuous effort to ensure the practices of the school support and encourage student learning.	• Appeals to "mindless precedent" sustain ineffective practices and procedures that interfere with learning.
• Parents are given timely information about the learning of their children and are provided with multiple avenues for becoming partners in their children's education.	• Parents are not informed regarding their students and play no role in promoting their education.

We know schools characterized by the conditions in the left column of the feature box are more likely to promote higher levels of learning than schools defined by the conditions in the right column. District leaders cannot be indifferent to the presence of conditions in their schools that have an adverse impact on student learning. They must establish clear expectations for improvement for the principals and staff of every school. District leaders who frame their loose-tight leadership with the big ideas of a PLC might establish such expectations by including the message shown in the feature box on pages 346–347 as the introduction to the Board policy manual, the faculty manual, and the job description of each principal. More importantly, they would communicate the message on a daily basis through both their words and actions.

Advice on Being Tight

Even leaders who recognize the need to be tight about the key conditions that promote student and adult learning can be ineffective in conveying the message and implementing the processes to foster those conditions. Appreciating the significance of the concept of loose-tight leadership does not assure skillfulness in applying the concept. We offer the following four keys to help leaders at the district level employ this powerful tool for shaping culture.

Key 1: District Leaders Must Use Every Aspect of an Effective Change Process and Present a Compelling Rationale for Moving Forward

Being tight does not absolve a leader from the responsibility of building consensus when people are being asked to change their practice. In chapter 5, we presented a list of mistakes leaders make when attempting to build consensus for change: They attempt to go it alone rather than build a guiding coalition, they use a forum that is ill-suited to the dialogue necessary to build consensus, they present and/or pool opinions rather than build shared knowledge, they allow for ambiguity about the standard to be met for moving forward, or they set an unrealistic standard for action. Effective leaders address these mistakes using the strategies presented in chapter 5 (see page 113).

A Commitment to Learning for All

We know the purpose of our schools is to ensure all our students learn at high levels, and certain things should happen in each school to demonstrate our commitment to that purpose. Systems must be in place to ensure the following:

1. Each teacher is clear on and committed to teaching the knowledge, skills, and dispositions all students are to learn for every unit of instruction.

2. Common formative assessments provide every teacher with frequent information regarding the learning of each student.

3. The school provides students who experience difficulty with additional time and support for learning in a timely, directive, and systematic way.

4. The school has a plan to extend and enrich the learning for students who are proficient.

5. Students understand what they are to learn and the criteria that will be used to assess their work.

6. The school has examined its procedures and practices to ensure it promotes rather than impedes learning for all.

A Collaborative Culture

Our schools will be organized into collaborative teams of professionals who work together interdependently to achieve common goals for which members are mutually accountable. Staff in our district will not work in isolation. Teams will be empowered to make important decisions regarding curriculum, pacing, instruction, and assessment, but they must make those decisions collaboratively and collectively rather than in isolation, and they must build shared knowledge of the most effective practices rather than pooling opinions before arriving at a decision.

(continued)

A Commitment to Learning for All (continued)

A Focus on Results

We will assess our effectiveness on the basis of evidence of results. To foster this results orientation, every school and every collaborative team within the school will be expected to create a SMART goal aligned with one or more of the district's goals. Every school will have systems in place to provide each teacher with timely feedback about the success of his or her students in meeting the agreed-upon learning standards on a valid common assessment in comparison to all other students in the course or grade level who are attempting to achieve the same standard. Every teacher and every team will be expected to use results to inform and impact their professional practice, guide the process of continuous improvement, and facilitate continuous adult learning.

Although these characteristics should be evident in each school, we also will extend considerable autonomy to each site and to teams within the school as they move forward with implementation. Each team can clarify the essential learnings of the district curriculum and determine how its members will pace content. Each team will create its own common formative assessments. The system of interventions and enrichment may vary from school to school. How teams are organized, when they meet, the norms they establish, and the goals they pursue may differ from one school to the next. We hope to encourage diversity in instructional techniques so individual teachers will have the autonomy to use the strategies they feel are most effective for them, as long as they can demonstrate those strategies lead to good results. Teams will determine the focus of their professional development, and they will have the opportunity to learn and grow as part of their routine work practices.

We expect to see these practices in all our schools because they are supported by research, proven to be effective, and endorsed by our professional organizations. Most importantly, they pass the test of common sense. So, how can we at the district office help to create these conditions in your school?

Effective leaders also encourage—rather than ignore or squash—disagreement because they recognize that when managed well, disagreements provide an opportunity to draw out assumptions, build shared knowledge, clarify priorities, and find common ground. They listen intently and respond to concerns. They recognize that there is more than one way to solve a problem and are open to exploring alternative strategies or timelines for implementation. They are willing to compromise on details while adhering tightly to core principles.

Central office leaders can use a number of different strategies in their efforts to persuade staff of the benefits of an improvement initiative. Howard Gardner (2006) offers seven strategies for changing someone's mind (including your own):

1. Reasoning and rationale thinking: "Doesn't it make sense that we can accomplish more by working together collaboratively than we can in isolation, by checking for student understanding through formative assessments rather than by waiting for the results of summative assessments, by creating timely school-wide systematic interventions when students experience difficulty rather than by expecting each teacher to try to figure out how to respond?"

2. Research: "I have shared the research with you that supports this initiative. I found it very compelling. Do you interpret the research another way? Do you have any contradictory research we could look at together?"

3. Resonance: "I know you believe in equity and fairness. Wouldn't it be more equitable and fair if we could assure students they will have access to the same guaranteed curriculum no matter who their teacher is, that their work will be assessed according to the same criteria, and that we have a consistent way of responding when they struggle to learn? Shouldn't we model the equity and fairness we say are important to us?"

4. Representational re-description: "I have presented you with the data regarding the large numbers of our students who are not being successful. Now let me put those numbers in human terms. Let me tell you some stories of the impact their failure to learn is having on their lives."

5. Rewards and resources: "I acknowledge this will be difficult. That is why I ask your help in identifying the resources you will need to be successful: time, training, materials support, and so on. Let's work together to identify the necessary resources, and I pledge I will do everything in my power to make them available."

6. Real-world events: "I understand you have misgivings and predict negative consequences if we implement this initiative. But let's visit some schools and districts that have done it successfully. You will hear the enthusiasm of the teachers as they explain how they and their students have benefited."

7. Require: "I understand you remain unconvinced, but this is the direction in which we are going, and this is what you must do to help us get there. I hope you will have a good experience as you work through the process, and I hope you will come to have a more positive disposition toward it."

Kerry Patterson and his colleagues (Patterson, Grenny, Maxfield, McMillan, & Switzler, 2008) also offer insights into changing the mind and the behavior of others in *Influencer: The Power to Change Anything*. Patterson contends the issue of persuading someone to change comes down to two essential questions: Is it worth it (is the change worthwhile or desirable), and can I do it (is the change feasible)? He then offers recommendations in three areas—personal, social, and structural—taken from research in psychology, social psychology, and organizational theory for each of the two questions to establish six sources of influence.

1. Influence personal motivation. Patterson and colleagues contend that verbal persuasion rarely works against resisters who "don't merely believe you are wrong; they need you to be wrong to preserve the status quo. And since the final judge exists in their own head, you lose every time" (p. 51). Their advice is emphatic: "*The great persuader is personal experience . . .* the mother of all cognitive map changes" (p. 51) and "the gold standard of change" (p. 57). They call for field trips to help people see the benefits of the behavior in the real world. If field trips are not possible, they suggest leaders create "vicarious experiences" through vibrant, credible stories and compelling testimonials. As they write, "A well-told narrative . . . changes people's view of how the world works because it presents a plausible, touching, and memorable flow of cause and effect that can alter people's view of the consequences of various actions or beliefs" (p. 59). A powerful story, one that evokes empathy, can help move a person from the role of critic to the role of participant. Ultimately, like so many others who have examined the change process, Patterson and colleagues contend that commitment to change follows rather than precedes new behavior. Thus, the task of the change leader is to immerse people in the new activity to create new personal experiences.

Leaders can also influence others when they create new motives. Patterson and colleagues caution leaders to fight against all forms of moral disengagement such as justification ("We can't expect these kids to learn given their socioeconomic status") or displaced responsibility ("I taught it, it is their job to learn it"), and to connect the new behavior to a resister's sense of values. This does not mean being preachy or judgmental. It means talking, and more importantly, listening to others to discover what they want and reframing the change so it links to a person's image of his or her higher self—the person he or she wants to be. It also means focusing on the human rather than the statistical consequences of failure to change (for example, stories of specific students rather than last year's test results) and helping people take their eyes off of their immediate demands to view the change as a personally defining moment within a larger moral issue. Learning by doing, seeking to understand through dialogue, and linking ideas to moral purpose is advice that should sound familiar to students of the PLC concept.

2. Enhance the personal ability of others. Because one of the pressing issues on the mind of someone being asked to change is, "Can I do it?" effective leaders help build capacity to build confidence. They set aside time for people to practice new vital behaviors. *Deliberate practice* is a critical element of this task. Deliberate practice requires complete attention, provides immediate feedback against a clear standard, and breaks mastery into several specific mini-goals.

The concept of deliberate practice has significant implications for school leaders. It calls upon them to clarify the high-leverage vital behaviors that improve teaching and learning. It means providing educators with very focused training in those behaviors over an extended period of time rather than offering the short-term, disjointed potpourri of offerings that characterizes professional development in so many districts. It then requires giving people time to practice with immediate and specific feedback against a clear standard. It calls for breaking complex skills and behaviors into short-term goals. Finally, it demands an organizational commitment to learning by doing. Patterson and colleagues stress the difference between *knowing* and *doing,* and urge leaders to over-invest in strategies that call upon people to learn skills by practicing the skills.

3. Harness the power of peer pressure. Patterson and colleagues contend that "no resource is more powerful and accessible" than the power of peer influence, and the most effective leaders "embrace and enlist" that power rather than "denying, lamenting, or attacking it" (p. 138). Effective leaders strive to create an environment where both formal and informal leaders constantly promote behavior essential to the change and skillfully confront behaviors that are misaligned with the change.

One strategy for creating such an environment is identifying and enlisting the support of the organization's "opinion leaders"—people who are considered knowledgeable, trustworthy, and generous with their time. Opinion leaders, who make up about 15% of the people in the organization, are socially connected and respected. Most importantly, "the rest of the population—over 85%—won't adopt the new practices *until opinion leaders do*" (p. 148). Patterson and colleagues insist it is not the merits of an idea that will determine its adoption but rather whether or not the opinion leaders endorse it. They conclude leaders should not worry about convincing everyone at once. Leaders must, however, spend disproportionate amounts of time with opinion leaders, establish open and trusting relationships, be amenable to their ideas, and call upon them for support. Finally, Patterson and colleagues caution that opinion leaders are not necessarily people with titles, nor are they people who jump immediately to embrace every new initiative. They can be identified simply by asking people throughout the organization who they believe are the most influential and respected people among their peers. Those whose names show up consistently are the opinion leaders.

Another strategy Patterson and colleagues recommend for bringing about changes in behavior, particularly when the change seems in conflict with long-standing norms, is to "transform taboo subjects into a routine part of the public discourse" (p. 155) because "when you make the undiscussable discussable, you openly embrace rather than fight the power of social influence" (p. 160). We saw evidence of this in a workshop we conducted for all the teachers and administrators of an entire school district. At every break, participants would approach us privately to express their pessimism regarding implementing the PLC concept, not because of the merits of the concept, but because of the lingering resentment over the unrelated outcome of the contract negotiations that had been completed 6 months earlier. Seventy percent of the teachers had voted to support the negotiated agreement, but those who had opposed it were bitter regarding both the outcome and the negotiations process. They suggested that neither the Board of Education nor the leaders of their own teachers' association had acted in good faith, and they were angry with colleagues who supported the vote and their state association for not supporting their position. They warned us the bitterness was so pervasive that an attempt to implement any improvement initiative was likely to be sabotaged.

After listening to this consistent refrain during every break throughout the 2 days, we publicly suggested there was an elephant in the room that should be addressed. We repeated the concerns that had been expressed and proposed that those concerns should be raised and resolved so the district could move forward rather than continue to focus on and complain about decisions made 6 months earlier. When we gave participants a few minutes to react to our observation, several came up to us privately to express their outrage and offense that we had posed the issue for consideration. The palpable animosity swirling around the room was, in their minds, not discussable. But as Patterson and colleagues write, "It is silence about the norm of silence that sustains the norm. If you can't talk about it, it will never go away" (p. 159). Changes in behavior will require changes in discourse, or as Harvard researchers Kegan and Lahey (2001) put it, changing the way we talk can change the way we work.

4. Find strength in numbers. Patterson and colleagues define social capital as *"the profound enabling power of an essential network of relationships"* (p. 174). In order to build social capital and increase the likelihood of successful change, they recommend organizing people into interdependent teams where the success or failure of the group depends upon contributions from each member. When the organizational structure requires people to work together, share ideas and materials, support one another in difficult moments, and contribute to collective goals, those people are more likely to hold each other accountable. The result is "synergy through non-voluntary interaction" (p. 183).

Patterson and colleagues also call for structures that allow more experienced members or members with particular expertise to serve as coaches, mentors, and trainers to others in the organization. These structures allow members throughout the organization to have real-time feedback from experts, which, again, is critical to changes in behavior.

The link between the recommendations of Patterson and colleagues in this area and our recommendations regarding school structures should be evident. When teachers work not in isolation but in teams (which we define as people working together interdependently to achieve a common goal for which members are mutually accountable), we help build their social capital. When, through the use of common assessments, it becomes evident that one member of the team has expertise in teaching a particular skill, that member can serve as a coach who provides real-time feedback to his or her colleagues. As Patterson and colleagues report, social psychologists discovered long ago that we are far more likely to hold ourselves accountable if we are members of a group. Finally, their call for "synergy through non-voluntary interaction" echoes our assertion that "collaboration by invitation, won't work!"

5. Design rewards and demand accountability. Patterson and colleagues emphasize that reward structures should be addressed only after considering other strategies to impact behavior such as intrinsic motivation and social support of peers. But effective leaders do use rewards, and when they do they make certain the rewards are directly linked to vital behaviors and valued processes. Patterson and colleagues advise leaders not to wait for phenomenal results, but to recognize and reward observable small improvement early in the change process because "even small rewards can be used to help people overcome some of the most profound and persistent problems" (p. 198). We will have a lot more to say about celebrating and rewarding small accomplishments in the final chapter.

Patterson and colleagues remind leaders, however, that "punishment sends a message, and so does its absence—so choose wisely" (p. 210). Failure to address those who refuse to engage in the vital behaviors sends a loud message to others that the behaviors are not so vital after all. They recommend that punishment be preceded by a "shot across the bow"—a clear warning to an individual of what *will* happen if he or she continues with the unacceptable behavior. As they write, "The point isn't that people need to be threatened in order to perform. The point is that if you aren't willing to go to the mat when people violate a core value . . . that value loses its moral force in the organization. On the other hand, you do send a powerful message when you hold employees accountable" (p. 216). Sounds a lot like the willingness to confront when people violate what we must be tight about, does it not?

6. Alter the environment to support the change. Patterson and colleagues argue that change in the structure and physical environment of an organization can make the right behavior easier and the wrong behavior more difficult. When the fundamental structure of the organization is the collaborative team, when time for collaboration is built into the weekly schedule, when members of a team work in close proximity to one another, they are far more likely to collaborate. As Patterson and colleagues write, "Often, all that is required to make good behavior inevitable is to structure it into your daily routine. If we have learned only one thing about today's overscheduled world it is that structure drives out lack of structure" (p. 250). If one team seems to be toxic, leaders would change the environment by reorganizing teams and assigning a toxic member to a high-functioning team.

Patterson and colleagues stress effective leaders also alter the environment by making sure vital information emerges from "dark nooks and crannies of the unknown into the light of day" (p. 230). He acknowledges that most organizations are awash in data. The challenge of leadership is not merely to pump out more data but to "mine the data stream"—to seek the kernels of gold, the critical data points that can change how people think and act. Effective leaders understand the importance of making information visible, timely, accurate, and relevant. As they write, "Instead of falling victim to data, they manage data religiously" (p. 232).

Finally, while each of these six strategies can help promote the vital behaviors, Patterson and colleagues argue the most effective leaders use all of the strategies in a continuous and comprehensive effort, rather than picking and choosing.

A comparison of these two extensive studies—Gardner and Patterson and colleagues—in the chart on page 357 offers great consistency for those seeking strategies for changing the mind and behavior of others.

Notice neither Gardner nor Patterson and colleagues suggest leaders begin the process of persuasion with "require." They are saying, however, leaders must be prepared to use that strategy if they are to bring about substantive change in their organizations. Psychologist Daniel Goleman came to the same conclusion. As Goleman (1998) wrote, "Persuasion, consensus building, and all the other arts of influence don't always do the job. Sometimes it simply comes down to using the power of one's position to get people to act. A common failing of leaders . . . is the failure to be emphatically assertive when necessary" (p. 190).

Effective leaders must recognize that school improvement cannot wait for everyone in the organization to have a favorable attitude toward the proposed change. As Robert Evans (1996) wrote, "If innovation is merely offered as a suggestion or left as a voluntary initiative, it generally fails. . . . It is insufficient simply to wait for changes in belief to produce changes in behavior; one must insist on some of the latter as a way to foster some of the former" (p. 244). There is abundant evidence in the fields of psychology, organizational development, and education that changes in attitudes follow rather than precede changes in behavior (Elmore, 2006; Fullan, 2007; Glasser, 1998; Kotter & Cohen, 2002; Pfeffer & Sutton, 2006; Reeves, 2006). Remember the conclusion of Patterson and his colleagues: "*The great persuader is personal experience*...the mother of all cognitive map changes" (p. 51). When work is designed to require people to *act* in new ways, new experiences are created for them. If those new experiences are positive, they can lead to new attitudes and assumptions over time.

Gardner's Advice (2006)	Patterson and Colleagues' Advice (2008)
• Reasoning and rational thinking	• Seek to understand. • Diagnose before you prescribe. • Mine the data stream to present the hard cold facts of actual real-life data.
• Research	• Review research of best practice to identify vital behaviors and conduct action research to find the positive deviants.
• Resonance	• Connect to individual values by linking ideas and behavior to the person an individual wants to be.
• Representational re-descriptions	• Move beyond data to stories. • Create empathy.
• Rewards and resources	• Use rewards after addressing intrinsic motivation and social supports. • Recognize small steps!
• Real-world events	• Take field trips to see the behavior at work in the real world.
• Require	• Insist resistant or incongruent behavior be changed. "Fire a shot across the bow" to warn of the specific consequences if the change is not forthcoming. • Use the power of peer pressure. Identify and create partnerships with opinion leaders and make the "undiscussables" discussable. • Create interdependent relationships through teams. • Change structures to support the desired change in behavior. • Build capacity through training, learning by doing, and real-time feedback.

Key 2: District Leaders Must Communicate Priorities Effectively, Consistently, and With One Voice

District leaders send mixed messages when they say the purpose of the organization is to ensure all students learn at high levels (as virtually all our mission statements claim), and then they allow people throughout the organization to opt out of practices that are clearly more effective at promoting learning than the prevailing practices. Thus, they fail to fulfill a fundamental responsibility of leadership. Marcus Buckingham (2005) has concluded the "one thing" leaders must always remember to be effective is the importance of clarity—clarity regarding the fundamental purpose of the organization; the future it must create to better fulfill that purpose; the most high-leverage strategies for creating that future; the indicators of progress it will monitor; the explicit standards, rubrics, and exemplars that illustrate the quality of work expected in the organization; and the specific ways each member of the organization can contribute both to its long-term purpose and short-term goals.

The challenge of clarity and congruence is greater in larger districts if different central office leaders fail to speak with one voice regarding priorities (Waters & Marzano, 2006). Patterson and colleagues (2008) concur that "solidarity" among leaders at all levels is one of "the most powerful forms of social capital" and a key element in bringing about change (p. 189). When different district administrators seem to be competing for the attention of those at the school site and pressing the different agendas of their respective offices, they create confusion and cynicism rather than coherence.

Central office leaders should, therefore, engage in periodic reviews of how clearly they are communicating priorities to people throughout their organizations. These reviews will be more powerful if principals and staff are asked to participate in anonymous surveys that give feedback to the central office. The following questions could be helpful in gathering honest feedback:

1. What systems have been put in place in our district to ensure priorities are addressed in each school?

    - Do we have systems for clarifying what students must learn?

    - Do we have systems for monitoring student learning?

    - Do we have systems for responding when students have difficulty?

    - Do we have systems for enriching and extending learning for students who are proficient?

    - Do we have systems for monitoring and supporting teams?

    - Do we have systems for providing each teacher and team with the timely information essential to continuous improvement?

2. What do we monitor in our district?

    - How do we monitor student learning?

    - How do we monitor the work and effectiveness of our collaborative teams?

    - How do we monitor the work and effectiveness of our building administrators?

    - How do we monitor the work and effectiveness of the central office?

3. What questions do we ask in our district?

    - What questions are we asking people to resolve through collective inquiry?

    - What questions drive the work of individuals and teams throughout our organizations?

4. How do we allocate resources (time, money, people) in our district?

- How do we provide time for intervention and enrichment for our students?

- How do we provide time for our collaborative teams to engage in collective inquiry?

- Are we using our resources most effectively?

5. What do we celebrate in our district?

- What process is in place to help identify schools and teams that are improving?

- How do we acknowledge and celebrate improvement?

- Who are the heroes in our district?

6. What are we willing to confront in our district?

- Have we recognized confronting resistance to the fundamental purpose and priority of our district is essential to our credibility?

- Have we recognized confronting resistance is essential to the clarity of our communication?

- Have we been willing to address the problem of principals or staff members who have resisted this initiative?

7. What do we model in our district?

- What evidence shows that the central office is committed to and focused on high levels of learning for all students?

- What evidence shows that we work together collaboratively?

- How does the central office gather and use evidence of results to inform and improve our own practice?

An example of effective communication. When administrators ask teachers to work as members of a PLC they are, in effect, asking teachers to participate in a process to focus on student learning, to work collaboratively, to agree on indicators they will track to monitor student learning, to share data on the achievement of their students, to be concerned about the learning of students outside of their own classrooms, and to help each other improve the current levels of performance. Administrators should demonstrate their commitment to that process by modeling it, and changing the focus of administrative meetings offers a perfect opportunity for such modeling.

The focus of administrative meetings in most districts is on managerial tasks rather than on leadership issues that impact learning. A central office could, however, use those meetings to help the district staff and principals function as their own PLC. At every meeting, one principal would be responsible for presenting to the group evidence of student learning in his or her school during the past 3 years. The principal would identify trends, highlight strengths, call attention to areas of concern, report on the SMART goal the school had established to address the concern, and discuss the specific strategies his or her school staff was considering to improve upon the results. The presenting principal would then invite district office staff and his or her colleagues to comment on their interpretations of the data, to ask clarifying questions, and to share any ideas or strategies they believed would help the school improve. Notice the focus is on evidence of student learning, administrators are working collaboratively, the entire group uses data to confront the brutal facts and explore strategies for improvement, and principals are expected to be concerned about and contribute to the success of other schools.

An article in the *Harvard Business Review* by W. Chan Kim and Renee Mauborgne (2003) examined how William Bratton, arguably the most successful police chief in America, used this identical process to achieve dramatic reductions in the crime rate of New York City. Bratton required mandatory attendance of his precinct captains at these strategy review meetings. The precinct captain selected to present data to the group was notified only 2 days prior to the meeting to emphasize

Bratton's expectation that each captain should be aware of the data for his or her precinct at all times.

This structured process clarified priorities to every leader in the department and created an intense focus on results. Participants were expected to help identify and resolve problems outside of their precincts and to learn from both the good and bad results that were occurring anywhere in the city. The focus of these meetings was not on ranking precincts because Bratton recognized New York would always have a best and worst precinct based on the crime data (that is, in order for one precinct to move up from the lowest ranking, another precinct must take its place). The emphasis instead was on which precincts were improving, an emphasis that allowed a high-crime precinct to be celebrated for a reduction in crime rates and challenged a low-crime precinct to engage in continuous improvement rather than rest on its laurels. The process gave everyone a chance to be recognized and celebrated, and most importantly, it increased the collective strength of the department. Over time, this management style filtered down through the ranks as captains created their own versions of the meeting for their precincts.

A superintendent and central office staff could adopt this process as the standard operating procedure for their administrative meetings. It would provide principals with a powerful model for transforming faculty meetings into team-led data analysis, dialogue, and problem-solving sessions. Fullan (2007) argues that for the PLC concept to spread across a district, a principal must be almost as concerned about the success of other schools as his or her own school. This format could foster that interdependence. Furthermore, it could give principals their own learning community and a powerful tool for their own ongoing development.

Key 3: District Leaders Must Limit Initiatives to Allow for the Sustained Focus Essential to a Change Initiative

When the Harvard Graduate School of Education and Harvard Business School collaborated in a joint project to develop a district-wide improvement strategy for central office leaders, they concluded that the biggest impediment to improving schools was the unmanageable number of initiatives and total lack of coherence (Olson, 2007). This project echoed the conclusion offered by Michael Fullan (2001) 6 years earlier when he asserted the main problem confronting educators is not the absence of innovation but the "presence of too many disconnected, episodic, piecemeal, and superficially adorned projects" (p. 109). Reeves (2006) agreed schools suffer from "initiative fatigue" and discovered the size of a district's strategic plan was actually inversely related to student achievement—the thicker the plan, the lower the results. Richard Elmore (2003) asserted that most districts are engaged in a frenetic amount of unconnected activities and initiatives characterized by volatility (jumping from one initiative to another in a relatively short period of time) and superficiality (choosing initiatives that have little impact on student achievement and implementing them in shallow ways).

Becky described the diverse and competing initiatives of a school district she consulted with in an article for *The School Administrator* (DuFour, 2003b):

> The director of staff development had mandated all professional development days should be devoted to training teachers in differentiated instruction and problem-based learning. The technology department had developed a new checklist requiring classroom teachers to assess each child's proficiency on numerous computer skills. The math coordinator had insisted that all K–12 teachers fully implement the newly adopted project-based math curriculum—even though most were unfamiliar with the concept. The assessment director had required all K–8 teachers to conduct time-intensive independent reading inventories on every student three times each year although teachers were not clear on how the results were to be used. The director of elementary education had d creed all schools must implement cognitive coaching by the end of the school year. (p. 15–16)

This district had lost sight of the fact that schools are staffed by mere mortals who have lives outside of their jobs. There are limits to the energy and effort even the most well-intentioned and enthusiastic educators can expend. The additional demands of every new initiative disperse the attention and resources of people throughout the organization, thereby reducing the likelihood of successful implementation of any initiative. As Pfeffer and Sutton (2006) concluded, "Leaders who push for fewer changes and push for them harder are more likely to have success than leaders who introduce so many changes that people become confused about which matter most and least to the company and how to spread their time and money among the initiatives" (p. 174). Ken Blanchard (2007) advises leaders to "spend ten times more energy reinforcing the change they just made than looking for the next great change to try" (p. 246). District leaders who hope to build the capacity of schools to function as PLCs should focus the entire organization's energies on that challenging task, coordinate all central office services to support it, declare a moratorium on new initiatives for several years, and allow staff in each school to determine the training and resources it requires to move forward with the initiative.

Key 4: District Leaders Must Help Teachers and Principals Build Their Collective Capacity to Raise Student Achievement by Embedding Ongoing Professional Development in the Routine Work of Every Educator

Once again, Elmore's concept of *reciprocal accountability* (2006) dictates a central office that expects the staff of a school to function as a PLC must commit to building the capacity of the staff to meet that expectation. Unfortunately, the way in which districts have typically approached professional development has not built capacity. Instead, it has contributed to teacher isolation in schools and a lack of coherence in districts.

In most districts, individual teachers enjoy tremendous discretion in choosing both the topics and providers of their professional development and are even offered financial incentives to pursue the advanced training of their choice. Many districts pay part of their teachers' tuition for graduate courses or workshop registration fees, and most advance their teachers on the salary schedule upon completion of graduate work. This happens even though there is little evidence that either graduate work or most workshops improve teacher quality (Haskins & Loeb, 2007). Thus, individual teachers are rewarded for pursuing random training through scores of disconnected providers in curricula of varying quality over which the district exercises no control. Rarely is there an attempt to align that training with school goals or district priorities or to reinforce it within the school.

It has been evident for some time that this approach to professional development is fundamentally flawed. John Goodlad (1983) addressed its ineffectiveness 25 years ago:

> We must build into each school a continuing attention to instruction and the curriculum. This does not occur when teachers are drawn out of schools as individuals to engage willy-nilly in workshops and courses and are then returned to the isolation of their classrooms and a school culture where how and what one teaches are not matters for peer-group analysis, discussion and improvement. Teaching must be taken out of its cloak of privacy and autonomy to become the business of the entire school and staff. (p. 557)

Goodlad's call for focused, collaborative, ongoing, and job-embedded professional development has been repeatedly reinforced by educational researchers and organizations. Consider the following from the research:

- Staff development should be conceived as ongoing and embedded in the process of developing and evaluating curriculum, instruction, and assessment. As teachers consult with one another in collectively developing, analyzing, and evaluating student work;

embedding assessment in their regular teaching practice; restructuring their school day; and transforming schools into learner-centered communities, a powerful form of learning occurs. An important part of staff development, then, should include time—along with the resources of research, information, and expertise—for teachers to work together on the development and implementation of school changes. (Darling-Hammond, 1995, p. 173)

- Learning is always an on-the-job phenomenon. Learning always occurs in a context where you are taking action. So we need to find ways to get teachers really working together; we need to create an environment where they can continually reflect on what they are doing and learn more and more what it takes to work as teams. (Senge & Kofman, 1995, p. 20)

- Teacher and administrator learning is more complex, deeper, and more fruitful in a social setting, where the participants can interact, test their ideas, challenge their inferences and interpretations, and process new information with each other. When one learns alone, the individual learner (plus a book, article, or video) is the sole source of new information and ideas. When new ideas are processed in interaction with others, multiple sources of knowledge and expertise expand and test the new concepts as part of the learning experience. The professional learning community provides a setting that is richer and more stimulating. (Southwest Educational Development Laboratory, 2000, p. 1)

- [In schools with model professional development] the very nature of staff development shifted from isolated learning and the occasional workshop to focused, on-going organizational learning built on collaborative reflection and joint action. . . Substantial progress is made only when teacher learning becomes embedded in the school day and the regular life of the school. (WestEd, 2000, p. 11)

- Staff development that improves the learning of all students organizes adults into learning communities whose goals are aligned with those of the school and district. . . . The most powerful forms of staff development occur in ongoing teams that meet on a regular basis, preferably several times a week, for the purposes of learning, joint lesson planning, and problem solving. These teams . . . operate with a commitment to the norms of continuous improvement and experimentation and engage their members in improving their daily work to advance the achievement of district and school goals for student learning. (National Staff Development Council, 2001)

- Recent research shows that the kinds of professional development that improve instructional capacity display four critical characteristics. . . . They are:

    - Ongoing

    - Embedded within context-specific needs of a particular setting

    - Aligned with reform initiatives

    - Grounded in a collaborative, inquiry-based approach to learning . . .

Effective professional development to improve classroom teaching also concentrates on high learning standards and on evidence of students' learning. It . . .

enables adult learners to expand on content knowledge and practice that is directly connected with the work of their students in the classroom.... Again, professional learning communities meet these criteria. (Annenberg Institute for School Reform, 2004, p. 1)

- The consensus view of effective professional development . . . derives from the assumption that learning is essentially a collaborative rather than an individual activity—that educators learn more powerfully in concert with others who are struggling with the same problems—and that the essential purpose of professional development should be the improvement of schools and school systems, not just the improvement of the individuals who work in them. (Elmore, 2003, p. 96)

- Professional development should be aligned with state and district goals and standards for student learning, and should become an everyday part of the school schedule rather than be conducted as a set of ad hoc events. The content of this professional development should be driven by frequent assessments that identify the specific topics that individual students are having trouble with, so that individual teacher's instructional practices can be altered to directly address these students' learning needs. Professional development activities should also involve opportunities for collaboration so that teachers can learn from each other. (The Teaching Commission, 2004, p. 49)

- Districts in the forefront of development promote "learning in context"—not just through workshops but through daily interactions in cultures designed for job embedded learning. . . . Capacity building . . .

is not just workshops and professional development for all. It is the daily habit of *working together*, and you can't learn this from a workshop or course. You need to learn by doing it and having mechanisms for getting better at it on purpose. (Fullan, 2005, p. 69)

- The more time teachers spend on professional development the more significantly they change their practice, and participating in professional learning communities optimizes the time spent on professional development. (American Educational Research Association, 2005, p. 4)

- School-based teacher learning communities align with current empirical evidence of the most effective professional development strategies. . . . Researchers agree that teachers learn best when they are involved in activities that: (a) focus on instruction and student learning specific to the settings in which they teach; (b) are sustained and continuous, rather than episodic; (c) provide opportunities for teachers to collaborate with colleagues inside and outside the school; (d) reflect teachers' influence about what and how they learn; and (e) help teachers develop theoretical understanding of the skills and knowledge they need to learn. (McLaughlin & Talbert, 2006, pp. 8–9)

The message is consistent and clear. The best professional development occurs in a social and collaborative setting rather than in isolation, is ongoing and sustained rather than infrequent and transitory, is job-embedded rather than external, occurs in the context of the real work of the school and classroom rather than in off-site workshops or courses, focuses on results (that is, evidence of improved student learning) rather than activities or perceptions, and is systematically aligned with school and district goals rather than random. In short, the best professional development takes place in professional learning communities.

Professional development often represents another classic case of the knowing-doing gap. Central office leaders who make any attempt to explore best practice in professional development will hear a consistent message—they will come to *know* the most powerful approaches to professional development, but too often they have failed to act on what they know.

If district offices are to play a role in building the capacity of school personnel to function as PLCs, they must redefine professional development and embrace a new approach to promoting adult learning. They must create structures and provide incentives to ensure educators are learning *together* in the context of their own schools and classrooms as part of their routine work practices. They must ensure professional development is specifically designed to improve student learning, and they must assess its effectiveness on the basis of results. They must stop thinking of professional development in terms of courses, workshops, or one-size-fits-all district-wide training and recognize the responsibility of the central office is to support the specific and timely learning needs of different collaborative teams, and provide training team-by-team that is "just in time" and "just what's needed" (National Commission on Teaching and America's Future, 2003, p. 28). For example, the second-grade team highlighted in chapter 7 whose formative test results demonstrated their students were struggling to learn a math concept benefited far more from the timely and focused help they received based on their specific need than they would have with professional development on a general topic determined by the central office.

We are not suggesting that a team, school, or district should rely exclusively on internal expertise or resources to promote adult learning. External experts, consultants, and facilitators can be powerful allies in building the capacity of an organization, and McLaughlin and Talbert (2006) argue an external facilitator may be essential to helping a staff learn to function as a PLC. It is, however, typically more powerful to bring the external resource into the school than it is to send isolated individuals from the school in search of external resources. We are not arguing that large-group or faculty-wide training can never be beneficial. In the right school culture, even the much-maligned "one-shot workshop" can serve as a catalyst for improvement if 1) it leads to collective inquiry and action research and 2) staff members have access to additional support and coaching as they move forward. But we *are* arguing the most powerful staff development will occur most often as part of the routine work practices of a collaborative team of teachers *if* the central office ensures the team is focused on the right work and provides the necessary encouragement, resources, and assistance to build the capacity of each team and school.

Finally, when the central office uses this approach to staff development, it honors the expertise and professionalism of the district's educators. Job-embedded professional development recognizes that very often the answers to the questions and challenges of schooling are to be found within the building and district, and when teams are able to determine their specific needs, professional development becomes something that is done *by* educators rather than *to* educators.

Positive Top-Down Leadership in Action

We conclude this chapter with a story of the different approaches taken by three districts to promote the PLC concept.

District A: The Autocratic Approach

District A had shown little interest in PLCs until one of its schools demonstrated remarkable gains in student achievement. When the faculty attributed the gains to their implementation of the PLC concept, the central office announced every school was now required to become a PLC. Unfortunately, the pronouncement was not accompanied by any attempt to clarify the term, by training, by time for faculties to do the work of PLCs, or by resources of any kind. The central office made no effort to monitor the progress of the initiative in any school and did nothing to model its own commitment to PLC practices. It continued to expect schools to address the plethora of other initiatives the district had launched over several years and dictated the topics and focus of every day designated for professional development. This central office did nothing to build the capacity of staff to improve student achievement, but it did cause a great deal of resentment toward the school that had been singled out for its success.

District B: The Laissez-Faire Approach

The superintendent of this large district became convinced of the merits of the PLC concept, and the Board of Education stipulated in its annual goals that every school would become a PLC. The district devoted considerable resources to the initiative, offering ongoing training for all principals and for a teacher team from each of its schools. Unfortunately, the central office did not speak with one voice regarding the priority of the initiative. Some directors supported principals, clarified expectations, monitored the progress of the schools for which they were responsible, and worked with the district's professional development department to coordinate training according to the specific needs of each school. Other directors left the initiative to the discretion of each principal they supervised, and many of their principals opted not to attend any of the training even though space, materials, and meals had been purchased for them. The schools served by those directors were not expected or required to foster a collaborative culture, to ensure teachers created common formative assessments, or to develop systems of interventions. At the end of 2 years, some schools in the district had made remarkable progress while others had made none.

District C: Loose-Tight Leadership at Work

The superintendent of District C had become convinced that the PLC concept offered the best hope for significant, sustained school improvement for his district. He arranged for 2 days of introductory training for the principal and a team of teachers from every school. He advised the teacher union representative of the training and invited her to attend. He actively participated in all of the training, and his entire central office leadership team attended as well.

The training was specifically designed to create a common vocabulary, build shared knowledge about the PLC concept, make a compelling case for the benefits of the concept, and give all participants the opportunity to express their concerns and questions. A segment of each day was devoted to "asking the superintendent," and everyone in the room was invited to present a question directly to the superintendent for an immediate and public response. The superintendent made certain to check in with his central office staff, principals, and teachers during lunch and breaks to get their perspectives on what they were learning.

By the end of the 2 days, there was palpable, widespread enthusiasm for the PLC concept. Then, in the midst of the initial enthusiasm, the union representative posed a critical question to the superintendent: "This all sounds fine, but are you saying we will be *required* to do this? Is this a top-down mandate?" It was a pivotal moment in the improvement process. His answer captured the essence of loose-tight leadership:

> Why wouldn't we do this? Is anyone aware of any evidence that this is detrimental to student learning, teacher effectiveness, or positive school cultures? This concept is supported by research, endorsed by our professional organizations, implemented with great success in schools around us, and it just makes sense. Knowing the commitment of the teachers in this district to do what is best for kids, how could we not go forward with this? I admit I am not certain regarding all the details of implementation, and I will need your ideas about how we can help all your colleagues become familiar with the concept and address their questions. I know all of us will need time and resources to move forward, and we will need to consider what we will remove from our plates if we

take on this challenge. But I propose this is the work we should be doing, and we need to build on the energy and enthusiasm in this room today and commit to doing whatever it takes to make this happen in our district.

Over the course of the next 2 years, the district supported ongoing training for every school in the district. Practices were aligned with the initiative, schedules were adjusted to provide teachers with time to engage in the work of PLCs, and the focus of administrative meetings changed to support principals in their implementation efforts. Central office staff met with concerned faculties and groups of teachers to address their questions. The central office distributed a questionnaire to every building administrator asking for his or her ideas for a "stop-doing list"—a list of things the central office should no longer require of schools so as to provide more time to work on implementing the PLC concept. Technology was purchased to ensure each school site had access to timely information. Each school was free to establish its own sequence and timeline for implementation. The focus of staff development days, which traditionally had been determined by the district, was now determined by collaborative teams within each school who were able to seek specific support and training based on their needs.

In 2 years, the district had the greatest gains in student achievement in the state in large part because the central office provided a clear, coherent strategy for improving student achievement, insisted that educators in each school focus on implementing that strategy, allowed schools and teams tremendous autonomy in the process of implementation, and built the capacity of staff to succeed by providing time, resources, and ongoing support based on the needs of each school.

Pressure and Support

There are responsibilities district leaders must address if they are to have a positive impact on student learning. They should utilize every component of an effective change process and present the rationale for the proposed initiative using a variety of strategies. They must be willing to listen to concerns, seek common ground, and compromise on the details of implementation. They must provide school sites with considerable autonomy as those sites move forward within clearly defined parameters. They must communicate clearly, ensuring there is congruence between their actions and their words. They must limit the number of initiatives they implement and provide adequate time for new practices and processes to become embedded in the culture of schools. They must demonstrate a sincere commitment to reciprocal accountability by providing the time, training, and resources necessary to build the capacity of their schools' staffs to accomplish what they have been asked to accomplish. They must recognize some schools will need far more support and direction than others to move forward. But, just as certainly, central office leaders must be prepared to insist that those within their organization heed rather than ignore clear evidence of the best, most promising strategies for accomplishing the purpose and priorities of the district. Educational leaders must provide both pressure and support if they are to play a role in improving their schools and districts.

Chapter 14

The Role of Parents and the Community in a Professional Learning Community

Almost every study supports the fact that parental involvement helps student performance, but defining what parental involvement means is one of the hardest tasks facing parents and educators today. What is the most effective way to do it?

—Monika Gutman

Nowhere is the two-way street of learning in more disrepair and in need of social reconstruction than in the relationships between parents, communities, and their schools.

—Michael Fullan

When George H.W. Bush convened the nation's governors to establish Goals 2000, the national goals American schools were to achieve by the millennium, they included the stipulation that "every school will promote partnerships that will increase parent involvement and participation in promoting the social, emotional, and academic growth of children" (United States Department of Education, 1995, p. 43). Within a few years, the Department of Education stipulated "every school will actively engage parents and families in a partnership which supports the academic work of children at home and shared educational decision making in the school" (United States Department of Education, 1995, p. 43). Despite these federal directives, educators have generally remained ambivalent about parent and community involvement in their schools. The two most frequent complaints we hear about parents when we work in districts are 1) "They don't get involved in their children's education," and 2) "They get too involved in their children's education." Like Goldilocks, educators seem to prefer parents who are neither too hot nor too cold, but "just right." They struggle, however, to articulate exactly what "just right" parental involvement might look like.

Educators committed to helping all students learn at high levels cannot overlook the extensive research base proclaiming the significant impact parents can have on student achievement. A positive partnership between the home and school has been one of the seven correlates of effective schools for almost 3 decades (Lezotte, 1991). More recently, Scheerens and Bosker (1997) cited this partnership as one of 10 factors associated with school effectiveness, and Marzano (2003) included it among five school-level factors impacting student achievement.

Other studies have been even more explicit and emphatic about the benefits of a strong partnership between schools and the parents and community they serve. Henderson and Berla (1995) and Henderson and Mapp (2002) report students whose parents are involved in their education are more likely to earn higher grades and test scores and enroll in higher level programs; be promoted, pass classes, and earn credits; attend school regularly; have better social skills; and graduate and go on to higher education. Epstein's ongoing studies have demonstrated that family involvement leads to better results for students, including higher achievement, better attendance, more course credits earned, more responsible preparation for class, and other indicators of success in school. A study of middle and high schools found that strong school-parent partnerships had positive correlations with students' grades, scores on achievement tests, attendance, behavior, and post-secondary planning (Epstein et al., 2002). The same study also revealed students were less likely to engage in risky or negative behavior and schools were able to provide a safer environment for learning when schools and parents formed partnerships to promote learning. A synthesis of the research conducted by the National Parent Teacher Association (2000) reported that when parents are involved in their children's education, students achieve more regardless of race or socioeconomic factors.

As Fullan (2007) concluded, "Emerging from this research is a message that is remarkable in its consistency: the closer the parent is to the education of the child, the greater the impact on child development and educational achievement" (p. 189). In short, the partnership between schools and parents represents such a powerful tool in promoting student learning that schools and districts simply cannot overlook it.

Creating a strong partnership with parents and families is certainly aligned with the assumptions and practices inherent in professional learning communities. In a PLC, people are asked to work collaboratively, share their knowledge to promote student learning, and embrace collective responsibility for students, instead of working in isolation. Although parents may lack content expertise or a deep understanding of the developmental needs of students at different ages, they still have insights about their own children that can contribute significantly to students' success and well-being in school. Furthermore, PLCs make a conscious effort to involve all staff members in important decisions because staff engagement and empowerment lead to greater ownership of and commitment to those decisions. The same principle applies to parents, who are far more likely to feel committed to their schools if they can participate in the educational process impacting their children.

Thus, there are compelling reasons for educators to establish partnerships with parents and families, but educators must be willing to redefine the nature of these partnerships. In the business world, forging a partnership can expand skills and expertise, offer a different perspective on key issues, increase available resources, provide a source of support in difficult times, and increase capacity to achieve mutual goals. An effective partnership is advantageous to all members because it increases the likelihood of the success of each person involved.

There is a tendency on the part of many educators, however, to define their partnership with parents in narrower terms. Educators believe it is their job to make the important decisions, and it is the job of parents to support them. Few people, however, would be attracted to a "partnership" that asks them to provide all the finances for the operation, yet demands their unquestioning support of all decisions made by their partner. Good partnerships, in schools as well as business, should be mutually beneficial.

Characteristics of Effective School-Family Partnerships

Many researchers and authors have considered the question, "What are the elements of an effective school-family partnership?" Marzano (2003) listed three features of such partnerships: effective two-way communication between the home and school, multiple opportunities for parents to participate in the school as volunteers, and specific structures that allow parents a voice in the governance of the school. Henderson and Mapp (2002) found schools that build strong partnerships focus on building a trusting collaborative relationship with family members, recognize and respect family needs and cultural differences, and embrace a philosophy of partnership where power and responsibility are shared. The National PTA has synthesized research to establish the following six standards of effective school-family partnerships.

Implement Regular, Two-Way, and Meaningful Communication Between Home and School

When teachers and schools establish meaningful two-way communication with families, parents are more aware of their children's progress, have a stronger belief in their ability to influence their children's learning, and become more involved in that learning (Epstein,

Coates, Clark-Salinas, Sanders, & Simon, 1997). The critical questions that drive the work of collaborative teams can also serve as a framework for meaningful communication between the school and home.

What Is It We Want Our Students to Learn?

Schools should provide parents with clear explanations about the specific knowledge, skills, and dispositions students will be expected to acquire in every course or grade level and a pacing guide to clarify when specific content will be addressed.

How Will We Know If Our Students Are Learning?

Parents are most interested in receiving information about the progress of their children. Parents who may be indifferent to newsletters announcing the dates of the winter concert are typically hungry for information about the academic status of their children. The need for *timely* information is imperative when it comes to reporting academic progress. Schools that leave parents in the dark do nothing to promote either greater student learning or stronger parent partnerships. Some of the most bitter and adversarial parents are those who were left uninformed as their children continued in a downward spiral of failure.

There are some promising developments for keeping parents informed of student learning. Standards-based report cards that attempt to clarify the specific standards students are expected to achieve and the degree to which an individual student is proficient are much better suited to meaningful communication than report cards that provide a single letter or score to depict student achievement. Technology is available that provides parents with real-time access to their children's indicators of progress while maintaining confidentiality about the achievement of other students. In many districts, parents with access to a computer are able to view teacher grade books online to check if their child is completing work and achieving success on assessments.

We will address the issue of engaging parents in the interventions for and enrichment of student learning in a later section of this chapter.

Schools must, however, do more than provide parents and community members with information; they must solicit helpful information from them as well.

For communication between home and school to be most effective, it must be two-way, providing both parties with an opportunity to seek clarification and respond to concerns. For example, bringing parents and community members into the school for parent breakfasts or luncheons hosted by staff and students can provide a forum for parents to have their questions asked and answered. Sending educators into the community for neighborhood coffees in the evening can encourage the dialogue that benefits both families and schools. School leaders can and should solicit opinions regarding the operation of the school and how it is perceived. This can be done through annual phone surveys of a random sampling of parents and community members, focus-group meetings, or assignments that call upon students to solicit ideas from their parents about ways to strengthen the school. Most importantly, schools should encourage parents to provide specific information about their children that could prove helpful in meeting their needs.

There is a perception in many communities that educators only reach out to residents when they want something, such as support for a building referendum, passage of a new tax rate, or to purchase magazines, candy bars, wrapping paper, or a myriad of other fundraising products. Sadly, that perception is quite valid in many communities.

Educators can take an important step in strengthening school-parent partnerships if, in their efforts to communicate with parents, they are committed to seeking to understand, and not merely seeking to be understood.

Offer Advice and Training Regarding Parenting Skills

Advocates of parental involvement in education begin with the assumption that such involvement is always beneficial. Recent research suggests, however, that involving parents in the educational process is not always positive, and that "more is not always better" (Pomerantz,

Moorman, & Litwack, 2007). Parent involvement can have an adverse impact on student learning if parents use a controlling style to pressure their children with commands, directives, or withdrawal of love; if they emphasize their children's innate ability and constantly compare them to other students; if they express negative emotions—frustration, anger, resentment—when monitoring homework; or if they convey negative beliefs and low opinions about their children's potential. Conversely, they support student learning if they allow their children a degree of autonomy, encourage them to initiate their own behavior, and help them to take an active role in solving their own problems; focus on effort rather than ability; stress the importance of perseverance in learning; convey learning as a positive experience; and communicate confidence in their children's potential to be successful in school if they work hard.

Most parents can benefit from advice about how they can play an effective role in the education of their children, and there is evidence that parents and educators may not agree about how to best support student learning. The Parent Institute surveyed teachers and parents to find out the most important things families could do to help children learn better in school. Respondents were presented with 19 options. Teachers rated "read to your child every day and have your child read to you" as the single most important thing a parent could do. Parents ranked it as number 15. Parents ranked "talk to your child and pay attention to what your child says to you" as their best way to support student learning and "help your child develop homework routines" as the second-best strategy. Educators ranked those strategies as 10th and 13th in their responses (Wherry, 2005). There is no reason to believe parents intuitively know what educators want from them; educators need to inform parents of their needs at the same time they ascertain what parents need from teachers.

Advice to parents, like feedback in general, works best when it is specific rather than general, but in offering that advice, educators must first build shared knowledge of best practice instead of pooling opinions or leaving the matter to the discretion of every professional in the building. For example, Stevenson High School convened a task force of parents to explore the topic, and after members examined the research, the task force developed a list of recommended "commitments" they urged every parent to endorse and model to serve as powerful partners in the education of their children (see pages 459–461 in the Appendix for a list of the parent commitments). The list is sent annually to every parent with a student enrolled at Stevenson and is referenced at every opportunity—parent conferences, neighborhood coffees, parent breakfasts, and so on. The Public School Parent's Network (2007) provides another example (although it is weak on specifics) with Project Appleseed's "The Parental Involvement Pledge"—a national movement to encourage every parent to sign a pledge to support the learning of their children. The pledge can be found at www.projectappleseed.org/pledge.html.

Schools should be particularly attentive to assisting parents during the transition years when children leave one level of schooling for another. For most parents, these transitions represent uncharted waters, and they benefit from information about what to expect from the school as well as what they might expect from their children. Educators who are proactive in addressing student and parent needs during times of transition demonstrate the importance of the school-family partnership, impact student and parent expectations in a positive way, and are more likely to sustain the partnership throughout the years the children are enrolled in that school (Epstein et al., 2002). High schools, for example, should have well-developed orientation programs for parents that begin early in eighth grade for entering freshmen. These programs should explain the school's programs, alert parents to concerns their students are likely to experience as they leave middle school, offer advice as to how parents can support their students, and advise parents how they and their students can access the support systems the school has created. This reaching out to parents should occur not only at formal programs at the high school but also through a variety of informal venues such as middle school PTA meetings, neighborhood coffees, and parent luncheons. High schools should also have a well-designed and coordinated program to assist parents with the transitions that occur as students graduate and enter higher education or the work force. Topics include the college selection and admission process, financial aid, scholarship options, the regulations of the National Collegiate Athletic Association for athletes, career exploration, and the emotional issues involved for both students and parents as young adults prepare to leave home.

Make Sure Parents Become Partners in the Education of Their Children

Parents are more likely to become involved as partners in the education of their children if they perceive the school has an inviting climate and that teachers sincerely desire to include them in the learning process. In fact, one study found parent perception of the school's openness to their involvement has a more significant impact on their participation than any sociodemographic variable. It also found that parent perception of teacher outreach to parents is the only statistically significant variable in predicting parent involvement both at home and at school (Patrikakou & Weissberg, 1998). A recent synthesis of the research on parent participation came to a similar conclusion (Hoover-Dempsey et al., 2005). Parent involvement increases when schools welcome parents into the teaching and learning process, communicate the importance of the parent's role in student success, and provide explicit strategies for parents to become involved in their children's learning. Teachers promote deeper parent involvement in the education of their children when they reach out to parents on a regular basis, make them aware of learning goals and the pacing of the curriculum, clarify expectations, and solicit parent perspectives on their children's interests and aptitudes.

Parents can play an active role in the school's intervention and enrichment process if they are given clear explanations of the knowledge, skills, and dispositions their students are to acquire in school, if they are given pacing guides that establish when various skills and content will be taught, and if they receive tutorial materials they can use at home to assess and reinforce their student's learning. We know of schools where teachers work together in collaborative teams to create these materials for parents. Then, on parent-teacher evenings, the entire team meets with the parents of their grade or course to review the materials and demonstrate how they can be used at home to support learning. The teachers then establish a simple weekly two-way communication strategy that enables parents to check one of three boxes during each unit of instruction indicating the parent's perception of their child's proficiency: "My student seems highly proficient in this skill," "My student is proficient in this skill," or "My student needs more help in acquiring this skill." Of course the type and depth of this involvement will depend to some extent on the age of the students and the content being taught. It is reasonable to ask parents to review multiplication facts with a third grader, but unrealistic to expect parents to assist a senior with his or her calculus homework. High school parents could, however, read the same novels as their children and engage them in the discussion of those novels, or raise specific questions about biology, history, or government to demonstrate their own intellectual curiosity and willingness to keep learning.

Schools committed to parent involvement will take into account the potential barriers that prevent parents from participating fully in the education of their children. Printed materials should be provided in the primary languages of parents. Transportation and childcare needs should be addressed. Program offerings should take into account the inflexible work hours many parents confront, and the school should function as a true community center as it coordinates community services for parents and families (Hoover-Dempsey et al, 2005).

Provide Multiple Opportunities for Parents to Volunteer in the School

A thriving program with community members who volunteer their time and talents to assisting educators is the very essence of a win-win situation. Community members benefit from witnessing the culture of the school on a personal level, from developing a deeper understanding of the responsibilities and challenges of students and educators, and from the positive feelings associated with helping others. Students benefit from the additional support and specialized expertise volunteers bring to the school. Educators benefit from the additional helping hands. There are, however, considerable obstacles that must be overcome to create effective volunteer programs (National Parent Teacher Association, 2000):

- **Concerns about confidentiality.** Volunteers repeatedly express the need to be better informed in order to be more confident and effective in their roles. Teachers and principals, on the other hand, often express concern with the ability of volunteers to maintain confidentiality.

- **Discipline.** Volunteers often express frustration about both the lack of training for responding to discipline issues and the ambiguity regarding their authority to discipline students. Educators, however, cite the unwillingness of volunteers to discipline unruly children.

- **Assignments.** Parents often report to being used in limited and inconsequential roles that are not valued or needed, while educators claim many parents are only interested in contributing to their own children's classrooms.

- **Legalities.** It is incumbent upon schools to conduct routine background checks on volunteers just as they would for new staff members, even though volunteers may be offended by what they perceive to be a violation of their privacy or the questioning of their character.

- **Recruitment.** Many educators believe community members interested in volunteering should take the initiative to come forward; however, community members often think the school should make an effort to recruit them for assignments that match their skills and interests.

The National PTA (2000) has identified seven steps to creating an effective volunteer program in schools:

- **Assess volunteer needs at the school.** Staff members should generate a list of possible volunteer assignments in classrooms and throughout the school. Staff should also consider ways for residents to contribute from their homes to include those whose work schedules or personal situations do not allow them to come to the school.

- **Train all staff in the effective use of volunteers.** Clarify the appropriate roles for volunteers and the responsibilities staff assume in the supervision of volunteers.

- **Set goals and objectives for volunteer assignments.** Educators enhance the effectiveness of volunteers when they create detailed job descriptions that help volunteers understand the specific tasks they are to accomplish and why they are asked to complete them. Volunteers should have a clear understanding of how they can help and why that help is important.

- **Recruit volunteers.** Schools should survey staff to identify their needs in regard to volunteers. In addition, it is helpful to survey community members to determine their interests, talents, and availability. A history teacher could help students reach a better understanding of Jim Crow laws if those with personal experience in coping with those laws were to address the class. Students in a building trades class could benefit from working with a retired carpenter. Parents with a journalism background might sponsor a student newspaper. Senior citizens might welcome the opportunity to read to students and to have students read to them. Finding the right fit between the school's needs and the volunteer's expertise and expectations is vital to an effective program. Some volunteers may be perfectly happy collating papers, while others would be disappointed in any assignment where they were not working directly with students. A volunteer who hopes to help children develop creative writing skills who is assigned instead to playground supervision will not remain a volunteer for long.

- **Train and provide orientation for volunteers.** Volunteers should not be expected to fend for themselves. Effective training and orientation enhances the likelihood the experience will benefit students and volunteers. Orientation should help volunteers understand school policy, procedures, and expectations. Training should give them the skills to enhance their effectiveness, particularly when they work with students. Volunteers should be asked for feedback on the training they receive and for suggestions about training they think would be beneficial.

- **Retain and recognize volunteers.** Volunteers are more likely to support the school if they feel they are making valuable contributions to students and staff and that their contributions are appreciated. Notes from principals, staff, and students remind volunteers they are appreciated, and a wall of fame showing pictures of outstanding volunteers celebrates their contribution in a very public way.

- **Evaluate the success of the volunteer program.** Ask the questions, "How will we know if we have an exemplary volunteer program?" and "What criteria will we use to assess its effectiveness?" Develop strategies for gathering and analyzing data on the impact of the program.

Include Parents in School Governance and Decision-Making

Seymour Sarason (1997) contends schools have functioned as fortified enclaves whose implicit message to parents has been, "Send us your children, stay out of our way, we know what needs to be done, you will some day thank us" (p. 73). Efforts certainly have been made to overcome this tradition. James Comer's School Development Program explicitly required parent participation on two of the three teams responsible for school governance (Joyner, Ben-Avie, & Comer 2004). Title I programs called for the creation of parent advisory councils. Districts that adopted the site-based management model typically included parents on their site-based councils, which made decisions for the schools. Many urban school reform models call for local school councils as a way to give parents a significant role in governance and to decentralize decision-making.

However, there is ample evidence that parent involvement in governance and decision-making can have negative rather than positive consequences. One study of 83 schools that used some form of parent involvement in site-based management found little evidence that the involvement had a positive effect on student achievement (Leithwood & Menzies, 1998). Once again, if uninformed people are asked to make decisions, they will make uninformed decisions. If educators are to engage parents in significant decisions, they must include them in the process to build shared knowledge of the current reality and best practice. If this crucial step is ignored, parent participation in governance and decision-making can do more harm than good.

Furthermore, many parents may be unwilling or unable to devote the time required to play an active role in ongoing governance. Chicago Public Schools, for example, launched a restructuring initiative to provide every school with a local school council, but has had a difficult time recruiting a sufficient number of parents to serve on the councils. Those same parents who may be unable to make a long-term commitment could, however, play a vital role in helping make decisions to improve their community schools through participation in short-term task forces.

Task forces are temporary groups of representative stakeholders convened to work on a specific, defined task or activity. Once the task has been completed, the group is dissolved. Members bring different perspectives and areas of expertise to the work and operate as an egalitarian rather than hierarchical group. Members are given a specific charge and a few guiding parameters within which they are asked to work, but they enjoy considerable freedom about how to approach their task.

For example, assume a district has decided it should develop more effective procedures for providing feedback to parents about the academic progress and achievement of their children. The district invites or recruits interested people to participate on a task force to address that objective. Members include someone from the Board of Education, teachers, administrators, parents, community members, and perhaps some older students. The task force is presented with the following charge and operating parameters:

> When parents receive frequent, timely, and precise feedback about the academic progress of their children, they can contribute more effectively to their children's learning and form a stronger partnership with educators. Therefore, the Academic Progress Task Force is hereby charged to 1) identify and recommend more effective procedures for reporting student progress to parents, and 2) help build consensus in support of its recommendations.
>
> Recommendations should be consistent with the district vision and values and represent research-based best practice. The task force should present an analysis of the financial impact of its recommendations and assess the time demands its recommendations will place on staff and parents. Members are reminded that they serve in an advisory capacity. They have no authority to make policy, establish procedures, or expend district funds. If, however, they identify strategies for improving feedback to parents and are able to build consensus in support of those strategies, they can have a profound and lasting positive effect on the education of children in this district. Finally, the task force is asked to present its

recommendations to the Board of Education within the next 6 months. Members may seek an extension of this timeline if they determine they need additional time to meet their charge.

Whereas many school governance structures involve just a few parents in the decision-making process, a school or district that establishes several task forces each year could involve many parents. Once again, with involvement comes increased ownership in and support for the organization and its decisions. Good ideas can come from sources other than just those at the top of an organization, and task forces expand the potential pool of good ideas. The use of task forces has been described as one of the most powerful tools available for effecting change in organizations (Waterman, 1993), and schools and districts should incorporate this powerful tool into their strategies to engage all stakeholders in the decision-making process.

Community members should also be able to initiate their own ideas for improving the school rather than merely waiting for invitations from the school to address topics selected by educators. Every school should provide well-publicized processes that enable parents to express their concerns, raise questions, or offer proposals. Schools should also have plans in place to solicit the parental perspective in the evaluation of programs, policies, procedures, and the culture of the school through formal surveys, focus groups, hotlines, websites, parent luncheons, neighborhood coffees, and regularly scheduled open forums.

Finally, parents are typically most anxious to play a role in decision-making when the decision directly involves their own child. Schools that solicit parental participation in those decisions are far more likely to build strong partnerships.

Collaborate With the Larger Community and Utilize Community Resources

Schools have traditionally been regarded as institutions that provide educational services to the children of the community for 7 hours each day, Monday through Friday, September through June. They can and should, however, be viewed as vital resources that contribute to the entire community throughout the entire school year.

Adlai Stevenson High School District 125 has created a "lifetime partnership" with its community that provides services and support to all segments of its community throughout all stages of life. Imagine Mr. and Mrs. Jones, residents of the district, have just found out they are going to have a baby. They enroll in the prenatal care and Lamaze classes offered as part of the adult-education program at Stevenson. Upon the birth of their son, Max, Mrs. Jones signs up for the "Mom and Tots" swim program offered at the school. When Max is 3, he is enrolled in the preschool program and receives very personal attention from the high-school students who participate in the childcare program. As a young boy, Max never misses the Children's Theater Program held at the school every fall and spring. He attends religious services at the school every weekend because his congregation is one of several to use the school facilities.

In elementary and middle school, Max participates in the athletic, drama, and music camps held at the high school each summer. In eighth grade, he attends the dress rehearsal performances of the high school's major theatrical productions and participates in programs to learn about the school's academic offerings and cocurricular opportunities. His eighth-grade graduation is held at the high school. By the time he enters Stevenson as a freshman, Max has been in the school and on the campus so often for so many different functions that it feels like his home away from home.

As a student, Max becomes a member of the 300 Club, an organization that arranges community service opportunities for students. He becomes an active volunteer, working after school and on weekends in a nursing home, a soup kitchen, and in his former elementary school as a tutor. Each year he participates in the annual Health Fair offered by the area medical community and the Fine Arts Festival offered by the community's Fine Arts Council. At the Career Exposition offered by the school's business partners, he signs up to assist in conducting an environmental study sponsored by the Forest Preserve. The school-business partnership also helps him determine his career choice after he participates in the job-shadowing program and is provided an internship in a veterinarian's office. At his high school graduation ceremony, he is among the hundreds of students recognized for devoting over 300 hours to serving his community while in high school.

Meanwhile, Max's parents are also very involved in life on the Stevenson campus. They participate in the ballroom dancing and yoga classes offered at the school through the Park District. They participate in financial seminars, cooking classes, computer classes, practical foreign language classes, and a host of other programs offered through the district's adult-education program. Mrs. Jones earns her master's degree through an evening program at the school made available through the district's partnership with a number of universities. Because Stevenson functions as the very hub of the community, the Jones family is able to benefit from its services throughout all the years they live in the district.

This scenario is not an unrealistic dream. It is the reality at Adlai Stevenson High School, and it shows the strong partnership between the school district and its community. Stevenson has made a conscious effort to bring community resources—social agencies, universities, businesses, park districts, foundations—into the school to benefit its constituents. It has also made an effort to extend its human resources into the community and to foster a sense of service in its students. For a quarter century, its students have been instrumental in coordinating the county's program to provide needy families with support during the holidays. Stevenson students represent one of the largest sources of donors for the blood drives sponsored by the Red Cross. They provide the county with its largest single source of election judges. They have been recognized at the local, state, and national levels for their extraordinary commitment to community service. This district's effort to collaborate with and coordinate services to the larger community has certainly been a factor in the ongoing support it has received from residents who have repeatedly voted to approve tax referenda to support the district and its programs.

Tips for Effective School-Family Partnerships

Joyce Epstein (2001), the director of the Center on School, Family, and Community Partnerships at Johns Hopkins University, has made the study of this topic her life's work. She offers the following insights among her conclusions:

- A comprehensive program of partnership includes activities of all six types of involvement presented by the National PTA.

- Developing partnerships is a process—not an event. Efforts to develop partnerships must be ongoing and seen as the regular work of leaders.

- Since the purpose of partnerships is to benefit children and enhance their learning, they should be assessed on the basis of results.

- Action teams should be established to develop and sustain effective school, family, and community partnerships. The process involves identifying team members, establishing structures, determining processes, writing plans, allocating budgets, and conducting evaluations. The process is too important to be left to chance or suffer from ambiguity regarding responsibility. Epstein (2005) considers defined leadership, teamwork, action plans, implementation of plans, funding, collegial support, evaluation, and networking to be the essential elements of high-quality partnership programs.

- Partnerships are for all families and are important for students at all grade levels. There is a dramatic decline in parent involvement as children advance through school. Data from the administration of the 2000 National Assessment of Educational Progress showed that nationally, 90% of fourth graders attended schools where a school official reported the majority of parents participated in parent-teacher conferences. Among eighth graders, the percentage dropped to 57% ("Parent Involvement"). Parents of middle school students often report thinking their children should be more self-reliant and also express a lack of confidence in their ability to help students with their schoolwork. The task of working with several teachers rather than a single elementary classroom teacher makes communicating with teachers more challenging. And, of course, many—if not most—middle school students do not want their parents to get involved in their schools (or their lives, for that matter). Nevertheless, evidence gathered from more than 1,000 schools and 125 school districts establishes that the benefits of parental involvement extend through high school (Epstein, 2005). Middle and high school educators are not exempt from the need to foster strong partnerships with parents.

Which Lens Will We Look Through?

To reiterate, all parents, regardless of race or income, education, or cultural background, want their children to do well in school (Henderson & Mapp, 2002), and the extent of their involvement in their children's education can have a significant impact on student achievement. Schools and the educators within them play a critical role in promoting that involvement. The way in which educators view their schools will determine their interest in and commitment to including parents as significant partners in the teaching and learning process.

So do educators believe their schools are based on the industrial model, or do they believe their schools are based on the service-industry model? The industrial model calls for uniformity, adherence to standardized processes, and protecting those processes from outside interference to ensure consistency. The service-industry model calls for individualization, soliciting the perspective of the customer, and then exceeding customer expectations.

Several years ago, Rick attended a banquet to celebrate the accomplishments of schools that had been involved in a state-funded grant program to improve their schools. Representatives of each staff issued brief reports on their most significant achievements. One school proudly reported the problem they had tackled was parents entering the building prior to the closing of school. The faculty task force in charge of school improvement devised a solution to this problem: They purchased time-sensitive locks that kept the parents outside. It was not difficult to ascertain which model this faculty used in looking at parents. If educators cling to the industrial model, they will consider parents an unwelcome interference; if they embrace the service-industry model, they will welcome parents as partners and be hungry for evidence about how parents perceive their schools.

In a service industry, every employee understands the importance of creating an inviting atmosphere and meeting the needs of each customer. To illustrate, let us look outside of education to a case study reported by Patterson, Grenny, Maxfield, McMillan, & Switzler (2008). When a large medical service center began gathering data on patients' perceptions of the quality of their treatment, administrators discovered the center's scores had declined consistently for 13 months. Patients did not think they were being treated with dignity and respect. The center created a task force that included representatives of every department and function in the hospital to examine the data and develop recommendations for resolving the problem. The task force searched the Web for research, interviewed dozens of patients and their families, and solicited ideas from employees throughout the hospital. Most importantly, they sifted through the center's data to identify "positive deviants"—people in their own organization who consistently received high scores from patients regarding the quality of their service. Eventually, the task force discovered those employees demonstrated five vital behaviors in all of their contacts: 1) They smiled, 2) they made eye contact, 3) they identified themselves, 4) they explained what they were doing and why, and 5) they ended every interaction with the question, "Is there anything else you need?" When these vital behaviors were taught to each of the 4,000 employees in the center, the quality scores began to rise, and they continued rising for 12 consecutive months as the center became best-in-class among its peers.

This case study is a classic example of a learning organization at work. The center was hungry for evidence of its effectiveness and developed strategies for gathering meaningful data. When the data revealed a problem, a collaborative team was established to build shared knowledge of best practice. The team explored the research, but it also looked for expertise within the organization. The team studied the positive deviants to determine the exact behaviors that led to their success, communicated its findings with people throughout the organization, trained people in the behaviors, monitored the impact of the training by gathering more information, and celebrated improvements.

If, on the other hand, hospital staff took the position that medical treatment required professional expertise and therefore patient perspectives were irrelevant, the hospital would have had no interest in exploring the issue. So there are two critical questions every school must address in its efforts to improve student achievement: "Do we perceive ourselves and does our community view our school as a service industry?" and "Will we adhere to learning-organization practices to determine how to best provide our service?"

Mountain Meadow Elementary: A Professional Learning Community

We conclude this chapter with the success story of an elementary school staff that embraced a service culture and created strong parent partnerships to transform their school.

Janel Keating, Deputy Superintendent of the White River School District, Buckley, Washington, and Former Principal of Mountain Meadow Elementary School

My school district, White River, lies at the base of Mount Rainier some 30 miles southeast of Seattle, Washington. When I was assigned to the principalship of Mountain Meadow Elementary School in 1998, only 58% of the school's students met the state standard in reading, 42% met the standard in math, and a dismal 19% met the standard in writing. That fall, when the state required schools to administer a reading assessment to each student entering second grade, only 46% of our students were reading at or above grade level.

Furthermore, because Mountain Meadow did not generate enough students from its own attendance zone, the school was designated as the "overflow" school that enrolled students from other attendance areas in the district. For example, in 1998, 120 students were transferred to our school from elementary schools around the district after the beginning of the school year. After spending 1 year with us, those students were sent back to their home schools. Each fall the next group of overflow students came to us, and at the end of the school year, they left.

One reason Mountain Meadow had room for students was because all the parents in the most affluent part of the community, the neighborhood where the school superintendent resided, sought waivers to enroll their children in an elementary school outside of the district. Quite obviously, some things needed to change at Mountain Meadow. We needed to create a school that parents wanted their children to attend. The question was where to start.

Our Journey to Becoming a Professional Learning Community

Our first step was to build shared knowledge by seeking out best practices. In the spring of 1999, we started studying the Effective Schools research of Larry Lezotte and others. After studying the research as well as our own Mountain Meadow data, we began to dream about the school we wanted to become and describe that school in vivid detail.

Next, we clarified the collective commitments each staff member would honor in order to create such a school. We decided to focus on reading as the first content area we would address, and we agreed the children most in need would receive the most help by the most skilled staff members. It sounds simple, but making it happen within a school community involves a mountain of work (no pun intended), cooperation, and commitment.

For example, we had to adjust the master schedule, which had traditionally reflected the preferences, convenience, and autonomy of each adult in order to align with the new priority of meeting the needs of students. The revised schedule provided a large block of uninterrupted instructional time for reading and writing and carved out additional time to address the needs of students who required more individualized support.

As the staff at Mountain Meadow moved forward with implementing other best practices within the PLC framework, the term *community* took on special significance. We understood that if we were to become the kind of school we dreamed of, we would need the help, support, and enthusiasm of the entire community—especially parents. We also realized it would be difficult to earn the support and allegiance of parents if their children were *not* learning. Perhaps most importantly, we acknowledged that establishing a strong parent partnership was contingent on our own ability to view parents and the community in a fundamentally different way. Like many educators, we had a tendency to complain about parents—their lack of involvement, their over-involvement, their unreasonable demands, and so on. In fact, each year on the day student assignments to a particular teacher were posted at school, teachers left the building through back doors to avoid interacting with parents.

The groundwork for building strong parent partnerships was laid when we conceded that parents were generally doing the best they could, that they acted in what they believed to be in their children's best interests, and that they entrusted their children to us with a fervent hope we would provide them with a positive experience, treat them with special care, encourage them, and ensure they learn. We decided to focus on what we had in common with parents—the sincere desire to help their children—and to make that shared desire the basis of our partnership.

Once again, we started with the end in mind. We asked such questions as the following:

- If our own children attended this school, what would we want the relationship between us and the school to look like?

- We say we want exemplary school-parent/community relations, but what would that look like if we really meant it?

- What commitments would each of us need to make to establish exemplary partnerships with our parents and community?

We then developed additional shared knowledge by using external resources to provide training for the entire staff in principles of customer service. Next, we worked collaboratively to create and implement a plan to foster strong partnerships with our parents and community through a collective commitment to customer service. Elements of the plan included the following:

- **Valet service.** Mountain Meadow's staff members were stationed at the drop off/pick up area of the school at the beginning and end of each school day. When cars pulled into that area, the door of the car was opened, parents were greeted by name, and their child was delivered to or from a caring adult. We wanted parents to feel as though we were waiting for their children to arrive. At the end of the day, the staff often shared highlights of the child's day with the parent, complimenting the work or progress of the child. Staff members made a point to express to parents how happy we were that their children attended our school.

- **A personal greeting.** We made a conscious effort to learn parents' names and to provide them with a personal greeting every time they came into our school.

- **"How may I help you?"** Every staff member made a commitment to greet any visitor to our school with the question, "How may I help you?" and to conclude the exchange by asking, "Has this helped you?" We wanted to provide personal attention to anyone who entered our school and to ensure we had listened and responded to his or her concerns. There would be no more retreating out back doors to avoid dealing with our public.

- **Positive phone calls.** Every week, each teacher filled out cards that highlighted individual children and something about their learning. These cards were turned into the office, and I made time each week to call home and share with parents what teachers had written about their children. Over the years, parents shared how they kept my voice messages of praise for their child, and many a beaming child has exclaimed in the hallway, "You called my house yesterday!" The child would often go on to explain that he or she was not used to hearing from teachers and the principal about positive things.

- **Mentors.** We created a mentor program to link adults in the community with our kids who could benefit from another positive adult role model. These adults provided a critical friend to students who needed extra attention. Mentors would meet with their students at lunch to listen, help students solve problems, acknowledge their accomplishments, encourage them, and assist them in setting short-term goals. This personal attention often helped students improve academically, and we soon discovered that students who previously had attendance issues never missed school on the days their mentors were scheduled to be there.

- **Volunteer programs.** We brainstormed to identify a variety of ways we could bring parents into our school as volunteers. Teachers began to welcome volunteers into their classrooms, but we also created opportunities beyond the classroom. Today, more than 200 parent volunteers work with students at Mountain

Meadow—in the library, on the playground, or in the recess room, as well as in classrooms. Parent volunteers are alerted to problems and then included in seeking solutions. For example, they have been trained to be particularly attentive to students who seem to be struggling to get along with others, and they focus on helping those students find a way to make better choices.

- **Volunteer training.** We realized if we were to tap into the full potential of volunteers to impact student learning, those volunteers would need training. Therefore, we began training parents to use specific intervention strategies with students, rather than just assigning them to collate and staple papers in the workroom. For example, Lynne, a parent volunteer, typically devoted her volunteer time to the usual copy, cut, and paste work for a classroom teacher; but once she was trained in the Read Naturally program, she began to provide Jordan with additional support in reading. She read with Jordan one-on-one on a daily basis and began gathering books from the library that she knew would hold his interest. As Jordan's behavior and reading improved dramatically, Lynne felt the tremendous satisfaction of knowing the connection she established with Jordan had made an important difference in his life.

- **Celebrations.** We understood that to change the perception of our school in the community, we needed to utilize the power of rituals, ceremonies, and celebrations. We traditionally had only celebrated the accomplishments of honor roll students at our assemblies, which meant most students were never recognized. We concluded that if we valued and appreciated *improvement* as well as *achievement,* we should publicly recognize both students who demonstrated marked improvement and those who had achieved milestones in their learning. We began monthly assemblies to recognize students for improved schoolwork, improved behavior, and improved attitude and to acknowledge students who had achieved specific benchmarks in reading. Each child was given an Olympic-type medal as part of this celebration. Parents were invited to join us for these celebrations, and the superintendent, deputy superintendent, or a member of the Board of Education often joined us to award the medals. This seismic shift in the focus and purpose of the ceremony meant every child in our school had the opportunity to be recognized and celebrated.

One morning a grandmother of several Mountain Meadow students arrived at the school and asked to see the principal. She shared the story of the recent death of her husband, the children's grandfather. She told me how touched her husband had been to come to the school to be a part of the improvement celebrations—celebrations that recognized his grandchildren and made him feel like a part of the school. She then presented me with a check large enough to cover the cost of the next thousand medals.

Our public recognition and celebrations were not limited to students. Adults were recognized too—frequently and publicly, both individually and in groups. Staff members and community volunteers were presented with constant reminders that their efforts were noted and appreciated.

- **Parents as partners.** The most important step we took in this effort to strengthen our partnership with parents was to demonstrate a sincere interest in giving them a voice in the education of their children. We knew parents had important insights about their own children, and we committed to including them in our planning and respecting them as "the experts" where their children were concerned. Our mantra became, "When in doubt, ask mom or dad." Each year we ask parents to complete a form indicating their child's interests, strengths, and weaknesses as learners, and any information that would help us create the best educational opportunity for their child.

Building Strong Partnerships

Many parents have expressed their gratitude for the care we have given their students and the strong partnerships we have forged with them and the community. The following letter submitted by the parents of Hannah, a Mountain Meadow student, illustrates how our efforts to promote strong parent partnerships have positively affected the lives of our students and their families.

It is difficult to capture the magic we experienced when enrolling our eldest child, Hannah, in first grade at Mountain Meadow Elementary. Sure, we had heard great things about the school, but we had no idea what a fantastic journey the entire family was about to embark upon. You see, Mountain Meadow doesn't just serve its students; it serves parents and the community as well.

It was in late August when we first took our daughter to Mountain Meadow for the ice cream social where Hannah would learn who her first-grade teacher would be. The prior spring, we had the opportunity to complete an "environmental request form," where we described our child and her specific skills and passions. We were thrilled to learn Hannah was assigned to Ms. Fast, the teacher we knew would fit our daughter's personality and skills. We were soon approached by Mrs. Keating, Mountain Meadow's principal, and she greeted us by name. She then knelt down to the children's level to greet Hannah and Ella, our then 3-year-old. She asked, "Hannah, aren't you thrilled about your new teacher? She loves to read just like you do, and she also loves to learn!" and then "Ella, you will be a Timber Wolf soon. I can't wait until you come to school here!" She hugged both kids, asked if we needed anything, and smiled as she walked away. We felt so special. Not only did she remember our names, but we knew that someone had actually read the form that we had so carefully prepared.

The most amazing part of the story was yet to come. We then watched as Mrs. Keating treated other parents the exact same way. The principal knew each and every parent and child by name, and made each individual family feel special with her willingness to truly listen and care about our children.

The teachers and staff at Mountain Meadow modeled the same behaviors as their leader, each one taking the time to listen, respond, and truly care about our child as a unique individual. The focus of the school is on what is in the child's best interest. If the current program couldn't meet the needs of a student, then that program would be modified. All students' needs are met; there is no other option.

Another parent wrote the following of Mountain Meadow Elementary:

This commitment to personalized service has become a part of the culture of the school. It echoes through the halls, it permeates the PTA—it is the gold medal of the community. We are incredibly thankful for the staff and administration at Mountain Meadow Elementary. They have provided our son, and every other student that walks the halls, with an incredible foundation for the future. I'm not sure if Mountain Meadow was blessed with good people from the get-go or if the culture facilitated this attitude. Regardless, I have great respect for all of my child's teachers—each has left his or her "brand" on his development.

Another family made a point to contact me about the experience of their daughter, Sara. During the first week of school, Sara's first-grade teacher had emailed them to request a conference to discuss Sara. The teacher explained that Sara had tested out of the curriculum, and she felt Sara would benefit from working in a more advanced reading program with another staff member for an hour each day. The parents, stunned that the teacher would be so aware of the ability and needs of their daughter after a week of school, readily agreed to her proposal. They soon discovered, however, that the personalization did not stop with reading. As the parents reviewed the "Friday Folder" Sara brought home with her each week, they discovered the teacher had substituted more complex math problems for the ones offered in the standard math materials. They expressed their amazement that the school was able to provide such individualized attention to each student. As another parent expressed, "Sometimes I feel like Michael is the only student at Mountain Meadow." Or, as a representative of a social service organization wrote after visiting the school, "Mountain Meadow is the Nordstrom of public education," comparing our commitment to service to the legendary store that serves as the standard for customer service in the retail world.

A Dramatic Improvement

Our collaborative culture, focus on each student's learning, attention to results, and strong school-parent partnerships soon led to significant improvements in student achievement. Within 3 years, the percentage of students meeting or exceeding the state proficiency standard increased from 58% to 98% in reading and from 42% to 92% in math. Furthermore, the improvements were sustained over time as reflected by the following percentages of students who met or exceeded state standards:

	Reading	Math
2004	100%	100%
2005	99%	95%
2006	100%	97%

Mountain Meadow Elementary was recognized as one of the highest academically performing elementary schools in Washington State. It became a showcase school with teachers and administrators frequently visiting from across the state. The "overflow" school—the one no one wanted to attend—became a school of choice in our community as parents clamored to transfer their children to Mountain Meadow. Parents of children initially sent to us because of overcrowding at their home schools were appealing to the district to stay at Mountain Meadow, even though they knew they would be responsible for transporting their children to and from school. The district even had to build an additional parking lot to handle the traffic created by all the students from both within and outside the district who now sought waivers seeking to attend. The PTA president resided in a neighboring school district, but she wanted her child to be educated at Mountain Meadow. The parents in the superintendent's neighborhood that had opted to educate their kids out of the district began enrolling their children in our school.

What Did We Learn?

Mountain Meadow's quest towards great school-parent/community relations has been a journey—a marathon rather than a sprint. We have not arrived yet, and actually never will. Each year we try to get better. We have, however, learned some important lessons along the way.

You must have a plan. All schools desire great school-community relations, but at Mountain Meadow, we learned that hoping was not enough. We needed a plan that would get us to where we wanted to go. We studied best practices in parent partnerships, described the ideal relationships we hoped to create, and then created and implemented a plan to move forward. We recognized the importance of learning by doing, so we experimented by trying some strategies to see what worked.

You must form genuine collaborative partnerships. It is very easy to settle for "collaboration lite" with parents if the goal is to keep them happy (or quiet). If, however, partnerships with parents are destined to have a positive impact on student learning, those partnerships must address significant issues. We discovered that when parents sense you genuinely desire a deeper, richer level of collaboration, they are much more willing to participate (and much more forgiving when you make mistakes).

Celebrate small wins. The faculty and staff of Mountain Meadow wanted really good things to happen really fast. We learned, however, that changing culture is difficult and complex work that takes place incrementally over time. So, it was important for us to highlight the successes we were having. By celebrating these "small wins," we helped people realize we were making progress on our journey. Without acknowledging and celebrating those wins, it would have been easy to get discouraged.

Realize that, ultimately, it is about the kids. This was our greatest lesson—it's about the kids! If a school does everything else right, but the kids are not learning, it will be impossible to have great school-parent/community relations. It is obvious: Parents care about *their* child. They want their child to attend a *great* school; however, to educate all students at high levels takes more than a teacher. It takes a team of teachers, it takes a school, it takes parents, and it takes the larger community. In fact, it takes all of us! The challenge for Mountain Meadow (and for every school) is to develop a community dedicated to raising the aspirations and achievement levels of all our children by *taking a hand, opening a mind, and touching a heart!*

So, I can say with complete certainty that the power of PLCs to impact the learning and lives of students is only magnified when the collaboration and sense of community extend beyond the schoolhouse walls and include parents and families. When parents and educators are linked together, they can forge a chain of learning that benefits all concerned. The eloquent words of one of our parents serve as tribute to the power of PLCs and are an appropriate conclusion to this chapter:

> *My youngest son currently attends Mountain Meadow Elementary, and my two older sons are alumni. I have often expressed to Janel Keating and other talented staff*

members at Mountain Meadow the gratitude we feel that our kids experienced their magic.

Until [I attended a] PLC conference, I simply saw this magic as a function of the compassion and commitment of these very creative professionals. Though there is no doubt they are exceptional, I realized that Janel had a deliberate plan all along and was quietly building effective structures of collaboration and cooperation at Mountain Meadow. She had been implementing PLCs that would go on to play a fundamental part in the success of my own kids.

So I say, "Way to go TEAM!" to Janel and the Mountain Meadow staff. There is amazing proof in my family, living data if you will, that the efforts of caring and committed PLCs can bring about very powerful results.

Chapter 15

Sustaining the Professional Learning Community Journey

The final challenge—and the one that solidifies success—is to build so much momentum that change is unstoppable, that everything reinforces the new behavior, that even the resistors get on board—exactly the momentum that develops in winning streaks.

—Rosabeth Moss Kanter

Imagine you go to the doctor to seek advice regarding how to lose weight. The doctor responds enthusiastically and confidently, assuring you she has *the* solution, a foolproof way for you to accomplish your goal. "It's simple," she says, "all you need to do is change your lifestyle to ensure you eat less and exercise more. If you adhere to that prescription over time, I guarantee you will lose weight." The doctor's logic is unassailable, and if you follow her succinct admonition to change your lifelong habits so you eat less and exercise more, you will indeed lose weight. Anyone who has ever attempted to make this transition, however, can attest to its difficulty.

Perhaps you picked up this book hoping it would provide you with a foolproof strategy for improving student achievement in your school or district. If so, we can assert enthusiastically and confidently you will improve student achievement when the staff of your school becomes proficient in doing the work of professional learning communities. We can offer an unambiguous answer to the question, "How can we improve student learning?" However, we recognize that applying this answer in the complex cultures of schools and districts is anything but easy. The cultural shifts that are necessary remind us of the advice offered to Blackthorne in the novel *Shōgun*, as he struggled to learn the customs and language of the Japanese: "It is all so simple, Anjin-san. Just change your concept of the world" (Clarell, 1986, p. 504). Developing schools and districts as PLCs is not easy precisely because educators will be called upon to change their concept of their world. Readers who are looking for "easy" would be advised to continue doing what you have always done, which is certainly less troublesome than substantive cultural change.

Of course, if you choose easy, you will not likely see any substantial changes in the current levels of learning or in the culture of your school or district.

We also want to avoid giving the impression there is a prescribed, step-by-step recipe or route to becoming a PLC. Developing the collective capacity to function as a PLC is *not* analogous to participating in a "road rally" in which you must proceed at a specified speed to the next stop in a prescribed order to reach your ultimate destination successfully. On the other hand, some critical issues must be addressed sooner rather than later if the school improvement journey is to proceed in a purposeful direction.

Consider this analogy: There is no "one right way" to drive from New York to San Francisco. People can choose very different routes and proceed at very different speeds depending on a number of variables and still arrive in the "City by the Bay." A family with small children and only one driver in an older car with high mileage will stop more frequently and at different places than a group of college students who share the driving responsibilities in a new car. One group of travelers may take a leisurely pace and stop to confirm directions multiple times while another will proceed with urgency. One group may elect to take a northern route while another opts for a southern route. Despite this flexibility, however, there are at least two absolute requirements for those who wish to take this cross-country trip. First, they must start the engine, take the car out of park, and put it in drive. Second, they must ultimately point the car toward the west.

Similarly, there is no "one right way" to proceed on the journey to become a PLC. A school with a single champion of the concept will proceed at a much different pace than a school with a guiding coalition of multiple leaders and widespread enthusiasm for moving forward. A school with a tradition of adults working in isolation may take a different path than a school in which adults are accustomed to working together. But while there may be no one right way to proceed, there are certain issues that ultimately must be addressed. Educators will never create PLCs until they take action and unless they move in the right direction.

To take the analogy one step further, those who begin the PLC journey should be wary of several dangerous detours and potholes that can lead to a complete breakdown and cancellation of the trip.

Dangerous Detour #1: We Need More Training Before We Can Begin

Often educators who are called upon to implement the PLC concept respond with the assertion they could not possibly undertake the task without extensive training over a long period of time. They assert they simply do not know how to work together collaboratively, identify essential curriculum, develop valid assessments, interpret achievement data, create systems of interventions and enrichment, reach out to parents, or trust one another. They could not possibly begin the endeavor until they have been buttressed by years of training.

Peter Block, one of the world's leading organizational theorists (2003), contends the question, "But *how* do we do this?" is a favorite defense against taking action because it looks for the answer outside of us. He considers the question an "indirect expression of our doubt that we know enough and are enough" (p. 5). He advises that people in organizations accomplish most by taking action and believing in their capacity to learn through their shared experiences and joint reflections on those experiences rather than waiting for more training, more knowledge, more skills, and more support to ensure greater certainty as a precondition for moving forward.

Pfeffer and Sutton (2000) came to a similar conclusion when they discovered organizations often substitute training for doing. They found the most effective organizations appreciate the power and necessity of *learning by doing* rather than *learning by training*. As they wrote, "Learning is best done by trying a lot of things, learning from what works and what does not, thinking about what was learned, and trying again. Enlightened trial and error outperforms the planning of flawless intellects" (p. 249). They concluded that the single most powerful strategy for eliminating the knowing-doing gap and developing deeper understanding is to learn by doing.

We often ask educators to reflect upon their own experience to illustrate the power of learning by doing. Most spent 4 or 5 years "training" to become teachers—taking coursework in content and pedagogy, observing teachers, and completing student teaching under the tutelage of a supervising teacher. But when we ask, "How many of you feel you learned more about the profession in your first semester of teaching than you did in the 4 or 5 years you devoted to *preparing* to become a teacher?" there is virtually universal agreement that it was doing the work of a teacher that provided the deepest understanding and most profound learning.

Educators will certainly need training as they proceed on the PLC journey, but the training is most relevant and valuable when it is delivered as they are engaged in doing the work of a PLC and is specific to the task at hand. As we have advised in the past, "When we wrote *Professional Learning Communities at Work*, we made a conscious decision to emphasize 'work' in order to stress the importance of an action orientation.

We did not refer to 'PLCs at training,' 'PLCs at study,' 'PLCs at reading,' or 'PLCs at staff development.' Now that we have had the opportunity to work with school systems throughout North America, we are more convinced than ever schools develop as PLCs when their staffs actually *work* at the process rather than train for the process" (DuFour, DuFour, Eaker, & Many, 2006, p. 198).

In our work with districts, we will typically spend several days with educators helping them to examine the PLC concept, answering their questions, and offering specific implementation strategies. It is not uncommon at that point for the district to request "advanced PLC training." Our response continues to be, "Advanced training is doing the work. Take steps to implement strategies and we will support you as you run into challenges, but further training at this point is merely procrastination." The training and professional development that often occur in schools and districts create the *illusion* of action rather than building capacity. Beware of substituting training, reading, or planning for *doing* the work of PLCs.

Dangerous Detour #2: Let's Find a Way to Shortcut Key Processes

Given the already crushing demands on their time, it is understandable that educators instinctively seek ways to shortcut key processes as they implement the PLC concept. Predictable refrains will include the following:

- "Our team doesn't have time to talk about essential curriculum, so just give us the state standards (or district curriculum, or textbook) as the guaranteed curriculum for our course or grade level."

- "We don't have the time or expertise to create common formative assessments as a team, so we will just use the district assessments (or the questions at the end of each chapter, or lobby for the purchase of commercial tests)."

- "Why bother sharing results from assessments when any differences between teachers are probably a function of the students in our classes? I will just look at my own data."

- "Shouldn't someone in the central office or the principal analyze results from assessments rather than our team?"

- "We understand collaboration is important, but if someone doesn't want to collaborate, shouldn't he or she be allowed to opt out of the process?"

- "If we provide students with additional time and support, aren't we really just enabling them?"

Questions like these get to the very heart of the PLC concept, and when the essence of PLC practice is compromised, the improvement process is almost certain to fail. The products created in a PLC—a clearly defined, guaranteed, and viable curriculum; formative assessments; analysis of data; and intervention plans—are not as important as the process that leads to their creation. If the process does not include the educators themselves, it robs them of the opportunity and absolves them of the responsibility to learn. As we wrote in *Learning by Doing*, "We are convinced that the most common cause of the demise of PLC initiatives is not the result of a single cataclysmic event, but rather repeated compromises regarding the fundamental premises of PLCs. There is no one fatal blow: PLCs die from a thousand small wounds" (DuFour, DuFour, Eaker, & Many, 2006, p. 195). Beware of compromises that violate the fundamental premise and practices of a PLC. Beware of allowing the powerful concept to die from a thousand small wounds.

Dangerous Detour #3: Someone Else Needs to Do It

There is an almost universal tendency for people at all levels of a school district to point out what others need to do to improve a school or district. A recurring reaction we hear from participants at the conclusion of one of our national institutes is "My _____ (superintendent, principal, department chairperson, board president, state legislator, governor, colleague) should have been here to learn what he/she needs to do to make this happen."

Author Terry Pratchett (2006) captured this tendency to assign responsibility to others when she wrote:

> It is so much easier to blame it on Them. It was bleakly depressing to think it might be Us. If it was Them, then nothing was anyone's fault. If it was Us, well I am one of Us. I've certainly never thought of myself as one of Them. No one ever thinks of himself as one of Them. We are always one of Us. It is Them that do the bad things" (p. 206).

Dennis Sparks (2007) contends educators are particularly prone to this tendency of assigning responsibility to others for improving their situation. As a result, they fall victim to a sense of resignation that robs them of the energy essential to improving their schools and districts. Elmore (2006, p. 127) also cites the "culture of passivity and helplessness that pervades many schools" as working against improvement. Kanter (2004) uses the similar phrase, "passivity and learned helplessness," to describe what she considers "one of the most damaging pathologies to people and the places they work." As she writes, "When people become resigned to their fate, nothing ever changes. When people are surrounded by pessimism—that feeling that they are the victims of uncontrollable forces around them—they drag others down with them, finding the worst in everything and resisting other peoples' ideas but offering none of their own" (p. 256).

Rick captures this cultural trait in his poem, "It's Not My Fault."

> "He doesn't have the skills we need,"
> the employer harrumphed with disgust.
> "The colleges are ivory towers
> so training him falls to us."

"It's not our fault," the professors cried.
"He was deficient in every way.
Remediation has become our task
because high schools fail kids today."

"But kids we get can't read or write.
He doesn't know things he should.
We high school teachers aren't at fault
The middle school's no damn good."

"We can't overcome six years of neglect,"
the middle school teachers explained.
"If elementary schools won't do their job
then they're the ones to blame."

"He wasn't school ready when he arrived,"
the K–5 teachers moaned.
"All we can do is babysit.
The fault lies in the home."

"It's really not the poor dear's fault,"
his mother was heard to say.
"He's a victim of his family tree . . .
His father's the same way."

Fortunately, people who have succumbed to "learned helplessness" are not doomed to a life of resignation; they can learn to develop a strong sense of self-efficacy (Seligman, 2006). School leaders help overcome a tradition of dependency and resignation when they create cognitive dissonance by identifying districts with similar student populations and resources that are outperforming their schools. For example, the province of Ontario has assigned every elementary school in the province into one of four quadrants on the basis of similar student populations and shows how students from schools in each quadrant perform on provincial exams in reading, writing, and math. The state of California assigns schools into deciles based on student populations and indicates where each school ranks in its decile on the basis of state assessments.

An even more effective strategy for creating cognitive dissonance is to create systems in each school to identify the "positive deviants"—the teachers who are consistently able to help students achieve at higher levels than colleagues who teach similar students (Richardson, 2004). It becomes increasingly difficult for educators to claim they have no impact on student achievement when they are confronted with evidence of similar districts, schools, and teachers who have been far more effective in helping all students learn. As Patterson and colleagues (2008) write, "Nothing changes the mind like the cold, hard world hitting it with actual real-life data" (p. 51). When information regarding student learning becomes easily accessible and openly shared among members of the same team, teachers and principals are able to discover and learn from their own positive deviants.

Yet another powerful strategy for overcoming dependency and resignation is to insist that educators focus within their own sphere of influence and identify and honor the collective commitments they will make to improve teaching and learning. Attention to this critical component of the foundation of a PLC can help educators heed Mahatma Gandhi's advice: "You must be the change you wish to see in the world."

Dangerous Detour #4: We Pick and Choose Programs Rather Than Work at Comprehensive Cultural Change

Kerry Patterson and colleagues (2008) describe a common mistake of those who visit high-performing organizations to learn about and replicate their practices. As they write, "They see a place that works, then they go home and adopt only one idea to add to their existing ineffective efforts. Of course this single element rarely adds enough horse power to create change, so their new and improved strategy fails, and the earnest change agents wonder why their efforts did not work" (p. 260).

For example, educators who visit the two exemplary middle schools of Kildeer Countryside School District 96 in Buffalo Grove, Illinois, to learn how they too can build continuous improvement into the culture of their school may become enamored with the schools' use of technology to provide parents with access to their child's grades, attendance, and homework. They return to their districts and lobby for the expenditure to replicate that technology. What they fail to grasp is that this tool to keep parents informed is only one small part of a comprehensive effort and collective commitment to help all students learn. Teachers in District 96 work in collaborative teams to develop a guaranteed and viable curriculum in every course and grade level. They create frequent common assessments to monitor student learning. They follow a plan for timely, directive, and systematic interventions to provide students with additional time and support for learning. They have examined all of their practices and aligned them to support high levels of learning for all students. Those who hope to emulate the success of District 96 or other high-performing districts or schools will not regard a school as a buffet from which to pick and choose but rather will recognize the need to develop a *comprehensive* approach to creating systematic, substantive, and lasting cultural change.

Dangerous Detour #5: We Quit When the Going Gets Tough

Change expert Rosabeth Moss Kanter (1999) concludes, "Years of study and experience show that the things that sustain change are not bold strokes but long marches." "Everything can look like a failure in the middle," Kanter advises (2005, p. 267). Predictable problems occur during every substantive improvement process, but in education, too often these difficulties are viewed as evidence of failure and a reason to abandon the effort.

Substantive change efforts do not proceed smoothly or in a linear fashion, and it is unrealistic and arrogant to assume *initial efforts* to improve a school or district represent *the final* solution. It is much more productive to think of the improvement process as action research, trial and error, and learning by doing. As Kouzes and Posner (2006) write, "The phrase, 'failure is not an option' is one of the dumbest clichés ever uttered. . . . In real life, when we're trying to do something we've never done before, we virtually never get it right the first time. . . . In real life, we make lots of mistakes when doing something new and different. In real life, failure is always an option" (p. 164).

The key to transforming initial failure into ultimate success is how people respond to the failure—how long they sustain their effort in the face of adversity (Kanter, 2004; Kouzes & Posner, 2006). As Kanter writes, "The dividing line between winning streaks and losing streaks is the choice of behavior in response to setbacks. The decision to build rather than retreat, to rally rather than get discouraged, involves viewing setbacks through an optimistic lens, as an opportunity to learn and move on. Optimists assume that negative events are temporary glitches rather than the permanent state of affairs that pessimists see, and that setbacks are due to specific causes that can be identified and fixed" (pp. 356–357).

When confronted with difficulty and uncertainty, it is natural for people to seek the security and comfort of the status quo. It will always be more comfortable, and easier, to focus on teaching rather than learning, to work in isolation rather than collaboratively, to use summative rather than formative assessments, to leave the question of responding to student difficulties to the discretion of each teacher rather than create a systematic response, to assign responsibility for results to others rather than ourselves, to care only about what happens in our room or our school rather than concern ourselves with the success and well-being of others, to cling to our assumptions and practices rather than examine them. It will always be easier to quit and return to the familiar than to persevere in the face of challenges, reversals, and disappointments.

Therefore, the key to success in implementing PLC concepts is demonstrating the discipline to endure at the hard work of change rather than retreating to the comfort of traditional practices. Collins (2001) found that companies who made the leap from good to great inevitably did so as a result of "a quiet deliberate process of figuring out what needed to be done to create the best future results and then taking those steps, one after another. By pushing in a constant direction over an extended period of time, they inevitably hit a point of breakthrough" (p. 169). Great results, he concluded, could only be achieved "through consistent, coherent effort over time" (p. 182). Kouzes and Posner (2006) discovered that it was not the absence of mistakes but rather the ability to learn from mistakes and integrate that learning into the next effort that was key to the success of organizations. Pfeffer and Sutton (2006) called upon leaders of substantive change to "embrace the mess, do the best you can with the knowledge and evidence at hand, learn as you go, and take action in the meantime" (p. 184). Goleman (1998) found the most effective leaders were resilient, celebrating effort and learning when things did not go well at the same time they considered how to make the situation better. Patterson et al. (2008) found the most influential leaders "interpret setbacks as opportunities to learn, as guides not breaks" (p. 129). Blanchard (2007) advised the key to organizational success is sticking with focused improvement initiatives rather than launching new ones.

Hugh Burkett (2006), director of the Center for Comprehensive School Reform and Improvement, offered this advice to educators: "I learned that a leader should choose carefully what to focus on and then stick with it. . . . I know that the urge to try something new is often born of a fear that we've chosen wrong and a frustration that we aren't getting quick results. . . . In hindsight, I see that moving forward and doing something innovative often won out over painstakingly measuring our progress and adjusting our strategies. My advice? Stay the course. Work the plan. Monitor progress and analyze results. It's not glamorous; it doesn't make headlines. But patience and persistence work when trying to achieve success at this most difficult of tasks" (p. 3).

Fullan (2007) concluded the advice about implementing change in organizations "all amounts to focus, persistence, implementation, monitoring, corrective action, and humility" (p. 121), and he advised districts to stay the course for a period of 10 years or more to transform school cultures. McLaughlin and Talbert (2006) decried the tendency of district leaders to launch new initiatives "in order to make a splash." They advised that building and sustaining learning communities is "neither flashy nor sexy . . . [but] entails slow, steady effort" (p. 114).

The message is consistent: Discipline, persistence, determination, and resilience are essential to substantive improvement initiatives. The challenge confronting leaders at all levels of schools and districts is to help people sustain their effort during the hard work of change rather than retreat to the comfort of the status quo. But how can this be done?

Sustained Effort Requires Creating Short-Term Wins

Let us return to the analogy of the cross-country car trip from New York to San Francisco. Two families, each made up of Mom, Dad, and a brother and sister ages 12 and 10 respectively, set out on the trip, but they take very different approaches to the experience. Mr. Smith considers San Francisco the reward for enduring an arduous and boring drive, and he is determined to complete it as quickly as possible so the family will have more time in California. He insists the family begin the trip in the middle of the night to avoid traffic. He drives relentlessly, 14 hours each day, despite the protestations of his wife and children. He suggests they stop at drive-through restaurants for meals so he can push on with minimal interruption. He resents stopping for bathroom breaks. He assures his family that San Francisco will be so wonderful that their experience there will be well worth the temporary discomfort they are experiencing. Tedium and tension grow in the car. The children are bickering, and midway through the trip, Mr. Smith and his wife have stopped speaking to one another. In Denver, she announces she and the children have no intention of continuing on the trip and will instead fly back home. Mr. Smith is left with an empty car.

The Williams family takes a different approach. Mr. Williams is determined to make the entire journey memorable, not merely the destination. His daughter, Julie, is an avid fan of classic rock, and so the family stops in Cleveland to visit the Rock and Roll Hall of Fame. In Chicago, they take time to attend the Grant Park Summer Shade Festival and visit the Museum of Science and Industry. In Denver, the family attends a Colorado Rockies baseball game, much to son Brandon's delight. In Utah, they rent mountain bikes for a day. Each member of the family has the opportunity to select a place for dinner one night during the trip. But the trip is not without its problems. A tire goes flat in Cleveland. Traffic in Chicago has them at a standstill. Mr. Williams takes a wrong turn coming out of Denver, and they are lost for several hours. Julie becomes nauseous on the curvy mountain roads of Utah. Despite these unforeseen problems, however, by the time the Williams family arrives in San Francisco, they have shared a wonderful week's worth of memories.

The difference between our two families is that Mr. Williams was attentive to the needs and interests of his family, and he made certain to build in stops along the way to honor their interests and celebrate their progress. This attention to breaking long journeys into incremental steps and then recognizing and celebrating the completion of those steps is crucial to sustaining the effort to transform schools and districts into PLCs. Consider the following advice, and identify the trend:

- In successful change efforts empowered people create short-term wins—victories that nourish faith in the change effort, emotionally reward the hard workers, keep the critics at bay, and build momentum. Without sufficient wins that are visible, timely, unambiguous and meaningful to others, change efforts inevitably run into serious problems. (Kotter & Cohen, 2002, p. 125)

- Many change plans underestimate the momentum generated by short-term wins. . . . Short-term wins have several benefits. First, they proactively address impact concerns (such as "Is the change working?"). Second, they provide good news early in the change effort, when good news is hard to come by. Third, they reinforce behavior changes made by early adopters. Fourth, they help sway those who are "on the fence" regarding action. (Blanchard, 2007, p. 238)

- Milestones that are identified, achieved, and celebrated represent an essential condition for building a learning organization. (Thompson, 2006, p. 98)

- The most effective change processes are incremental—they break down big prolems into small, doable steps and get a person to say "yes" numerous times, not just once. They plan for small wins that form the basis for a consistent pattern of winning that appeals to people's desire to belong to a successful venture. A series of small wins provides a foundation of stable building blocks for change. (Kouzes & Posner, 1987, p. 218–219)

- Specific goals should be designed to allow teams to achieve small wins as they pursue their common purpose. Small wins are invaluable to building members' commitment and overcoming the obstacles that get in the way of achieving a meaningful, long-term purpose. (Katzenbach & Smith, 1993, p. 54)

- There is no motivator more powerful than frequent successes. By replacing large-scale, amorphous improvement objectives with short-term, incremental projects that quickly yield tangible results, managers and employees can enjoy the psychological fruits of success. (Schaffer & Thomson, 1998, p. 203)

- When people see tangible results, however incremental at first, and see how the results flow from the overall concept, they will line up with enthusiasm. People want to be a part of a winning team. They want to contribute to producing visible, tangible results. When they feel the magic of momentum, when they begin to see tangible results—that's when they get on board. (Collins, 2001, p. 175)

- Reward small improvements in behavior along the way. Don't wait until people achieve phenomenal results. (Patterson, Grenny, Maxfield, McMillan, & Switzler, 2008, p. 205)

- Win small. Win early. Win often. . . . People can't argue with success. (Hamel, 2002, p. 202)

Sustained Effort Requires Celebrating Short-Term Wins

It is not merely the achievement of small victories but the recognition of those victories and the people behind them that sustain momentum for change. As Kotter and Cohen (2002) cautioned, "The more visible the victories are the more they help the change process. What you don't know about is not a win" (p. 129).

Each year employees report their biggest complaint is that their efforts and achievements go unrecognized (Patterson et al., 2008). This tendency to "astonishingly undercommunicate" appreciation and positive regard robs organizations of the vitality needed to sustain improvement (Kegan & Lahey, 2001). The need to feel that what we do matters and is valued by others represents one of our "deepest hungers" because it "can confirm for us that we matter as a person" and because "it connects us to other people" (Kegan & Lahey, 2001, p. 92). Kouzes and

Posner (2006) advised, "There are few if any needs more basic than to be noticed, recognized, and appreciated for our efforts. . . . Extraordinary achievements never bloom in barren and unappreciative settings" (p. 44).

A sense of significance, competence, and connections represent vital human longings, and those who hope to embark on the PLC journey are strongly advised to use public recognition and celebration of achievement, effort, and improvement to address those needs and to sustain the journey. As Kanter (1999) writes, "Remembering to recognize, reward, and celebrate accomplishments is a critical leadership skill. And it is probably the most underutilized motivational tool in organizations. There is no limit to how much recognition you can provide, and it is often free. Recognition brings the change cycle to its logical conclusion, but it also motivates people to attempt change again."

Final Thoughts

In some of our workshops, we have asked participants to think of and describe the very best teachers they have ever had. The following are some of the comments that have appeared on virtually every list:

- "He took a personal interest in me. He cared about me as a person."

- "She had a contagious enthusiasm, a passion for her subject and for teaching that was infectious."

- "He was energizing. He made learning fun."

- "She had high expectations for me. She demanded my best."

- "He believed in me and made me believe in myself."

- "She never gave up on me. She was tenacious, always encouraging me and expressing her confidence that I would succeed."

The common themes, stated over and over again, are personal connections, enthusiasm for the work, high standards coupled with high expectations for success, and constant encouragement and support. The teachers our participants described believed in themselves as well as their students, and their belief resulted in students who felt empowered, more confident that their efforts held the key to their success. Saphier (2005) describes such teachers as "spiritual leaders" who are able to "mobilize students' desire to learn, build their confidence and belief in themselves, and teach them how to exert effective effort" (p. 16). Teachers who lack self-efficacy, who attribute their students' failure to learn to external forces, or who hold their students in low regard never make this list.

We have also asked participants to think of the very best leader they have known. Their responses, inevitably, echo those of the group that described their best teacher. The point has often been made that great leaders are great teachers and great teachers are great leaders (Gardner, 1988; Tichy, 1997; Pfeffer & Sutton, 2006). And like great teachers, great leaders believe not only in themselves, but also in those they serve. School leaders who have no regard for the ability of those with whom they work, or worse, hold them in contempt, will never lead a PLC.

As Kanter (2004) writes, "self-confidence is not the real secret of leadership. The more essential ingredient is confidence in other people" (p. 328). Fullan (2008) goes even further when he argues the first of six secrets for leading the change process is to love employees as much as customers. Students may rightfully be considered the primary customer of the school, but those who hope to serve those customers cannot be indifferent to the needs, concerns, and capacity of those who are called upon to educate them. As our friend and colleague Mike Mattos has said, "If you help all students learn at the cost of destroying teachers, ultimately you will fail" (DuFour, Eaker, & DuFour, 2007).

We have grave concerns about some of the school reform efforts in vogue today. Efforts that set out to improve schools by applying more and more severe sanctions, by prescribing what teachers in every classroom must say and do on any given day of the school year, or by providing the incentive of merit pay for those who excel are based on the premise that educators have simply not chosen to put forth the effort to raise student achievement. They resort to the stick and the carrot to evoke the prerequisite effort. We believe the underlying premise of these strategies is fundamentally wrong. The problems confronting public education have never been a result of lack of effort or lack of caring among educators. We have taken good people and put them into bad systems. It is time to quit blaming the people and to transform the system. Educators must play the key role in that transformation.

We have spent the past decade arguing on behalf of the PLC concept specifically because it honors rather than denigrates educators. Certainly educators are not blameless for the conditions in the systems in which they work. As a profession, we have been slow to close the gap between knowing what needs to be done to improve schools and actually doing what needs to be done. Educators must acknowledge that often, the primary cause for our inaction has been conflict from within rather than the opposition of external forces. But if those conditions are to be improved, this nation must invest in, support, and develop the capacity of teachers, principals, and central office staff. If contemporary schools are to reflect fundamentally different assumptions than schools of the past, if they are to reflect a genuine commitment to high levels of learning for all students, if they are to be places of collective inquiry and collaborative efforts, it will be because of rather than in spite of the educators within them. We hope this book makes a small contribution to that transformation.

Appendix

Indicators of Student Achievement: Our Current Reality

Our School's Grade Distributions			
	2006	2007	2008
A	9%	10%	11%
B	16%	16%	15%
C	38%	36%	34%
D	20%	19%	21%
F	17%	19%	19%
Percentage A/B versus D/F	25/37	26/38	26/40

State Reading Assessment Achievement Results			
	2006	2007	2008
	Our Students/ State	Our Students/ State	Our Students/ State
Academic Warning	10%/8%	9%/7%	13%/6%
Below Standard	30%/34%	30%/33%	26%/30%
Meets Standard	46%/46%	48%/48%	46%/50%
Exceeds Standard	14%/12%	13%/12%	15%/14%

State Writing Assessment Achievement Results			
	2006	**2007**	**2008**
	Our Students/ State	Our Students/ State	Our Students/ State
Academic Warning	5%/6%	6%/5%	7%/5%
Below Standard	29%/35%	30%/32%	31%/30%
Meets Standard	50%/50%	48%/50%	44%/49%
Exceeds Standard	16%/9%	16%/13%	18%/16%

State Math Assessment Achievement Results			
	2006	**2007**	**2008**
	Our Students/ State	Our Students/ State	Our Students/ State
Academic Warning	4%/9%	3%/8%	3%/6%
Below Standard	16%/37%	17%/36%	15%/36%
Meets Standard	59%/45%	60%/46%	60%/47%
Exceeds Standard	21%/9%	20%/10%	22%/11%

State Science Assessment Achievement Results			
	2006	2007	2008
	Our Students/ State	Our Students/ State	Our Students/ State
Academic Warning	11%/12%	12%/11%	11%/10%
Below Standard	39%/38%	38%/37%	37%/36%
Meets Standard	39%/39%	39%/41%	41%/42%
Exceeds Standard	11%/11%	11%/11%	11%/12%

State Social Studies Assessment Achievement Results			
	2006	2007	2008
	Our Students/ State	Our Students/ State	Our Students/ State
Academic Warning	8%/9%	8%/8%	8%/7%
Below Standard	30%/33%	31%/32%	32%/30%
Meets Standard	49%/46%	50%/48%	48%/50%
Exceeds Standard	13%/12%	11%/12%	12%/13%

National Indicator: ACT Scores			
	2006	**2007**	**2008**
% of Our Students Taking the Test	65	64	63
	Mean Score	Mean Score	Mean Score
Our Composite	21.6	21.5	21.4
State Composite	21.4	21.5	21.6
National Composite	21.0	21.0	21.0
Our ACT English	21.4	21.3	21.3
State English	21.2	21.3	21.5
National English	20.9	20.9	20.9
Our ACT Math	22.1	22.0	22.1
State Math	21.0	21.0	21.3
National Math	20.8	20.8	20.9
Our ACT Reading	21.3	21.2	21.1
State Reading	21.0	21.1	21.2
National Reading	21.1	21.1	21.1
Our ACT Science	20.9	21.0	20.9
State Science	21.0	21.2	21.4
National Science	20.9	20.9	21.0

National Indicator: Advanced Placement Test Results			
	2006	2007	2008
Number of Students	88	84	83
Number of Exams	133	130	129
Percentage of Honor Students	78%	80%	78%
Percent Scoring 4 or 5	25%	28%	21%
Percent Scoring 3	53%	52%	57%
Percent Scoring 1 or 2	22%	20%	22%
Percentage of Seniors Completing an AP Course	22%	21%	20%

State Test Ranking Among Five Comparable Schools			
1 = Highest Performance; 5 = Lowest Performance			
	2006	2007	2008
Reading	5	5	5
Writing	5	4	4
Math	3	2	3
Science	5	5	5
Social Studies	4	5	5

ACT Ranking Among Five Comparable Schools			
1 = Highest Performance; 5 = Lowest Performance			
	2006	2007	2008
Reading	5	5	5
English	5	4	4
Math	3	2	3
Science Reasoning	5	5	5

Synthesis of Research on the Characteristics of Effective Schools

Effective Schools research began in the 1970s by Ron Edmonds, Larry Lezotte, Wilbur Brookover, Michael Rutter, and others as an attempt to find schools that were consistently more effective in helping all students learn regardless of race or poverty. It was one of the first research models that disaggregated data. The following list, developed in the 1990s, summarizes what Lezotte (1991) has called the second generation of research on effective schools. It includes seven "correlates"—factors that are correlated with effective schools.

Correlate 1: Safe and Orderly Environment

Effective schools have an orderly, purposeful, businesslike environment that is conducive to learning without being oppressive. Students work together cooperatively, respect human diversity, and appreciate democratic values.

Correlate 2: Climate of High Expectations for Success

The staff in an effective school demonstrates its belief that all students can attain mastery of the essential school skills. Teachers develop and implement a wide array of varied strategies to ensure that students achieve mastery. The school responds to and assists students who do not learn.

Correlate 3: Instructional Leadership

The principal in an effective school functions as an instructional leader who communicates the school's mission to students, teachers, and community. However, leadership is widely dispersed, and the principal functions as a leader of leaders—a coach, a partner, and a cheerleader.

Correlate 4: Clear and Focused Mission

The staff understands and is committed to the mission of the school, to its instructional goals, and to its priorities. They design and deliver a curriculum that goes beyond low-level skills and is responsive to the need for higher levels of learning for all students.

Correlate 5: Opportunity to Learn and Student Time on Task

In an effective school, a significant amount of classroom time is allocated to instruction in essential skills. The school is willing to declare that some things are more important than others and to abandon some less important areas of content in order to have enough time for material that is valued more.

Correlate 6: Frequent Monitoring of Student Progress

In an effective school, student progress is measured frequently through a variety of assessment procedures. Teachers recognize the need for alignment between what is taught and what is tested. There is less emphasis on standardized, norm-referenced, paper-pencil tests and more on authentic, curricular-based, criterion-referenced measures of student mastery.

Correlate 7: Home-School Relations

Parents in effective schools understand and support the school's mission and play an important role in achieving the mission. There is enough trust and communication between teachers and parents to enable parents to serve as full partners in working toward the mutual goal of providing children with a high-quality education.

Synthesis of Research on Indicators of a Productive School Culture

Researchers conducted what they referred to as a "meta-analysis" of studies that had been done on productive school cultures to determine that these cultures were characterized by the following (Georgiades, Fuentes, & Snyder, 1983):

1. Predispositions

    - A student-centered orientation with frequent monitoring of each student's success

    - An improvement orientation—a commitment to continuous improvement

    - A success orientation with high expectations

2. Collaborative work behavior including a focus on common goals, continuous dialogue among staff, shared decision-making, planned action, and periodic reflection and feedback

3. Professional productivity

    - A strong knowledge base supported by staff development

    - A sense of group goals and commitments

    - A focused, involved, and concerned staff

Successful School Improvement

The Center on Organization and Restructuring of Schools conducted a 5-year study in the early 1990s that included analysis of data from more than 1,500 elementary, middle, and high schools throughout the United States. The Center also conducted field research in 44 schools in 16 states. Schools that were successful in linking their improvement initiatives with improved student learning were characterized by the following (Newman & Wehlage, 1995):

1. They focus on an agreed-upon vision of what students should learn.

2. Their teachings require students to think, to develop in-depth understanding, and to apply academic learning to important, realistic problems.

3. They function as professional learning communities in which teachers . . .

   - Are guided by a clear, commonly held, shared purpose for student learning.

   - Feel a sense of collective responsibility for student learning.

   - Collaborate with one another to promote student learning.

   - Enjoy increased autonomy at the school site.

Professional Learning Communities Required to Improve Schools

Another analysis of the data collected by the Center on Organization and Restructuring of Schools agreed that the development of PLCs was critical to improving schools and elaborated on the conditions that led to successful PLCs. Researchers found that teachers in a PLC are committed to the following (Kruse, Seashore Louis, & Bryk, 1994):

1. Reflective dialogue based on a shared set of norms, beliefs, and values that allow them to critique their individual and collective performance

2. De-privatization of practice that requires teachers to share, observe, and discuss each other's methods and philosophies

3. Collective focus on student learning fueled by the belief that all students can learn and that staff members have a mutual obligation to make sure students learn

4. Collaboration that moves beyond dialogue about students to producing materials that improve instruction, curriculum, and assessment for students

5. Shared norms and values that affirm common ground on critical educational issues and a collective focus on student learning

The study also reported that these five factors are supported by structural conditions such as time to meet during the school day, teachers organized into collaborative teams that work together interdependently to achieve common goals, open communication within and across teams, and teacher autonomy guided by a shared sense of purpose, priorities, and norms. Social resources that support PLCs include commitment to continuous improvement, high levels of trust and respect, sharing of effective teaching practices, supportive leadership, and focused orientation for those new to the school.

What Works: School Factors That Increase Student Achievement

Translating 35 Years of Research Into Action

Robert Marzano (2003) synthesized research conducted over 35 years on school-level factors that impact student achievement. He concluded that schools can have a tremendous impact on student achievement if they apply the lessons of the research, which include the following:

1. A Guaranteed and Viable Curriculum (Opportunity to Learn)

The school identifies essential curriculum content. It then makes certain the content is sequenced appropriately and can be addressed adequately in the available instructional time. The school ensures teachers cover the essential content and protect instructional time.

2. Challenging Goals and Effective Feedback

The school establishes challenging goals to be achieved by all students and monitors each student's progress on specific knowledge and skills on a frequent basis. Students receive timely feedback at least once per quarter. The school emphasizes formative assessment.

3. Parent and Community Involvement

The school establishes timely, two-way communication systems with parents, develops strategies to involve parents and community in the learning process, and allows parents and community some voice in key school decisions.

4. Safe and Orderly Environment

The school establishes clear rules and procedures for general behavior and consistently enforces consequences for violations of those rules. It develops programs to teach self-discipline and responsibility and creates systems for early detection of students at risk of violent or extreme behavior.

5. Collegiality and Professionalism

The school culture encourages norms of collegiality and professionalism. Teachers are involved in making decisions and establishing policies for the school. The school's approach to staff development promotes active learning and ongoing discussion within the context of a specific subject area or assignment.

Practices of Improving Schools and Districts

Doug Reeves (2006) has identified what he refers to as 90/90/90 schools and districts—places that have a student population of 90% minority and 90% poverty and yet have over 90% of their students achieving at high levels on various measures of proficiency. He found that improving schools and districts share the following characteristics:

1. The school and district promote distributed leadership rather than relying on a single charismatic leader.

2. There is a holistic approach to accountability with frequent monitoring of valued outcomes in an attempt to establish both cause and effect.

3. Every subject area emphasizes nonfiction writing.

4. Frequent common assessments are integral parts of the teaching, leadership, and learning cycles.

5. The school implements a plan for timely and decisive intervention when students do not learn.

6. Student achievement data are easily accessible and openly shared among teachers who work collaboratively to improve their individual and collective performance.

Six Characteristics of High-Performing Organizations

Ken Blanchard (2007) has summarized the lessons learned from his 25 years of consulting with organizations on how to improve their performance. He found the most effective organizations attend to each of the following six areas:

1. Shared Information and Open Communication

The information needed to make informed decisions is readily available to people and is openly communicated.

2. Compelling Vision

A compelling vision creates a deliberate, highly focused culture that drives people within the organization toward the intended results. They can describe a clear picture of what they intend to create, and everyone is aligned and going in the same direction.

3. Ongoing Learning

Continuous, job-embedded learning is built into the routine practices of the organization.

4. Relentless Focus on Customer Results

High-performing organizations understand who their customers are and measure results accordingly. They produce outstanding results, in part, because of an almost obsessive focus on results.

5. Energizing Systems and Structures

The systems, structures, processes, and practices in high-performing organizations are aligned to support the organization's purpose, vision, and goals. The systems and structures help people accomplish their jobs more easily.

6. Shared Power, High Involvement, and Collaborative Teams

Power and decision-making are shared and distributed throughout the organization, not guarded at the top of the hierarchy. Participation, collaboration, and teamwork are a way of life. People are empowered with clear boundaries of autonomy. There is a strong sense of individual and collective efficacy that foster high expectations.

Adlai Stevenson High School Vision Statement

The very first policy in the Board Policy Manual of Adlai Stevenson High School District 125 articulates the vision of the school the district is attempting to create. Each constituency then articulates the collective commitments its members have made to bring this vision to life.

Stevenson High School is an exemplary learning community school. To ensure future development and growth, the school must have a clear sense of the goals it is trying to accomplish, the characteristics of the school it seeks to become, and the contributions the various stakeholders in the school will make in order to transform ideals into reality. The following vision statement is intended to provide the standards Stevenson High School should strive to achieve and maintain.

I. Curriculum, Instruction, and Assessment

An exemplary learning community provides students with a common coherent curriculum complemented with a variety of elective courses and cocurricular activities. This balanced program stimulates intellectual curiosity, requires students to demonstrate they have learned how to learn, and leads students to develop into productive and responsible citizens. The school articulates the outcomes it seeks for all of its students and monitors and assesses each student's attainment of those outcomes through a variety of indicators. In such a school:

a. The curriculum addresses important academic content and essential life skills.

b. The curriculum broadens each student's perspective in order to understand and appreciate diversity.

c. Instructional strategies reflect best practice and stimulate student engagement.

d. Instructional practice promotes and integrates appropriate technology to enhance curricular outcomes and cocurricular pursuits.

e. Assessment is an ongoing practice containing both formative and summative components.

f. Assessment is used to ensure quality learning and to inform teachers and teams regarding curricular and instructional decision-making.

g. Curriculum, instructional practice, and assessment recognize and accommodate individual differences, interests, and abilities.

h. Curriculum, instructional practice, and assessment reflect the district's support of innovation and commitment to continuous improvement.

II. Emphasis on the Individual Student: Equity and Access for *All*

An exemplary learning community recognizes and values the importance of the individual student. Staff members are committed to understanding the uniqueness of each student. In the final analysis, the effectiveness of any school is based on the conduct, character, and achievement of its students. In an exemplary learning community, these qualities are a result of genuine concern for the individual student. In such a school:

a. Each student will be provided the information, assistance, and support to develop appropriate educational and career goals for transitioning to and through high school.

b. Attention will be paid to the whole student, including academic progress, behavior, and emotional well-being, with the initiation of appropriate services as needed.

   c. Staff will facilitate students' development of the skills necessary to become independent, lifelong learners.

   d. Staff will guide students in accepting increasing responsibility for their learning, decisions, and actions.

   e. Each student is encouraged to explore and take advantage of the variety of opportunities for participation in the curricular and cocurricular programs.

   f. Students will fulfill the expectation to be actively engaged and give their best efforts, intellectually and ethically, to their academic and cocurricular pursuits.

   g. All members of the Stevenson learning community will conduct themselves in a way that contributes to a safe and orderly environment that respects the rights of others within a diverse community.

III. Working Within a Professional Learning Community

An exemplary learning community operates on the premise that success for every student is dependent upon the people in the organization. Therefore, the Board, administration, and staff are committed to recruiting, developing, and retaining individuals with exceptional expertise in their respective fields and a passionate commitment to the school as a professional learning community. In such a school, the Board, administration, and staff:

   a. Actively promote and honor the district's vision, values, and goals.

   b. Have high standards and expectations for student success and engage in reflection and collective inquiry regarding best practices.

   c. Are committed to contributing to high-performing collaborative teams.

   d. Model the importance of lifelong learning through a commitment to ongoing professional development.

e. Are committed to collective inquiry and reflection on the results of student achievement in order to improve student learning.

f. Are committed to a high level of mutual support and trust between all members of the learning community.

IV. A Culture for Learning

An exemplary learning community creates a safe, caring environment and fosters a culture that promotes collaboration, enables staff and students to explore their full learning potentials, and results in meaningful learning experiences. This culture contributes to a shared sense of pride in the school. In such a school:

a. There is a commitment to maintain an emotionally and physically safe, supportive environment.

b. Well-maintained physical facilities meet the needs of all members of the Stevenson community and reflect pride in the school.

c. There is an ongoing effort to provide a school that is free of alcohol, other drugs, and violence.

d. The diverse community of students and staff treats each other with mutual respect, consideration, and acceptance.

e. There is open and ongoing communication between all members of the Stevenson community.

f. Staff and students are encouraged to participate in curricular and cocurricular challenges in order to promote personal growth.

g. Individual and collective effort and achievement are promoted, recognized, and celebrated.

h. Learning is recognized as dynamic and socially constructed, requiring student engagement, collaboration, and supportive relationships with one's peers and teachers.

V. Community Engagement

An exemplary learning community values the importance of collaborative relationships with its extended community—families, residents, businesses, government agencies, and other educational systems. It strives to develop a strong commitment between the community and the school. In such a school:

a. The extended community shares and promotes the vision and values of the school.

b. The extended community provides the various resources that enable the school to offer exemplary academic and cocurricular programs and expects effective stewardship of those resources.

c. The community and the school value and recognize the mutual benefit of exchanging information and feedback.

d. The community is encouraged to utilize school resources and facilities.

e. Parents play an active role in the education of their children, monitor their children's academic performance, and work collaboratively and positively with staff to maximize their children's educational experience.

f. The school, business community, and other organizations collaborate to provide authentic learning experiences for students and staff, thereby reinforcing the relevance of the academic and cocurricular programs.

g. The school continually seeks effective partnerships with sender districts and institutions of higher education.

h. The school serves as a lighthouse, interacting and collaborating with the educational community at large.

i. The school provides opportunities for students to serve and participate within the extended community.

Stevenson High School Board/ Administrative Leadership Team Collective Commitments

The Board and Administrative Leadership Team of Stevenson High School are committed to the education and well-being of each student. As part of a professional learning community, we have identified the following values in order to guide the policies, procedures, programs, priorities, and day-to-day decisions of the district. The team will honor, advance, and protect these values. We will also acknowledge and address behaviors that are inconsistent with the district's vision and goals.

- We will model and advance the behaviors established in the Stevenson Vision Statement to all members of the Stevenson community. These behaviors include:
  - Active promotion of the District's vision, values, and goals
  - High standards and expectations for student success and engagement in reflection and collective inquiry regarding best practices
  - A commitment to the contribution toward high-performing collaborative teams
  - A commitment to lifelong learning through ongoing professional development and growth
  - A commitment to collective inquiry and reflection on the results of student achievement in order to improve student learning
  - A commitment to a high level of mutual support and trust between all members of the learning community
- We will recruit and retain individuals who are best suited to advance the vision and goals of the district, and we will create conditions which support their ongoing professional growth.

- We will facilitate the development of curricular and cocurricular programs that result in high levels of student engagement, address student needs and interests, integrate technology when appropriate for achieving program goals, and enable students to understand and appreciate diversity.

- We will model, monitor, and enforce student and adult behaviors that contribute to a safe and orderly environment while respecting the rights of others within a diverse community.

- We will develop and implement policies, programs, and procedures to monitor and support collective achievement and individual student success.

- We will develop and implement policies, programs, and procedures that result in increased responsibility for student learning, decisions, and actions.

- We will recognize and celebrate the individual and collective efforts and achievements of the Stevenson community.

- We will fulfill our responsibilities for good stewardship by managing the district's resources in a manner that addresses the needs of the community, establishes community partnerships, and builds community support.

- We will fulfill our responsibility as leaders of a lighthouse school, providing effective interaction and collaboration with the educational community at large.

These commitments are designed to help the Board/Administrative Leadership Team serve the advancement of the five components of the Vision Document: Curriculum, Instruction, and Assessment; Emphasis on the Individual Student: Equity and Access for All; Working Within a Professional Learning Community; A Culture for Learning; and Community Engagement.

Stevenson High School Faculty Collective Commitments

We have established these guiding principles as a basis for our values as teachers and professionals at Stevenson High School. They are intended as a means for informal personal reflection and are not intended to be used in the formal evaluation process. They represent our *shared purpose* and will continue to guide us as educators.

- We will develop curriculum and instructional strategies that utilize various resources, which will promote active involvement of students, and provide for their varied experiences as well as their individual abilities and talents.

- We will assist each student in his or her transition into high school, through high school, and beyond by providing appropriate instruction, monitoring his or her progress, and offering guidance and support services tailored to individual needs.

- We will model the importance of lifelong learning through our ongoing professional development.

- We will collaborate with one another to create conditions that provide equity and promote student success.

- We will act in a professional manner with integrity and honesty and develop relationships characterized by caring and respect—relationships that will lead to a rewarding professional experience.

- We will provide a supportive school atmosphere where everyone feels emotionally, physically, and intellectually safe.

- We will hold high expectations for student achievement and character, and will guide students to make responsible choices for their lives and the learning process.

- We will care for our physical environment and school property and will expect the same of students.

- We will communicate with parents and each other about students and encourage parents to be positively involved in their children's education.

Stevenson High School Support Staff Collective Commitments

As members of the Stevenson High School support staff, we affirm our active participation in helping Stevenson achieve its mission to become an exemplary learning community. In fulfilling our respective responsibilities, we share the following common commitments:

- We will support the collective effort to create the school described in Stevenson's Vision Document.

- We will foster a safe, nurturing, responsible, and positive environment that is conducive to the academic, ethical, and social growth of each individual student.

- We will continue to develop and support positive relationships with our colleagues, students, and community.

- We will show appreciation for cultural diversity and be sensitive to the thoughts and opinions of others.

- We will participate in effective and open communication throughout the school and community.

- We will pursue a commitment to continuous improvement in our performance.

- We will honor our commitment to lifelong learning.

- We will demonstrate pride and ownership in the school taking responsibility for informed decision-making.

- We will develop a sense of responsibility and mutual respect in each student.

- We will celebrate school accomplishments and promote school spirit.

Collective Commitments for Stevenson Students

For more than 30 years, Stevenson High School has been building a tradition of excellence. As a student of Stevenson, you are asked to help contribute to that tradition. By maintaining high personal expectations for success, utilizing open communication with staff and fellow students, and following the guidelines listed below, you both increase your opportunities for success and help make Stevenson an excellent school. To ensure this success, we will:

- Take responsibility for our education, decisions, and actions.

- Act in a manner that best represents ourselves, our school, and our community.

- Be active in the school and community.

- Maintain a balance between academics, cocurricular activities, and other endeavors, continually giving our best efforts to each.

- Respect our fellow students and their activities.

- Respect cultural diversity, individuality, and the choices and rights of others.

- Promote a safe and healthy learning environment.

Collective Commitments for Stevenson Parents

We, as parents, must first become familiar with the established vision statement of Stevenson High School. We can contribute to the pursuit of that vision and the success of our children when we do the following:

1. Become informed and knowledgeable about the curricular, co-curricular, and student support programs available to students by

   - Carefully reviewing school publications such as the Curriculum Coursebook, Cocurricular Handbook, and Student Guidebook

   - Attending and participating in parent information programs sponsored by the school

   - Reading *The Minuteman* each month

   - Reading/using the Stevenson website

2. Assist our children in making important educational decisions by

   - Helping them set educational goals that are appropriate to their individual capabilities, interests, and needs

   - Participating in the course selection process

   - Encouraging involvement in school activities

   - Helping our children identify and pursue post-secondary education and career goals

3. Engage in open and timely communication with the school by

   - Responding to the school's feedback about our children's academic progress and behavior

- Advising school personnel of any special circumstances or needs of our children

- Being proactive in asking questions, expressing concerns, and seeking information

4. Become actively involved in the life of the school by

- Attending school programs

- Participating in parent support groups such as the Patriot Parent Association, Booster Clubs, task forces, and so on

- Volunteering in the school

- Acting as an advocate for quality education within the community

- Utilizing the resources of the school through adult education and community access programs

- Promoting Stevenson to the extended community

5. Help our children become responsible, self-reliant members of the school community by

- Teaching them to accept responsibility for their own learning, decisions, and behavior

- Insisting they observe the rules of the school

- Demonstrating respect, consideration, and cooperation in dealing with others and expecting our children to do the same

6. Create a supportive environment for learning in our homes by

- Modeling the importance of lifelong learning

- Providing a quiet time and place for study

- Helping our students make connections between their learning experiences and their everyday lives

- Expecting achievement and offering encouragement and praise

7. Promote healthy lifestyles by

- Modeling and supporting responsible lifestyle choices

- Monitoring the activities of our children and responding to behavior which jeopardizes their health and well-being

- Becoming informed of the risks associated with teenage use of alcohol, tobacco, and other drugs

- Discussing and developing family rules that prohibit illegal use of alcohol, tobacco, and other drugs

Key Terms and Concepts in a PLC

action orientation: A predisposition to learn by doing; moving quickly to turn aspirations into actions and visions into realities. Members of PLCs understand that the most powerful learning always occurs in a context of taking action, and they value engagement and reflective experience as the most effective teachers.

adaptive challenges: Challenges for which the solution is not apparent; challenges that cause us to experiment, discover, adjust, and adapt (Heifetz & Linsky, 2002). Adaptive challenges may also be described as second-order change.

attainable goals: Goals perceived as achievable by those who set them. Attainable goals are intended to document incremental progress and build momentum and self-efficacy through short-term wins.

balanced assessment: An assessment strategy that recognizes no single assessment yields the comprehensive results necessary to inform and improve practice and foster school and system accountability; therefore, balanced assessments utilize multiple measures of student achievement including formative assessments *for* learning and summative assessments *of* learning. Balanced assessment also refers to using different types of formative assessments based upon the knowledge and/or skills students are called upon to demonstrate. Rather than relying exclusively on one kind of assessment, schools and teams develop multiple ways for students to demonstrate proficiency.

building shared knowledge: Learning together. When members of PLCs are called upon to resolve an issue or make a decision, they consistently attempt to learn together by clarifying questions and accessing the same information and knowledge base. Members of a PLC, by definition, will *learn* together.

capacity building: Developing the collective ability—the dispositions, knowledge, skills, motivation, and resources—to act together to bring about positive change (Fullan, 2005a, p. 4).

collaboration: A *systematic* process in which people work together, *interdependently*, to analyze and *impact* professional practice in order to improve individual and collective results. In a PLC, collaboration focuses on the critical questions of learning: What is it we want each student to learn? How will we know when each student has learned it? How will we respond when a student experiences difficulty in learning? How will we enrich and extend the learning for students who are proficient?

collective inquiry: The process of building shared knowledge by clarifying the questions that a group will explore together. In PLCs, collaborative teams engage in collective inquiry into both best practices regarding teaching and learning as well as the reality of the current practices and conditions in their schools or districts.

common formative assessment: An assessment typically created collaboratively by a team of teachers responsible for the same grade level or course. Common formative assessments are used frequently throughout the year to identify (1) individual students who need additional time and support for learning, (2) the teaching strategies most effective in helping students acquire the intended knowledge and skills, (3) program concerns—areas in which students generally are having difficulty achieving the intended standard—and (4) improvement goals for individual teachers and the team.

community: A group linked by common interests. Whereas the term "organization" tends to emphasize structure and efficiency, "community" suggests shared purpose, mutual cooperation, and supportive relationships.

consensus: Consensus is achieved when (1) all points of view have been heard and (2) the will of the group is evident even to those who most oppose it.

continuous improvement process: The ongoing cycle of planning, doing, checking, and acting designed to improve results—constantly. In a PLC, this ongoing cycle includes gathering evidence of current levels of student learning, developing strategies and ideas to build on strengths and address weaknesses in that learning, implementing those strategies and ideas, analyzing the impact of the changes to discover what was effective and what was not, and applying the new knowledge in the next cycle of continuous improvement.

criterion-referenced assessment: An assessment used to determine if a student or group of students have met a specific standard or intended learning outcome (Ainsworth & Viegut, 2006).

crucial conversation: Dialogue in which "the stakes are high, opinions vary, and emotions run strong" (Patterson, Grenny, McMillan, & Switzler, 2002, p. 3).

curriculum leverage: The skills, knowledge, and dispositions that will assist the student in becoming proficient in other areas of the curriculum and other academic disciplines (Reeves, 2002).

data versus information: Data represent facts or figures that, standing alone, will not inform practice or lead to informed decisions. To transform data into information requires putting data in context, and this typically requires a basis of comparison.

dispersed leadership: Leadership that is widely distributed throughout a school rather than vested in an individual person or position. Emphasis is placed on developing the capacity of people throughout the school to assume leadership roles and to become "leaders of leaders."

DRIP Syndrome (Data Rich/Information Poor): The problem of an abundance of data that does nothing to inform practice because it is not presented in context through the use of relevant comparisons.

essential learning: The critical skills, knowledge, and dispositions each student must acquire as a result of each course, grade level, and unit of instruction. Essential learning may also be referred to as essential outcomes or power standards.

first-order change: Innovation that is incremental, representing the next step on an established path and operating within existing paradigms. The change can be implemented by using the existing knowledge and skills of the staff. The goal of first-order change is to help us get better at what we are already doing (Marzano, Waters, & McNulty, 2005).

formative assessment: An assessment *for* learning used to advance and not merely monitor each student's learning (Stiggins, 2002). Formative assessments are used to ensure any student who experiences difficulty reaching or exceeding proficiency is given additional time and support as well as additional opportunities to demonstrate his or her learning. Formative assessments are also used to help students monitor their own progress toward an intended standard of proficiency.

foundation of a professional learning community: PLCs rest upon a shared *mission* of high levels of learning for all students. In order to achieve that mission, educators create a common *vision* of the school they must create, develop *values* or *collective commitments* regarding what they will do to create such a school, and use *goals* as measurable milestones to monitor their progress.

"Genius of And": The ability to reject the "Tyranny of Or" and embrace paradox. Embracing the Genius of And allows an individual to avoid the choice between A *or* B and to choose both A *and* B at the same time (Collins & Porras, 1997). A commitment to simultaneous loose and tight leadership serves as an example of the Genius of And.

goals: Measurable milestones that can be used to assess progress in advancing toward a vision. Goals establish targets and timelines to answer the question, "What results do we seek, and how will we know we are making progress?"

guaranteed and viable curriculum: A curriculum that (1) gives students access to the same essential learning regardless of who is teaching the class *and* (2) can be taught in the time allotted (Marzano, 2003).

guiding coalition: An alliance of key members of an organization who are specifically charged to lead a change process through the predictable turmoil. Members of the alliance should have shared objectives and high levels of trust.

high expectations: The confident belief that all students can attain mastery of the essential learning and that the staff has the capability to help all students achieve that mastery. "High expectations for success will be judged, not only by the initial staff beliefs and behaviors, but also by the organization's response when some students do not learn" (Lezotte, 1991, p. 4).

knowing-doing gap: The disconnect between knowledge and action, the mystery of why knowledge of what needs to be done so frequently fails to result in action or behavior consistent with that knowledge (Pfeffer & Sutton, 2000).

Law of the Few: The ability of a small close-knit group of people to champion an idea or proposal until it reaches a tipping point and spreads like an epidemic throughout an organization (Gladwell, 2002).

learning: The acquisition of new knowledge or skills through ongoing action and perpetual curiosity. Members of a PLC engage in the ongoing study and constant reflective practice that characterize an organization committed to continuous improvement.

learning organization: "Organizations where people continually expand their capacities to create the results they truly desire, where new and expansive patterns of thinking are nurtured, where collective aspiration is set free, and where people are continually learning how to learn together" (Senge, 1990, p. 3).

mission: The fundamental purpose of an organization. Mission answers the question, "Why do we exist?"

moral purpose: "Acting with the intention of making a positive difference in the lives of employees, customers, and society as a whole" (Fullan, 2001, p. 3). Fullan lists a commitment to moral purpose as a critical element of effective leadership and contends leadership must be ultimately assessed by the extent to which it awakens and mobilizes the moral purpose of those within the organization.

norm-referenced assessment: An assessment designed to compare the performance of an individual or group with a larger "norm" group typically representing a national sample with a wide and diverse cross-section of students (Ainsworth & Viegut, 2006).

positive deviants: Individuals, schools, and districts "whose behavior and practices lead to solutions to problems that others in the group who have access to exactly the same resources have not yet been able to solve. . . . They provide demonstrable evidence that a solution exists within the community for the problem" (Jerry Sternin of Save the Children, quoted in Richardson, 2004).

power standard: The knowledge, skills, and dispositions that have *endurance, leverage,* and are essential in preparing students for *readiness* at the next level (Reeves, 2002); the most essential learning or outcomes.

professional: Someone with expertise in a specialized field, an individual who has not only pursued advanced training to enter the field, but who is also expected to remain current in its evolving knowledge base.

professional development: A lifelong, collaborative learning process that nourishes the growth of individuals, teams, and the school through a daily job-embedded, learner-centered, focused approach (National Staff Development Council, 2001).

professional learning community (PLC): Educators committed to working collaboratively in ongoing processes of collective inquiry and action research to achieve better results for the students they serve. Professional learning communities operate under the assumption that the key to improved learning for students is continuous job-embedded learning for educators.

readiness for the next level of learning/prerequisite knowledge: The skills, knowledge, and dispositions essential for success in the next unit, course, or grade level (Reeves, 2002).

reciprocal accountability: "For every increment of performance we ask of educators, there is an equal responsibility to provide them with the capacity to meet that expectation" (Elmore, 2006, p. 93). For example, principals of professional learning communities recognize they have an obligation to provide staff with the resources, training, mentoring, and support to help them successfully accomplish what they have been asked to do.

results orientation: A focus on outcomes rather than inputs or intentions. In PLCs, members are committed to achieving desired results and are hungry for evidence that their efforts are producing the intended outcomes.

school culture: The assumptions, beliefs, values, and habits that constitute the norm for the school and guide the work of the educators within it.

school structure: The policies, procedures, rules, and hierarchical relationships within the school.

second-order change: Innovation that represents a dramatic departure from the expected and familiar. It is perceived as a break from the past, is inconsistent with existing paradigms, may seem to be at conflict with prevailing practices and norms, and will require the acquisition of new knowledge and new skills (Marzano,Waters, & McNulty, 2005). Also called "disruptive change."

simultaneous loose and tight leadership: A leadership concept in which leaders encourage autonomy and creativity (loose) within well-defined parameters and priorities that must be honored (tight). The concept has also been referred to as "directed empowerment" (Waterman, 1987) and a "culture of discipline with an ethic of entrepreneurship" (Collins, 2001, p. 124).

SMART goals: Goals that are Strategic and Specific, Measurable, Attainable, Results-oriented, and Timebound (Conzemius & O'Neill, 2005).

stretch goals: Goals intended to inspire, to capture the imagination of people within the organization, to stimulate creativity and innovation, and to serve as a unifying focal point of effort. Stretch goals are so ambitious that they typically cannot be achieved without significant changes in practice. Stretch goals are also referred to as BHAGs: Big, Hairy, Audacious Goals (Collins & Porras, 1997).

summative assessment: An assessment *of* learning (Stiggins, 2002) designed to provide a final measure to determine if learning goals have been met (Ainsworth & Viegut, 2006). Summative assessments yield a dichotomy: pass or fail, proficient or not proficient. Additional support is typically not forthcoming.

systematic intervention: A school-wide plan that ensures every student in every course or grade level will receive additional time and support for learning as soon as he or she experiences difficulty in acquiring essential knowledge and skills. The intervention occurs during the school day, and students are required rather than invited to devote the extra time and secure the extra support for learning.

systematic process: A specific effort to organize the combination of related parts into a coherent whole in a methodical, deliberate, and orderly way toward a particular aim.

teachable point of view: A succinct explanation of an organization's purpose and direction that can be illustrated through stories that engage others emotionally and intellectually (Tichy, 1997).

team: A group of people working *interdependently* to achieve a *common goal* for which members are held *mutually accountable*. Collaborative teams are the fundamental building blocks of PLCs.

team norms: "Ground rules or habits that govern a group" (Goleman, 2002, p. 173). In PLCs, norms represent protocols or commitments developed by each team to guide members in working together. Norms help team members clarify expectations regarding how they will work together to achieve their shared goals.

time management: The ability to organize and execute one's time around priorities (Covey, 1989).

"Tyranny of Or": "The rational view that cannot easily accept paradox, that cannot live with two seemingly contradictory forces at the same time. We must be A or B but not both" (Collins & Porras, 1997, p. 44).

values: The specific attitudes, behaviors, and commitments that must be demonstrated in order to advance the organization's vision. Articulated values answer the question, "How must we behave in order to make our shared vision a reality?"

vision: A realistic, credible, attractive future for an organization. Vision answers the question, "What do we hope to become at some point in the future?"

References and Resources

ACT. (2006). *Retention/completion summary tables.* Accessed at http://www. act.org/path/policy/pdf/retain_trends.pdf on March 14, 2008.

Ainsworth, L. (2007). Common formative assessments: The centerpiece of an integrated standards-based assessment system. In D. Reeves (Ed.), *Ahead of the curve: The power of assessment to transform teaching and learning* (pp. 79–99). Bloomington, IN: Solution Tree.

Ainsworth, L., & Viegut, D. (2006). *Common formative assessments: An essential part of the integrated whole.* Thousand Oaks, CA: Corwin Press.

Alsalam, N., & Ogle, L. (1990). The condition of education. In L. Ogle (Ed.), *National Center for Educational Statistics.* Washington, DC: U.S. Government Printing Office.

Amabile, T., & Kramer, S. (2007, May). Inner work life: Understanding the subtext of business performance. *Harvard Business Review, 85*(5), 72–83.

American Educational Research Association. (2005, Summer). Teaching teachers: Professional development to improve student achievement. *Research Points: Essential Information for Educational Policy, 3*(1), 1–4.

American Institute for Research and SRI International. (2005). *Executive summary: Evaluation of the Bill and Melinda Gates Foundation's high school grants, 2001–2004.* Accessed at http://www.gatesfoundation.org/nr/downloads/ed/evaluation/Year%203%20Final%20Reports/Exec%20 Summary.pdf on March 14, 2008.

American Institute for Research and SRI International. (2006). *Evaluation of the Bill and Melinda Gates Foundation's high school grants initiative: 2001–2005, final report.* Accessed at http://www.gatesfoundation.org/nr/downloads/Ed/researchevaluation/Year4EvaluationAIRSRI.pdf on March 14, 2008.

Annenberg Institute for School Reform. (2004). *Professional learning communties: Professional development strategies that improve instruction.* Accessed at http://www.annenberginstitute.org/images/ProfLearning.pdf on December 11, 2007.

Appelbaum, D. (2002, February). *The need for district support for school reform: What the research says.* Washington, DC: National Clearinghouse for Comprehensive School Reform.

Autry, J. (2001). *The servant leader: How to build a creative team, develop great morale, and improve bottom-line performance.* New York: Three Rivers Press.

Axelrod, R. (2002). *Terms of engagement: Changing the way we change organizations.* San Francisco: Berrett-Koehler.

Bardwick, J. (1996). Peacetime management and wartime leadership. In F. Hesselbein, M. Goldsmith, & R. Beckhard (Eds.), *The leader of the future* (pp. 131–140). San Francisco: Jossey-Bass.

Barth, R. (1991). Restructuring schools: Some questions for teachers and principals. *Phi Delta Kappan, 73*(2), 123–128.

Barth, R. (2001). *Learning by heart.* San Francisco: Jossey-Bass.

Barth, R. (2006). Improving relationships inside the schoolhouse. *Educational Leadership, 63*(6), 8–13.

Bennis, W. (1997*). Organizing genius: The secrets of creative collaboration.* Cambridge, MA.: Perseus Books.

Bennis, W. (2003). *On becoming a leader.* New York: Basic Books.

Bennis, W., & Nanus, B. (1985). *Leaders: The strategies for taking charge.* New York: Harper & Row.

Bestor, A. (1953). *Educational wastelands: The retreat from learning in our public schools.* Champaign: University of Illinois Press.

Black, P., Harrison, C., Lee, C., Marshall, B., & Wiliam, D. (2004). Working inside the black box: Assessment for learning in the classroom. *Phi Delta Kappan, 86*(1), 9–19.

Black, P., & Wiliam, D. (1998). The formative purpose: Assessment must first promote learning. In M. Wilson (Ed.), *Towards coherence between classroom assessment and accountability. 103rd yearbook of the National Society for the Study of Education* (pp. 20–50). Chicago: University of Chicago Press for the NSSE.

Blanchard, K. (1996). Turning the organization upside down. In F. Hesselbein, M., Goldsmith, & R. Beckhard (Eds.), *The Leader of the future* (pp. 81–88). San Francisco: Jossey-Bass.

Blanchard, K. (2007). *Leading at a higher level: Blanchard on leadership and creating high performing organizations.* Upper Saddle River, NJ: Prentice Hall.

Block, P. (2003). *The answer to how is yes: Acting on what matters.* San Francisco: Berrett-Koehler.

Bolman, L., & Deal, T. (1996). *Leading with soul: An uncommon journey of spirit.* San Francisco: Jossey-Bass.

Bolman, L., & Deal, T. (2000). *Escape from cluelessness: A guide for the organizationally challenged.* New York: AMACOM.

Bossidy, L., & Charan, R. (2002). *Execution: The discipline of getting things done.* New York: Crown Business.

Bracey, G. (2006, July/August). Put to the test: Believing the worst. *Stanford Magazine.* Accessed at http://www.stanfordalumni.org/news/ magazine/2006/julaug/features/nclb.html on March 14, 2008.

Brookover, W., & Lezotte, L. (1979). *Changes in school characteristics coincident with changes in student achievement* (occasional paper number 17). East Lansing, MI: Michigan State University, Institute for Research on Teaching. Accessed at http://ed-web2.educ.msu.edu/irtlarchive/ OP017.pdf on December 11, 2007.

Brooks, D. (2006, October 6). Pillars of cultural capital. *New York Times.*

Brophy, J. (2004). *Motivating students to learn* (2nd ed.). Mahwah, NJ: Lawrence Earlbaum Associates.

Brophy, J., & Good, T. (2002). *Looking in classrooms* (9th ed.). Boston: Allyn & Bacon.

Buckingham, M. (2005). *The one thing you need to know . . . about great managing, great leading and sustained individual success.* New York: Free Press.

Buffum, A., Mattos, M., & Weber, C. (in press). *Pyramid of response to intervention: RTI, PLCs, and how to respond when kids don't learn.* Bloomington, IN: Solution Tree.

Burkett, H. (2006, May). Six don'ts of school improvement. *Center for Comprehensive School Reform Newsletter.* Accessed at http://www.centerforcsri.org/index.php?option=com_content&task=view&id=325&Itemid=5 on March 14, 2008.

Bush: NCLB not meant to punish schools, but to help them. (2007, April 12). *CNN.* Accessed at http://www.districtadministration.com/newssummary.aspx?news=yes&postid=18883 on March 24, 2008.

Bush, G. H. W. (1989, September 28). Joint statement on the education summit with the nation's governors at Charlottesville, Virginia. Accessed at http://bushlibrary.tamu.edu/research/public_papers.php?id=971&year=1989&month=all on March 29, 2008.

Bush, G. H. W. (1991, April 18). Address to the nation on the National Education Strategy. Accessed at http://bushlibrary.tamu.edu/research/public_papers.php?id=2895&year=&month= on March 29, 2008

Bush, G. W. (2003). President discusses education reform in Washington DC, July 1, 2003. Speech delivered at Kipp D.C. Key Academy. Accessed at http://www.whitehouse.gov/news/releases/2003/07/20030701-3.html on March 14, 2008.

Byrne, R. (2006). *The Secret.* New York: Atria Books/Beyond Words.

Carey, G., & Frohnen, B. (1998). (Eds.) *Community and tradition: Conservative perspectives on the American experience.* Lanham, MD: Rowman & Littlefield.

Cawelti, G. (2003). The new effective schools. In W. Owings & L. Kaplan (Eds.), *Best practices, best thinking and emerging issues in school leadership.* Thousand Oaks, CA: Corwin Press.

Cawelti, G., & Protheroe, N. (2001). *High student achievement: How six school districts changed into high-performing systems.* Arlington, VA: Educational Research Service.

Center for Evaluation and Education Policy. (2006, February). *Evaluation of the Cleveland scholarship and tutoring program: Summary report, 1998–2004.* Bloomington, IN: Author.

Champy, J. (1995). *Reengineering management: The mandate for new leadership.* New York: Harper Collins.

Chappuis, J. (2005). Helping students understand assessment. *Educational Leadership, 63*(3), 39–43.

Chubb, J. (Ed.). (2005). *Within our reach: How America can educate every child: Findings and recommendations of the Hoover Institution's Koret Task Force on K–12 education.* Palo Alto, CA: Hoover Press.

Clavell, J. (1986). *Shogun* (2nd ed.). New York: Dell.

Clinton, W. (2007). Middlebury College graduation address, May 7, 2007. Accessed at http://www.middlebury.edu/about/newsevents/archive/2007/newsevents_633158738134202567.htm on March 14, 2008.

Cole, R., & Schlechty, P. (1993). Teachers as trailblazers in restructuring. *Education Digest, 58*(6), 8.

College Board. (2007). *Advanced placement: Report to the nation 2007.* Accessed at http://www.collegeboard.com/prod_downloads/about/news_info/ap/2007/2007_ap-report-nation.pdf on March 14, 2008.

Collins, J. (2001). *Good to great: Why some companies make the leap . . . and others don't.* New York: Harper Business.

Collins, J., & Porras, J. (1997). *Built to last: Successful habits of visionary companies.* New York: Harper Business.

Colliton, J. (2005). *Professional learning communities and the NCA school improvement process.* Accessed at http://www.ncacasi.org/enews/articles_apr05/prof_learning.pdf on March 14, 2008.

Comer, J., Joyner, E., & Ben-Avie, M. (2004). *Essential understandings of the Yale school development program.* Accessed at http://www.med.yale.edu/comer/downloads/Joyner-TransformingRevChapter02.pdf on March 14, 2008.

Commission on No Child Left Behind. (2007). *Beyond NCLB: Fulfilling the promise to our nation's children.* Washington, DC: The Aspen Institute.

Conant, J. (1959). *The American high school today: A first report to interested citizens.* New York: McGraw-Hill.

Consortium on Productivity in the Schools. (1995). *Using what we have to get the schools we need.* New York: Teachers College Press.

Conzemius, A., & O'Neill, J. (2005). *The handbook for SMART school teams.* Bloomington, IN: Solution Tree (formerly National Educational Service).

Cotton, K. (2000). *The schooling practices that matter most.* Alexandria, VA: Association for Supervision and Curriculum Development.

Cotton, K. (2003). *Principals and student achievement: What the research says.* Alexandria, VA: Association for Supervision and Curriculum Development.

Council of Chief School Officers. (2002). *Expecting success: A study of five high-poverty schools.* Washington, DC: Council of Chief School Officers.

Covey, S. (1989). *The seven habits of highly effective people: Powerful lessons in personal change.* New York: Fireside.

Covey, S. (1996). Three roles of the leader in the new paradigm. In F. Hesselbein, M. Goldsmith, & R. Beckhard (Eds.), *The leader of the future (pp. 149–160).* San Francisco: Jossey-Bass.

Covey, S. (2002). Foreword. In K. Patterson, J. Grenny, R. McMillan, & A. Switzler (Eds.), *Crucial conversations: Tools for talking when stakes are high* (pp. xi–xiv). New York: McGraw-Hill.

Covey, S., Merrill, A., & Merrill, R. (1996). *First things first: To live, to love, to learn, to leave a legacy.* New York: Fireside.

Cremin, L. (1991). *Popular education and its discontents.* New York: Harper-Collins.

Csikszentmihalyi, M. (1997). *Finding flow: The psychology of engagement with everyday life.* New York: Basic Books.

Danielson, C. (2007). *Enhancing professional practice: A framework for teaching* (2nd ed.). Alexandria, VA: Association for Supervision and Curriculum Development.

Darling-Hammond, L. (1995). Policy for restructuring. In A. Lieberman (Ed.), *The work of restructuring schools: Building from the ground up* (pp. 157–175). New York: Teachers College Press.

Darling-Hammond, L. (1996). What matters most: A competent teacher for every child. *Phi Delta Kappan, 78*(3), 193–200.

Darling-Hammond, L. (2001). *The right to learn: A blueprint for creating schools that work.* San Francisco: Jossey-Bass.

Deal, T., & Key, M. K. (1998). *Corporate celebration: Play, purpose and profit at work.* San Francisco: Berrett-Koehler.

Decrane, A. (1996). A constitutional model of leadership. In F. Hesselbein, M. Goldsmith, & R. Beckhard (Eds.), *The leader of the future.* San Francisco: Jossey-Bass.

Deming, W. E. (2000). *Out of the crisis.* Cambridge, MA: MIT Press.

Deutschman, A. (2007). Three keys to change. *Fast Company.* Accessed at http://www.fastcompany.com/articles/2007/01/change-or-die.html on March 14, 2008.

Dewey, J. (1916). *Democracy and education: An introduction to the philosophy of education.* New York: Macmillan.

Dolan, P. (1994). *Restructuring our schools: A primer on systemic change.* Kansas City, KS: Systems and Organizations.

Drucker, P. (1992). *Managing for the future: The 1990s and beyond.* New York: Truman Talley.

Drucker, P. (1996). Not enough generals were killed. In F. Hesselbein, M. Goldsmith, & R. Beckhard (Eds.), *The leader of the future* (pp. xi–xvi). San Francisco: Jossey-Bass.

Druskat, V., & Wolf, S. (2001). Group emotional intelligence and its influence on group effectiveness. In C. Chernis & D. Goleman (Eds.), *The emotionally intelligent workplace: How to select for, measure, and improve emotional intelligence in individual groups and organizations* (pp. 132–156). San Francisco: Jossey-Bass.

DuFour, R. (2003a). Building a professional learning community. *The School Administrator, 60*(5), 13–18.

DuFour, R. (2003b). Central office support for learning communities. *The School Administrator, 60*(5), 15–16.

DuFour, R. (2007). Once upon a time: A tale of excellence in assessment. In D. Reeves (Ed.), *Ahead of the curve: The power of assessment to transform teaching and learning* (pp. 253–267). Bloomington, IN: Solution Tree.

DuFour, R., & Burnette, B. (2002, Summer). Pull out negativity by its roots. *Journal of Staff Development, 23*(3), 27–30.

DuFour, R., DuFour, R., & Eaker, R. (Eds.) (2005). *On common ground: The power of professional learning communities.* Bloomington, IN: Solution Tree (formerly National Educational Service).

DuFour, R., DuFour, R., Eaker, R., & Karhanek, G. (2004). *Whatever it takes: How a professional learning community responds when kids don't learn.* Bloomington, IN: Solution Tree (formerly National Educational Service).

DuFour, R., DuFour, R., Eaker, R., & Many, T. (2006). *Learning by doing: A handbook for professional learning communities at work.* Bloomington, IN: Solution Tree.

DuFour, R., & Eaker, R. (1998). *Professional learning communities at work: Best practices for enhancing student achievement.* Bloomington, IN: Solution Tree (formerly National Educational Service).

DuFour, R., Eaker, R., & DuFour, R. (2007). *The power of professional learning communities at work: Bringing the big ideas to life.* Bloomington, IN: Solution Tree.

Earl, L., & LeMahieu, P. (1997). Rethinking assessment and accountability. In A. Hargreaves (Ed.), *Rethinking educational change with heart and mind* (pp. 149–168). Alexandria, VA: Association for Supervision and Curriculum Development.

Eastwood, K., & Seashore Louis, K. (1992). Restructuring that lasts: Managing the performance dip. *Journal of School Leadership, 2*(2), 213–224.

Eden, D. (1990). *Pygmalion in management: Productivity as a self-fulfilling prophecy.* Lanham, MD: Lexington.

Edmonds, R. (1979, October). Effective schools for the urban poor. *Educational Leadership, 37*(1), 15–18, 20–24.

Education Commission of the States. (2007). *Demographics.* Accessed at http://www.ecs.org/html/IssueSectionasp?issueid=31&s=Overview on March 14, 2008.

Educational Research Service. (2004). *Handbook of research on improving student achievement* (3rd ed.). Alexandria, VA: Author.

Elmore, R. (2000). *Building a new structure for school leadership.* Washington, DC: The Albert Shanker Institute. Accessed at http://www.ashankerinst.org/Downloads/building.pdf on January 24, 2003.

Elmore, R. (2002, January/February). The limits of change. *Harvard Education Letter.* Accessed at http://www.edletter.org/past/issues/2002-jf/limitsofchange.shtml on January 6, 2006.

Elmore, R. (2003). *Knowing the right thing to do: School improvement and performance-based accountability.* Washington, DC: NGA Center for Best Practices.

Elmore, R. (2004). *The hollow core of leadership in practice.* Unpublished manuscript, Harvard University Graduate School of Education.

Elmore, R. (2006). *School reform from the inside out: Policy, practice, and performance.* Cambridge, MA: Harvard Education Press.

Epstein, J. (2001). *School, family, and community partnerships: Preparing educators and improving schools.* Boulder, CO: Westview Press.

Epstein, J. (2005). *Developing and sustaining research-based programs of school, family, and community partnerships: A summary of five years of*

National Network of Partnership Schools research. Accessed at http://www.csos.jhu.edu/P2000/pdf/Research%20Summary.pdf on March 14, 2008.

Epstein, J., Coates, L., Clark-Salinas, K., Sanders, M., & Simon, B. (1997). *Partnership 2000 schools' manual: Improving school-family connections.* Baltimore: Johns Hopkins University.

Epstein, J., Sanders, M., Simon, B., Salinas, K., Ansom, N., & Van Voorthis, F. (2002). *School, family, and community partnerships: Your handbook for action* (2nd ed.). Thousand Oaks, CA: Corwin Press.

Evans, R. (1996). *The human side of school change: Reform, resistance and the real-life problems of innovation (hard cover ed.).* San Francisco: Jossey-Bass.

Evans, R. (2001). *The human side of school change: Reform, resistance and the real-life problems of innovation.* San Francisco: Jossey-Bass.

Farhi, P. (2007, January 24). Five myths about U.S. kids outclassed by the rest of the world. *Washington Post,* p. B2.

Farkas, S., Johnson, J., Foleno, T., Duffett, A., & Foley, P. (2000). *A sense of calling: Who teaches and why—A report from Public Agenda.* New York: Public Agenda.

Feldman, S. (1998). *A teacher quality manifesto.* Accessed at http://www.aft.org/pubs-reports/american_educator/issues/fall98/feldman.htm on March 14, 2008.

Finn, C. (2006). March of the pessimists. *Thomas Fordham Foundation, The Education Gadfly.* Accessed at http://www.edexcellence.net/foundation/gadfly/issue.cfm?id=253#2962 on August 17, 2006.

Fiske, E. (1992). *Smart schools, smart kids: Why do some schools work?* New York: Simon & Schuster.

Flesch, R. (1955). *Why Johnny can't read: And what you can do about it.* New York: Harper & Brothers.

Frankl, V. (1959). *Man's search for meaning.* New York: Pocket Books.

Fullan, M. (1993). *Change forces: Probing the depths of educational reform.* London: Falmer Press.

Fullan, M. (1997). Emotion and hope. Constructive concepts for complex times. In A. Hargreaves (Ed.), *Rethinking educational change with heart and mind* (pp. 14–33). Alexandria, VA: Association for Supervision and Curriculum Development.

Fullan, M. (2001). *Leading in a culture of change.* San Francisco: Jossey-Bass.

Fullan, M. (2004, April). New lessons for districtwide reform. *Educational Leadership, 61*(7), 42–46.

Fullan, M. (2005a). *Leadership and sustainability: System thinkers in action.* Thousand Oaks, CA: Corwin Press.

Fullan, M. (2005b). Professional learning communities writ large. In R. DuFour, R. Eaker, & R. DuFour (Eds.), *On common ground: The power of professional learning communities* (pp. 209–223). Bloomington, IN: Solution Tree (formerly National Educational Service).

Fullan, M. (2006). *Turnaround leadership.* San Francisco: Jossey-Bass.

Fullan, M. (2007). *The new meaning of educational change* (4th ed.). New York: Teachers College Press.

Fullan, M. (2008). *The six secrets of change: What the best organizations do to help their organizations survive and thrive.* San Francisco: Jossey-Bass.

Fuller, B., Wright, J., Gesicki, K., & Kaeng, E. (2007). Gauging growth: How to judge No Child Left Behind. *Educational Researcher, 36*(5), 268–278.

Fuller, H., & Mitchell, G. (2006). A culture of complaint. *Education Next, 3.* Accessed at http://www.hoover.org/publications/ednext/3211456.html on March 14, 2008.

Fulton, K., Yoon, I., & Lee, C. (2005). *Induction into learning communities.* Washington, DC: National Commission on Teaching and America's Future.

Gardner, H. (1990). *Leading minds.* New York: Basic Books.

Gardner, H. (2006). *Changing minds: The art and science of changing our own and other people's minds.* Boston: Harvard Business School.

Gardner, H., & Laskin, E. (1996). *Leading minds: An anatomy of leadership.* New York: HarperCollins.

Gardner, J. (1988). *Leadership: An overview.* Washington, DC: Independent Sector.

Garmston, R., & Wellman, B. (1999). *The adaptive school: A sourcebook for developing collaborative groups.* Norwood, MA: Christopher-Gordon.

Georgiades, W., Fuentes, E., & Snyder, K. (1983). *A meta-analysis of productive school cultures.* Houston: University of Texas.

Gerstner, L., Semerad, R., Doyle, D., & Johnston, W. (1995). *Reinventing education: Entrepreneurship in America's public schools.* New York: Penguin Books.

Ginott, H. (1972). *Teacher and child: A book for parents and teachers.* New York: Macmillan.

Gladwell, M. (2002). *The tipping point: How little things can make a big difference.* New York: Back Bay Books.

Glasser, W. (1998). *The quality school.* New York: HarperCollins.

Goals 2000. (1998). *Reforming education to improve student achievement.* Accessed at http://www.ed.gov/pubs/G2KReforming/index.html on March 14, 2008.

Goddard, R., Hoy, W., & Hoy, A. (1994). Collective efficacy beliefs: Theoretical developments, empirical evidence, and future directions. *Educational Researcher, 33*(3), 3–13.

Goldberg, M., & Cross, C. (2005). Time out. *Edutopia Magazine.* Accessed at http://email.e-mailnetworks.com/ct/ct.php?t=1018842&c=56178407 1&m=m&type=3 on August 18, 2005.

Goldring, E., Porter, A., Murphy, J., Elliott, S., & Cravens, X. (2007). *Assessing learning-centered leadership: Connections to research, professional standards, and current practices.* Accessed at http://www. wallacefoundation.org/NR/rdonlyres/2D4629AE-6592–4FDD-9206-D23A2B19EAC5/0/AssessingLearningCenteredLeadership.pdf on March 14, 2008.

Goldsmith, M. (1996). Ask, learn, follow up, and grow. In F. Hesselbein, M. Goldsmith, & R. Beckhard (Eds.), *The leader of the future* (pp. 227–240). San Francisco: Jossey-Bass.

Goleman, D. (1995). *Emotional intelligence: Why it can matter more than IQ.* New York: Bantam Books.

Goleman, D. (1998). *Working with emotional intelligence.* New York: Bantam Books.

Goleman, D. (2002). *Primal leadership: Realizing the power of emotional intelligence.* Boston: Harvard Business School.

Goodlad, J. (1983, April). A study of schooling: Some implications for school improvement. *Phi Delta Kappan, 64*(8), 552–558.

Goodlad, J. (1984). *A place called school: Prospects for the future.* New York: McGraw-Hill.

Goodlad, J. (2004). *A place called school: Twentieth anniversary.* New York: McGraw-Hill.

Greene, J. (2006). A "comprehensive" problem. *Education Next, 1.* Accessed at http://www.hoover.org/publications/ednext/3212516.html on March 14, 2008.

Gutman, M. (1995, Spring). Beyond the bake sale. *America's Agenda, 5*(1), 21–25.

Hall, G., & Hord, S. (1987). *Change in schools: Facilitating the process.* Albany: State University of New York Press.

Hallinger, P. (2007, August 13). Leadership for learning. Presentation at annual conference of Australian Council for Educational Research, Melbourne, Australia.

Hallinger, P., & Murphy, J. (1985). Assessing the instructional management behaviors of principals. *Elementary School Journal, 86*(2), 217–247.

Hamel, G. (2002). *Leading the revolution.* Cambridge, MA: Harvard Business School.

Handy, C. (1995). Managing the dream. In S. Chawala & J. Renesch (Eds.), *Learning organizations: Developing cultures for tomorrow's workplace* (pp. 55–56). New York: Productivity Press.

Handy, C. (1996). The new language of organizing and its implications for leaders. In F. Hesselbein, M. Goldsmith, & R. Beckhard (Eds.), *The leader of the future* (pp. 3–10). San Francisco: Jossey-Bass.

Hargreaves, A. (2004). Broader purpose calls for higher understanding: An interview with Andy Hargreaves. *Journal of Staff Development, 25*(2), 46–50.

Hargreaves, A., & Fink, D. (2006). *Sustainable leadership*. San Francisco: Jossey-Bass.

Hargrove, T., & Stempel, G. (2007). *Scripps Howard News Service*. Accessed at http://www.scrippsnews.com/node/23421 on May 30, 2007.

Haskins, R., & Loeb, S. (2007, Spring). A plan to improve the quality of teaching in American schools. *The Future of Children Policy Brief.* Accessed at http://www.futureofchildren.org/usr_doc/FOC_Brief_Spring2007.pdf on March 14, 2008.

Hattie, J. (1992). Measuring the effects of learning. *Australian Journal of Education, 36*(1), 5–13.

Haycock, K. (1998). Good teaching matters. . . . A lot. *Thinking K–16, 3*(2), 1–14.

Heifetz, R., & Linsky, M. (2002). *Leadership on the line: Staying alive through the dangers of leading*. Boston: Harvard Business School.

Henderson, A., & Berla, N. (1995). *A new generation of evidence: The family is critical to student achievement*. Washington, DC: The Center for Law and Education.

Henderson, A., & Mapp, K. (2002). *A new wave of evidence: The impact to school, family, and community connections on student achievement*. Austin, TX: Southwest Educational Development Laboratory.

Hernez-Broome, G., & Hughes, R. (2004). Leadership development: Past, present, and future. *Human Resource Planning, 27*(1), 24–32.

Heskett, J., & Schlesinger, L. (1996). Leaders who shape and keep performance-oriented culture. In F. Hesselbein, M. Goldsmith, & R. Beckhard (Eds.), *The leader of the future* (pp. 111–120). San Francisco: Jossey-Bass.

Hirsch, E. D. (1996). *The schools we need: And why we don't have them.* New York: Doubleday.

Hoover-Dempsey, K., Walker, J., Sandler, H., Whetsel, D., Green, C., Wilkins, A., & Closson, K. (2005, November). Why do parents become involved? Research findings and implications. *Elementary School Journal, 106*(2), 105–130.

Hord, S. (1997). Professional learning communities: Communities of continuous inquiry and improvement. *Southwest Educational Development Laboratory.* Accessed at http://www.sedl.org/pubs/change34/ on March 14, 2008.

Hord, S., Rutherford, W., Huling-Austin, L., & Hall, G. (1987). *Taking charge of change.* Alexandria, VA: Association for Supervision and Curriculum Development.

Hoxby, C. (2001, Winter). Rising tide. *Education Next, 1*(4), 69–74. Accessed at http://www.hoover.org/publications/ednext/3399061.html on March 24, 2008.

Institute of Education Sciences. (2004). *Highlights from the trends in international mathematics and science study.* Accessed at http://www.nces.ed.gov/pubs2005/timss03/summary.asp on March 14, 2008.

Interstate New Teacher Assessment and Support Consortium. (1992). *Model standards for beginning teacher licensing, assessments, and development: A resource for state dialogue.* Accessed at http://www.ccsso.org/content/pdfs/corestrd.pdf on March 17, 2008.

Interstate School Leaders Licensure Consortium. (1996). *Standards for school leaders.* Washington, DC: Council of Chief State School Officers.

Jacobs, H. (1997). *Mapping the big picture: Integrating curriculum and assessment K–12.* Alexandria, VA: Association for Supervision and Curriculum Development.

Jacobs, H. (2001). New trends in curriculum: An interview with Heidi Hayes Jacobs. *Independent School, 61*(1), 18–24.

Janofsky, M. (2005, July 16). Students say high schools let them down. *New York Times.* Accessed at http://www.nytimes.com/2005/07/16/education/16STUDENTS.html?ei=5090&en=38235abc122acecb&ex=1279166400&partner=rssuserland&emc=rss&pagewanted=print on March 17, 2008.

Jefferson, T. (1782). *Notes on the state of Virginia.* Accessed at http://www.yale.edu/lawweb/avalon/jevifram.htm on March 17, 2008.

Johnson, D., & Johnson, R. (1994). An overview of cooperative learning. In J. Thousand, A. Villa, & A. Nevin (Eds.), *Creativity and collaborative learning.* Baltimore: Brookes Press. Accessed at http://www.cooperation.org/pages/overviewpaper.html on March 17, 2008.

Johnson, D., Johnson, R., & Stanne, M. (2000). *Cooperative learning methods: A meta-analysis.* Accessed at http://www.co-operation.org/pages/clmethods.html on March 17, 2008.

Joyce, B., & Showers, B. (1995, May). Learning experiences in staff development. *The Developer* (National Staff Development Council), p. 3.

Joyner, E., Ben-Avie, M., & Comer, J. (Eds.). (2004). Essential understandings of the Yale school development program. *Transforming school leadership and management to support student learning and development: The field guide to Comer schools in action.* Thousand Oaks, CA: Corwin Press.

Kanold, T. (2006). The continuous improvement wheel of a professional learning community. *Journal of Staff Development, 27*(2), 16–21.

Kanter, R. (1995). Mastering change. In S. Chawala & J. Renesch (Eds.), *Learning organizations: Developing cultures for tomorrow's workplace.* New York: Productivity Press.

Kanter, R. (1997, October 23). Leading the change-adept organization with concepts, competence, and connections. Keynote address presented at the Lessons in Leadership Conference, Boston.

Kanter, R. (1999, Summer). The enduring skills of change leaders. *Leader to Leader, 13,* 15–22. Accessed at http://www.leadertoleader.org/knowledgecenter/journal.aspx?ArticleID=50 on March 24, 2006.

Kanter, R. (2004). *Confidence: How winning streaks and losing streaks begin and end.* New York: Three Rivers Press.

Kanter, R. (2005, Winter). How leaders gain (and lose) confidence. *Leader to Leader, 35,* 21–27.

Katzenbach J., & Smith, D. (1993). *The wisdom of teams: Creating the high-performance organization.* Boston: Harvard Business School.

Kegan, R., & Lahey, L. (2001). *How the way we talk can change the way we work: Seven languages for transformation.* San Francisco: Jossey-Bass.

Kendal, J., & Marzano, R. (2000). *Content knowledge: A compendium of standards and benchmarks for K–12 education* (3rd ed.). Alexandria, VA: Association for Supervision and Curriculum Development.

Kennedy, J. (1962, June 11). Commencement address at Yale University. Accessed at http://www.jfklibrary.org/historical+resources/archives/reference+desk/speeches/jfk/003POF03Yale06111962.htm on March 17, 2008.

Kim, W., & Mauborgne, R. (2003, April 1). Tipping point leadership. *Harvard Business Review, 81*(4), 61–69.

Klein, S., Medrich, E., & Perez-Ferreiro, V. (1996). *Fitting the pieces: Education reform that works.* Washington, DC: United States Department of Education.

Kolta, G. (2007, January 3). A surprising secret to a longer life: Stay in school. *New York Times.* Accessed at http://www.nytimes.com/2007/01/03/health/03aging.html?ex=1325480400&en=b8ffe64abf1b1466&ei=5088&partner=rssnyt&emc=rss on March 17, 2008.

Kotter, J. (1996). *Leading change.* Boston: Harvard Business School.

Kotter, J. (1998, Fall). Winning at change. *Leader to Leader, 10,* 27–33.

Kotter, J., & Cohen, D. (2002). *Leading change.* Boston: Harvard Business School.

Kouzes, J., & Posner, B. (1987). *The leadership challenge: How to get extraordinary things done in organizations.* San Francisco: Jossey-Bass.

Kouzes, J., & Posner, B. (1996). Seven lessons for leading the voyage to the future. In F. Hesselbein, M. Goldsmith, & R. Beckhard (Eds.), *The leader of the future* (pp. 99–110). San Francisco: Jossey-Bass.

Kouzes, J., & Posner, B. (1999). *Encouraging the heart: A leader's guide to rewarding and recognizing others.* San Francisco: Jossey-Bass.

Kouzes, J., & Posner, B. (2003, Spring). Challenge is the opportunity for greatness. *Leader to Leader, 28,* 16–23.

Kouzes, J., & Posner, B. (2006). *A leader's legacy.* San Francisco: Jossey-Bass.

Kruse, S., Seashore Louis, K., & Bryk, A. (1994, Spring). Building professional learning community in schools. *Issues in Restructuring Schools, 6,* 3–6. Accessed at http://www.wcer.wisc.edu/archive/cors/issues% 5Fin%5FRestructuring%5FSchools/issues_NO_6_SPRING_1994.pdf on March 17, 2008.

Kruse, S., Seashore Louis, K., & Bryk, A. (1995). *Building professional learning community in schools.* Madison, WI: Center for School Organization and Restructuring.

Lazerson, M., & Grubb, W. N. (Eds.). (1974). *American education and vocationalism: A documentary history.* New York: Teachers College Press.

Lee, V., & Burkham, D. (2002, September 30). *Inequality at the starting gate: Social background differences in achievement as children begin school.* Washington, DC: Economic Policy Institute.

Leiserson, G., & Rohaly, J. (2006, November 15). The distribution of the 2001–2006 tax cuts. *The Urban Institute.* Accessed at http://www. urban.org/publications/411378.html on March 17, 2008.

Leithwood, K., & Menzies, T. (1998). Forms and effects of school-based management: A review. *Educational Policy, 12*(3), 325–346.

Leithwood, K., Seashore Louis, K., Anderson, S., & Wahlstrom, K. (2004). *How leadership influences student learning.* New York: Wallace Foundation.

Lemann, N. (2000). *The big test: The secret history of the American meritocracy.* New York: Farrar, Straus, and Giroux.

Lencioni, P. (2003, Summer). The trouble with teamwork. *Leader to Leader,* *29*, 35–40.

Lencioni, P. (2005). *Overcoming the five dysfunctions of a team: A field guide.* San Francisco: Jossey-Bass.

Levine, D. (2003). *Building classroom communities: Strategies for developing a culture of caring.* Bloomington, IN: Solution Tree (formerly National Educational Service).

Lezotte, L. (1991). *Correlates of effective schools: The first and second generation.* Okemos, MI: Effective Schools Products. Accessed at http://www.effectiveschools.com/Correlates.pdf on January 6, 2006.

Lezotte, L. (1997). *Learning for all.* Okemos, MI: Effective Schools Products.

Lezotte, L. (2001). *Revolutionary and evolutionary: The effective schools movement.* Accessed at http://www.effectiveschools.com/downloads/RevEv.pdf on March 17, 2008.

Lezotte, L. (2005). More effective schools: Professional learning communities in action. In R. DuFour, R. Eaker, & R. DuFour (Eds.), *On common ground: The power of professional learning communities* (pp. 177–191). Bloomington, IN: Solution Tree (formerly National Educational Service).

Lickona, T., & Davidson, M. (2005). *Smart and good high schools: Integrating excellence and ethics for success in school, work, and beyond.* Cortland, New York: Center for the 4th and 5th Rs (Respect and Responsibility), and Washington, DC: Character Education Partnership.

Lieberman, A. (1995). Restructuring schools: The dynamics of changing practice, structure, and culture. In A. Lieberman (Ed.), *The work of restructuring schools: Building from the ground up* (pp. 1–17). New York: Teachers College Press.

Little, J. (1990). The persistence of privacy: Autonomy and initiative in teachers' professional relations. *Teachers College Record, 91*(4), 509–536.

Little, J., Gearhart, M., Curry, M., & Kafka, J. (2003). Looking at student work for teacher learning, teacher community, and school reform. *Phi Delta Kappan, 83*(5), 184–192.

Lortie, D. (1975). *Schoolteacher: A sociological study*. Chicago: University of Chicago Press.

Louis, K., Kruse, S., & Marks, H. (1996). Schoolwide professional community. In F. Newmann (Ed.), *Authentic achievement: Restructuring schools for intellectual quality* (pp. 179–204). San Francisco: Jossey-Bass.

Louis, K., Kruse, S., & Raywid, M. (1996, May). Putting teachers at the center of reform. *NASSP Bulletin*.

Louis, K., & Marks, H. (1998). Does professional learning community affect the classroom teachers' work and student experience in restructured schools? *American Journal of Education, 106*(4), 532–575.

Lubienski, C., & Lubienski, S. (2006). *Charter, private, public schools and academic achievement: New evidence from NAEP mathematics data*. National Center for the Study of Privatization in Education. New York: Teachers College Press. Accessed at http://www.ncspe.org/readrel.php?set=pub&cat=126 on March 17, 2008.

Mandl, A., & Sethi, D. (1996). Either/or yields to the theory of both. In F. Hesselbein, M. Goldsmith, & R. Beckhard (Eds.), *The leader of the future* (pp. 257–264). San Francisco: Jossey-Bass.

Marks, H., Doanne, K., & Secada, W. (1996). Support for student achievement. In F. Newmann (Ed.), *Authentic achievement: Restructuring schools for intellectual quality* (pp. 209–227). San Francisco: Jossey-Bass.

Marzano, R. (2003). *What works in schools: Translating research into action*. Alexandria, VA: Association for Supervision and Curriculum Development.

Marzano, R. (2006). *Classroom assessment and grading that work*. Alexandria, VA: Association for Supervision and Curriculum Development.

Marzano, R. (2007). *The art and science of teaching: A comprehensive framework for effective instruction*. Alexandria, VA: Association for Supervision and Curriculum Development.

Marzano, R., Pickering, D., & Pollock, J. (2001). *Classroom instruction that works*. Alexandria, VA: Association for Supervision and Curriculum Development.

Marzano, R., & Umphrey, J. (2008). Producing learning: A conversation with Robert Marzano. *Principal Leadership, 8*(5), 16–20.

Marzano, R., Waters, T., & McNulty, B. (2005). *School leadership that works.* Alexandria, VA: Association for Supervision and Curriculum Development.

Matthews, D. (1997, June). The lack of a public for public schools. *Phi Delta Kappan, 78*(10), 740–743.

Maxwell, J. (1995). *Developing the leaders around you: How to help others reach their full potential.* Nashville, TN: Thomas Nelson.

Maxwell, J. (1998). *The 21 irrefutable laws of leadership: Follow them and people will follow you.* Nashville, TN: Thomas Nelson.

McKinney, M. (2005, Fall). *The persistence of vision.* Accessed at http://www.leadershipnow.com/Persistence_of_Vision.html on March 29, 2008.

McLaughlin, M., & Talbert, J. (2001). *Professional communities and the work of high school teaching.* Chicago: University of Chicago Press.

McLaughlin, M., & Talbert, J. (2006). *Building school-based teacher learning communities: Professional strategies to improve student achievement.* New York: Teachers College Press.

McTighe, J., & Wiggins, G. (2004). *Understanding by design: Professional development workbook.* Alexandria, VA: Association for Supervision and Curriculum Development.

McVee, M. B., Dunsmore, K., & Gavalek, J. R. (2005). Schema theory revisited. *Review of Educational Research, 75*(4), 531–566.

Mehlinger, H. (1995). *School reform in the information age.* Bloomington, IN: Indiana University Center for Excellence in Education.

Mintzberg, H. (1994). *The rise and fall of strategic planning.* New York: Free Press.

Mizell, H. (2007, Summer). Narrow the focus, expand the possibilities. *Journal of Staff Development, 28*(3), 18–22.

Moe, T. (Ed.). (2001). *A primer on America's schools.* Stanford, CA: Hoover Institution Press.

Moe, T. (2006, July/August). Put to the test: Thriving on failure. *Stanford Magazine.* Accessed at http://www.stanfordalumni.org/news/magazine/2006/julaug/features/nclb.html on March 17, 2008.

Morrissey, M. (2000). *Professional learning communities: An ongoing exploration.* Accessed at http://www.sedl.org/pubs/change45/1.html on March 17, 2008.

Naisbitt, J., & Aburdene, P. (1985). *Reinventing the corporation: Transforming your job and your company for the new information society.* New York: Warner Books.

Nanus, B. (1992). *Visionary leadership.* San Francisco: Jossey-Bass.

National Assessment of Educational Progress. (2007). *Results from the 2005 NAEP high school transcript study.* Accessed at http://www.nces.ed.gov/whatsnew/commissioner/remarks2007/2_22_2007.asp on March 29, 2008.

National Association of Elementary School Principals. (2001). *Leading learning communities: Standards for what principals should know and be able to do.* Accessed at http://www.naesp.org/client_files/LLC-Exec-Sum.pdf on August 14, 2007.

National Association of Secondary School Principals. (2004). *Breaking ranks II: Strategies for leading high school reform.* Reston, VA: Author.

National Association of Secondary School Principals. (2006). *Breaking ranks in the middle: Strategies for leading middle level reform.* Reston, VA: Author.

National Association of Secondary School Principals and the Carnegie Foundation for the Advancement of Teaching. (1996). *Breaking ranks: Changing an American institution.* Reston, VA: Author.

National Board for Professional Teaching Standards. (2007a). *The five core standards.* Accessed at http://www.nbpts.org/the_standards/the_five_core_propositions on August 14, 2007.

National Board for Professional Teaching Standards. (2007b). *History.* Accessed at http://www.nbpts.org/about_us/mission_and_history/history on August 14, 2007.

National Center for Education Statistics (NCES). (2005). *Digest of education statistics.* Accessed at http://nces.ed.gov/programs/digest/d05/ on March 17, 2008.

National Center for Education Statistics (NCES). (2006). *Comparing private schools and public schools using hierarchal linear models.* United States Department of Education. Accessed at nces.ed.gov/nationsreportcard//pdf/studies/2006461.pdf on March 17, 2008.

National Center for Education Statistics (NCES). (2007). *Results from the 2005 NAEP high school transcript study.* Accessed at http://www.nces.ed.gov/whatsnew/commissioner/remarks2007/2_22_2007.asp on March 17, 2008.

National Center for Research on Evaluation, Standards and Student Testing. (2006). Accessed at http://www.cse.ucla.edu on January 6, 2006.

National Center on Education and the Economy. (2007). *Tough choices or tough times: The report of the new commission on the skills of the American workforce.* San Francisco: Jossey-Bass.

National Commission on Excellence in Education. (1983, April). *A nation at risk.* Accessed at http://www.ed.gov/pubs/NatAtRisk/risk.html on March 17, 2008.

National Commission on Teaching and America's Future. (1996). *What matters most: Teaching and America's future.* Washington, DC: Author.

National Commission on Teaching and America's Future. (2003). *No dream denied: A pledge to America's children.* Washington, DC: Author.

National Commission on Teaching and America's Future. (2005). *Induction into learning communities.* Washington, DC: Author. Accessed at http://www.nctaf.org/resources/research_and_reports/nctaf_research_reports/ on March 24, 2008.

National Council of Teachers of English. (2006, April). *NCTE principles of adolescent literacy reform: A policy research brief.* Accessed at http://www.ncte.org/library/files/about_NCTE/Overview/Adol-Lit-Brief.pdf on March 17, 2008.

National Council of Teachers of Mathematics (in press). *Principles and standards for mathematics education leaders.* Reston, VA: Author.

National Education Association. (2003). *School quality: NEA's KEYS initiative.* Accessed at http://www.nea.org/schoolquality/index.html on January 6, 2006.

National Education Association. (2005). *Classroom assessment practices.* Accessed at http://www.nea.org/accountability/assessment.html on March 17, 2008.

National Education Association. (2007). *School quality: NEA's keys initiative.* Accessed at http://www.nea.org/schoolquality/key2.html on March 17, 2008.

National Middle School Association. (2003). *This we believe: Successful schools for young adolescents: A position paper.* Westerville, OH: Author.

National Middle School Association. (2006). *National Middle School Association's position statement on the professional preparation of middle level teachers.* Accessed at http://www.nmsa.org/AboutNMSA/PositionStatements/ProfessionalPreparation/tabid/287/default.aspx on March 17, 2008.

National Parent Teacher Association. (2000). *Building successful partnerships: A guide for developing parent and family involvement programs.* Bloomington, IN: Solution Tree (formerly National Educational Service).

National Science Teachers Association. (2006). *NSTA position paper: Professional development in science education.* Accessed at http://www.nsta.org/about/positions/profdev.aspx on March 17, 2008.

National Staff Development Council. (2001). *The NSDC standards: Collaboration skills.* Accessed at http://www.nsdc.org/standards/collaborationskills.cfm on March 17, 2008.

National Staff Development Council. (2007). *The NSDC standards: Learning communities.* Accessed at http://www.nsdc.org/standards/learningcommunities.cfm on January 6, 2007.

New Commission on the Skills of the American Workforce. (2007). *Tough choices or tough times.* National Center on Education and the Economy. Accessed at http://skillscommission.org/pdf/exec_sum/ToughChoices_EXECSUM.pdf on March 17, 2008.

Newmann, F., & Associates. (1996). *Authentic achievement: Restructuring schools for intellectual quality.* San Francisco: Jossey-Bass.

Newmann, F., & Wehlage, G. (1995). *Successful school restructuring: A report to the public and educators by the Center for Restructuring Schools.* Madison: University of Wisconsin Press.

Newmann, F., & Wehlage, G. (1996). Restructuring for authentic student achievement. In F. Newmann (Ed.), *Authentic achievement: Restructuring schools for intellectual quality* (pp. 286–301). San Francisco: Jossey-Bass.

Olson, L. (2007, June 26). Harvard project boils down ingredients for district success. *Education Week.* Accessed at http://www.edweek.org/ew/articles/2007/06/26/43pelp_web.h26.html?qs=harvard+project+boils on March 17, 2008.

O'Neil, J. (1995, April). On schools becoming learning organizations: A conversation with Peter Senge. *Educational Leadership, 52*(7), 20–23.

Pacenza, M. (2007). *Flawed from the start: The history of the SAT.* Accessed at journalism.nyu.edu/pubzone/race_class/edu-matt3.htm on March 17, 2008.

Parent involvement. (2004, September 21). *Education Week.* Accessed at http://www.edweek.org/rc/issues/parent-involvement/ on March 24, 2008.

Partnership for 21st Century Skills. (2007). *Framework for 21st century learning: Communication and collaboration.* Accessed at http://www.21stcenturyskills.org/index.php?option=com_content&task=view&id=261&Itemid=120 on March 17, 2008.

Patrikakou, E., & Weissberg, R. (1998). *Parents' perceptions of teacher outreach and parent involvement in children's education.* Accessed at http://www.temple.edu/lss/htmlpublications/publications/pubs98–14.htm on March 17, 2008.

Patterson, K., Grenny, J., Maxfield, D., McMillan, R., & Switzler, A. (2008). *Influencer: The power to change anything.* New York: McGraw-Hill.

Patterson, K., Grenny, J., McMillan, R., & Switzler, A. (2002). *Crucial conversations: Tools for talking when stakes are high.* New York: McGraw-Hill.

Perkins, D. (1992). *Smart schools: From training memories to educating minds.* New York: Free Press.

Perkins, D. (2003). *King Arthur's roundtable.* New York: John Wiley & Sons.

Perkinson, H. (1979). *The imperfect panacea: American faith in education, 1865–1965.* New York: Random House.

Peters, T. (1987). *Thriving on chaos: A handbook for a management revolution.* New York: Knopf.

Peters, T., & Austin, N. (1985). *A passion for excellence: The leadership difference.* New York: Random House.

Peters, T., & Waterman, R. (1982). *In search of excellence: Lessons from America's best-run companies.* New York: Harper and Row.

Petrilli, M. (2007, January 4). Is No Child Left Behind's birthday worth celebrating? *Education Gadfly, 7*(1). Accessed at http://www.fordhamfoundation.org/foundation/gadfly/issue.cfm?edition=&id=271#3177 on March 17, 2008.

Pfeffer, J., & Sutton, R. (2000). *The knowing-doing gap: How smart companies turn knowledge into action.* Boston: Harvard Business School.

Pfeffer, J., & Sutton, R. (2006). *Hard facts, dangerous half-truths and total nonsense: Profiting from evidence-based management.* Boston: Harvard Business School.

Pinchot, G., & Pinchot, E. (1993). *The end of bureaucracy and the rise of the intelligent organization.* San Francisco: Berrett-Koehler.

Pomerantz, E., Moorman, E., & Litwack, S. (2007, September). The how, whom, and why of parents' involvement in children's academic lives: More is not always better. *Review of Educational Research, 77*(3), 373–410.

Popham, W. J. (2001). *Classroom assessment: What teachers need to know* (3rd ed.). Boston: Allyn & Bacon.

Popham, W. J. (2001). *The truth about testing: An educator's call to action.* Alexandria, VA: Association for Supervision and Curriculum Development.

Popham, W. J. (2003). The seductive allure of data. *Educational Leadership, 60*(5), 48–51.

Popham, W. J. (2004, November). Curriculum matters. *American School Board Journal.* Accessed at http://www.asbj.com/MainMenuCategory/Archive/2004/November.aspx on March 24, 2008.

Popham, W. J. (2005, April). F for assessment: Standardized testing fails. *Edutopia Magazine.* Accessed at http://www.edutopia.org/magazine/apr05 on March 24, 2008.

Pratchett, T. (2006). *Jingo.* London: Transworld.

Pratt, A., Tripp, C., Fraser, R., Warnock, J., & Curtis, R. (2008). *The skillful leader II: Confronting conditions that undermine learning.* Acton, MA: Ready About Press.

Protecting mediocre teachers. (2005, December 9). *Chicago Tribune.*

Public Education Leadership Project at Harvard University. (2007). Accessed at http://www.hbs.edu/pelp/framework.html on March 17, 2008.

Public School Parents Network. (2007). *Project Appleseed.* Accessed at http://www.projectappleseed.org/chklst.html on March 24, 2008.

Purkey, S., & Smith, M. (1983). Effective schools: A review. *Elementary School Journal, 83*(4), 427–452.

Ratner, G. (2007). Why the No Child Left Behind Act needs to be restructured to accomplish its goals and how to do it. *University of the District of Columbia Law Review, 9*(1). Accessed at http://www.citizenseffectiveschools.org/udclawreview.pdf on March 17, 2008.

Ravitch, D. (2007a). AACTE warned of efforts to harm public education. *Education Week.* Accessed at http://www.edweek.org/ew/articles/2007/03/07/26aactenote.h26.html on March 17, 2008.

Ravitch, D. (2007b). *The future of NCLB.* Accessed at http://www.huffingtonpost.com/diane-ravitch/the-future-of-nclb_b_44227.html on March 24, 2008.

Reeves, D. (2000). *Accountability in action: A blueprint for learning organizations.* Denver: Advanced Learning Press.

Reeves, D. (2002). *The leader's guide to standards: A blueprint for educational equity and excellence.* San Francisco: John Wiley & Sons.

Reeves, D. (2004). *Accountability for learning: How teachers and school leaders can take charge.* Alexandria, VA: Association for Supervision and Curriculum Development.

Reeves, D. (2005). Putting it all together: Standards, assessment, and accountability in successful professional learning communities. In R. DuFour, R. Eaker, & R. DuFour (Eds.), *On common ground: The power of professional learning communities* (pp. 45–63). Bloomington, IN: Solution Tree (formerly National Educational Service).

Reeves, D. (2006). *The learning leader.* Alexandria, VA: Association for Supervision and Curriculum Development.

Reeves, D. (Ed.). (2007). *Ahead of the curve: The power of assessment to transform teaching and learning.* Bloomington, IN: Solution Tree.

Richardson, J. (2004). *From the inside out: Learning from the positive deviance in your organization.* Oxford, OH: National Staff Development Council.

Rippa, S. A. (1974). *Education in a free society: An American history.* New York: David McKay Company.

Rose, L., & Gallup, A. (2006). The 38th Annual Phi Delta Kappa Gallup Poll of the public's attitudes toward the public schools. *Phi Delta Kappan, 88*(1), 41–56.

Rose, L., & Gallup, A. (2007). The 39th annual Phi Delta Kappa Gallup Poll of the public's attitudes toward the public schools. *Phi Delta Kappan, 89*(1), 33–48.

Rosenholtz, S. J. (1986). Organizational conditions of teacher learning. *Teaching and Teacher Education, 2*(2), 91–104.

Rosenholtz, S. (1989). *Teachers' workplace: The social organizations of schools.* New York: Longman.

Rothstein, R. (2004). *Class and schools: Using social, economic, and educational reform to close the black-white achievement gap.* Washington, DC: Economic Policy Institute.

Rothstein, R. (2006). *Response to Chester Finn.* Accessed at http://www. epinet.org/webfeatures/viewpoints/200608_rothstein_finn/ rothsteinresponse_to_finn.pdf on March 17, 2008.

Rudalevige, A. (2003, Fall). The politics of No Child Left Behind: Did the need to build consensus give too much leeway to state capitals? *Education Next, 3*(4), 63–69.

Sagor, R. (1997). Collaborative action research for educational change. In A. Hargreaves (Ed.), *Rethinking educational change with heart and mind.* Alexandria, VA: Association for Supervision and Curriculum Development.

Saphier, J. (2005). *John Adams' promise: How to have good schools for all our children, not just for some.* Acton, MA: Research for Better Teaching.

Saphier, J., Haley-Speca, M. A., & Gower, R. (2008). *The skillful teacher: Building your teaching skills* (6th ed.). Acton, MA: Research for Better Teaching.

Sarason, S. (1995). Foreword. In A. Lieberman (Ed.), *The work of restructuring schools: Building from the ground up.* New York: Teachers College Press.

Sarason, S. (1996). *Revisiting the culture of the school and the problem of change.* New York: Teachers College Press.

Sarason, S. (1997). *How schools might be governed and why.* New York: Teachers College Press.

Schaffer, R., & Thomson, H. (1998). Successful change programs begin with results. *Harvard Business Review on Change* (pp. 189–214). Boston: Harvard Business School.

Scheerens, J., & Bosker, R. (1997). *The foundations of educational effectiveness.* New York: Elsevier.

Schein, E. (1992). *Organizational culture and leadership.* San Francisco: Jossey-Bass.

Schein, E. (1996). Leadership and organizational culture. In F. Hesselbein, M. Goldsmith, & R. Beckhard (Eds.), *The leader of the future* (pp. 59–70). San Francisco: Jossey-Bass.

Schemo, D. (2006, August 9). It takes more than schools to close the achievement gap. *New York Times.* Accessed at http://www.nytimes.com/2006/08/09/education/09education.html?_r=1&scp=1&sq=It+takes+more+than+schools+to+close+the+achievement+gap&st=nyt&oref=slogin on March 24, 2008.

Schlechty, P. (1990). *Schools for the 21st century: Leadership imperatives for educational reform.* San Francisco: Jossey-Bass.

Schlechty, P. (1997). *Inventing better schools: An action plan for educational reform.* San Francisco: Jossey-Bass.

Schlechty, P. (2005). *Creating the capacity to support innovations: Occasional paper #2.* Louisville, KY: Schlechty Center for Leadership in School Reform. Accessed at http://www.schlechtycenter.org/pdfs/support-inn.pdf on March 17, 2008.

Schmoker, M. (1999). *Results: The key to continuous school improvement* (2nd ed.). Alexandria, VA: Association for Supervision and Curriculum Development.

Schmoker, M. (2003). First things first: Demystifying data analysis. *Educational Leadership, 60*(5), 22–24.

Schmoker, M. (2004a). Learning communities at the crossroads: A response to Joyce and Cook. *Phi Delta Kappan, 86*(1), 84, 85–89.

Schmoker, M. (2004b). Start here for improving teaching and learning. *School Administrator, 61*(10), 48–49.

Schmoker, M. (2004c). Tipping point: From feckless reform to substantive instructional improvement. *Phi Delta Kappan, 85*(6), 424–432.

Schmoker, M. (2005). Here and now: Improving teaching and learning. In R. DuFour, R. Eaker, & R. DuFour (Eds.), *On common ground: The power of professional learning communities* (pp. 135–153). Bloomington, IN: Solution Tree (formerly National Educational Service).

Schmoker, M. (2006). *Results now: How we can achieve unprecedented improvements in teaching and learning.* Alexandria, VA: Association for Supervision and Curriculum Development.

Secrets of the SAT. (2007). *Frontline.* Accessed at http://www.pbs.org/wgbh/pages/frontline/shows/sats/where/history.html on March 14, 2008.

Seligman, M. (2006). *Learned optimism: How to change your mind and your life.* New York: Vintage Books.

Selznick, P. (1957). *Leadership in administration: A sociological interpretation.* New York: Harper & Row.

Senge, P. (1990). *The fifth discipline: The art and practice of the learning organization.* New York: Currency Doubleday.

Senge, P., Kleiner, A., Roberts, C., Ross, R., & Smith, B. (1994). *The fifth discipline fieldbook: Strategies and tools for building a learning organization.* New York: Currency Doubleday.

Senge, P., & Kofman, F. (1995). Communities of commitment: The heart of learning organizations. In S. Chawla & J. Renesch (Eds.), *Learning organizations: Developing cultures for tomorrow's workplace* (pp. 15–44). New York: Productivity Press.

Sergiovanni, T. (1994). *Building community in schools.* San Francisco: Jossey-Bass.

Sergiovanni, T. (2001). *The principalship: A reflective practice perspective.* Needham Heights, MA: Allyn & Bacon.

Sergiovanni, T. (2005). *Strengthening the heartbeat: Leading and learning together in schools.* San Francisco: Jossey-Bass.

Shannon, G., & Bylsma, P. (2004). *Characteristics of improved school districts: Themes from research.* Olympia, WA: Office of the Superintendent of Instruction.

Sherman, A., & Aron-Dine, A. (2007). *New CBO data show income inequality continues to widen.* Center on Budget and Policy Priorities. Accessed at http://www.cbpp.org/1–23–07inc.htm on January 23, 2007.

Short, B. (2004). *The harsh truth about public schools.* Vallecito, CA: Chalcedon/Ross House Books.

Smith, T. (2006). *Trends in national spending priorities, 1973–2006.* General Social Survey, National Opinion Research Center, University of

Chicago. Accessed at www.news.uchicago.edu/releases/07/070110. gss-report.pdf on March 17, 2008.

Smith, W., & Andrews, R. (1989). *Instructional leadership: How principals make a difference.* Alexandria, VA: Association for Supervision and Curriculum Development.

Snyder, C. R. (1991). The will and the ways: Development and validation of an individual-differences measure of hope. *Journal of Personality and Social Psychology, 60*(4), 570–585.

Somé, M. (1996). Ritual, the sacred, and community. In L. Mahdi, N. Christopher, & M. Meade (Eds.), *Crossroads: The quest for contemporary rites of passage* (pp. 17–26). Peru, IL: Open Court Publishing.

Southern Regional Education Board. (2000). *Things that matter most in improving student learning.* Atlanta, GA: Author.

Southwest Educational Development Laboratory. (2002). *Professional learning communities: An ongoing exploration.* Southwest Educational Development Laboratory. Accessed at http://www.sedl.org/pubs/change45/1.html on March 17, 2008.

Sparks, D. (2005). Leading for transformation in teaching, learning, and relationships. In R. DuFour, R. Eaker, & R. DuFour (Eds.), *On common ground: The power of professional learning communities* (pp. 155–175). Bloomington, IN: Solution Tree (formerly National Educational Service).

Sparks, D. (2007). *Leading for results: Transforming, teaching, learning and relationships in schools.* Thousand Oaks, CA: Corwin Press.

Steere, W. (1996). Key leadership challenges for present and future executives. In F. Hesselbein, M. Goldsmith, & R. Beckhard (Eds.), *The leader of the future* (pp. 265-272). San Francisco: Jossey-Bass.

Steinberg, L. (1996, July 11). Failure outside the classroom. *Wall Street Journal.* Accessed at http://media.hoover.org/documents/0817928723_117.pdf on March 24, 2008.

Stevenson, H., & Stigler, J. (1992). *The learning gap: Why our schools are failing and what we can learn from Japanese and Chinese education.* New York: Simon & Schuster.

Stiggins, R. (1999). Assessment, student confidence, and school success. *Phi Delta Kappan, 81*(3), 191–198.

Stiggins, R. (2001). *Student-involved classroom assessment* (3rd ed.). Upper Saddle River, NJ: Prentice Hall.

Stiggins, R. (2002). Assessment crisis: The absence of assessment for learning. *Phi Delta Kappan, 83*(10), 758–765.

Stiggins, R. (2004). New assessment beliefs for a new school mission. *Phi Delta Kappan, 86*(1), 22–27.

Stiggins, R. (2005). Assessment for learning: Building a culture of confident learners. In R. DuFour, R. Eaker, & R. DuFour (Eds.), *On common ground: The power of professional learning communities* (pp. 65–83). Bloomington, IN: Solution Tree (formerly National Educational Service).

Stiggins, R. (2007). Assessment *for* learning: An essential foundation of productive instruction. In D. Reeves (Ed.), *Ahead of the Curve: The power of assessment to transform teaching and learning* (pp. 59–76). Bloomington, IN: Solution Tree.

Stover, D. (2007). NCLB—Act II. *American School Board Journal.* Accessed at http://www.asbj.com/MainMenuCategory/Archive/2007/January.aspx on March 24, 2008.

Straus, D. (2002). *How to make collaboration work: Powerful ways to build consensus, solve problems, and make decisions.* San Francisco: Berrett-Koehler.

Surowiecki, J. (2004). *The wisdom of crowds.* New York: Doubleday.

Symonds, K. (2004). *Perspectives on the gaps: Fostering the academic success of minority and low-income students.* Naperville, IL: North Central Regional Educational Laboratory.

The Teaching Commission. (2004). *Teaching at risk: A call to action.* New York: The Teaching Center. Accessed at http://www.csl.usf.edu/teaching%20at%20risk.pdf on March 17, 2008.

Teixeira, R. (2006, September 18). What the public really wants on education. *The Century Foundation.* Accessed at http://www.tcf.org/list. asp?type=PB&pubid=577 on March 17, 2008.

Thompson, J. (2006). The renaissance of learning in business. In S. Chawala & J. Renesch (Eds.), *Learning organizations: Developing cultures for tomorrow's workplace* (pp. 85–100). New York: Productivity Press.

Tichy, N. (1997). *The leadership engine: How winning companies build leaders at every level.* New York: Harper Business.

Toppo, G. (2007). *How Bush education law has changed our schools.* Accessed at http://www.usatoday.com/news/education/2007-01-07-no-child_x. htm on March 17, 2008.

Turtel, J. (2005). *Public school, public menace: How public schools lie to parents and betray our children.* Staten Island, NY: Liberty Books.

Tyack, D., & Cuban, L. (1995). *Tinkering toward utopia: A century of public school reform.* Cambridge, MA: Harvard University Press.

Ulrich, D. (1996). Credibility × capability. In F. Hesselbein, M. Goldsmith, & R. Beckhard (Eds.), *The leader of the future* (pp. 209–222). San Francisco: Jossey-Bass.

UNICEF. (2007). *Child poverty in perspective: An overview of child well-being in rich countries—A comprehensive assessment of the lives and well-being of children and adolescents in the economically advanced nations.* Florence Italy: Innocenti Research Centre. Accessed at http://www. unicef.org/media/files/ChildPovertyReport.pdf on March 17, 2008.

United States Census Bureau. (2006a). *Current population survey: Educational attainment in the United States.* Accessed at http://www.census.gov/ population/www/socdemo/educ-attn.html on March 17, 2008.

United States Census Bureau. (2006b). *A half-century of learning: Historical census statistics on educational attainment in the United States, 1940–2000.* Accessed at http://www.census.gov/population/www/ socdemo/education/introphct41.html on March 29, 2008.

United States Department of Education. (1995). *An invitation to your community: Building community partnerships for learning.* Washington, DC: U.S. Government Printing Office.

United States Department of Education. (1999, August). *A first look at what we can learn from high performing school districts: An analysis of TIMSS data from the First in the World Consortium.* Accessed at http://www.ed.gov/pubs/FirstLook/What.html on March 17, 2008.

United States Department of Education. (2002). *No Child Left Behind Act.* Accessed at http://www.ed.gov/policy/elsec/leg/esea02/index.html on March 17, 2008.

United States Department of Education. (2007). *Smaller learning communities program.* Accessed at http://www.ed.gov/programs/slcp/index.html on March 17, 2008.

Vonnegut, K. (1973). *Breakfast of champions.* New York: Delta Books.

Warren Little, J. (1990). The persistence of privacy: Autonomy and initiative in teachers' professional relations. *Teachers College Record, 91*(4), 509–536.

Waterman, R. (1987). *The renewal factor: How the best get and keep the competitive edge.* New York: Bantam Books.

Waterman, R. (1993). *Adhocracy.* New York: W. W. Norton.

Waters, T., & Marzano, R. (2006). *School district leadership that works: The effect of superintendent leadership on student achievement.* Denver, CO: Mid-Continent Research for Education and Learning.

Wehlage, G., Newmann, F., & Secada, W. (1996). Standards for authentic achievement and pedagogy. In F. Newmann (Ed.), *Authentic achievement: Restructuring schools for intellectual quality* (pp. 21–48). San Francisco: Jossey-Bass.

West, M. (2005, December). *No Child Left Behind: How to give it a passing grade.* Brookings Institution. Accessed at http://www.brookings.edu/papers/2005/12education_west.aspx on March 17, 2008.

WestEd. (2000). *Teachers who learn, kids who achieve: A look at schools with model professional development.* San Francisco: Author.

Wheatley, M. (1999). Goodbye command and control. In F. Hesselbein & P. Cohen (Eds.), *Leader to leader* (pp. 151–162). San Francisco: Jossey-Bass.

Wheelis, A. (1973). *How people change.* New York: Harper & Row.

Wherry, J. (2005, March/April). Do you have a parent involvement disconnect? *Principal, 84*(4), 6.

Whittle, C. (2006). Dramatic growth is possible: Untangling education's Gordian knot. *Education Next, 2.* Accessed at http://www.hoover.org/publications/ednext/3210466.html on March 18, 2008.

Wiliam, D., & Thompson, M. (2007). Integrating assessment with learning: What will it take to make it work? In C. A. Dwyer (Ed.), *The future of assessment: Shaping teaching and learning.* Mahwah, NJ: Lawrence Erlbaum Associates.

Wright, S., Horn, S., & Sanders, W. (1997). Teacher and classroom context effects on student achievement: Implications for teacher evaluation. *Journal of Personnel Evaluation in Education, 11*(1), 57–67.

Zuckerman, M. (2006, June 12). Rich man, poor man. *U.S. News & World Report,* 70–71.

Index

A

Aburdene, P., 124
Academic Coaching at Eastview (ACE) program, 252
accountability
    in change process, 354–355
    in collective commitments, 154–156
accreditation, PLCs and, 78
ACT exams, 259
action orientation, 16, 165, 167, 413–415
    collective commitments and, 151
    common goals and, 159
    defined, 463
    importance of, 25–26
action research, 14
actions
    aligning with mission, 115–119, 317–324
    disconnect with mission, 113–115
Adams, Henry, 332
adaptive challenges, 463
Addley, Alan, 2, 251
adequate yearly progress (AYP), 37–39
Adlai Stevenson High School example
    classroom learning communities, 296–299
    collective commitments, 149–151, 453–461
    community involvement, 393–395
    intervention systems, 253, 259, 261, 263–264
    school-family partnership, 384
    vision statements, 448–452
administrative leadership team collective

commitments (Adlai Stevenson High School example), 453–454
administrative meetings, focus of, 360–362
Advanced Placement courses, 52
Advanced Placement exams, 259, 261
AFT (American Federation of Teachers), 58, 76
Ahead of the Curve: The Power of Assessment to Transform Teaching and Learning (Reeves), 221
aligning actions and mission, 115–119, 317–324
ambiguity, avoiding in collective commitments, 157–158
American Federation of Teachers (AFT), 58, 76
Anderson, Steve, 339
Aspen Institute, 42
assessments. *see also* common formative assessments; formative assessments; summative assessments
    balanced assessments, 463
    cultural changes regarding, 93
    international assessments, 53–54
    national assessments, 51–53
    norm-referenced assessments, 468
    principles of good, 222–223
    for sorting students, 199–202
    standards for, 40–41
    student-monitored assessments, 289–292
attainable goals, 463
Axelrod, Richard, 29
AYP (adequate yearly progress), 37–39

B

balanced assessments, 463

Barth, Roland, 1, 3, 90, 177

behavioral change
   in change process, 350–357
   in cultural change, 107–109

behaviors, collective commitments as, 158

beliefs, avoiding collective commitments as, 158

Berla, N., 378

Berra, Yogi, 120

best practices for learning, 343–344

Bestor, Arthur, 33

big ideas in a PLC, 18–19

Black, Paul, 3, 26, 218, 223

blaming others, avoiding, 416–419

Blanchard, Ken, 3, 91, 101, 120, 121, 147, 159, 364, 422, 446

Block, Peter, 413

Blue Ribbon Award, 149

Boones Mill Elementary School example (leadership of principals), 328–330

Bosker, R., 378

bottom-up leadership in cultural change, 105–107

Bracey, Gerald, 39

Bratton, William, 361

Breaking Ranks II (NASSP), 77

Breaking Ranks in the Middle (NASSP), 78

Breaking Ranks (NASSP), 307

Brigham, Carl, 200

Brookover, Wilbur, 438

Brophy, Jere, 224

Buckingham, Marcus, 3, 358

Burkett, Hugh, 422

Bush, George H.W., 35, 43, 62, 377

Bush, George W., 37, 43

buy-in, ownership versus, 326

Byrnes, Rhonda, 104

C

Canter, Lee, 287

capacity building, 464

catalysts for change process, 102–104

celebrating short-term wins, 426–427

Center for Creative Leadership, 312

Center on Organization and Restructuring of Schools, 441, 442

central office, role of, 28, 337–375

Champy, James, 3, 159

change process. *see also* cultural change
   catalysts for, 102–104
   central office's role in, 337–357
   discipline in, 420–423
   failure in, 66, 97–102
   short-term wins in, 423–427
   structural changes, 89–90

charismatic leadership, 324

"Charles Darwin" teachers, 243

charter schools, impact on achievement, 46

Chauncey, Henry, 200

Chicago Bulls basketball team analogy (collaboration), 180–181

"Chicago Cub fan" teachers, 244

Chicago marathon analogy (collaboration), 180

Chicago Public Schools example (parental involvement), 390

child study team, Helen Harvey Elementary School example, 279–280

clarity of results, lack of, 65

Classroom Assessment: What Teachers Need to Know (Popham), 221

classrooms
   collaborative norms in, 284–288
   formative assessments in, 205–208
   as learning communities, 28, 283–299

coalition in change process, 99

Cobbs, Bernice, 2, 246, 328, 328–330

Cohen, D., 104, 426

coherence provided by principals, 317–324

collaboration, 15–16, 18
   critical questions of learning, 183–187
   defined, 464
   guiding, importance of, 27–28
   half-truths of, 182–183
   importance of, 173–177
   knowing-doing gap in, 171–178
   shift toward in a PLC, 94–95

collaborative norms, in classrooms, 284–288

collaborative teams
  classroom learning communities versus, 295
  common formative assessments by, 208–216
  creating common formative assessments, 220–225
  critical issues for consideration, 313–315
  group processing and, 294–295
  intervention systems and, 256–257
  reciprocal accountability, 312–317
  requirements for, 178–181
  sharing knowledge versus pooling opinions, 187–189
  Westlawn Elementary example, 189–197
collective commitments, 147–151
  Adlai Stevenson High School example, 149–151, 453–461
  in cultural change, 156
  developing, 157–158
  importance of, 151–156
collective inquiry, 16, 464
College Board, 52
Collins, Jim, 3, 106, 107, 241, 243, 324, 422
Comer, James, 389
Commission on Instructionally Supportive Assessment, 40
Commission on No Child Left Behind, 42
commitments, in classroom learning communities, 286–288. *see also* collective commitments
common formative assessments, 26, 208–216
  created by collaborative teams, 220–225
  defined, 464
  usage examples, 216–220
  Westlawn Elementary example, 191–193
common goals. *see* goals
common language, need for, 28–29
communication, effective
  of central office, 358–362
  in change process, 99–100
  in school-family partnership, 380–382
community, defined, 20, 465
community involvement of schools, 392–395. *see also* school-family partnership
comparison data, provided by common formative assessments, 213–215
complacency in change process, 99
complexity of education reform, 63–64
Conant, James, 200
consensus
  defined, 465
  importance of defining, 129–130
  unanimity versus, 130
consensus building
  common mistakes in, 122–130
  in creating vision, 120–121
  difficulty of, 139–140
  illustration of, 130–139
conservative politicians, NCLB views of, 45–47
Consortium on Productivity in the Schools, 57
continuous improvement process, 17, 465
continuous learning, 18
cooperative learning, 291–296
Correlates of Effective Schools, 438–439
Cotton, Kathleen, 307
Council of Chief State School Officers, 73
covenants, collective commitments as, 154–156
creating short-term wins, 423–426
Cremin, Lawrence, 56
criterion-referenced assessment, 465
critical issues for team consideration, reproducible, 314–315
crucial conversation, 465
Cuban, Larry, 57, 105, 106
cultural change
  behavioral change in, 107–109
  collective commitments in, 156
  common mistakes in, 99–102
  comprehensive nature of, 419–420
  difficulty of, 92, 96
  importance of, 90–92, 326
  leadership strategies in, 105–107
  as organic, 109–110
  for PLCs, list of, 93–95
  rooting change process in, 101

culture (of school). *see* school culture

curriculum. *see* standards

curriculum leverage, 465

D

dangerous detours, 413–423

Danielson, Charlotte, 3, 322

data, information versus, 26–27, 465

data picture, reproducible, 125–127

Davidson, Matthew, 113, 163

DE-S3P (Diagnostic, Explicit, and Systematic Student Support Program), 247

decision-making, parental involvement in, 389–392

deliberate practice, 351

Deming, W. Edwards, 87, 183

Deutschman, Alan, 103

Dewey, Dick, 2, 333, 333–334

Dewey, John, 33

diagnostic feedback, formative feedback versus, 207

"diplementation," 327–328

directed empowerment. *see* loose-tight leadership

discipline in change process, 420–423

discussion of taboo topics, 352–353

dispersed leadership, 330–332. *see also* loose-tight leadership

defined, 466

importance of, 122–123

by principals, 309–317

disruptive change. *see* second-order change

distribution of leadership, 28

district-level vision, school-level vision versus, 140–141

district office. *see* central office, role of

Dockery, Kim, 195

DRIP Syndrome (Data Rich/Information Poor), 26, 466

Drucker, Peter, 3, 308

E

E.J. Swint Elementary School example (leadership of principals), 327–328

Eastview High School example

intervention systems, 252

leadership of principals, 333–334

economy, education and, 55–57

education reform. *see also* public education

history of, 31–44

impact of, 45–62

loss of confidence in, 57–62

reasons for failure of, 62–66

viewed as failure, 51

education standards. *see* standards

education system, changing unwritten rules of, 86–87

Educational Research Services, 188

Educational Testing Services, 200

Educational Wastelands (Bestor), 33

Effective Schools research, 337, 438–439

efficiency of common formative assessments, 212–213

Einstein, Albert, 31, 163

elementary school principals, standards for, 306

Elizabeth Vaughan Elementary School example (leadership of principals), 332–333

Elmore, Richard, 3, 58, 89, 108, 156, 171, 173, 214, 318, 363, 364, 417

Emerson, Ralph Waldo, 13, 21

empowerment of collective commitments, 152

endorsements of PLCs, 72–79

enrichment programs, 258–260, 274–277

Epstein, Joyce, 378, 395

equity in common formative assessments, 213

essential learning, 466

evaluating

teachers, 321–324

vision statements, 142–143

Evans, Robert, 104, 337, 356

excellence movement (education reform), 34–35, 64

F

factory model of education, 32–33

failure of change process, reasons for, 97–102

failure, response to, 420–423

fear, as catalyst for change, 102–104

feedback. *see* assessments

Finn, Chester, 50

"First in the World" (FiW) consortium, 54

first-order change, 466

Flesch, Rodolf, 34

formative assessments (*for* learning). *see also* common formative assessments
  classroom usage of, 205–208
  defined, 466
  summative assessments versus, 202–204

Forum on Educational Accountability, 41–42

foundation of professional learning community, 466

four pillars of a PLC, 164–165

Freeport Intermediate School example
  intervention systems, 250
  leadership of principals, 330–332

Fullan, Michael, 1, 2, 3, 58, 63, 64, 91, 96, 105, 108, 110, 144, 162, 183, 197, 214, 264, 307, 324, 325, 363, 377, 379, 423, 428

Fulton, Kathleen, 169

funding for NCLB, lack of, 41

G

Gardner, Howard, 3, 10, 29, 348, 356–357

Gardner, John, 3, 104

"Genius of And," 106–107, 141, 467

Gandhi, Mahatma, 419

Ginott, Haim, 283

Glasser, William, 283, 287, 293

goals
  common, 6, 15, 147–167
  defined, 467
  nonmeasurable goals, 163–164
  reducing number of, 161–163
  SMART goals, 159–161, 470

Goals 2000, 35–36, 377

Goleman, Daniel, 3, 356, 422

Goodlad, John, 172, 337, 365

governance, parental involvement in, 389–392

Granby Memorial High School example (intervention systems), 251–252

Grenny, J., 397

group processing in cooperative learning, 294–295

guaranteed and viable curriculum, 467

guiding coalition, 122–123, 467

Gutman, Monika, 377

H

half-truths, 25

Hallinger, Philip, 304, 309

Handbook of Research on Improving Student Achievement (Educational Research Services), 188

Hargreaves, Andy, 3, 92

Harper, Ron, 181

Harrison, C., 218, 223

Helen Harvey Elementary School example (intervention systems), 271–280

Henderson, A., 378, 380

"Henry Higgins" teachers, 244

high expectations, 253–255, 467

high-performing organizations, characteristics of, 446–447

high school graduation rates, 51–52

"highly qualified" teachers, defining, 42

history of education reform, 31–44

hope, as catalyst for change, 102–104

I

IEA (International Association for the Evaluation of Educational Achievement), 53

impact of education reform, 45–62

implementation dips, 327–328

improvement process. *see* change process; cultural change

industrial model, service-industry model versus, 396–398

Influencer: The Power to Change Anything (Patterson, et al.), 349

information
  data versus, 26–27, 465
  gathering for consensus building,
    124–129
  importance of, 26–27
  managing, 355
  provided by common formative
    assessments, 213–215
initiative overload, avoiding, 362–364
instructional leaders, 309
INTASC (Interstate New Teacher
  Assessment and Support Consortium),
  73
interaction in cooperative learning, 294
interdependence, 178–181, 293–294
internal focus of collective commitments,
  152–154
international assessments, 53–54
International Association for the
  Evaluation of Educational Achievement
  (IEA), 53
interpersonal skills in cooperative
  learning (students), 293–296
Interstate New Teacher Assessment and
  Support Consortium (INTASC), 73
Interstate School Leaders Licensure
  Consortium, 305
intervention systems
  cautions concerning, 255–257
  common formative assessments in, 216
  defined, 470–471
  examples of, 246–253, 271–280
  high expectations in, 253–255
  lack of, 241–246
  objections to, 258–269
  RTI (Response to Intervention), 269–271
IQ tests, 200
isolation of teachers, 169–178, 182
"It's Not My Fault" (poem), 417–418

J

Jackson, Phil, 180
Jefferson, Thomas, 31–32
Jessie, Lillie, 2, 332, 332–333
Johannsen, Tom, 131, 134
Johnson, D., 293, 295

Johnson, Lyndon, 62
Johnson, R., 293, 295
Jordan, Michael, 180, 181

K

Kanter, Rosabeth Moss, 3, 104, 169, 411,
  417, 420, 421, 427, 428
Keating, Janel, 2, 116, 399
Kegan, Robert, 3, 28, 353
Kennedy, John F., 24
Kerr, Steve, 181
Keynes, John Maynard, 89
Keys to Excellence (NEA), 75–76
Kierkegaard, Søren, 30
Kildeer Countryside School District 96
  example
    comprehensive cultural change, 420
    intervention systems, 248–249, 258
Kim, W. Chan, 361
King, Dennis, 2
knowing-doing gap, 79–82
  defined, 467
  evidence of, 343–344
  overcoming, 413–415
  in professional development, 370
  teacher isolation and, 171–178
The Knowing-Doing Gap (Pfeffer and
  Sutton), 79
Kofman, Fred, 17, 311
Kotter, John, 3, 99, 101, 102, 104, 142, 426
Kouzes, James, 3, 29, 113, 124, 301, 317,
  334, 421, 422, 426
Kruse, S., 311
Kukoc, Tony, 181

L

Lahay, Lisa Laskow, 28, 353
language precision, importance of, 28–29
Law of Legacy, 330
Law of the Few, 467
leadership. see also dispersed leadership
  characteristics of great leaders, 427
  cultural change strategies, 105–107
  distribution of, 28
  examples of principals, 324–335
  responsibilities of principals, 304–308

Leading Learning Communities: Standards for What Principals Should Know and Be Able to Do (National Association of Elementary School Principals), 77
learning
  best practices for, 343–344
  continuous learning, 18
  cooperative learning, 291–296
  defined, 19, 468
  lack of. *see* intervention systems
  monitoring. *see* assessments
  questions of, 183–187
learning by doing. *see* action orientation
learning communities, classrooms as, 283–299. *see also* PLCs (professional learning communities)
learning leaders, 321
learning organizations, 468
learning outcomes, defining for students, 288–289
Lee, Christine, 169, 218, 223
Leithwood, K., 305
Levey Middle School example (intervention systems), 249–250
Lezotte, Larry, 1, 3, 186, 254, 399, 438
liberal politicians, NCLB views of, 47–50
Lickona, Thomas, 113, 163
Lieberman, Anne, 172
Limbaugh, Rush, 341
local school system, public support for, 54–55
longevity, effect of education on, 61
loose leadership in cultural change, 105–107
loose-tight leadership. *see also* dispersed leadership
  defined, 470
  example of, 372–374
  role of, 341–371
Lortie, Dan, 172
Louis, K., 69, 311
Lyn, Hannah, 271–280

M

Mapp, K., 378, 380
Marks, H., 69, 311

Marsh, B., 218, 223
Marzano, Robert, 3, 184, 186, 187, 296, 307, 310, 311, 340, 342, 378, 380, 443
Maslow, Abraham, 269
Mattos, Mike, 2, 251, 325, 325–327, 428
Mauborgne, Renee, 361
Maxfield, D., 397
Maxwell, John C., 330
McLaughlin, Milbrey, 3, 301, 310, 370, 423
McMillan, R., 397
McNulty, B., 307, 310, 311
mental models, as barriers to change, 21–25
mission
  aligning actions with, 115–119, 317–324
  defined, 468
  disconnect with actions, 113–115
  vision versus, 119
Moe, Terry, 31, 47
monitoring learning. *see* assessments
moral purpose, 468
Mountain Meadow Elementary School example (school-family partnership), 398–410
Muhammad, Anthony, 2, 249
Murphy, Joseph, 304
mythology, as barrier to change, 21–25

N

NAEP (National Assessment of Educational Progress), 39–40
Naisbitt, J., 124
Nanus, Burt, 3, 119
NASSP (National Association of Secondary School Principals), 77, 250, 307
A Nation at Risk (National Commission on Excellence in Education), 34
National Assessment of Educational Progress (NAEP), 39–40
national assessments, 51–53
National Association of Elementary School Principals (NAESP), 77
National Association of Secondary School Principals (NASSP), 77, 250, 307
National Board for Professional Teaching Standards, 73

National Center for Education Statistics (NCES), 46

National Clearinghouse for Comprehensive School Reform, 338

National Commission on Excellence in Education, 34

National Commission on Teaching and America's Future, 72, 110, 172

National Council of Teachers of English (NCTE), 74

National Council of Teachers of Mathematics (NCTM), 74

National Education Association, 33, 75

National Forum to Accelerate Middle-Grades Reform, 250

National Middle School Association, 77

National PTA, 379, 380, 388

National Science Teachers Association, 74

National Staff Development Council, 78

NCA (North Central Association Commission on Accreditation and School Improvement), 78

NCES (National Center for Education Statistics), 46

NCLB (No Child Left Behind), 37–64

NCTE (National Council of Teachers of English), 74

NCTM (National Council of Teachers of Mathematics), 74

NEA (National Education Association), 33, 75

New American School, 149

New Commission on the Skills of the American Workforce, 65

Newmann, Fred, 3

Newsweek, 252

Nin, Anaïs, 21

90/90/90 schools and districts, 445

No Child Left Behind (NCLB), 37–64

nonmeasurable goals, 163–164

norm-referenced assessments, 468

norms, collaborative norms in classrooms, 284–288

North Central Association Commission on Accreditation and School Improvement (NCA), 78

O

obstacles, addressing, 100

opinion leaders, 351–352

organization, defined, 20

organizational endorsements of PLCs, 72–79

ownership, buy-in versus, 326

P

Papillion-LaVista High School example (intervention systems), 262–263

parallel play, 177–178

The Parent Institute, 383

parent involvement

Adlai Stevenson High School example, 459–461

fostering, 385–386

Helen Harvey Elementary School example, 277–278

role in PLCs, 377–410

parenting skills training, 382–385

partnership. *see* school-family partnership

Partnership for 21st Century Skills, 295

Patterson, Kerry, 3, 10, 349, 350, 351, 352, 353, 354, 355, 356, 358, 397, 419, 422

peer pressure, 351–353

Perkins, D., 222

perseverance, lack of, 65–66

The Persistence of Privacy (Little), 172

personal motivation in change process, 350–351

Petrilli, Michael, 43

Pfeffer, Jeffrey, 3, 25, 67, 79, 108, 114, 155, 181, 199, 224, 325, 343, 364, 414, 422

Pickering, D., 296

Pioneer Middle School example

intervention systems, 250–251, 258–259

leadership of principals, 325–327

Pippen, Scottie, 181

PLCs (professional learning communities)

central office's role in, 337–375

characteristics of, 15–17, 326–327, 442–443

cultural changes necessary for, 93–95

defined, 14, 469
foundation of, 164–167
four pillars of, 164–165
framework for, 18–19
obstacles to sustaining, 413–423
organizational endorsements of, 72–79
parents' role in, 377–410
principals' role in, 301–335
research supporting, 68–72
sustaining, 411–429
terminology, 19–20
unwritten rules of, 82–86
vision, creating, 120–121. *see also* consensus building
Pollock, J., 296
"Pontius Pilate" teachers, 243
pooling opinions, shared knowledge versus, 124–129, 187–189
Popham, W. James, 41, 184, 221, 222, 224
Porras, Jerry, 3, 106
positive deviants, 397, 468
Posner, Barry, 3, 29, 113, 124, 301, 317, 334, 421, 422, 426
poverty, impact on achievement, 47–50
power standard, 468
Pratchett, Terry, 417
precision of language, importance of, 28–29
prerequisite knowledge, 469
principals
leadership examples of, 324–335
role in PLCs, 301–335
support for PLCs, 77–78
prioritizing education standards, 184–186
productive school cultures, 440
professional, defined, 19, 469
professional development
of assessment skills, 215
central office's role in, 364–371
cultural changes to, 95
defined, 469
professional learning communities. *see* PLCs
professional organizations, collaboration endorsement of, 175–177
professional teaching standards, 72–77
Progress in International Reading

Literacy Study, 53
progressive education model, 33
public education, success of, 51–54. *see also* education reform
Public School Parent's Network, 384
public support for local school system, 54–55
purpose. *see* mission
Putnam City High School example (intervention systems), 268–269
pyramid of interventions, 251–253, 267–270

R

R.H. Dana Elementary School example (intervention systems), 247–248
Ravitch, Diane, 43, 63
readiness, 469
reciprocal accountability, 312–317, 364, 469
reculturing. *see* cultural change
Reeves, Doug, 1, 3, 26, 161, 185, 186, 199, 202, 209, 221, 224, 241, 363, 445
research studies
central office role, 337–341
effective schools, characteristics of, 438–439
PLCs, support for, 68–72
principal's role, 301–304
productive school cultures, 440
professional development, 365–369
school-family partnerships, 377–379
student achievement factors, 443–444
Response to Intervention (RTI), 269–271
responsibility
abdicating, 416–419
in cooperative learning, 294
primary responsibility of principals, 308–309
teaching, 260–265
restructuring movement (education reform), 35–37, 64
results, lack of clarity on, 65
results orientation, 17–19, 469
retaining teachers, 86–87
reward systems in change process, 354–355

rich-poor gap, 48–49
Ritchie, Sara, 131, 134
Roberts, C., 141
Rodman, Dennis, 180
Rosenholtz, Susan, 130, 172
Rothstein, Richard, 47, 49, 50
RTI (Response to Intervention), 269–271
Rutter, Michael, 438

S

Sale-Davis, Clara, 2, 250, 330, 330–332
Saphier, Jonathon, 1, 13, 188, 428
Sarason, Seymour, 3, 58, 96, 172, 389
SAT (Scholastic Aptitude Test), 52, 200
Schaumburg School District 54 example
  (goal-setting), 160–161
schedule conflicts, 265–269
Scheerens, J., 378
Schein, Edgar, 90
Schlechty, Phil, 3, 58, 65, 92, 106
Schmoker, Mike, 1, 3, 67, 147
Scholastic Aptitude Test (SAT), 52, 200
school culture
  aligning with mission, 317–324
  defined, 469
  productive school cultures, 440
  reshaping, 21–25. see also cultural
    change
school-family partnership, 377–410
  characteristics of, 380–395
  Mountain Meadow Elementary School
    example, 398–410
  tips for, 395–396
school-level vision, district-level vision
  versus, 140–141
school reform. see education reform
school structure, 470. see also structural
  changes
schools
  community involvement of, 392–395
  fundamental purpose of, 18
  PLCs, unwritten rules, 82–86
  unwritten rules of, 79–82
Seashore Louis, Karen, 3, 305
second-order change, 92, 470. see also
  adaptive challenges

The Secret (Byrne), 104
SEDL (Southwest Educational
  Development Laboratory), 75
Senge, Peter, 3, 17, 164, 311
Sergiovanni, Tom, 1, 20, 150, 154, 311, 333
service-industry model, industrial model
  versus, 396–398
shared knowledge
  building, 464
  creating common formative
    assessments, 220–225
  pooling opinions versus, 124–129,
    187–189
shared leadership, 310
shared mission, 15, 326
shared purpose, 15
shared values. see collective commitments
shared vision. see vision
Shōgun, 412
short-term wins in change process, 100,
  423–427
shortcuts, avoiding, 415–416
Simpson's Paradox, 52
simultaneous loose and tight leadership.
  see loose-tight leadership
small-group dialogues, 132–134
small-group forums in building
  consensus, 123–124
small-group skills in cooperative
  learning, 294
SMART goals, 159–161, 470
Smith, Bryan, 120, 141
Snow Creek Elementary School example
  intervention systems, 246–247
  leadership of principals, 328–330
social capital, 353–354
sorting students, assessments for,
  199–202
Southwest Educational Development
  Laboratory (SEDL), 75
Sparks, Dennis, 1, 3, 417
specials integration, 278–279
specificity in collective commitments,
  157–158
SPEED intervention criteria, 248–249

standards
   for assessments, 40–41
   for elementary school principals, 306
   prioritizing, 184–186
state standards, disparity among, 39–40
Stiggins, Rick, 1, 3, 26, 205, 221, 224, 289
stories
   power of, 29–30, 333–334
   teacher isolation, 182
stretch goals, 470
structural changes, 89–90, 355
student achievement factors, 443–444
Student-Involved Classroom Assessment
   (Stiggins), 221
students. *see also* classrooms
   Adlai Stevenson High School example
      (collective commitments), 458
   defining learning outcomes for,
      288–289
   effect of PLCs on, 71
   high expectations for, 253–255
   lack of learning. *see* intervention
      systems
   participation in learning assessments,
      289–292
   response to, 94
   sorting by assessments, 199–202
   workplace skills needed by, 295–296
summative assessments (*of* learning)
   defined, 470
   formative assessments versus, 202–204
support staff collective commitments
   (Adlai Stevenson High School example),
   457
Surowiecki, J., 61
sustaining PLCs, 411–429
Sutton, Robert, 3, 25, 67, 79, 108, 114,
   155, 181, 199, 224, 325, 343, 364, 414,
   422
Switzler, A., 397
systematic interventions. *see* intervention
   systems
systematic process, 471
systematic responses, importance of, 27

T

Talbert, Joan, 301, 310, 370, 423
task forces, 390–392
taxes, effect on rich-poor gap, 48–49
Taylor, Fredrick Winslow, 32
teachable point of view, 471
teacher unions, 47
teachers. *see also* classrooms
   Adlai Stevenson High School example
      (collective commitments), 455–456
   characteristics of great teachers,
      427–428
   common formative assessments by,
      208–216
   cultural changes regarding, 94
   effect of PLCs on, 70–71
   evaluations by principals, 321–324
   "highly qualified" teachers, defining,
      42
   isolation of, 169–178, 182
   professional standards for, 72–77
   responses to student lack of learning,
      241–246
   retaining, 86–87
   sharing knowledge versus pooling
      opinions, 187–189
   teams. *see* collaborative teams
   unwritten rules for, 79–82
   unwritten rules of PLCs, 82–86
team norms, 471
teams, defined, 471. *see also*
   collaboration; collaborative teams
Ten Star Award, 252
tests. *see* assessments
This We Believe (National Middle School
   Association), 77
Thompson, Marnie, 206, 207, 211, 215
Thoreau, Henry David, 13
Tichy, Noel, 18, 29
tight leadership. *see* top-down leadership
time management, 332–333, 471
TIMSS (Trends in International
   Mathematics and Science Study), 53
top-down excellence movement. *see*
   excellence movement (education reform)

top-down leadership
  in cultural change, 105–107
  examples of, 371–374
  role of, 341–371
training
  over-reliance on, 413–415
  in parenting skills, 382–385
transformational leadership, 309
Trends in International Mathematics and
  Science Study (TIMSS), 53
Twadell, Eric, 2
The 21 Irrefutable Laws of Leadership
  (Maxwell), 330
Tyack, David, 57, 105, 106
"Tyranny of Or," 106, 141, 163, 471

U

unanimity, consensus versus, 130
unrealistic expectations for education
  reform, 62–63
unwritten rules
  changing, 86–87
  of PLCs, 82–86
  of schools, 79–82
urgency, sense of. *see* fear

V

values, defined, 471. *see also* collective
  commitments
victory, declaring in change process, 100
vision
  benefits of, 143–144
  in change process, 99
  creating, 120–121. *see also* consensus
    building
  defined, 472
  development over time, 144–145

evaluating, 142–143
guiding questions for, 141–142
importance of, 119–120
mission versus, 119
school-level versus district-level,
  140–141
vision statements, Adlai Stevenson High
  School example, 448–452
volunteer programs, 386–389
Vonnegut, Kurt, 13
vouchers, impact on achievement, 46

W

Wahlstrom, K., 305
Warren Little, Judith, 3, 172
Waterman, Robert, 3, 213
Waters, T., 307, 310, 311, 340, 342
Websites for PLC information, 78
Weber, Chris, 247
Wentroth, Don, 268
Westlawn Elementary example
    collaborative teams, 189–197
    student participation in learning
      assessments, 290
Whatever It Takes (DuFour, et al.), 243,
  260
Why Johnny Can't Read (Flesch), 33
Wilde, Oscar, 325
Wiliam, Dylan, 3, 26, 206, 207, 211, 215,
  218, 223
Williams, Ken, 2, 130–134, 327, 327–328
Wong, Harry, 287
workplace skills needed by students,
  295–296

Y

Yoon, Irene, 169

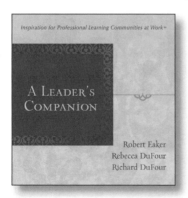